LAW IN THE SERVICE OF HUMAN DIGNITY

The accelerating pace of international law developments in multiple fora present a challenge for studying, influencing, and predicting these changes. This volume assembles essays from over twenty-five notable jurists, academics, and practitioners from around the world who offer new insights regarding the jurisprudence of world trade law, the changing landscape of investment arbitration, and other vital topics in international adjudication. These essays are assembled in celebration of Justice Florentino Feliciano of the Philippines, who continues to be one of the most inspirational figures in the international law community. This collection will be of special interest to analysts of the World Trade Organization as the contributors include six current or former members of the WTO Appellate Body, as well as several leading trade law commentators. Among the key issues discussed are the WTO environmental cases, trade and human rights, and potential reforms of the WTO dispute system.

STEVE CHARNOVITZ is Associate Professor of Law at George Washington University Law School. Previously, he practised law at Wilmer Cutler Pickering Hale and Dorr LLP.

DEBRA P. STEGER is Professor of Law at University of Ottawa Faculty of Law. She is currently Chair of the Trade and Customs Law Committee of the International Bar Association.

PETER VAN DEN BOSSCHE is Professor of International Economic Law and Head of the Department of International and European Law at Maastricht University.

LAW IN THE SERVICE OF HUMAN DIGNITY

Essays in Honour of Florentino Feliciano

edited by

STEVE CHARNOVITZ, DEBRA P. STEGER AND PETER VAN DEN BOSSCHE

CAMBRIDGE
UNIVERSITY PRESS

CAMBRIDGE UNIVERSITY PRESS
Cambridge, New York, Melbourne, Madrid, Cape Town, Singapore, São Paulo

CAMBRIDGE UNIVERSITY PRESS
The Edinburgh Building, Cambridge CB2 2RU, UK

Published in the United States of America by Cambridge University Press, New York

www.cambridge.org
Information on this title: www.cambridge.org/9780521852531

First published 2005

Printed in the United Kingdom at the University Press, Cambridge

A catalogue record for this book is available from the British Library

ISBN-13 978-0-521-85253-1 hardback
ISBN-10 0-521-85253-6 hardback

CONTENTS

CONTRIBUTORS

M. AUERBACH-ZIOGAS holds BCL/LLB from McGill University in Montréal, Canada. He is a member of the Bar of New York.

JAMES BACCHUS is a former Chairman of the WTO Appellate Body. He currently practises law as the Chairman of the Global Trade Practice Group of Greenberg Traurig, PA in Orlando, USA. He is also a Professor at Vanderbilt University Law School. He had previously been a Member of the United States Congress and before that served as a Special Assistant to the United States Trade Representative.

LUIZ OLAVO BAPTISTA is Member of the WTO Appellate Body, Professor of International Trade Law at the University of São Paulo Law School and senior partner at the L. O. Baptista Law Firm, in São Paulo. He is also a Member of the Permanent Court of Arbitration at The Hague and of the International Chamber of Commerce Institute for International Trade Practices.

LAURENCE BOISSON DE CHAZOURNES is Professor at the Law Faculty of the University of Geneva and Head of the Department of Public International Law and International Organisation at the Graduate Institute of International Studies, also in Geneva. Previously, she worked as a senior counsel in the World Bank's legal department as well as a consultant for various international organizations including the United Nations and the WTO.

RUDOLF DOLZER is the Director of the Institute for International Law at the University of Bonn, Germany. Some of his previous positions include a research fellowship at the Max Planck Institute of Comparative Public Law and International Law and membership of the German Parliament's Commissions of Enquiry into 'Protection of Atmosphere' and 'Globalization'.

ROSALYN HIGGINS is a Judge of the International Court of Justice, The Hague. Before taking this post, she taught international law at the University of London. Queen's Counsel and Bencher of the Inner Temple, she practised in England and before international tribunals, including the International Court of Justice, the European Court of Human Rights, and the European Court of Justice.

JOHN H. JACKSON is University Professor at Georgetown University and Director of the Institute of International Economic Law at the same university. He is also the editor in chief of the *Journal of International Economic Law* and a member of the board of editors of other international law journals. He was recently appointed to the WTO Consultative Board.

CHARLOTTE KU is the Executive Vice President and Executive Director of the American Society of International Law in Washington, DC. In the past, she was a visiting professor at the School of Advanced International Studies, Johns Hopkins University, Nanjing (China) and an Assistant Professor of Government and Foreign Affairs at the University of Virginia.

BARBARA KWIATKOWSKA is Professor of International Law of the Sea at the University of Utrecht, the Netherlands. She is also a Deputy Director of the Netherlands Institute for the Law of the Sea (NILOS), Utrecht, Editor in Chief of the *International Organizations Yearbook*, and Co-Director of the Rhodes Oceans Academy. She specializes in ICJ jurisprudence and serves as a member of leading journals on the international law of the sea and many other professional societies.

JULIO A. LACARTE is a former Member and the first Chairman of the WTO Appellate Body. Some of his previous posts include Minister of Industry and Trade of Uruguay, Uruguay's Ambassador to several countries, Uruguay's Permanent Representative to the GATT, Deputy Executive Secretary of the GATT, and high level positions at the United Nations.

MITSUO MATSUSHITA is a former WTO Appellate Body Member. He is currently Professor Emeritus at Tokyo University and counsel to Nagashima, Ohno & Tsunematsu, an international law firm in Tokyo. He has been teaching at a number of universities in Japan, the USA, and Europe. He also serves as a Member of the Office of the Ombudsman of Trade and Investment, which is part of the Japanese government.

ARMAND DE MESTRAL holds the Jean Monnet Chair in the Law of International Economic Integration and is Co-Director of the Institute of European Studies at McGill University in Montréal, Canada. In the past, he was also Director of the Institute of Comparative Law and Acting Director of the Institute of Air and Space Law, also at McGill University.

SAID EL-NAGGAR was a Member of the WTO Appellate Body and Professor Emeritus of Economics at Cairo University. His previous positions included Executive Director of the World Bank representing the Arab countries and President of the New Civic Forum, an Egyptian civic and human rights organization. Dr. El-Naggar passed away in April 2004.

FRANCISCO ORREGO VICUÑA is Professor of International Law at the University of Chile Law School and Institute of International Studies. He is also a member of the Institut de Droit International and a Judge and former President of the World Bank Administrative Tribunal.

LEO PALMA is Deputy Director of the Advisory Centre on WTO Law in Geneva. In the past he was Attaché for WTO Legal Affairs, and before that Labor Attaché, at the Philippine Mission in Geneva. Previously he had worked as a business executive and legal counsel in the Philippines.

ERNST-ULRICH PETERSMANN is Professor of International and European Law at the European University Institute, Florence. He previously taught at many universities around the world and was a legal adviser at the GATT and the WTO, as well as Secretary, Member or Chairman of GATT and WTO dispute settlement panels.

M. C. W. PINTO is an attorney of the Supreme Court of Sri Lanka and a barrister of the Inner Temple. His works have been published extensively and for a number of years he was an editor of the *Asian Yearbook of International Law*.

W. MICHAEL REISMAN is the Myres S. McDougal Professor of International Law at Yale Law School. He is also a member of the Board of Directors of the Foreign Policy Association, the Executive Council of the American Society of International Law, and Honorary Editor and former Editor in Chief of the *American Journal of International Law*.

HÉLÈNE RUIZ FABRI is Professor of International Law at the University of Paris I (Panthéon-Sorbonne) and Director of the Institute of Comparative Studies of Paris, as well as Member of the National

Committee on evaluation of public scientific, cultural, and professional institutions. She also acted as a consultant for the Council of Europe and other national and international bodies.

GIORGIO SACERDOTI is a Member of the Appellate Body and Professor of International Law and Jean Monnet Chair of European Law at the Bocconi University, Milan.

PHILIPPE SANDS is Professor of Law and Director of the Centre for International Courts and Tribunals (CICT) at University College London. He is a silk at Matrix Chambers, London, having been appointed as Queen's Counsel in 2003. He has also been a member of the Irish Bar since 2003.

STEPHEN M. SCHWEBEL served as a Judge of the International Court of Justice 1981–2000, and as its President 1997–2000. He spent some years in private practice, taught at Harvard Law School and the School of Advanced International Studies of the Johns Hopkins University and served as a Deputy Legal Adviser of the US State Department as well as a member of the UN International Law Commission. He has been President of the Administrative Tribunal of the International Monetary Fund since 1994. He is an active international arbitrator.

DEBRA P. STEGER is Executive in Residence at the University of Ottawa Faculty of Law. She was previously Senior Counsel at Thomas & Partners (Ottawa), and prior to that the first Director of the WTO Appellate Body Secretariat. During the Uruguay Round of multilateral trade negotiations she served as senior negotiator and principal legal advisor for the Canadian government.

BRIGITTE STERN is Professor of International Law at the University of Paris I (Panthéon-Sorbonne). She is Adjunct Professor at the Graduate Institute of International Studies in Geneva and Vice-President of the United Nations Administrative Tribunal.

TULLIO TREVES is a Judge at the International Tribunal for the Law of the Sea in Hamburg, Germany. He has been a member of the Tribunal since 1996. Having been President of the Seabed Disputes Chamber between 1999 and 2002, he was appointed as President of the Chamber for Marine Environment Disputes in 2002. He is a Professor at the University of Milan.

PETER VAN DEN BOSSCHE is Professor of International Economic Law, Head of the International and European Law Department and Director of the *Magister Iuris Communis* programme at Maastricht University in the Netherlands. Previously he was Counsellor to the Appellate Body of the WTO and served as Acting Director of the Appellate Body Secretariat.

GUIGUO WANG is Professor (Chair) of Chinese and Comparative Law at the City University of Hong Kong. He is a member of the International Institute of Comparative Law in The Hague, Chairman of the Hong Kong WTO Research Institute and Distinguished Professor of Law at Hunan Normal University Faculty of Law (China).

PREFACE

This volume of essays seeks to honour a remarkable, true renaissance man, Justice Florentino P. Feliciano. We are privileged to know him as a jurist, a teacher, a scholar, a lawyer, a loyal citizen of his beloved country, the Philippines, and a citizen of the world. He has had multiple careers of achievement and positive legacy in so many fields that it is hard to imagine how one individual could accomplish it all. He was a Justice of the Philippines Supreme Court from 1986 to 1995, thereafter, he was one of the first seven members of the World Trade Organization's Appellate Body from 1995 to 2001 and its Chairman in 2000 to 2001. For years he has been one of the world's most experienced international legal scholars and arbitrators. He is highly respected in the international law community having been, among many other distinctions, an associé de l'Institut de Droit International for almost forty years and a Member of the Curatorium of the Hague Academy of International Law. A short biographical note on Justice Feliciano and a bibliography of his publications is included in this volume.

Justice Feliciano ('Toy' to his many friends and colleagues around the world) is a very humble, kind and thoughtful gentleman. He is a principled and religious man, with a passion for justice, equality, and the rule of law, both in his own country and in the international community. He has an unparalleled intellect and curiosity about the world around him, but he is also an extremely meticulous and careful thinker – a person who must learn all that he can about a particular subject before taking any decision. In other words, he is the perfect judge. He can, at times, be fearsome, particularly when he is sitting on the bench and preparing to ask a penetrating question of an unsuspecting counsel. He likes to introduce his inquisition with the simple, humble words: 'I'm just a judge from a little country'. Many an experienced counsel has learned that this is just the beginning of a challenging, intellectual inquiry on the merits of a particular legal argument.

As befitting a volume about the progressive development of international law in a globalized world, our contributors hail from all over the world. We have divided this rich collection of essays into four parts.

The first part, entitled 'Reflections', presents essays about Justice Feliciano and his contributions to international law by some of his closest colleagues and friends. Included in this collection are essays by Professor Michael Reisman of Yale Law School, Justice Feliciano's alma mater, on his philosophy of judicial function, and an essay by Judge Rosalyn Higgins, who was a student at Yale with Justice Feliciano and is now a Judge of the International Court of Justice, in which she offers her personal reflections on her friendship with him going back forty-five years. The other essays in this section were written by two of Justice Feliciano's former colleagues on the WTO Appellate Body: Ambassador Julio A. Lacarte and the Honorable James Bacchus.

The second section of WTO 'Insights' contains several essays about international trade law and the current issues facing the WTO. Each of these essays provides new analysis and many offer innovative policy proposals. It is particularly fitting that Professor John Jackson chose to write about the environment-related jurisprudence of the WTO, as Justice Feliciano heard and decided important cases dealing with the environment, including the very first case, *US – Reformulated Gasoline*, and the much publicized *US – Shrimp* case.

The third section addresses the changing landscape of international investment arbitration and contains papers by well-known scholars and jurists. Included in this part is a contribution by Judge Stephen M. Schwebel, who served two decades on the International Court of Justice and was its President for three years before he retired.

The fourth section looks at new challenges in international arbitration and contains several essays by highly-regarded scholars and jurists on various topics of public international law and the practice of international tribunals.

A book project of this depth and scope takes years from start to finish, and we, the editors, have very much enjoyed this endeavour and especially our communication with each of the participants. As is almost inevitable in a multiyear project of this sort, some participants have passed away. One of them, Professor Robert E. Hudec, had intended to do a study of the negotiation of Part IV of the General Agreement on Tariffs and Trade based on the notes he kept as an American trade official at that time. Sadly, Bob passed away, and his paper was never written.

On the other hand, our volume does include an excellent essay by Professor Said El-Naggar, one of the original seven members of the Appellate Body and a close friend of Toy's, who had finished his essay on the WTO participation of developing countries shortly before he passed away in April 2004. Professors Hudec and El-Naggar were legends in international economics and law, and both shared a passion for interdisplinary studies of international trade law, policy, and economics.

In addition to all of the contributors, we want to thank the individuals and organizations who have made this book possible. We wish to especially acknowledge the helpful advice and encouragement from Professor Maria Lourdes Sereno, who has been privileged to have Justice Feliciano as her special mentor ever since she went to work with his law firm as a young lawyer over twenty years ago. We received editing assistance from Natalia Bayurova, Jan Bohanes, Lisa Coen, Carol Ní Ghiollarnáth, Adéshola Odusanya, Iain Sandford, and Arun Venkataraman. The Global Environment and Trade Study and the Faculty of Law of Maastricht University provided financial assistance. We also wish to thank Finola O'Sullivan and the editors at Cambridge University Press for supporting this project and helping us see it through to fruition.

This project, for us, has been a labour of love, affection, admiration, and respect for a man whom we hold in the highest esteem. We have enjoyed working together – this book is the result of a dedicated collaboration across continents and time zones. It is an example of international cooperation in honour of a truly international jurist and scholar.

STEVE CHARNOVITZ
George Washington University Law School

DEBRA P. STEGER
University of Ottawa Faculty of Law

PETER VAN DEN BOSSCHE
Maastricht University Faculty of Law

September 2004

BIOGRAPHICAL NOTE

JUSTICE FLORENTINO P. FELICIANO

Justice Florentino P. Feliciano was born in Manila, the Philippines, in 1928. Following his undergraduate BA and LLB degrees at the University of the Philippines, Justice Feliciano obtained a Master of Laws (LLM) and a Doctor of Juridical Science (JSD) at Yale University. He was subsequently awarded a Doctor of Laws (LLD) by Misamis University in the Philippines. He won the prestigious Carolinda Waters Prize in International Law at Yale Law School in both 1953 and 1955.

Justice Feliciano, or 'Toy' as he unassumingly prefers to be addressed by peers and subordinates alike, was admitted to the Philippine Bar in 1953. After working with the Department of Justice in the Philippines, and after lecturing in law at (amongst others) the University of the Philippines and Yale, Justice Feliciano embarked upon a long and illustrious legal career during which he has advised upon, and adjudicated over, many different areas of law in many international jurisdictions.

He was a partner at SyCip Salazar Hernandez & Gatmaitan (formerly SyCip Salazar Feliciano & Hernandez) for nearly twenty years, and became the firm's Co-Managing Partner in 1981 and its Managing Partner in 1983. During his time as a partner at that firm, Justice Feliciano advised many national and international corporations on their activities on a wide spectrum of legal issues.

After many years in private practice, Justice Feliciano was appointed as an Associate Justice of the Supreme Court of the Philippines in 1986, following which he became a Senior Associate Justice in 1994. While at the Supreme Court, he decided a number of cases dealing with a broad range of legal issues, including commercial law, tax law, commercial arbitration, and the administration and recognition of domestic and foreign arbitral awards.

Following his outstanding work at the Supreme Court, Justice Feliciano became a member of the newly established Appellate Body of the World Trade Organization in 1995. The Appellate Body, the highest international tribunal for trade disputes, hears appeals from WTO panel cases. Justice Feliciano was Chairman of the Appellate Body in 2000–1. During this period, he contributed immensely to the burgeoning jurisprudence of international trade law.

Justice Feliciano is also well-known in the field of international arbitration. He has acted as both an arbitrator and as counsel for parties in numerous international commercial and investment arbitration disputes. In addition to his work for (amongst others) the International Chamber of Commerce (ICC) and the International Centre for the Settlement of Investment Disputes (ICSID), Justice Feliciano has served as the President in a Stockholm Arbitration Institute case and as a Member of the Arbitration Tribunal under Chapter XV of the 1982 United Nations Convention on the Law of the Sea (UNCLOS). He served on the Asian Development Bank Administrative Tribunal from 1991 to 1995.

Justice Feliciano is currently Senior Counsel at SyCip Salazar Hernandez & Gatmaitan. He is a member of the World Bank Administrative Tribunal and a member of the Senior Advisory Council on the South East Asian Programme on Ocean Law and Policy. In addition, he is a member of the ICC Panel of Arbitrators, the ICSID Roster of Arbitrators and Conciliators, the Panel of Accredited Arbitrators of the China International Economic Trade Law Arbitration Committee (Beijing); the Japan Commercial Arbitration Association (Tokyo); the World Trade Law Association's Governing Council (London); the International Development Law Institute (Rome); and the International Institute of Humanitarian Law (San Remo).

He was elected to the Institut de Droit International and the Curatorium of the Hague Academy of International Law.

In addition to his international service, Justice Feliciano has held a number of positions of honour in the Philippines. These include the Philippine Society of International Law (President from 1975 to 1983), the House of Representatives' Electoral Tribunal (1988 to 1993, Chairman from 1993 to 1995), the Senate Electoral Tribunal (1995), and the Philippine Council for Foreign Relations. He is currently a member of the editorial board of the *Philippine Yearbook of International Law* and a member of the editorial advisory board of the *Journal of International Economic Law*. In July 2003, Justice Feliciano was appointed by President Arroyo of the Philippines as the Chairman of a special fact-finding commission to look into the causes of the 2003 mutiny in Makati, the Philippines.

ABBREVIATIONS

AAA	American Arbitration Association
ACWL	Advisory Centre on WTO Law
ADA	WTO Anti-dumping Agreement
AoA	WTO Agreement on Agriculture
ATC	WTO Agreement on Textiles and Clothing
BIT	bilateral investment treaty
CCAMLR	Convention on the Conservation of Antarctic Marine Living Resources 1980
CFI	Court of First Instance
CIETAC	China International Economic and Trade Arbitration Centre
DS	dispute settlement
DSB	Dispute Settlement Body
DSU	Dispute Settlement Understanding
ECHR	European Convention on Human Rights
ECJ	European Court of Justice
ECOWAS	Economic Community of West African States
ECtHR	European Court of Human Rights
EEZ	exclusive economic zone
EFTA	European Free Trade Association
EU	European Union
FDI	foreign direct investment
FTA	free trade area
GATS	General Agreement on Trade in Services
GATT	General Agreement on Tariffs and Trade
GMO	genetically modified organism
GSP	Generalized System of Preferences
ICC	International Chamber of Commerce
ICCt	International Criminal Court
ICISS	International Commission on Intervention and State Sovereignty

ICSID	International Centre for Settlement of Investment Disputes
ICTR	International Criminal Tribunal for Rwanda
ICTY	International Criminal Tribunal for the former Yugoslavia
ILA	WTO Agreement on Import Licencing Procedures
ILO	International Labor Organization
IMF	International Monetary Fund
ITLOS	International Tribunal for the Law of the Sea
ITO	International Trade Organization
IUUF	illegal, uncontrolled, undeclared fishing
MAI	Multilateral Agreement on Investment
MFA	Multifibre Arrangement
MFN	most-favoured nation
NAMA	non-agricultural market access
NGO	non-government organization
NTB	non-tariff barrier
PCIJ	Permanent Court of International Justice
SA	WTO Agreement on Safeguards
SCM Agreement	WTO Subsidies and Countervailing Measures Agreement
SIAC	Singapore International Arbitration Centre
SPS Agreement	WTO Sanitary and Phytosanitary Measures Agreement
TBT	technical barriers to trade
TBT Agreement	WTO Technical Barriers to Trade Agreement
TRIMS Agreement	WTO Agreement on Trade-Related Investment Measures
TRIPS Agreement	WTO Agreement on Trade-Related Intellectual Property Rights
TS	territorial sea
UN	United Nations
UNCED	UN Conference on Environment and Development
UNCITRAL	UN Commission for International Trade Law
UNCLOS	UN Convention on the Law of the Sea
UNCTAD	UN Conference on Trade and Development
WTO	World Trade Organization

PART I

Reflections on the contributions of Florentino Feliciano to international law

1

A Judge's Judge: Justice Florentino P. Feliciano's Philosophy of the Judicial Function

W. MICHAEL REISMAN

Florentino P. Feliciano is a towering scholar in international law. He has written authoritatively in virtually every area of international law and legal theory, from the law of the sea and, especially, the problems of archipelagos, to human rights law, where his work on refugees and coerced movements of peoples is remarkable for its insights, to environmental law, international economic law, and the law of war, in which his magisterial work with Myres S. McDougal continues to be the essential *vade mecum* for practitioners and students.[1] A student who knew Feliciano only from his extraordinary corpus of written work would have expected a scholar, stockaded behind books in some corner of an ivory tower, jealous of every minute that could be devoted to even more scholarly inquiry. That student would be surprised to encounter quite a different person, for Feliciano has been anything but retiring. He has been an outstanding teacher, practitioner, diplomat, citizen of his country, region and the world, and, above all, judge.

Every role that Feliciano has played has enriched his scholarship and his scholarship has analysed and reflected on each successive role for which he has been a participant-observer. But the role of judge has been central to his intellectual evolution. Indeed, long before he was a Justice of the Philippine Supreme Court and long before he was the Chair of the seven Members of the Appellate Body of the World Trade Organization, the most striking impression that Feliciano made on one was his judiciousness. So it was no surprise that, upon elevation to the bench, as he had done in each previous phase in his career, he would turn his thought to an examination of the role of the judge, informed by the understanding he had acquired in all of his previous experiences, and produce penetrating essays on the judicial function. This is in the great tradition of Holmes, Cardozo, and others. But

[1] See Bibliography of Works by Florentino Feliciano.

other judges who have used their own experiences and insights to analyse the judicial role have done so from a purely domestic perspective. No one has done so from the vantage of both a seasoned domestic and a seasoned international judge. For this reason, Feliciano the judge, and his work on judging, are unique and a particularly valuable source for the student of legal decision.

In an address to the judicial orientation programme of the Philippine Supreme Court on 14 January 1994, Justice Feliciano explained to newly appointed judges the qualities that they would have to nurture in themselves and bring to bear on their assignments for the proper discharge of their office. He identified four characteristics or, as he described them, 'qualities of mind and heart', that the judge required. The first was humility, both personal and with respect to the role of the judge itself:

> A judge must, in the first place, be a man of humility. This is a fundamental requirement which manifests itself in many different ways. Perhaps the most important dimension of humility in a judge is the willingness to listen to both parties, to consider carefully their respective views of the facts and their understanding of the applicable legal principle or norm, before he reaches a conclusion. In a real sense, the observance of the requirements of due process is an exercise in humility for the judge.
>
> There are other dimensions of judicial humility. The judge should have a clear understanding not only of his own personal limitations but also of the limitations of professional competence and of the judicial process itself. A truly humble judge should be able to resist the shimmering vision of an 'imperial judiciary' and should come to realize that he has neither the commission nor the competence to solve all the problems of the nation and that there are other 'workers in the vineyard', the members of the Executive and Legislative Departments who make and execute the laws which the judge is to apply.[2]

The second quality of mind and heart was learning:

> In the second place, the judge must be a man of learning. The law has always been a learned profession and the judge must render, not justice according to his own private lights, but justice *according to law*. The judge then must have a natural love of learning. He must be willing to invest a considerable amount of time and effort learning about the craft and profession of judging, and in informing himself about recent developments in the law and new norms and caselaw he must apply to the controversies before him. He must also inform

[2] Florentino P. Feliciano, 'Qualities of a Good Judge', address before the 28th Judicial Orientation Program, Supreme Court, Manila, 14 January 1994.

> himself about the community in which he lives, the social concerns, the politics and economics and the notions of moral rectitude obtaining in that community, the stuff out of which human controversies arise and eventually come before the judge. The judge must be learned but he is not a lonely scholar in a library nor a scientist isolated in a laboratory. He must be a man of his times.[3]

The third quality was sensitivity to the social values in the law:

> A judge must be sensitive to the basic social values which are embodied in the legal norms and principles he must apply and which the law seeks to promote and protect through the judicial process. He must, in other words, become aware that his decisions have consequences for human values. In those areas which are open to the exercise of judicial discretion, the judge in making his choices should give effect to the values which have been incorporated in the moral code and social mores of the community. His decisions, in other words, should not reflect merely his own individual caprices nor his private conceptions of a desirable social or economic or political program.[4]

The fourth quality was personal morality and integrity:

> A fourth characteristic which I believe a judge must have, relates to the fact that our community requires very high standards of personal morality and integrity from judges. A judge passes judgment upon his fellow human beings. To be morally entitled to do so, to merit respect for his judgments, our society demands more from a judge than from those who are subject to the authority and jurisdiction of the judge. It is not easy to be a good man; it is even more difficult to be a good judge, for he must constantly strive to be better, morally speaking, than the average person or the man of average goodness. The quality of justice a judge renders is necessarily reflective of the quality of the judge as a moral person, as a principled man.[5]

In another article, Justice Feliciano related these issues of character and quality to a method, marked by patience and a scientific disposition. He counselled a method which is 'tentative and discursive . . . analyzing, testing and reviewing provisional characterizations, revising, sometimes rejecting, preliminary conclusions before settling upon definitive ones'.[6] As he put it:

[3] *Ibid.* at p. 3. [4] *Ibid.* at pp. 3–4. [5] *Ibid.* at p. 4.

[6] Florentino P. Feliciano, 'The Application of Law: Some Recurring Aspects of the Process of Judicial Review and Decision Making' (1992) *American Journal of Jurisprudence* 37 at 36–7.

> The judge proceeding in this cautiously tentative manner is thereby acting out his impartiality and open mind and his willingness to examine and consider the evidence and the arguments submitted by the contending parties. He is, in other words, consciously deferring a conclusion, until such evidence and arguments have been factored in his own judgmental process.[7]

These instructions to acolyte judges have a universal validity. They are also a portrait of Florentino P. Feliciano.

In his distinguished Sherrill Lecture, which he delivered on 4 December 1990 at the Yale Law School, Justice Feliciano elaborated the methodology which the judge, whose personal characteristics he had described, had to deploy in order to properly discharge the obligations of his office. I had the privilege of hearing Judge Feliciano deliver the lecture and, like everyone else in the packed hall, realized that I was witness to a major event in legal scholarship. Subsequently published as an essay, Justice Feliciano's lecture ranks with Cardozo's *The Nature of the Judicial Process* in its ambition, but goes far beyond it in depth of analysis. The lecture proposed to do nothing less than 'to explore the thrust and implications of the intellectual activities summed up as the "application of law" which take place within, and as part and parcel of, the process of judicial review and, more broadly, the judicial process itself'.[8]

Justice Feliciano turned his attention, specifically, to the intellectual operation involved in the application of legal prescriptions. He explained that this task has a number of temporal dimensions. In the short term, the judge must decide a case within definite time limits. In the longer run, he must clarify and develop a body of law. This is, of course, akin to Judge Friendly's 'law-making' function, but Justice Feliciano has made clear that whatever the nominal philosophy of the judge in question – positivist, naturalist, historicist, or socialist – there is no way of evading this part of the intellectual assignment.

To be sure, as Justice Feliciano teaches us, the law pretends to be retrospective, always purporting to look back for authority. In fact, it is, ineluctably, a process of making choices, which are, of course, informed by expressions of policy from the past but require far more from the judge than their rote application. As Justice Feliciano put it:

[7] *Ibid.* at 37. [8] *Ibid.* at 17.

> Human choice is inherent in the functioning of the judicial process as we know it, that freedom of choice is exercised by the judge in the course of applying authoritative policy to the facts before him.[9]

Few judges acknowledge this and many more may be unaware of it. But Justice Feliciano has been there and warns us that 'the rhetoric of judicial decision is frequently different from the rhetoric of the preceding deliberations in a collegiate or multi-judge court'.[10]

Justice Feliciano gently disagreed with Justice Cardozo and Judge Clark with respect to the number of cases requiring choice. His learned predecessors had thought that the vast majority of the cases coming before them were 'predestined' because, as Judge Clark put it, there are 'vast and important areas of the law where there is little debate as to the substantive principles, and the cases, if not foredoomed from the start, deal only with the procedure'.[11] Justice Feliciano instructs us that even there, the choices that still remain to be made, indeed, are ineluctable. As he says, the more the judge knows about an area, the more options or alternatives in decision he will perceive.[12] He draws attention to Karl Llewellyn's staggering compendium of ways that appellate courts shape old law into new without acknowledging it, perhaps without themselves being fully aware of it.

So, like it or not and admit it or not, the application function inexorably includes a component of choice by the applier. Is this choice to be effected by untrammelled exercise of discretion, in some sort of quintessential 'creative act'? In his Sherrill Lecture, Justice Feliciano pointed out that the freedom of the judge is not absolute. Nonetheless, there is always an element of choice and the question is how it is to be performed. Whatever the degree of consciousness of the judge about these tasks, he is engaged in three distinct operations when applying legal norms in a case before him: first, he must determine the operative facts; secondly, he must determine the applicable legal or normative prescriptions; and thirdly, he must relate the prescriptions to the operative facts.[13] Nor are these tasks performed in a linear sequence.

[9] *Ibid.* at 35. [10] *Ibid.*

[11] 'The Limits of Judicial Objectivity' (1963) *American University Law Review* 3.

[12] Florentino P. Feliciano, 'The Application of Law: Some Recurring Aspects of the Process of Judicial Review and Decision Making' (1992) *American Journal of Jurisprudence* 41.

[13] *Ibid.* at 36.

For Justice Feliciano, the method of choice required is a very disciplined exercise of judgment. As he writes:

> The most important task of the judge is to become very clear as to what community values or interests are engaged, and in what degree, in the case before him, given the facts provisionally designated as operative and the legal norms tentatively deemed applicable. He must be able to apprehend such values and translate them into terms sufficiently concrete and operational so as to be able to relate them to both the facts and the probably applicable authoritative policy. The detailed relating of basic community interests to the facts and the norm or norms provisionally applicable may be done through, and in the course of, carrying out the other tasks of application.
>
> He must then draw upon the wisdom of the past and examine the previous applications of the potentially applicable precedent to ascertain what principles, more or less general, have emerged from what beginnings and in what directions precedent and principle may be developing. The past decisions or potential precedents, whether they agree or are apparently in conflict with one another, would have to be scrutinized to lay bare the factors or conditions which may rationally explain the results reached in different decisions and the shape of the general principle which has emerged or may be emerging. These factors might relate, for instance, to the presence or absence of certain critical facts; the relative importance of the values at stake and the anticipatable impacts upon such values; the size and other characteristics of the groupings of people affected by particular decisions; the tranquillity or the condition of crisis (e.g., insurgency or social unrest or economic depression) prevailing in society at the time; the degree of persuasiveness or ineptness of the analogies used in past decisions; and so on. Further, the judge must seek to anticipate and estimate possible future consequences upon the community of each alternative in decision that he sees open to him. Finally, he must seek to design a decision, with an appropriate mode of explication, which promises the greatest net value advantage to the parties and to the community at large.[14]

In free societies, a key source of community values is the authoritative communications of legislative, executive, and administrative bodies. But, if the answer to the question before a court were readily available in these formal expressions of the law, there would be little requirement for judicial choice. As Justice Feliciano points out:

[14] *Ibid.* at 42–3.

> The task of clarifying and specifying community values is not necessarily exhausted by examination of the value content of the legal norms tentatively designated as applicable by the judge. The policy guidance yielded by that examination might not be adequate or sufficiently specific to bring him to the critical point of decision. . . . In this and other types of situations, the task of clarification and specification needs to continue.[15]

So the judge may be obliged to consult more general community values. Faced with this challenge, some scholars have retreated to logical exercises. Professor Wechsler made famous the notion of 'neutral principles'. My former colleague, Judge Bork, insisted that the judge eschew clarification of values and rely upon strict logic, which, he believes, 'has a life of its own' and can be applied rigorously to a text in order to squeeze out answers. My former colleague, Harry Wellington, suggests that in these circumstances the judge need do no more than repair to 'conventional morality'[16] as a reliable indication of shared community values, a pluralization of Lord Devlin's 'man on the Clapham omnibus'. But as Judge Skelly Wright observed, 'how are we to evaluate the "neutrality" of line-drawing except by reference to some sort of value choices?'

Justice Feliciano cuts through this. He observes that consensus on conventional morality dissolves quickly when one puts it under the microscope of social inquiry. Indeed, most of the critical issues in complex modern societies are marked by heterogeneity of view rather than homogeneity. Hanging on the straps of that Clapham omnibus are many different men (and women), each distinguished by factors as diverse as personality, culture, class, sexual orientation, and crisis exposure. Their inner worlds, their identifications, their matter-of-fact expectations of past and future, and their value demands, may vary greatly. Hence Justice Feliciano explains that the judge may have to engage in an integration of many different moral views in order to determine what the supplementary material available from his inquiry is. He may also turn to the body of international human rights law, which, happily, the United States Supreme Court has at long last begun to do.[17]

All of these exercises essentially involve the integration of others' views. It seems to me clear, from a review of all of Justice Feliciano's

[15] *Ibid*. at 47.

[16] Harry H. Wellington, 'Common Law Rules and Constitutional Double Standards: Some Notes on Adjudication' (1973)*Yale Law Journal* 244.

[17] *Grutter* v. *Bollinger*, 123 S.Ct. 2325 (2003).

work, that he also believes that the judge may, in some circumstances, be obliged to postulate values for the community and apply them even if they are inconsistent with the other more conventional sources. This supplementing and corrective function may involve an integration of competing interests or the superordination of one of those over the other. Such integrative solutions are often referred to as 'balancing', a term borrowed from hydraulics, which seems to import a mechanical operation. In fact, 'balancing' conceals a great deal of choice. As Myres McDougal eloquently wrote:

> A rational concern for long-term interests in the real world commonly includes, further, a concern for the next steps, or immediate consequences. The effective accommodation of opposing interests must require, beyond verbal abstractions, the balancing and integration of value demands in social process.[18]

Justice Feliciano concluded his remarkable Sherrill Lecture with the following words:

> In the end, of course, much depends upon the judges themselves, their qualities of mind and heart, the substance of their attachment to the best traditions of the judicial and legal professions, their courage and sensitivity and commitment to the values of free human beings in a society that is both productive and caring and, ultimately, their view of the relation of man to the universe.[19]

This tribute to Justice Feliciano and his extraordinary contribution to our understanding of the judicial process began with his identification of the necessary characteristics of the judge. And properly so. For Justice Feliciano has demonstrated to us more than anyone else that adjudication is not an impersonal process of 'rule-crunching'. In the end, it is the judge, drawing upon a lifetime's personal resources of knowledge, character and courage, who must decide. In all the judicial functions that Justice Feliciano has performed, as Justice of the Supreme Court of the Philippines, as Member of the Appellate Body of the World Trade Organization, and as international arbitrator in innumerable cases, the international community can be grateful for the character, knowledge, courage, and judiciousness that he has brought to bear.

[18] M. McDougal, 'The Application of Constitutive Prescriptions: An Addendum to Justice Cardozo', *Thirty-third Annual Benjamin N. Cardozo Lecture Delivered Before the Association of the Bar of the City of New York on October 13, 1977* (1978), p. 17.

[19] *Supra* n. 6 at p. 56.

2

The Benign First Mate

ROSALYN HIGGINS

Toy Feliciano's life in the law is a silent rebuttal to those who contend that a policy-oriented approach to law is but a façade for politics, that it is a tool for the powerful, and that it is in essence a front for the views of the State Department. As a member of the 'invisible college' of Yale Law School lawyers, he has throughout his life shown how this approach can be put to the service of values that are universal. His life and work also illustrate how those values can be promoted in full conformity with deep scholarship.

I first met Toy when I was a graduate student at Yale from 1959–61. He was already established there as a teacher and known to be collaborating with Myres McDougal in the preparation of *Law and Minimum World Public Order*. I was at that stage in my life where I had left the safe moorings of black-letter law and was being tossed about in the turbulent waters of policy science. Moreover, the captain of the ship on which I now found myself was at once magnificent and terrifying. Toy Feliciano seemed to me a sort of benign first mate, who certainly understood the course on which we were set and how we were to get there, but who might still be talked to in the 'language of the old country'. My enduring memory of him in those early Yale years was of a person who was gentle, kind, and thoroughly competent. I have never had occasion to revise those early impressions.

Toy had already numbered among the 'associates' who in 1987 wrote with McDougal *Studies in World Public Order*. The co-authored *Law and Minimum World Public Order*, which appeared in 1961, was shortly followed by the *International Law of War* in 1964. When, thirty-five years later, Toy spoke at McDougal's Memorial gathering, he spoke of this collaboration as an 'honour, which I have treasured throughout my life'.

However, he decided to proceed with his life's work outside of academia and returned to the Philippines as a member of the law firm SyCip Salazar Feliciano & Hernandez. He became immersed in a different range of issues – including trade and corporate law, anti-dumping, intellectual property, banking and insurance services, shipping and telecommunications. This combination of expertise in what today we might call international trade law, and in public international law, was later to assist the World Trade Organization in a very special way.

The standing in which Toy was regarded in his own homeland was evidenced by his elevation to the Supreme Court of the Philippines in 1986. After nine years the call came from the World Trade Organization to serve on its Appellate Body. For six years – which included a period as Chairman – he brought his special combination of skills to bear on the problems of major importance referred to that Body. Toy Feliciano was one of the exceptional persons in the World Trade Organization who truly knew international trade matters and also public international law. Only very occasionally have these two fields of expertise been combined in a single person. Those who follow these matters know that he has played a central role in ensuring that the Appellate Body adjudicates not on the basis of the 1994 World Trade Organization rules and procedures alone, but ultimately by reference to international law more generally. Feliciano has written[1] that the panels and Appellate Body are bound to interpret the WTO agreements having regard to the customary rules of international law – which has frequently been held to include the Vienna Convention on the Law of Treaties.

He has already affirmed this in the *United States – Gasoline* matter, in which he was the Presiding Member. The Appellate Body held that the panel below had overlooked a fundamental rule of treaty interpretation, namely that embodied in Article 31 of the Vienna Convention. It added that its decision 'reflects a measure of recognition that the *General Agreement* [i.e., the General Agreement on Tariffs and Trade of 1994] is not to be read in clinical isolation from public international law'.[2] A further insistence that the law of the World Trade Organization finds its place in the wider body of international law is to be found in the

[1] Florentino Feliciano and Peter L. H. Van den Bossche, 'The Dispute Settlement System of the World Trade Organization: Institutions, Process and Practice' in Niels M. Blokker and Henry G. Schermers (eds), *Proliferation of International Organizations: Legal Issues* (Kluwer Law International, The Hague, 2001), p. 314.

[2] Appellate Body Report, *United States – Standards for Reformulated and Conventional Gasoline* ('*US – Gasoline*'), WT/DS2/AB/R, 20 May 1996, p. 17.

United States – Import Prohibition of Certain Shrimp and Shrimp Products case, over which he presided.[3]

It should not be forgotten that Feliciano was elected an associé de l'Institut de Droit International astonishingly early, in 1965. From 1965 until 2001 he has served, almost without pause, on a series of commissions, the variety of which testify as to the breadth of his knowledge. A variety of Reports and Resolutions have benefited from his input: the application of the laws of war to the military operations of the United Nations and regional organizations (Resolutions 54-II, 449 and 56, 540); the legal conditions for capital investments in developing countries and related agreements (no resolutions adopted); the proper law of the contract in agreements between a state and a private foreign entity (Resolution 58-II, 192); the law applicable to joint international state or quasi-state enterprises of an economic nature (Resolution 61-II, 268); the distribution between states of the spheres of action, independent of their territorial delimitation (no resolutions adopted); the autonomy of the parties in international contracts between private persons or entities (Resolution 64-II, 382); the effects of obligations of one company of a transnational group upon the other companies of that group (Resolution 66-II, 462); the application of international humanitarian law and fundamental human rights in armed conflicts in which non-state entities are parties (Resolution 86-II, 386); immunities from jurisdiction and execution of heads of state and of government in international law (Resolution 69, 742). In all of these he was able to offer knowledge and constructive insights.

Throughout all of this remarkable career, Toy Feliciano has remained essentially unchanged as a person: kind, unassuming, attentive to others. And in all of his work he has adhered to the promises he made to Myres McDougal in 1958: to 'reject . . . "bright line" formulations or catchy phrases that seemed to permit a decision maker, with apparent ease, to decide quickly', but instead to 'engage in explicit, systematic, and contextual examination . . . [and to appraise in] terms of short- and long-term goals of the community of nations'.[4]

I am delighted that he is being honoured with this *Liber Amicorum*.

[3] Appellate Body Report, *United States – Import Prohibition of Certain Shrimp and Shrimp Products*, WT/DS58/AB/R, 12 October 1998, paragraph 158.

[4] (1998–9) *Yale Law Journal*, 949.

3

The Aristotelian

JAMES BACCHUS

Florentino Feliciano smiles down on me nowadays from the wall of the chambers of the Appellate Body of the World Trade Organization with the same small smile he wore on the day we first met at the WTO all those years ago.

'Call me Toy', he said. So I did. We all did.

Everyone everywhere calls him 'Toy'. Everyone everywhere has always called him 'Toy'. Florentino Feliciano was one of the most distinguished jurists on the planet long before there was such a thing as an Appellate Body or a WTO, and yet, then as now, far and wide, he has been always simply 'Toy'.

'Toy' is a familiar nickname in the Philippines. For my friend Florentino, it is a nickname he has had since his childhood. This is fitting; for it was in his childhood in the Philippines that the beginnings were made of the great judge that Toy became.

Born in 1928, Toy was thirteen when the Japanese attacked Pearl Harbor. A few weeks later, Japanese forces overran and occupied the Filipino capital of Manila. The occupation forces closed the Catholic school where American Jesuits had been teaching the teenager Toy.

This, however, was not the end of Toy's wartime education. Toy's father, an engineer and geologist who taught at the University of the Philippines for thirty-nine years, had studied in the USA in the 1930s at the University of Chicago. He had brought back home with him to the Philippines the five-foot shelf of classic works of science, philosophy, history, and literature that the University of Chicago called the 'Great Books'.

The 'Great Books' programme of the University of Chicago was one of the great experiments in American education of the twentieth century. In the 1930s, the university's president, Robert Hutchins, and his prolific philosopher friend, Mortimer Adler, had set out to create a new

This chapter was previously published in James Bacchus, *Trade and Freedom* (Cameron May, London, 2004).

collegiate curriculum at Chicago that would focus on the 'great ideas' of the 'Great Books' in the Western tradition. They denounced much of what then passed for higher education; they deplored narrow specialization and they sought to impart instead the general enlightenment that they believed would surely come from an immersion in the 'Great Books' of the Western liberal tradition.[1]

Hutchins advocated restructuring undergraduate education based on 'a course of study consisting of the greatest books of the western world and the arts of reading, writing, thinking, and speaking, together with mathematics, the best exemplar of the processes of human reason'.[2] Similarly, Adler maintained that a direct relationship with the 'Great Books' would enable and empower people 'to lead the distinctively human life of reason'.[3]

Hutchins and Adler never fully succeeded in incorporating the 'Great Books' into the curriculum at Chicago. Although the 'Great Books' continue to have many enthusiasts, the ideal of a liberal arts education that would open individual minds to the vast potential of human reason through exposure to the 'great ideas' in the 'Great Books' remains, in most places, only an ideal.[4]

But that was not so for Toy Feliciano in the Japanese-occupied Philippines of the Second World War. With all the schools closed, Toy continued his schooling at home by reading his way through his father's five-foot shelf of 'Great Books'. He participated also in informal study sessions on the 'Great Books'. These sessions employed the Socratic method of constant questioning – just as Hutchins and Adler had recommended.

In this methodical approach to learning, as any lawyer who ever argued before him in later years would surely assume, Toy shined.

Through this youthful experience, through this immersion in the great thoughts in all the 'Great Books', Toy chose the life of reason. He

[1] For a brief perspective on the 'Great Books' programme at the University of Chicago, see 'The Great Ideas: The University of Chicago and the Ideal of Liberal Education', an Exhibit in the Department of Special Collections, University of Chicago Library (1 May 2002–6 September 2002), online at www.lib.uchicago.edu/e/spcl/excat/ideasint.html

[2] Robert Hutchins, *The Higher Learning in America* (Yale University Press, New Haven, 1936).

[3] Mortimer Adler, *How To Read a Book: The Art of Getting a Liberal Education* (Simon & Schuster, New York, 1940).

[4] For an autobiographical retrospective by Adler, see Mortimer Adler, *Philosopher at Large: An Intellectual Autobiography* (Macmillan, New York, 1977).

recalls now, 'I did an enormous amount of reading which was ordinarily done in college'. He adds, 'I also learned how to think.' Plato, Lucretius, Aurelius, Plotinus, Montaigne, Bacon, Hobbes, Locke, Smith, Jefferson, and Mill: the reading of these, and more, were all, for Toy, part of learning how to think and to reason while he waited for the war to end.

But none of the classic authors of the 'Great Books' impressed him more, or influenced him more, than the ancient Greek philosopher Aristotle. None of them, as Toy has told me many times, left more of an imprint on his own way of thinking than Aristotle. Soon after I met him, Toy told me, for the first of many times, 'I am an Aristotelian'.

The Aristotelian view became Toy's view. The Aristotelian way became Toy's way. Observation. Classification. Definition. Cause. Purpose. Connection. Logic. Always logic. A predisposition to proceed from particular facts to universal conclusions. A deep feeling for the natural world. And a passion, always a passion, for the natural laws that imply the existence of what Toy likes to call 'natural justice'. These are the constant ways of Toy, the Aristotelian.

To this, as it relates to law, and especially as it relates to how he sees law as a judge, must be added the additional ways of thinking that Toy learned following the war as a law student at Yale from his teacher and long-time mentor, the late Professor Myres McDougal. Professor 'Mac' McDougal was the guiding light of the 'New Haven' school of jurisprudence in the 1950s. He had served as an aide to Harry Hopkins during the New Deal, had been an early advocate of the human rights efforts of the new United Nations, and, when Toy arrived in New Haven, had already begun his considerable intellectual and other efforts to re-invent legal thinking.

McDougal saw law as an open-ended process of never-ending give and take. He saw it as a process of continuous interaction in an ever-evolving world in which individual decision-makers of all kinds weigh competing ideas of what law should be in 'demand and response' to the world's constant changes.[5] McDougal saw law as consisting primarily of individual human decisions, as being 'a process of decision',[6] and thus he saw the judicial process as a process in which the judge plays, necessarily, a very human role.

[5] See, e.g., Myres S. McDougal, 'The Hydrogen Bomb Tests' (1955) 49 *American Journal of International Law* 357.

[6] Myres S. McDougal, 'Preface' to Harold D. Lasswell and Myres S. McDougal, *Jurisprudence for a Free Society: Studies in Law, Science and Policy* (Student Edition, 1997), v [1992].

At Yale, Toy worked with McDougal on his classic book on the law of war (one of the 'Great Books' of international law). Toy recalled later that, as a young Filipino who had lived through the Japanese occupation of his homeland, he had little faith at the outset of their work together in the existence of something that might justifiably be called a 'law' of war. With McDougal's guidance, he changed his mind.

In Aristotelian fashion, Toy later helped McDougal identify and categorize the processes of decision-making and the major types of controversies that lead to war. Then, with two Yale degrees in hand, he went home. Yet even from afar, 'Mac' McDougal remained his friend and his mentor for decades to come. Toy's father had died while Toy was at Yale, and McDougal became a 'father figure' for the young Filipino.[7]

Back in the Philippines, Toy quickly became one of the most successful international lawyers in the Philippines and in all of Asia. He continued to write. He served as an arbitrator. He represented individuals and companies with worldwide interests. He built one of the most successful law firms in his developing country.

The government of the Philippines at the time was in the hands of Ferdinand Marcos. Originally elected and re-elected as President, Marcos had abandoned democracy, declared martial law, and established a corrupt and oppressive dictatorship in 1972. Twice, the Marcos Government wanted to nominate Toy for the Supreme Court of the Philippines. Twice, in his quiet way, he avoided the nomination. Years later, in typical understatement, and in his typically quiet voice, Toy said to me, 'I did not support Mr Marcos. Mr Marcos did not support the rule of law'.

The people's revolt in the Philippines, in February 1986, finally toppled Marcos after more than twenty years in power and put the ousted dictator on a helicopter to a well-deserved exile. Six months later, the new, and democratic, President of the Philippines, Carazon Aquino, named Florentino Feliciano to the country's Supreme Court. He served with distinction on the court until shortly before I first saw him smiling in Geneva in 1995.

Of the seven of us who were first appointed to the Appellate Body by the Members of the WTO in 1995, Toy alone had previously been a judge. Perhaps partly for that reason, of all of us, Toy most looks like a judge. Always impeccably dressed – wearing an immaculate white shirt,

[7] Florentino P. Feliciano, 'In Memoriam', 'Tributes: Myres S. McDougal' (1999) 108, (5) *Yale Law Journal* 947 at 951.

a neatly knotted tie, a gray sweater vest, and a permanently pensive air – he is always supremely judicial. When he shifts back and forth between his two pairs of glasses – the one for reading and the other for judging – and when he peers over at me in utter thoughtfulness, he looks every bit a judge.

Moreover, Toy not only *looks* like a judge. He *acts* like a judge. And he has never been averse to urging his colleagues to act like judges too. When Toy especially wants to get my attention, he calls me 'James'. Politely he asks, 'You don't mind if I call you James, do you?' I never do. 'James', he has often told me, 'act like a judge. Think like a judge. Be a judge.'

With Toy's help, I have tried. We all have. In his six years on the Appellate Body, Toy showed us all how to be a judge. In his time at the round table of the Appellate Body, Toy tried his best also to teach us all his Aristotelian ways. He brought to the round table of the Appellate Body what can only be described as an Aristotelian zeal for the task of interpreting the WTO Treaty when judging appeals in WTO disputes.

Like the medieval Schoolmen who followed Aristotle, Toy schooled us all in the methodical rigours of a logical approach to legal reasoning. It was Aristotle, after all, who invented formal logic. Toy implored us to think logically. He urged us, in his frequent phrase, to 'put leg over leg until the dog reaches Dover'. He counselled us to have the patience to explore every conceivable angle of a legal issue until we 'broke the camel's back'. These quaint phrases from his genteel tradition revealed the inner workings of a rational and ordered mind.

Yet, unlike the Schoolmen, Toy beseeched us also to look beyond logic. Unlike them, he refused to divorce speculation from observation. He refused to allow us ever to descend, like the medieval Scholastics of lore, to the intellectual indulgence of Thomistic angel-counting. Remembering Aristotle's focus on the natural world, and no doubt remembering also McDougal's emphasis on the critical personal role of an individual legal decision-maker, Toy encouraged us always to focus on the observable facts, and he reminded us always to be mindful of the consequences of our decisions 'in the real world where people live and work and die'.[8]

Toy has an empathy for others that seems, to me, to be missing in Aristotle. Aristotle defended slavery. Aristotle accepted the abject subjugation of women. Even allowing for the great gulf of several millennia between then and now, Aristotle does not seem in his writings – to me at least – to be especially concerned about anything resembling what we

[8] Appellate Body Report, *European Communities – Measures Concerning Meat and Meat Products (Hormones)*, WT/DS26/AB/R, 13 February 1998, paragraph 187.

would see today as social justice. In contrast, for Toy, justice is an ever-present concern. For my friend Toy, with his abiding passion for 'natural justice', no sparrow can ever be allowed to fall in vain.

And, for Toy, justice can best be secured by the best combination of words. One of those whose writings can be found among the 'Great Books' is Thomas Jefferson. Like Jefferson, Toy is blessed with a felicitous pen. He would write with a quill pen if he had one. Like Jefferson, too, Toy can be inventive with words. He has even been known to *invent* a word or two for purposes of prose effect along the way. When we pointed out to him once that a 'word' he had employed in one of his pleasingly elegant passages was not, in fact, a word at all, Toy was not fazed. He simply replied, 'Well, it should be.'

Peering out over his 'judging' glasses, looking down from his appellate perch on some wary lawyer who has already been arguing before him for hours, seemingly futilely, in some exhausting oral hearing, Toy can appear imperious indeed. The worst for the weary appellate advocate, though, comes when Toy pauses in an interrogation and, with a disarming smile, says softly, 'I'm just an old judge from a small country'. Word quickly spread beyond Geneva to all those who might one day argue before Florentino Feliciano that what this simple, unassuming sentence really means is: 'Watch out!' For it is in what follows that modest phrase that Toy truly begins to teach the fine points of Aristotelian logic. It is then when he begins his most merciless judicial inquisition.

In his spare time, while on the Appellate Body, Toy encouraged me to read, and reread, the 'Great Books'. He urged me to make my own way through Hutchins' and Adler's five-foot shelf. 'It is all there, James', he would say. 'Read Aristotle.' At his urging, I did. With his tutelage, I became a poor Alexander to his latter-day Aristotle, and I savoured a special sense of accomplishment when, shortly before he retired from the Appellate Body, I was able to convince my friend Toy of the merit of my position on a legal question of causation by citing Aristotle's principle of the 'final cause'.[9]

Aristotle's passion for independent inquiry is mirrored in Toy's own passion for both independence and inquiry. Toy thinks independently;

[9] As Toy certainly knows, Aristotle said that each thing or event has four causes: the material cause, the efficient cause, the formal cause, and the final cause. The 'final cause' is the purpose – the goal or full development of an object. For more on this, see Aristotle, *The Ethics of Aristotle: The Nicomachean Ethics* (Penguin Classics, New York, 1955), Appendix E, p. 355.

he thinks for himself. Toy conducts his own inquiry; he acts for himself. Thinking and acting for himself, he endeavours to master every single detail of every single case. Toy gives exhaustive consideration to every single argument, no matter how seemingly far-fetched. He gives elaborate consideration to every single fact, no matter how seemingly tangential. In his passion for justice, Toy wants to get it all just right. He wants to get the dog to Dover. He wants to break the camel's back. He insists, however, on doing it in just the right way.

Toy's insistence on doing it in just the right way is just one example of the intellectual integrity he has absorbed from Aristotle and from many of the other authors of the 'Great Books' that he read so diligently in his youth, and that he still reads so devotedly even today. Florentino Feliciano is marked, perhaps most of all, by an utter and singular intellectual honesty that keeps him from saying, or doing, or joining in, anything that he is not fully persuaded *is* just right. This helps explain the singular satisfaction that I have always felt on those occasions when Toy has been persuaded by my own diligent efforts to join in a consensus on the Appellate Body. On those occasions, because of Toy, we have had added intellectual assurance that our reasoning and our result were both just right.

Aristotle's ideal of the good life is explained in his treatise entitled *The Nicomachean Ethics*. His equally famous treatise, *Politics*, is really a sort of sequel to this treatise on ethics (regrettably, nowadays, many politicians tend to forget which of the two comes first). Aristotle saw our powers of reason as separating us from all other living things and, thus, as central to what should be our thinking on ethics. Thus, as he explains in *The Nicomachean Ethics*, he believed that the good life, the virtuous life, is one filled to the brim with activities which require the fullest exercise of the uniquely human powers of reason. In particular, he thought the highest good in human life could be achieved through a life of rational, philosophical contemplation.[10] The Greeks called this highest good '*eudaimonia*'. We call this 'happiness'.

As an Aristotelian, Toy goes along with all of this. He seemed to see our collective struggle on the Appellate Body to find the right answer at our table on the legal issues raised in appeals in WTO dispute settlement as a shared experience in rational, philosophical contemplation. He seemed never to be happier than when we were labouring together to

[10] *Ibid.* at pp. 328–35.

fathom the farthest reaches of the possible implications of our mutual decision-making. This, to Toy, is happiness.

Yet Toy is mindful also that Aristotle spoke as well of the virtue of 'the doctrine of the Mean'.[11] According to Aristotle, a desirable 'mean' for living is to be found in a path of moderation between the excesses of two extremes. This 'mean', according to Aristotle, is 'relative' to each of us, and is thus, presumably, 'relative' to our individual circumstances and to our individual abilities.[12] It is the moderate middle way. It is the path of prudence and practical wisdom that seeks a balance between all the pushes and all the pulls of all the varied extremes that compete for our attention and for our allegiance as we strive to live a life of reason. In following this Aristotelian path, 'virtue aims to hit the mean'.[13]

And so, despite his compulsion to immerse himself in the contemplation of the law, despite his determination to divine every last shade of meaning from every single legal issue we ever faced, despite his devotion to wringing every last drop of substance from every last point – however peripheral – that was ever made at our table, and despite his diehard dedication to a life lived – in every waking moment – in, and for, and ever amid, his abiding love of the law, Toy did his best, in his years on the Appellate Body, to aim to hit the mean.

Sometimes he even found his target.

Toy loves pizza almost as much as he loves the law. And once, with typical Aristotelian precision, he and our colleague on the Appellate Body, his Japanese friend Mitsuo Matsushita, tore themselves away from the legal mysteries of the WTO Treaty long enough to conduct, evening after evening, and pizzeria after pizzeria, a mutual, methodical search for the best Italian pizza in the French-Swiss environs of Geneva, Switzerland. Finally, in the veranda restaurant of a small hotel near the Cornavin train station, they found what they were seeking.

'I've tried them all, James', Toy reported back to me, while no doubt recalling all the observations and all the classifications he had made of comparative 'pizza-ness' in his gastronomic journeys throughout Geneva. With a smile of satisfaction, he explained that, at this restaurant, 'the mozzarella is the best, and the crust is just right'. Later, he and I shared a pizza on his newfound veranda. Toy was right – as he was so often right.

He had found the perfect Aristotelian pizza.

[11] *Ibid.* at pp. 100–10. [12] *Ibid.* at p. 100. [13] *Ibid.* at p. 101.

4

Trade and Economic Justice According to Law

JULIO A. LACARTE

The massive increase in commitments arising from the Uruguay Round was instrumental in leading governments to realize that they needed to ensure proper fulfilment by others of the hard-earned concessions that they had negotiated, even though this meant that they themselves would be bound by the same rules. The Understanding on Rules and Procedures Governing the Settlement of Disputes, commonly referred to as 'the Dispute Settlement Understanding' or DSU, which forms an integral part of the Agreement Establishing the World Trade Organization and which signified a substantial change and improvement on the pre-existing GATT provisions, was intended to respond to this perceived need. One of its main innovations was the incorporation of an appeals stage in WTO dispute settlement.

The establishment of the Appellate Body represented a noticeable departure from past GATT practice, not only by bringing in a new level in dispute settlement, but also because it meant that governments accepted the existence of a mechanism that would be at the very least semi-judicial in nature, whose rulings would be definitive and which would function independently of all pressures, political or otherwise.

Conceivably, there were many who felt that dispute settlement in the WTO would go on very much as it had done previously in the GATT and that the Appellate Body would operate only sporadically, when some particularly thorny issue came up, or when a special need to have recourse to it would arise. In practice, any such expectations were not realized. From the very beginning, WTO members repeatedly appealed panel rulings, and the result was – and continues to be – that an overwhelming majority of panel reports are eventually submitted to the Appellate Body.

The seven original members of the Appellate Body could not foresee these events. They had been selected according to geographical distribution and personal competence criteria, and in general knew little about each other, precisely because they had been drawn from areas as diverse as the judicature, intergovernmental organizations, government service, diplomacy, and political life. Clearly, the Appellate Body would need to feel its way forward, justify fully the trust deposited in it and acquire with as little delay as possible a degree of authority commensurate with its duties.

My colleagues had been generous enough to elect me as first Chairman of the Appellate Body, presumably due to my previous experience in GATT affairs and in the Uruguay Round, and I felt we had to blend our seven differing personalities and backgrounds into a coherent, solid group with as little delay as possible. Ensuring harmony among members, channelling discussions constructively, setting up practical procedures to study our cases, and reaching generally acceptable findings without sacrificing individual views, were ambitious objectives but there seemed to be no alternative if the Appellate Body were to attain early the degree of recognition conditions required.

The prompt drafting and approval of the Working Procedures for Appellate Review, which the DSU entrusts to the Appellate Body, represented an essential first step. These Procedures were an initial test that the Appellate Body would undergo, and the manner in which it overcame it would be the object of careful perusal by governments and academics.

This text was given urgent priority, and the fact that it has stood the test of time over nine years with very minor amendments would seem to indicate that it responded well to general expectations.

One of the concepts incorporated into the Working Procedures is that of 'collegiality'. This means that, while a Division made up of three members is responsible for the case on which it sits, the Working Procedures foresee an exchange of views with the other four members, in the course of which the Division has the benefit of the views of its remaining colleagues. The four non-members of the Division are obliged to read, analyse and know all the documentation of the case just as well as the Division, because otherwise they would be quite unable to participate intelligently and usefully in the 'collegiate' consultation. In practice, this has proven to be an extremely efficient way to meet two aims that were in the mind of Appellate Body members from the outset: to utilize fully the human resources of the Appellate Body and to weld its members together through intensive joint work and debate.

It can be said – as with any other similar, newly-created organ – that members of the Appellate Body had to learn how to get along and cooperate with each other. Irrespective of their previous professional experience, they were in a new medium that posed its own unique challenges and demands. It soon transpired that there existed a solid base for this understanding; without exception, the seven were experienced in many walks of life, well-equipped, and desirous of putting in an unstinting effort to make the Appellate Body a success.

The institutional arrangements originally set up by the WTO for the Appellate Body, which remain in force, require that its members be permanently on call, although their overall remuneration is significantly lower than that of other equivalent tribunals. The obvious consequence of this situation is that Appellate Body members must often renounce other more lucrative assignments that could interfere with their WTO-imposed availability. All of those who made up the first Appellate Body were naturally well aware of these conditions, and their acceptance of the appointment meant the implicit acceptance of the financial sacrifice involved.

Over the two terms during which I was part of the Appellate Body, never once did one of my colleagues excuse himself from his obligations to the WTO. This devotion to the formal commitment accepted when being sworn in on appointment, was certainly one of the most potent reasons why the Appellate Body – through a joint and unstinting effort which never measured hours, days, or weeks of work – was formed into a coherent and efficient organ for fairness and equity in world trade.

Practically from the beginning, it was clear to me at least, and I believe also to the others, that we had the makings of a good team and, in this respect, I would be more than unfair if I did not stress the extreme dedication, professional capacity, and unwavering loyalty of our Secretariat Director, Debra Steger, who had become intimately familiar with the DSU as a member of the Uruguay Round Negotiating Group that had drafted it.

Each of my former colleagues has his own individuality; each contributed strongly to the common cause; and I have kept innumerable fond memories of barbed exchanges, apparently insurmountable disagreements, and final texts reached in an atmosphere of reciprocal tolerance and respect.

Within this framework, I would wish to refer to Judge Florentino Feliciano. It did not take us long to find out that he was an individual whose whole formation, experience, intellectual inclination, and single-minded purpose revolved around the interpretation and the application of the law. Some years ago, the Appellate Body was described as 'unflinching' when it had to take difficult decisions likely to provoke controversy due to the importance of the interests involved. The members of the Appellate Body did, indeed, feel that their conduct justified this description. In retrospect, no one merited this more than Justice Feliciano.

Experience soon showed that one of his outstanding characteristics is his unwavering determination to get to the bottom of each and every issue, applying the most rigorous intellectual and professional standards. He neither conceives nor accepts half-measures. His enormous experience and fertile mind are quick to explore differing avenues in all their conceivable permutations, pushing ever for clarification and testing implacably all lines of reasoning. The hearings with parties to a dispute were a privileged venue to exercise these characteristics, as more than one legal counsel whose presentation apparently was not fully satisfactory in terms of its logical coherence, would surely testify. There, all members of the Appellate Body were strongly inquisitorial, but none more so than Justice Feliciano.

These demands Justice Feliciano imposes upon himself are extreme; he must be fully convinced he has explored all possible avenues and exhausted all sources of information before he reaches any conclusion. To the superficial observer, this pattern of behaviour could be mistaken for stubbornness, since in the absence of conviction agreement is inconceivable. Appellate Body members knew better: the process of conviction was ever-present, through long debates and exchanges of views. Given the nature of the work, internal Appellate Body discussions are often long, and occasionally seemingly unending. Varying opinions and interpretations arise and they give rise to vigorous debate.

Obviously, all seven members expected and received the respect due to their background and their personal competence; but, within these parameters, I felt more than once as we reached our conclusions in regard to a particular dispute, that if the ever-demanding Florentino Feliciano was in agreement, then we could be confident we had extracted the most from ourselves in exploring every avenue and blending our individual efforts into a solid ruling.

When three of us – Claus-Dieter Ehlermann, Florentino Feliciano, and I – took our leave of the Appellate Body on concluding our respective terms of office, we were invited to pronounce some parting words before the assembled members of the WTO. All three of us had regrets at leaving our colleagues, with whom we had shared so many stimulating intellectual endeavours and set up such firm links of reciprocal appreciation. It was also a moment in which we felt impelled to endeavour to bid a farewell in which we should leave some lasting legacy to the WTO and to our successors. In his address, Justice Feliciano stressed the significance of the creation of the Appellate Body, as a firm step towards a system that seeks to realize, as he put it, trade and economic justice according to law. And he regretted that there remained then, as there remain now, many aspects of international relations where such an advance was quite inconceivable. He went on to refer to the independence and impartiality of both individuals and institutions as a necessary requirement of the system, and in expressing these concepts he set out what had been, in effect, the guiding light of his six-year term of service at the heart of the world trading community: the respect and application of the rule of law through independent and vigorously unyielding impartiality.

Not very long ago, the President of the Philippines appointed Florentino Feliciano to head a high-level commission enquiry into internal events that had put the country's political stability at stake. The conclusions contained in the committee's report bear the imprint of his deeply-felt patriotism and principles, as he once again served his country by upholding the pillars of republican democracy.

I suspect that Justice Feliciano will continue, with his untiring energy and enthusiasm, to play an important role in many fields of juridical endeavour for a long time to come. He brought to the WTO brilliant academic credentials, membership of the most prestigious professional associations, recognition as an internationally accredited arbitrator, editorships, professorships, consultancies, lectures, government service, a thriving law practice, many publications on an astonishing variety of issues, and distinguished service at the highest level in his country's judiciary. In total: a highly disciplined mind answering to solid moral principles, a passion for the law, and a seemingly bottomless fund of rich and varied experience. All these accomplishments and virtues remain intact, ready and willing to be utilized for the advancement of our societies.

The forces of destiny that brought us together at the WTO have allowed us to keep in touch since, and even to plan jointly for the future. It will be a privilege for me to follow his footsteps closely with the admiration he deserves, and to feel I have in him a good and loyal friend.

PART II

Insights into the World Trade Organization

5

Justice Feliciano and the WTO Environmental Cases: Laying the Foundations of a 'Constitutional Jurisprudence' with Implications for Developing Countries

JOHN H. JACKSON

Introduction

The World Trade Organization (WTO), established by the results of the Uruguay Round of trade negotiations (1986–94), has put in place one of the most far-reaching systems of international dispute settlement that has ever existed. After only eight and one-half years of experience, as of July 2003, this system had received 295 complaints and completed 126 reports, including 79 first level panel reports (resulting from 92 complaints) and 47 Appellate Body reports, plus a series of reports of post-decision procedural controversies. Only 26 first level panel reports have *not* been appealed. (The total of Appellate Body reports plus first level panel reports that were not appealed is thus $47 + 26 = 73$, which represents the cases completed through the final report stage.) These reports total more than 22,000 pages of jurisprudence, comprising an extraordinary body of analysis and reasoning with many implications for international law and international economic relations.[1]

This dispute settlement (DS) system, with its unique appeal procedure, is proving to be the centrepiece of the new trade organization, provoking both firm praise and acerbic criticism. With its basis of compulsory jurisdiction, combined with findings in reports that are virtually automatically approved (and thus binding on the nation state), WTO member disputants, diplomats, and national political leaders are manifesting uneasiness about the power of the

[1] See Kara Leitner and Simon Lester, 'WTO Dispute Settlement 1995–2002: A Statistical Analysis' (2003) 6 *J. Int'l Econ. L.* 251.

system.[2] Various proposals for change have been made, and although the new trade negotiation round launched at Doha, Qatar, in November 2001 has been charged with considering reforms, it is nevertheless unclear whether the round will actually make any fundamental changes to the DS system.[3]

One of the curious, and potentially meaningful, characteristics of the work of the DS system in its first eight years is the emphasis that has emerged in the cases on environmental and food safety regulatory issues. With at least six cases completed with adopted reports on these subjects, and a major new case involving genetically modified organisms (GMOs) now in process, one can reasonably observe from the penetrating analysis in those reports, that the most significant systemic or 'constitutional' issues of the WTO jurisprudence have been issues emerging from these cases. This could be partly a result of the importance of environmental issues for trade policy, and also due to the significance of the many treaty clauses in the Uruguay Round texts that deal with the subject. Clearly, the issues involved have very great significance for developing countries, maybe relatively more significance for them than for richer WTO members.

This chapter will discuss how we arrived at this state of affairs and present some reflections on the longer-term significance of these observations, with particular reference to developing countries. The second part will briefly overview the background of the WTO DS system, while the third part will outline the current structure of that system and its record so far. The fourth part will describe the cases on environment (including food safety) and the fifth part will conclude with some perceptions and perspectives, identifying some of the key systemic subjects addressed by this jurisprudence, which have profound implications for the future of the WTO (and for international law generally).

One of the conclusions that engages this brief study (as indicated below) is that Florentino Feliciano, during his Appellate Body tenure of six years (1995–2001) as a member of the first Appellate Body roster (the 'founding' group), had a profound influence on the development of WTO Appellate Body jurisprudence, with his particularly heavy role in the four most critical cases of the six 'environmental' cases studied herein.

[2] John H. Jackson, 'Dispute Settlement and the WTO: Emerging Problems' (1998) 1 *J. Int'l Econ. L.* 329.

[3] See WTO Document Series TN/DS/ . . . for negotiating proposals regarding WTO dispute settlement reform in the current negotiating round.

Background and history of the WTO dispute settlement system

For 400 years or more, international law and international relations have given a preeminent position to the 'nation state' as the active participant and subject of such law and relations, albeit with profound shifts in attitudes towards this preeminence evolving over much of that time, and accelerated greatly by the Second World War and its aftermath.[4] One feature of this system has been a reluctance to design a dispute settlement system that could impose judgments on sovereign nation states without their approval. Various institutions have been created to move tentatively in that direction, such as the World Court and various arbitral tribunals.

Regarding international trade relations, the first major, multilateral, broad-based institution to develop rules designed to enhance the liberal trade policies of effective international markets was the General Agreement on Tariffs and Trade (GATT). This agreement was developed primarily as a mechanism to lower tariffs by reciprocal agreements, as part of a proposed International Trade Organization (ITO). When the ITO failed to come into force, the more narrowly conceived GATT, which had been adopted, became the *de facto* core institution for the enhancement of multilateral trade cooperation. In this agreement there were only three paragraphs relating explicitly to dispute settlement and there existed various opposing ideas about what those paragraphs meant. Nevertheless, through a series of specific cases and procedural innovations, the GATT dispute settlement system evolved into a sophisticated, and rather elaborate, set of procedures. These procedures were reasonably successful in enhancing compliance with, and effectiveness of, the GATT rules and for providing some measure of predictability and reliability of such rules for national trade policies and for entrepreneurs.[5]

4 See e.g., John H. Jackson, *The World Trading System: Law and Policy of International Economic Relations* (2nd edn., MIT Press, 1997); John H. Jackson, *The Jurisprudence of the GATT and the WTO: Insights on Treaty Law and Economic Relations* (Cambridge University Press, 2000).

5 Understanding on Rules and Procedures Governing the Settlement of Disputes (DSU) in World Trade Organization, *The Legal Texts: The Results of the Uruguay Round of Multilateral Trade Negotiations* (1999), Annex 2, Article 3.2. See John H. Jackson, *The World Trade Organization: Constitution and Jurisprudence* (Chatham House Papers, Royal Institute of International Affairs, London, 1998).

By the 1980s, however, it became clear that tariffs were not the real problem for effective liberal trade, but rather 'non-tariff measures' were increasingly important. Such non-tariff measures were often internal national regulatory rules and measures that posed conflicts between broader international trade policies, on the one hand, and national (often more parochial) policies on the other hand. In short, the GATT and its DS system were increasingly forced to confront issues that heretofore had fallen totally within nation state internal sovereign prerogatives. Thus, it was not surprising that the strains put upon the GATT DS system were exposing weaknesses in that system that threatened to undermine its effectiveness. A 'consensus' system of decision-making in the GATT led to situations where any government could block the effectiveness of the DS system and of the very rules themselves. A losing party to a DS procedure, for example, could block the approval of that GATT panel report. Governments began to search for a way around this and other difficulties.

The eighth, and last, GATT trade round, the 'Uruguay Round', formulated a new set of DS procedures in a text called the 'Dispute Settlement Understanding' (DSU), annexed to the WTO Charter as Annex 2. This text provided for virtually automatic adoption (no blocking permitted) of panel reports, but also established a right of appeal to an Appellate Body whose report was also adopted without allowing blocking by one or a few nations.[6]

With that, some would argue, a new era of international law was evolving, and the impact on the older traditional concepts of sovereignty became more apparent.

The dispute settlement system structure in brief, and the record so far

The DS system, while not nominally termed a 'court' or 'tribunal' or even 'arbitration', nevertheless has many characteristics of a juridical body and has been evolving procedures essential for its efficient and fair working. The system has gradually taken on more characteristics of a court or tribunal, leading critics to worry about the 'judicialization' or 'legalization' of the WTO/GATT.

Complaints are brought by one or more members of the WTO (only nation states or independent customs territories are WTO members).

[6] See DSU Articles 16 and 17.

The DSU requires the disputants to enter into consultations for a short while to determine whether a settlement can be reached. If a settlement cannot be reached, a panel is formed, usually consisting of three persons acting independent of government direction, and often selected by extensive negotiation among the disputants. This panel receives written submissions, listens to oral arguments, and after several phases of this, it writes a report with its findings.

As noted, this report is duly, and almost automatically, adopted by the Dispute Settlement Body (which supervises the whole procedure), unless one of the disputing parties appeals. If appeal is made, it goes to the Appellate Body, which consists of a roster of seven individuals (also acting independently), three of whom are chosen to serve as the Division that decides any particular appeal. The Appellate Body members serve for terms of four years, which can be renewed once, although at the start, lots were drawn to assign three of the original Appellate Body roster members to a two-year term so that rotation would occur for about half of the roster at any given time.

The Appellate Body Division selected for the case then receives submissions and hears oral arguments. A practice (sometimes called 'collegiality') has developed that all seven of the Appellate Body roster will study and discuss every case, although only the three selected for the Division will actually decide the case and write the report. This report then also goes to the Dispute Settlement Body which adopts it by procedures similar to that provided for a first level panel report (no blocking allowed).

The DSU provides that 'opinions expressed in the Appellate Body report by individuals serving on the Appellate Body should be anonymous'. Thus, the influence or impact by a particular Appellate Body Division member cannot be explicitly attributed, although certain 'surmises' can be hypothesized. It seems clear from indications from Appellate Body members that there is usually a very lively and constructive discussion among the three Division members. Drafting of the report is a collective effort, although it is most likely that in some instances certain individuals will play a key role for certain parts of a report, and the Presiding Member of a Division may assume an overall responsibility that could weigh heavily.

With these cautious observations in mind, it is quite remarkable to ascertain from the records that, of the six cases focused upon here, Feliciano was a Division member for four Appellate Body reports. Moreover, those four reports are easily the most significant (see overview below) and furthermore, it turns out that in those four cases, Feliciano was the Presiding Member! It would thus be hard to overstate the important role he played in these jurisprudential developments.

Environmental cases contribute fundamentally to the jurisprudence

Overview of cases relating to environmental issues

As mentioned, the over 22,000 pages of WTO DS reports contain an enormously rich jurisprudence, with analysis which often goes more deeply into the perplexing human and government policy questions than perhaps anything before experienced in international law. Of the seventy-nine cases with final reports adopted, the six involving significant environmental (including health and food safety) issues are not a particularly high percentage of the total cases. In terms of the importance of the systemic and 'constitutional' issues addressed, however, these cases hold a prime place in this jurisprudence, grappling with a series of perplexing questions which have puzzled scholars, officials, and other practitioners for centuries. This grappling, moreover, in this author's opinion, has dug further and deeper than that of any similar body of international jurisprudence. Questions addressed include: the appropriate role of sovereign nations compared to international institutions (which leads into questions of governance and democratic legitimacy); the puzzles of how to evaluate scientific facts and their implications; how to design institutional rules for a juridical procedure; and the amount of deference which the DS system should give to nation state measures.

I begin an overview of the cases that are discussed in this section with an extremely brief (and thus general) abstract of the facts and issues:

1. Appellate Body Report, *United States – Standards for Reformulated and Conventional Gasoline*, WT/DS2/AB/R, 20 May 1996. AB Division = Presiding Member Feliciano, Members: Christopher Beeby and Mitsuo Matsushita. Question of whether US government environmental regulations concerning the composition of gasoline treated imports less favourably than domestic products. Held: They did.
2. Appellate Body Report, *European Communities – Measures Concerning Meat and Meat Products (Hormones)*, WT/DS26/AB/R, 13 February 1998. AB Division = Presiding Member Feliciano, Members: Claus-Dieter

Ehlermann, Mitsuo Matsushita. Question of whether European Union regulation banning sale of domestic beef and banning imports of beef, which beef had been treated with artificial growth hormones, was WTO consistent. Held: EU had not adequately followed procedures for a risk assessment, as required by the WTO Agreement on Sanitary and Phytosanitary Measures ('SPS Agreement'). The EU has endeavoured to revise and carry out its procedures so as to claim they now fulfil the WTO requirements.

3. Appellate Body Report, *Australia – Measures Affecting Importation of Salmon*, WT/DS18/AB/R, 6 November 1998. AB Division = Presiding Member Ehlermann, Members: Beeby, Said El-Naggar. Australia imposed a ban on imports of dead salmon if they had not been 'heat treated' to prevent the spread of certain diseases, but had not conducted a 'risk assessment' required by the SPS Agreement. After GATT consultations, Australia performed a risk assessment to certain types of salmon, and concluded not to permit imports of all 'uncooked' (non-heat treated) salmon. The Appellate Body concluded that Australia's measures were inconsistent with the SPS Agreement, and criticized the risk assessment as inadequate.
4. Appellate Body Report, *United States – Import Prohibition of Certain Shrimp and Shrimp Products*, WT/DS58/AB/R, 6 November 1998. AB Division = Presiding Member Feliciano, Members: James Bacchus, Julio Lacarte Muró. Question of whether US government restrictions on imports of shrimp that the sellers could not demonstrate had been harvested in a manner that would not kill turtles, were permissible under the WTO rules. Held: US original regulations (but not the statute) were inconsistent with the WTO requirements. However, after the US government redid the regulations to take into account the Appellate Body report requirements, to attempt multilateral negotiated solutions, and to give exporting nations a fair chance to comment and obtain changes in the regulations, the regulations were deemed consistent with the WTO rules.
5. Appellate Body Report, *Japan – Measures Affecting Agricultural Products (Japan – Agricultural Products II)*, WT/DS76/AB/R, 19 March 1999. AB Division = Presiding Member Beeby, Members: Lacarte Muró, Matsushita. Japan maintained a regulation requiring testing of certain fruit imports to prevent them from introducing an insect pest not found in Japan. The Appellate Body ruled that the 'varietal testing requirement' was without sufficient scientific evidence and thus inconsistent with the SPS Agreement. The Appellate Body also

ruled that Japan failed to justify its measures by Article 5.7 of the SPS Agreement, regarding provisional measures pending additional scientific evidence, since Japan did not show that the requirements of Article 5.7 had been met.

6. Appellate Body Report, *European Communities – Measures Affecting Asbestos and Asbestos-Containing Products*, WT/DS135/AB/R, 5 April 2001. AB Division = Presiding Member Feliciano, Members: Bacchus, Ehlermann. Question of whether a French ban on imported asbestos of certain types, while another type produced domestically could be sold, was consistent with the WTO rules. The panel had ruled against the EU, arguing that the GATT Article III:4 requirement of national treatment was violated, and that GATT Article XX exceptions could not defend the ban. The Appellate Body, however, held that the two products (domestic and imported) had important different characteristics which made them not 'like products', so Article III was not violated and there was no need to seek an exception in Article XX.
7. *European Communities – Biotech Products.* In May 2003, the USA and some other WTO members brought a case against the EU regarding the EU and member state regulations which allegedly have prevented imports of most foods involving GMOs, in a manner contrary to the WTO rules. This promises also to be a highly significant case.[7]

From these all too short descriptions, it is hard to appreciate the importance of the analysis and rationale, but the details in these cases raise a series of significant questions, only a few of which can be mentioned here. The six cases already brought involved three subsets of issues.

First, there are two cases that deal with environmental policies more generally and globally. These are *US – Gasoline* and *US – Shrimp*, both relating to imported products that, in strikingly different ways, affect the environment (clean air and endangered species). Secondly, there are three cases that deal with regulations regarding imported foodstuffs (*Australia – Salmon*, *Japan – Agricultural Products II* (fruits and nuts), and *EC – Hormones* (treated beef)). Thirdly, there is a case related to human health for imported material that is not a food (*EC – Asbestos*). It is

[7] WTO Consultations Request, *European Communities – Measures Affecting the Approval and Marketing of Biotech Products*, Request by the USA, WT/DS291/1, 13 May 2003; Request by Canada, WT/DS292/1, 13 May 2003; Request by Argentina, WT/DS293/1, 14 May 2003.

interesting to note that all these cases were appealed and thus engaged the attention of the WTO Appellate Body. (The percentage of WTO cases that are appealed has been declining, and overall, 26 first-level panel reports have been adopted *without* appeal, which is now 33 per cent of the total cases that have been decided.) It is also interesting to note that all but one of these cases so far has ruled that a WTO member was not in full compliance with the WTO Treaty rules.

Structure of the legal arguments

All the cases listed above have dealt principally with one or more of three treaty texts of the WTO, namely GATT Article III, paragraph 4 regarding 'national treatment'; GATT Article XX, which contains a series of exceptions to other GATT and WTO rules; and the SPS Agreement. In each of these treaty texts, there is a tension between the desires of nation states to maintain what they call 'sovereignty' and to regulate economic matters without intervention of international law or institutions. This tension is one of the core jurisprudential questions that runs throughout virtually all of the WTO jurisprudence. In the area of environment and foodstuffs, this tension seems particularly acute because domestic interests are very concerned, and often very articulate and well organized, with a desire to preserve regulations of their nation states (or of the European Union, as the case may be) which these domestic interests have been involved with establishing, or which involve some very profound domestic citizen and cultural attitudes. What do these treaty texts say?

GATT Article III deals primarily with the concept of 'national treatment', which means that governments are required to treat imported goods equal to their treatment of domestically produced goods, although the wording says that treatment shall be 'no less favourable' than the domestic treatment. Article III develops this concept with respect to several different types of measures, including internal taxation, but most important for the environmental cases is paragraph 4, which includes exceptionally broad language that says that imported products 'shall be accorded treatment no less favourable than that accorded to like products of national origin in respect of all laws, and of regulations and requirements affecting their internal sale, offering for sale, purchase, transportation, distribution, or use'. This is language that has been unchanged since the very first drafts of the GATT in 1947, and is drawn, virtually unchanged, from a number of bilateral trade treaties over the preceding several decades. It seems clear that, when applied, this international law obligation can impact quite deeply on internal regulatory decisions. This is in contrast to statements heard more recently, from political and other interests, that the GATT originally was intended to treat only border measures (tariffs, etc.) affecting trade.

GATT Article XX contains a series of exceptions. We see from the language of the article, and from the thrust of jurisprudence, beginning in the GATT era and continuing into the WTO, that if a country's measures affecting imports turn out to be consistent with the GATT, there is no need to turn to Article XX. On the other hand, if the measures are inconsistent with Article III or any other article of the GATT (such as Article XI, which prohibits most import restraining measures at the border), then governments are entitled to invoke the exceptions list of Article XX. In this case, the Appellate Body has articulated a relatively strict analysis process, requiring two steps for a government to be able to claim an exception. The first step is to look at the specific list of exceptions in paragraphs (a) through (j) of Article XX, such as paragraph (b), which makes an exception for measures 'necessary to protect human, animal, or plant life or health'. If none of the exceptions (a) through (j) can be judged to embrace the importing nation's measure, then its search for an exception fails. But if it does find an exception that it can claim, then it must also pass the requirements of the 'chapeau' of Article XX, which is a preamble paragraph that sets forth general criteria that apply even if a specific exception would embrace a measure. This general criteria prohibits measures which 'constitute a means of arbitrary or unjustifiable discrimination between countries . . . or a disguised restriction on international trade'.

This treaty text of the chapeau, and the interpretations of the Appellate Body, obviously leaves a fair amount of leeway for decisions of a juridical type body. And it is here that the tension between nation state 'sovereignty' and international obligation become most accentuated. The *US – Shrimp* case is an outstanding example and exposition of some of the different kinds of policy approaches that can affect the outcome of a case.

The SPS Agreement is new text resulting from the Uruguay Round negotiation and addressed to 'improve the human health, animal health, and phytosanitary situation in all members'. It applies to all 'sanitary and phytosanitary measures', and those are defined rather elaborately in Annex A of the SPS text, as measures applied, for example, to 'protect animal or plant life or health', or 'protect human or animal life or health', etc., followed by a list of risks such as the spread of pests, disease-carrying organisms, additives, contaminants, and so forth. The SPS Agreement requires that SPS measures be applied 'only to the extent necessary to protect human, animal or plant life or health', and that it be based on 'scientific principles'. However, the jurisprudence suggests that this does not have to be majority science, quantifiable science, or even sound science, but must have 'some science' to support it. It also sets forth an important concept of the necessity of an 'assessment of risk', which will affect a determination of the 'appropriate level of sanitary or phytosanitary protection'. It is the risk assessments that have been examined in great detail. It is clear from the jurisprudence that the SPS Agreement differs from GATT Article III, 'national treatment', in the sense that it is not confined as tightly to questions of 'discrimination', but on the other hand, seems to have a threshold standard of even non-discriminatory measures for their 'appropriate level'. Thus it is, that cases that involve foodstuffs, which generally fall under the SPS Agreement, focus almost entirely on the SPS text, without much, if any, need to address GATT Article III or XX. To some extent, the SPS Agreement parallels language in Article XX, so that there are very similar concepts against 'arbitrarily or unjustifiably discriminating', or using a 'disguised restriction on international trade'.

Conclusions, implications, and perceptions

The WTO dispute settlement system is, by years of application, still in its infancy. But by number of pages of its jurisprudence and the intricate analysis and extensive reasoning, its jurisprudence is, in certain ways, many times as mature and refined as most other international law juridical institutions. It is interesting, but not surprising, how central the 'environmental cases' of the dispute settlement system are to this evolving jurisprudence. Many people feel that the directions of WTO jurisprudence have been quite constructive, carefully balancing between relatively contradictory policy directions in a way that could be said to enhance, or even optimize, the impact of the policies on the competing goals which it has had to mediate. But in any event, it is quite clear that the WTO dispute settlement system has a potential major impact on environmental rules in the world, and that it has something to teach both the environmental advocates and the trade policy advocates.[8]

[8] There is already a huge body of literature regarding all of the cases and issues mentioned in this chapter. See www.worldtradelaw.net and particularly the 'Dispute Settlement Commentary' for each case, which has a list of some of the salient literature regarding each case, at the end of the relevant commentary.

However, this WTO jurisprudence may have its most profound implications both for the WTO and for general international law and international relations because of some of the systemic or 'constitutional' issues it covers. Only a few of these issues can be mentioned here:

1. In the very first of these cases, and indeed the first of any WTO case to proceed through all stages of the reports and appeal, *US – Gasoline*, the Appellate Body set forth some very basic concepts about the nature of WTO law and jurisprudence. In particular, it made it clear that general international law was relevant, and that the WTO jurisprudence was a part of that general international law. In that regard, the Appellate Body noted that the DSU itself called for the system to use the customary international law norms of treaty interpretation, and the Appellate Body noted that that generally referred to the description of such norms found in the text of the Vienna Convention on the Law of Treaties (even though not all parties to the WTO have ratified that treaty). This foreclosed some speculative academic theories that were advanced during the GATT years, that the GATT and its system might be a totally separate regime, not related to general international law. Clearly, the findings of the Appellate Body in *US – Gasoline* do not solve all the issues of the relationship of general international law to WTO law, but a starting point was set forth in that case.

2. In *US – Shrimp*, the Appellate Body report contains perhaps the most extensive and most significant jurisprudence yet so far in the WTO system, regarding basic constitutional issues. Among the many issues covered by this report was the enunciation of a principle in the particular facts of that case, which led the Appellate Body to rely upon certain treaty activity and norms that were separate from, but related to, the WTO. In doing so, the Appellate Body also relied upon goals mentioned in the preamble to the text of the WTO Charter, to establish the approach of the Appellate Body to take into account the fundamental policy goals that were not just trade goals. The Appellate Body admonished the first level panel for focusing too much and only on trade, and entertained these other goals in the process of interpreting some crucial language at the beginning of GATT Article XX (the so-called 'chapeau'). This was truly extraordinary language, and a constitutional door opener for approaches that require a broader perspective than just the four corners of the very extensive GATT/WTO treaty language.

3. This consideration of non-trade policy goals in juxtaposition with the trade goals, then led logically to the Appellate Body's inference that it had to 'balance' the various goals. This notion that the Appellate Body

would exercise this balancing process certainly worried certain nation states that would argue that such a balancing process should better be left to 'sovereigns'.

4. In the process of interpretation, the Appellate Body mentioned, in connection with one of the norms it was exploring, the application of an 'evolutionary approach' to interpretation of treaty norms. Again, this opens the door to greater discretion on the part of the Appellate Body and the WTO dispute settlement system, in how it will go about interpreting the essential treaty clauses of this system.

5. The Appellate Body explicitly overruled the first level panel when the latter embraced strongly the notion that 'multilateralism' was part of the basic norms of the WTO system. The Appellate Body noted that this could not be found in the text of the agreements, and then the Appellate Body went on to opine, in a very crucial paragraph (paragraph 121), that, in some circumstances, a unilateral approach might be justified under the overall framework of the exceptions of GATT Article XX. Indeed, in later stages of the same case, after the USA had revised its regulations, the Appellate Body upheld the USA's later unilateral action, noting that the USA had complied with a series of criteria which had been set forth in the original Appellate Body opinion.

6. Fundamental to a number of cases, perhaps most prominently *EC – Hormones*, but also involved in *US – Shrimp* and other cases, was the recurring question of how the WTO dispute settlement system at either the first level or the appellate level should ascertain scientific judgment and then evaluate the different levels or different approaches of the science which was before it and crucial for its findings. The *EC – Hormones* first level panel designed a special procedure for ascertaining scientific information and this was approved by the Appellate Body, although it did not fit under some of the scientific fact-finding ideas expressed in the DSU. Instead, a more general clause (DSU Article 13) was relied upon since this clause gave very broad authority to the panels to call upon outside sources for information and technical advice. Clearly, the question of science, and how to handle it, is one that is going to pervade much of the future jurisprudence of the WTO, and it is certainly very central to the 'GMO' case (or cases likely to occur in further proceedings).

One could further outline other fundamental jurisprudential issues, but given the constraints of this chapter, that is not feasible. However, a word about how all of this might affect developing countries is in order.

It can be noted that in only two of the six cases already decided were developing countries actual disputants (although there were some additional developing countries involved as third parties). These two cases were the *US – Gasoline*, which was brought by Brazil and Venezuela, and *US – Shrimp*, which was brought by four developing countries, India, Malaysia, Pakistan, and Thailand. Both of those cases ruled against a developed country defendant, which happened to be the USA in both instances. In *US – Gasoline*, the USA was able to comply by changing administrative action and this was an interesting and reasonably important signal of a powerful trading country's attitude towards the dispute settlement system in its very first case. In *US – Shrimp*, the USA again was held to be in non-compliance, for a variety of reasons specified, and the complaining developing countries were initially elated by the first level panel's holdings in that regard. The Appellate Body, however, modified those holdings very fundamentally, and constrained the reach of the first level panel opinion, by indicating a number of specific aspects of the US regulatory approach which were at fault. When the USA then corrected those aspects to the satisfaction of the Appellate Body, the Appellate Body judged that the USA could proceed with its unilateral constraint (which had an 'extra-territorial reach').

However, the fundamental issues listed for all six cases discussed above have implications for all member states of the WTO, including the developing countries. Clearly, there is a tension between the apparent or alleged 'regulatory authority' of the WTO, and the issues are more complex than many member states would like them to be. With particular reference to the environmental issues, developing countries have been exceedingly antagonistic to the introduction of any environmental justification for trade restraints. They fear (justifiably, as *US – Gasoline* indicated) that industrialized countries would likely use environmental regulatory arguments as an excuse for limiting imports from developing countries, and do so in a way that would be heavily influenced by protectionist sentiments rather than 'sound science', or other, more objective, criteria. *US – Gasoline* was the ideal demonstration of that activity by an industrialized country. In that case, however, the WTO jurisprudence rose to the occasion and branded the American approach as inappropriate, resulting in compliance by the USA.

The other cases, particularly *US – Shrimp* and *EC – Hormones*, raise issues that are more complex and not so clearly decided for one side or the other. A major issue in *EC – Hormones* was deference, or 'standard of review', with the Appellate Body outlining some approaches, rejecting extremes of *de novo* or complete deference, but not giving very much guidance on the line that would be drawn in between as to the appropriate approaches on these crucial questions of deference.

Thus, the true importance of the jurisprudence of these six cases is not necessarily targeted towards developing countries, but embraces developing countries as part of the total constituency of the WTO membership. It is this author's view that the Appellate Body has generally been correct in its approach, and has admirably struggled with the nuances and intricacies that are called for, both by the treaty text involved, and by broader policies of 'object and purpose' of the Treaties.

Finally, it seems clear that this jurisprudence, as intricate and as elaborate as it already is, is still only a starting point for a trail that promises to be rather long.

6

International Trade Law, Human Rights and Theories of Justice

ERNST-ULRICH PETERSMANN

Florentino Feliciano and I met for the first time in a symposium on the Judicial Settlement of International Disputes at the Max-Planck Institute for Comparative Public Law and International Law at Heidelberg in July 1972. As assistant of the director of the Institute, Professor Mosler, I had just published a long article on 'The New Law of North-South Trade' and the emerging International Development Law in the *Heidelberg Journal of International Law.*[1] During the evening excursion on a riverboat down the Neckar river, I sat at the same table as Florentino and asked him about his conference intervention on why developing countries were so reluctant to submit to the jurisdiction of the International Centre for the Settlement of Investment Disputes.[2] We engaged in a lively discussion on the difficulties of realizing 'social justice' through international law.

When we later met again in the World Trade Organization (WTO) where I worked as legal adviser for less-developed WTO members, the role of less-developed countries in international law (e.g., as plaintiffs or defendants in WTO dispute settlement proceedings) continued to be one of the central themes of our discussions. Should international law and the WTO legal system be perceived as a law of states, a law of peoples, or as a cosmopolitan law of individuals? Can the WTO effectively serve general citizen interests as long as WTO negotiations are one-sidedly 'producer-driven' and the constitutional safeguards of 'input legitimacy' (such as human rights, democratic procedures) and of 'output legitimacy' (such as promotion of general consumer welfare)

[1] E. U. Petersmann, 'Das Neue Recht des Nord-Süd-Handels' in (1972) *Zeitschrift für ausländisches öffentliches Recht und Völkerrecht* 339.

[2] See the comments by F. Feliciano in *Judicial Settlement of International Disputes* (Max-Planck Institute for Comparative Public Law and International Law, 1974), pp. 129 *et seq.*, 169 *et seq.*

are not mentioned in WTO law? Do the WTO's 'Development Round negotiations' risk to fail without more leadership by the European Union (EU) and the USA for taking justice-related claims of the less-developed majority of WTO member countries, and the perceived lack of legitimacy of power-oriented WTO negotiations, more seriously?

Justice as objective of international law

According to James Madison, 'justice is the end of government. It is the end of civil society. It ever has been and will be pursued until it is obtained, or until liberty be lost in the pursuit'.[3] The United Nations (UN) Charter and numerous other international treaties recognize 'justice' as a central objective of international law. International rules and institutions that are perceived as unjust are unlikely to shape the conduct of governments and of their citizens effectively.[4]

Even though justice is acknowledged as a common objective in numerous international treaties and national constitutions, the legal principles and procedures for realizing justice differ from treaty to treaty and from country to country. Legal theories of justice likewise differ considerably depending on their underlying worldviews and moral and legal value premises.[5]

For example, in the rights-based libertarian tradition, justice relates to 'natural individual rights' and corresponding limitations on government powers in order to protect the autonomy and independence of individuals who, as explained by Immanuel Kant, must be treated as ends in themselves and never merely as means for securing benefit to some other person. While Anglo-American libertarians (like John Locke and Robert Nozick) conceive human rights (e.g. to life, liberty, and property) and legitimate government powers narrowly, modern European constitutional theories seek to protect human liberty and personal self-development broadly as maximum equal freedom subject to democratic legislation that must protect and balance human rights in a non-discriminatory and proportionate manner.[6]

[3] James Madison in *The Federalist Papers* (1961), no. 51.

[4] See e.g., Americo Beviglia Zampetti, 'Democratic Legitimacy in the World Trade Organization: the Justice Dimension' (2003) *Journal of World Trade* 105.

[5] For an overview of the diverse theories of justice see, e.g., T. Campbell, *Justice* (2nd edn., 2000).

[6] See E. U. Petersmann, 'Taking Human Dignity, Poverty and Empowerment of Individuals More Seriously' in (2002) *European Journal of International Law* 845.

John Rawls' conception of 'justice as fairness' and 'procedural justice'[7] proceeds from a rational constitutional choice among individuals behind a 'veil of uncertainty' in order to define the basic rights and liberties of free and equal citizens in a constitutional democracy. According to Rawls' 'welfare liberalism', rational citizens would give priority to maximum equal liberty as the 'first principle of justice', but would also recognize the 'principle of fair equality of opportunity' and a 'difference principle' aimed at guaranteeing basic social needs for poor people. The latter 'secondary principles of social justice' are rationally necessary for defining 'the appropriate distribution of the benefits and burdens of social co-operation'[8] so as to secure a socially just distribution of welfare essential for moral and rational self-development of every person.

Utilitarian theories of justice justify individual liberty and equal opportunities for unfettered exchange between individuals not in terms of constitutional contracts, but as result-oriented mechanisms for attaining 'welfare' in the sense of the greatest happiness of the greatest number. Yet, whether market-driven distributions of goods and income can maximize not only utility and efficiency but also 'justice' remains controversial because only human conduct – but arguably not market-mechanisms (e.g., prices) – can be 'unjust'.

Communitarian theories of justice regard all values as embedded in a particular social culture and put emphasis on 'deliberative democracy' and other democratic procedures (rather than on individual freedom) for determining social and political community values.

Meritorian theories of justice combine notions of equality, desert, and 'corrective justice' (e.g., punishment and compensation for injuries) in order to 'give every man his due'. Justice requires treating individuals as rational agents responsible for their actions and, therefore, rewarding or punishing their conduct.

The modern universal recognition of human rights constitutionally limits foreign policies by recognizing common moral and legal core values, such as respect for human dignity, equal human worth, democratic self-government, and access to courts. Justice is becoming a matter of universal and 'inalienable' human rights, democratic governance, and positive national and international constitutional law in order to empower individuals and protect individual and democratic self-development across frontiers. Democratic legislation defining, balancing, and implementing constitutional rights may legitimately differ

[7] J. Rawls, *A Theory of Justice* (1973), p. 85. [8] *Ibid.* at p. 4.

from country to country. Yet, there is an 'inalienable core' of human rights that can no longer be lawfully taken away by governments. Beyond the 'self-evident' rights to life, liberty, and property recognized in virtually all modern constitutional democracies as well as in international human rights law, also the human rights requirements of democratic governance and social justice can no longer be ignored by any worldwide organization that claims social legitimacy and respect for its rules.

Justice as empowerment and protection of individuals through constitutional rights: three basic principles

The universal recognition of 'inalienable' human rights deriving from 'human dignity' requires the interpretation of national and international law as a functional unity for promoting individual and democratic autonomy and diversity. The 'principles of justice' and 'procedures of justification' offered by modern 'theories of justice' tend to focus on three social problems: (1) principles and rules for the just allocation of equal freedoms and other basic rights of individuals in order to protect 'human dignity' and peaceful cooperation among free citizens; (2) principles and rules for the just distribution of scarce resources through voluntary cooperation and governmental correction of 'market failures'; (3) principles and rules for a just constitutional order protecting general citizen interests against 'government failures'.

Maximum equal freedoms as the first principle of justice

The liberal claim, in Article 1 of the French Declaration of the Rights of Man and the Citizen of 1789, that 'All men are born and remain free and equal in their rights', has become universally recognized in numerous UN human rights instruments: 'All human beings are born free and equal in dignity and rights' (Universal Declaration of Human Rights (UDHR) Article 1). The universal recognition of an 'inalienable core' of human rights can and should be construed as a new 'constitutional contract' fundamentally limiting the traditionally state-centred structures and contents of public international law.

The French Declaration defined liberty in terms of maximum equal freedom: 'Liberty is the power to do anything which does not harm another; hence the only limits to the exercise of each man's natural rights are those which secure to other members of society the enjoyment of the same rights. These limits may be fixed only by statute law' (Article 4). This constitutional guarantee of equal individual freedom subject to democratic legislation is recognized in most constitutional democracies, and also in international human rights law, either in terms of individual rights to maximum equal freedom (e.g., German Basic Law Article 2:1) or in terms of a constitutional requirement, often unwritten (e.g., in the constitutional law of the USA and some other Anglo-Saxon countries), of a legislative basis for restrictions of freedom and other human rights (e.g., UDHR Article 29). Respect for maximum equal 'liberties to be' is of existential importance for personal self-development in dignity and, as explained in Immanuel Kant's moral theory of the 'categorical imperative' as well as in John Rawls' theory of justice, constitutes the first principle of justice.

'Liberties to be' must be distinguished from *instrumental freedoms* (e.g., 'liberties to have', produce, acquire, sell or consume) which, unlike 'dignity', may have a 'price' (in Kant's terms). Yet, also economic liberties (such as free choice of one's profession) and property rights have an 'inalienable' core in view of their existential necessity for personal self-development. As respect for human dignity requires the treatment of human beings as ends in themselves and as legal subjects rather than mere objects of government policies (or as means to securing benefits to some other person), individuals should be recognized as legal subjects in all fields of international law, just as they are recognized as citizens and holders of individual rights in all fields of EU law and of constitutional democracies.[9] Hence, whereas some Anglo-American constitutional theories on inalienable human rights to life, liberty, and property tend to conceptualize individual liberty narrowly (e.g., in terms of basic personal freedoms of bodily movement and democratic liberties), EU law rightly recognizes individual producers, investors, traders, consumers, and other 'EU citizens' as legal subjects of European integration law inside the EU.

Social solidarity rights as the second principle of justice

Wherever existential liberty rights are protected, markets for mutually beneficial social cooperation and competition emerge spontaneously in response to consumer demand for scarce goods and services. As most people can survive only by trading the fruits of their labour in exchange for other goods and services, freedom of trade constitutes one of the

[9] For a criticism of the neglect of economic individual rights and of the perception, favoured notably by Anglo-Saxon lawyers, of individuals as mere objects of governmental trade policies, see E. U. Petersmann, *Theories of Justice, Human Rights and the Constitution of International Markets* (EUI Working Paper Law No. 2003/17, 2003).

most existential human liberties. Based on 'the principle of an open market with free competition' (see EC Treaty Articles 4, 98, 105, 157) and 'freedom to conduct a business in accordance with Community law and national laws' (EU Charter of Fundamental Rights Article 16), national and European constitutional law in the EU protects free movement of goods, services, persons, capital, related payments, and non-discrimination as individual fundamental rights[10] and corresponding government obligations so as to guarantee an 'internal market . . . without internal frontiers in which the free movement of goods, persons, services and capital is ensured' (EC Treaty Article 14). Just as 'human dignity' is indivisible, the 'indivisibility' of all human rights is recognized in EU law as well as in international law.[11]

The market freedoms guaranteed by the EC Treaty constitution can be understood as agreed extensions of 'freedom of trade' deriving ultimately from a basic 'right to liberty' (EU Charter of Fundamental Rights Article 6). In constitutional democracies and also in EC law, instrumental 'process freedoms' are subject to numerous rules and government interventions aimed at correcting 'market failures' and supplying 'public goods', including 'a system ensuring that competition in the internal market is not distorted' (EC Treaty Articles 3g, 81 *et seq.*), 'environmental protection . . . with a view to promoting sustainable development' (Articles 6, 174 *et seq.*), 'fundamental social rights' (Article 136 *et seq.*), and health and consumer protection (Article 152 *et seq.*). As market-based distributions of resources may not enable each individual to live a life in dignity, market freedoms need to be supplemented by a variety of solidarity obligations to promote, for example, 'social security and social protection of workers' (EC Treaty Article 137 EC), 'equal pay for male and female workers for equal work' (Article 141), and other social guarantees of personal self-development in dignity. Such social rights to satisfaction of the basic needs ('distributive

[10] See e.g., Case 240/83, *ADBHU* [1985] ECR 531, paragraph 9: 'the principles of free movement of goods and freedom of competition, together with freedom of trade as a fundamental right, are general principles of Community law of which the Court ensures observance'. The freedom of movements of workers and other persons, access to employment, and the right of establishment have been described by the European Court of Justice as 'fundamental freedoms' (Case C-55/94, *Gebhard* [1995] ECR I-4165, paragraph 37).

[11] For example, in the 1993 Vienna Declaration of the World Conference on Human Rights (see paragraph 5: 'All human rights are universal, indivisible, and interdependent and interrelated').

justice'), as they are today recognized also in regional and worldwide human rights treaties, may legitimately vary depending on the resources and social preferences of the local, national, or international community concerned.

Constitutional rights to democratic governance and constitutional order as the third principle of justice

National and international human rights law recognizes (e.g., in UDHR Article 29) the need for democratic legislation and constitutional rules protecting, implementing, and balancing human rights (e.g., on the basis of constitutional principles of non-discrimination, necessity, proportionality, due process of law, individual access to courts, and democratic governance).The democratic balancing processes, implementing legislation and institutions may legitimately differ from country to country depending on the preferences of their citizens and of their democratic institutions. They must be guided, however, by human rights – not only in their function as *individual rights* (e.g., of a 'negative', 'positive', procedural, or participatory nature) and corresponding obligations of national governments and intergovernmental organizations to respect and protect human rights, but also as *objective principles* of constitutional order to be respected by public and private actors in all areas of the polity and of the economy. As emphasized by the European Court of Human Rights, human rights treaties have become part of an objective 'constitutional order' based no longer exclusively on states, but also on individuals as legal subjects.[12]

Human rights, and the corresponding obligations of governments, do not end at national borders. UN human rights law recognizes that 'everyone is entitled to a social and international order in which the rights and freedoms . . . can be fully realized'.[13] Enjoyment of human rights depends on production and distribution of scarce goods and services whose availability, quality, and accessibility can be increased through international trade. As the division of labour necessary for satisfying consumer demand requires constitutional rules limiting 'market failures' and enabling the collective supply of 'public goods' (such as

[12] See European Court of Human Rights, *Loizidou* v. *Turkey* (Preliminary Objections), 23 March 1995, paragraph 75.

[13] UDHR Article 28. See also UN General Assembly Declaration 41/128, 4 December 1986 on the 'Right to Development'.

'democratic peace'), UN human rights instruments also rightly emphasize that 'democracy, development and respect for human rights and fundamental freedoms are interdependent and mutually reinforcing'.[14] The widespread poverty and human rights violations outside market-based democracies demonstrate, however, that these human rights objectives are not effectively realized in many UN member states. How can the WTO protect more effectively the human rights obligations which all of its member states have voluntarily accepted by ratifying regional or worldwide human rights treaties and other human rights instruments?

The human rights approach to WTO law advocated by the UN High Commissioner for Human Rights

Neither the UN Charter nor the law of UN specialized agencies guarantees a stable legal framework for a welfare-increasing, international division of labour based on the rule of law and compulsory international jurisdiction for the peaceful settlement of disputes. For more than half a century, UN law has manifestly failed to realize, in the majority of its 191 UN member states, its declared objectives of 'universal respect for, and observance of, human rights and fundamental freedoms for all' and 'creation of conditions of stability and wellbeing which are necessary for peaceful and friendly relations among nations' (UN Charter Article 55). Recent UN resolutions recognize the interrelationships between human rights, consumer-driven competition, and citizen-driven democracies.[15] Yet, even though the poverty and security problems in many 'failed states' are often due to inadequate respect for human rights, the UN and UN specialized agencies refrain from linking access to UN institutions to respect for human rights and constitutional democracy.

The UN High Commissioner for Human Rights has recently begun analysing human rights dimensions of the WTO Agreements on Trade-Related Intellectual Property Rights (TRIPS),[16] the Agreement on

[14] Vienna Declaration, *supra* n. 11 at paragraph 8. These interrelationships are explained in E. U. Petersmann, 'Constitutional Economics, Human Rights and the Future of the WTO' in (2003) 58 *Swiss Review of International Economic Relations (Aussenwirtschaft)* 49.

[15] See *Ibid.*

[16] *The Impact of the Agreement on Trade-Related Aspects of Intellectual Property Rights on Human Rights*, E/CN.4/Sub.2/2001/13, 27 June 2001.

Agriculture (AOA),[17] and the General Agreement on Trade in Services (GATS).[18] The reports call for a 'human rights approach to trade' which:

(i) sets the promotion and protection of human rights as objectives of trade liberalization, not exceptions;
(ii) examines the effect of trade liberalization on individuals and seeks to devise trade law and policy to take into account the rights of all individuals, in particular vulnerable individuals and groups;
(iii) emphasizes the role of the state in the process of liberalization, not only as negotiators of trade law and setters of trade policy, but also as the primary duty bearer of human rights;
(iv) seeks consistency between the progressive liberalization of trade and the progressive realization of human rights;
(v) requires a constant examination of the impact of trade liberalization on the enjoyment of human rights;
(vi) promotes international cooperation for the realization of human rights and freedoms in the context of trade liberalization.[19]

The High Commissioner emphasizes the human rights obligations of all WTO members deriving, *inter alia*, from the ratification, by every WTO member state, of one or more of the six major worldwide UN human rights conventions. The reports differentiate between obligations to respect human rights (e.g., by refraining from interfering in the enjoyment of such rights), to protect human rights (e.g., by preventing violations of such rights by third parties), and to fulfil human rights (e.g., by taking appropriate legislative, administrative, budgetary, judicial, and other measures towards the full realization of such rights). As enjoyment of human rights (e.g., to food, health, education, and development) depends on availability, accessibility, acceptability, and quality of traded goods and services, the relevance of WTO rules on market access, on limitations of 'market failures' as well as of 'government failures' for the protection and fulfilment of human rights, is acknowledged and discussed. The reports underline that what are referred to – in numerous WTO provisions – as *rights* of WTO members to regulate, may in fact be *duties* to regulate under human rights law (e.g., so as to

[17] *Globalization and its Impact on the Full Enjoyment of Human Rights*, E/CN.4/2002/54, 15 January 2002.
[18] *Liberalization of Trade in Services and Human Rights*, E/CN.4/Sub.2/2002/9, 18 June 2002.
[19] *Ibid.* at p. 2.

protect and fulfil human rights of access to water, medicines, health, and educational services at affordable prices). The UN High Commissioner suggests recognizing the promotion of human rights as an objective of the WTO so as to ensure that trade rules and policies advance the protection and promotion of human rights.

How to transform the WTO Agreement into a 'just international economic constitution'?

The ever increasing number of international treaties constituting worldwide organizations, the legal primacy of their respective 'constitutional charters' over 'secondary law' and, in the case of the UN Charter, also over other conflicting treaty rules (see UN Charter Article 103), and the separation and mutual 'checks and balances' among the legislative, executive, and judicial organs of international organizations – sometimes with compulsory international jurisdiction (e.g., in the WTO and the Law of the Sea Convention) – have promoted the emergence of 'international constitutional law' also on the worldwide level.[20] This progressive 'constitutionalization' is not limited to international treaty law but, as illustrated by the universal recognition of *ius cogens*, of *erga omnes* obligations, and of an 'inalienable core' of human rights – extends also to general international law. Yet, in contrast to the ever more comprehensive multilevel constitutional restraints on abuses of national policy powers in Europe, the USA remains committed to national – rather than international – constitutionalism, relying on its national military and economic power and 'USA sovereignty' more than before (e.g., in the early post-war period when the USA led the initiatives for creating the Bretton-Woods institutions, the UN and the GATT).

The law of some worldwide and regional organizations, such as the UN Charter and the constitutions of the International Labour Organizations (ILO), the World Health Organization, and the UN Education, Scientific and Cultural Organization, explicitly refer to human rights. Yet, the general international law requirement to construe international treaties in conformity with other international law

[20] See e.g., E. U. Petersmann, 'Constitutionalism, International Law and "We the Peoples of the United Nation"' in H. J. Cremer *et al.*, *Tradition und Weltoffenheit des Rechts, Festschrift für Steinberger* (2001), pp. 291–320.

rules applicable among the parties concerned[21] requires construing also the law of other international organizations in conformity with the human rights obligations of their member states.

The 1994 Agreement Establishing the WTO includes all four categories of constitutional elements in modern international law. First, the WTO establishes international organs with legislative, executive, and judicial powers which interact in an interdependent legal framework of 'checks and balances' (albeit *sui generis*, compared with national constitutions). Secondly, the legal primacy of constitutional rules over post-constitutional legislation is reflected in the legal requirement that, in the event of a conflict between the WTO Agreement and any of the numerous multilateral trade agreements annexed to it, 'the provisions of this Agreement shall prevail to the extent of the conflict' (Article XVI:3). Thirdly, the substantive WTO guarantees of freedom of trade, non-discriminatory conditions of competition, rule of law, and access to courts – albeit addressed to states rather than to individuals and without legally requiring 'direct effect' of WTO rules inside domestic legal systems – serve 'constitutional functions' for protecting freedom, non-discrimination, rule of law, and access to courts not only in intergovernmental relations among states, but indirectly also for the benefit of competing producers, investors, traders, consumers, and their respective governments in the 'cosmopolitan' division of labour across frontiers. Fourthly, the constitutional principle of access to justice is reflected in the compulsory jurisdiction of WTO dispute settlement bodies which has given rise to hundreds of WTO dispute settlement proceedings and WTO jurisprudence clarifying and further developing WTO rules, thereby progressively extending legal security and the rule of law across frontiers. Like the EC courts and the European Court of Human Rights, WTO dispute settlement bodies also increasingly apply general international law principles (e.g., of good faith, proportionality, due process of law) that are not specifically mentioned in WTO law. Human rights, however, are neither referred to in the 'WTO Constitution' nor, so far, in the legal findings of WTO dispute settlement bodies.[22]

In their 1996 Singapore Ministerial Declaration, WTO members renewed their commitment to the observance of internationally recognized core labour standards, affirmed their support for the ILO's work in

[21] See Vienna Convention on the Law of Treaties Article 31 which, according to the WTO Appellate Body, reflects customary rules of international treaty interpretation.

[22] See E. U. Petersmann, 'Human Rights and the Law of the WTO' in (2003) *Journal of World Trade* 242.

promoting these standards, and rejected protectionist abuses of such standards. In a similar way, WTO members could enhance the 'input legitimacy' of WTO rules and WTO negotiations by a WTO Ministerial Declaration (1) renewing the commitment of WTO members to respect universal human rights in all policy areas; (2) affirming their support for the progressive development of human rights through the competent UN and other human rights bodies; and (3) supporting the need for harnessing the complementary functions of WTO rules and human rights for welfare-increasing cooperation among free citizens based on consumer-driven competition, democratic governance, respect for human rights, and social justice.

Such a pledge by WTO members to respect human rights could – without creating new legal obligations or new WTO competencies – improve also the limited 'output legitimacy' of WTO rules and WTO negotiations by acknowledging that the numerous 'public interest clauses' in WTO law are flexible enough to enable WTO members to respect human rights obligations in the trade policy area and to take into account the social adjustment problems of international trade (e.g., for small subsistence farmers in poor countries, for other 'losers' in international competition, or for sick people depending on access to medicines at affordable prices). It could also contribute to limiting the one-sided 'producer bias' of WTO rules by acknowledging that the legitimacy of WTO rules depends on serving the interests of all human beings with due respect for human rights. Just as the WTO Ministerial Declaration on core labour standards helped the ILO to reach consensus on the 1998 ILO Declaration on Fundamental Principles and Rights at Work and on using ILO dispute settlement proceedings more effectively (e.g., vis-à-vis Myanmar), a positive WTO response to the UN proposals for a 'human rights approach to trade' could promote mutual synergies between human rights law and international trade law similar to those in European integration law.

Human rights and the WTO dispute settlement system

Even though the jurisdiction of WTO dispute settlement bodies is limited to the 'covered agreements' listed in Appendix 1 to the WTO Dispute Settlement Understanding, human rights may be 'relevant context' for the interpretation and application of WTO rules. Just as the European Court of Justice had to construe EC Treaty rules with due regard to general human rights long before human rights provisions were included into the EC Treaty, it may be only a matter of time until WTO bodies will have to respond to legal arguments that human rights (e.g., to food, health, education, freedom of opinion and of information, prohibition of child and slave labour, liberty, property, non-discrimination, access to courts, democratic governance) may be 'relevant legal context' for interpreting WTO rules. Yet, should WTO members leave the delicate clarification of the potential impact of human rights obligations of WTO members on the interpretation of WTO rules to the 'judicial branch' of the WTO?

In the several hundred dispute settlement proceedings under the GATT 1947 and the WTO, not a single dispute settlement report (e.g., by a panel, working party, the Appellate Body, arbitration awards) has so far identified a conflict between the GATT/WTO rules and human rights. Although the 'primary law' of the WTO does not explicitly refer to human rights, there are no reasons to presuppose *systemic* conflicts – at the international level of legal principles – for instance:

- between the non-discrimination requirements of human rights (which may call for 'positive discrimination') and those of WTO law (which permits e.g., subsidies, tax benefits, and other preferential treatment in favour of poor people, vulnerable minorities and suppliers of 'essential services');
- between the human rights to liberty, property, food, and health and the WTO guarantees of freedom of trade and protection of property rights (which permit, for example, compulsory licences and other limitations in order to prevent 'abuses' of property rights);
- among the human rights guarantees of due process of law and access to justice and the related government obligations and procedural guarantees in WTO law; or
- between the numerous 'general exceptions' in WTO law and the human rights obligations of WTO members.

Yet, this *prima facie* consistency of WTO rules and universal human rights at the level of international law in no way precludes conflicts among human rights and *national* trade laws and policies, especially in poor non-democratic countries. Unfortunately, academics and international organizations often neglect to examine whether the human rights obligations of WTO members are adequately taken into account in domestic trade laws and policies. A WTO Ministerial Declaration recognizing the need to respect universal human rights in the trade policy area should be without prejudice to the legitimate diversity of views on the interpretation and scope of human rights and on their relevance for the WTO. The WTO should remain an economic organization and leave international 'human rights assessments' and the interpretation and monitoring of human rights to specialized human rights bodies and to national governments. Yet, in contrast to the far too narrow interpretation of human rights and 'international justice' in John Rawls' conception of a *Law of Peoples* governing international relations between liberal and non-liberal societies,[23] national and international judges must ensure that, also in the application of WTO rules, no individual is denied respect for the 'inalienable core' of universal human rights.[24] We all owe gratitude to Justice Feliciano that, as a national and international judge, he has defended international justice and mutually beneficial cooperation among citizens across frontiers.

23 See J. Rawls, *The Law of Peoples* (1999), ch. 10. The eight principles of the 'Law of Peoples' which, according to Rawls (at p. 37), would result from a constitutional contract among representatives of liberal and 'decent' peoples, correspond essentially to existing international law principles. Rawls fails to explain convincingly why the need for tolerance vis-à-vis non-liberal peoples requires 'peoples-based' rather than 'individuals-based' rules of international justice, and how such tolerance can justify the limitations of human rights in non-liberal peoples. Modern international human rights law already appears to go far beyond Rawls' minimal concept of human rights.

24 The incoherence between the universalizable 'principles of individual justice' advocated in John Rawls' *Theory of Justice* and his later arguments in favour of an international 'Law of Peoples' tolerating 'decent', albeit non-liberal societies has often been criticized (e.g., by F. Teson, *A Philosophy of International Law* (1998), ch. 4). Even from a state-centred (rather than cosmopolitan or people-centred) conception of public international law, John Rawls' narrow interpretation of human rights and of 'the international political world as we see it' (*Law of Peoples*, p. 83) appears inconsistent with the progressive expansion, since the 1993 Vienna Declaration on Human Rights, of the 'inalienable core' of human rights universally recognized in national, regional, and worldwide legal instruments as constitutional limits of tolerance vis-à-vis non-liberal governments.

7

Developing Countries and the International Trading System

SAID EL-NAGGAR

Birth of the GATT

The purpose of this chapter is to try to answer a fundamental question, namely, the extent to which the rules and objectives of WTO, and the GATT before it, are consistent or inconsistent with the development of developing countries. Stated differently, what are the benefits and risks inherent in an open, rule-based international trading system?

Three pillars of the world economy were set up in the aftermath of the Second World War. The Bretton Woods conference of 1944 resulted in the establishment of the International Bank for Reconstruction and Development (World Bank) and the International Monetary Fund (IMF). The first was to aim, after the reconstruction of the devastation caused by the war, towards facilitating the flow of international capital from developed to developing countries. The second is to regulate the international monetary relationship, including foreign exchange and balance of payments policies of member countries. The two Bretton Woods institutions were supposed to be complemented by the creation of the International Trade Organization (ITO), charged with the task of regulating international trade relations. For that purpose, the Havana Conference was convened in 1947. It resulted in the Havana Charter, aiming at creating the ITO. The Havana Charter was not ratified by the US Congress. As a consequence, the ITO never saw the light of day. The objection of the US Congress to the Havana Charter was principally due to the fact that the Charter was seen as too much of an interventionist document. By way of illustration, it called for stabilizing prices of primary commodities through international commodity agreements. It also called for control of restrictive business practices in

Dr. El-Naggar passed away in April 2004.

international trade. None of these functions was acceptable to the USA. This is in addition to the protectionist posture of some powerful private interest groups in the USA, such as labour unions. However, some participants in the Havana Conference wanted to save certain non-controversial parts of the Havana Charter. Accordingly, they agreed on what came to be known as the GATT, i.e. the General Agreement on Tariffs and Trade, which has its roots in the chapter on commercial policy of the Havana Charter. The GATT, which came into force on 1 January 1948, was supposed to be a provisional stopgap measure pending a permanent and a more comprehensive trade agreement. But what was regarded as a provisional measure has remained right up to the present time, even after the World Trade Organization (WTO) and the Uruguay Round agreements came into force on 1 January 1995.

Unlike the World Bank and the IMF, which were fully-fledged international organizations, the GATT was no more than an international treaty. It lacked the basic components of an international organization. There was no hierarchical structure, such as an executive board or a board of governors, and no formal mechanism for decision-making. It was a mere international agreement endowed with a small technical secretariat whose functions did not go beyond preparing tariff negotiating conferences. Thus, participants in the GATT were referred to as 'contracting parties', not as members of an organization. To the credit of those 'contracting parties', the GATT developed, over time, its own institutions and mechanisms on a pragmatic basis in response to actual needs. Bit by bit and a small step at a time, the GATT became indistinguishable from any other international organization. In what follows I shall deal with the GATT as if it were an international organization. For ease and simplicity of expression, I shall speak of the 'establishment of GATT', not the 'conclusion of a treaty', and of members, not 'contracting parties'.

Non-discrimination in international trade

One of the basic objectives of the GATT is non-discrimination among trading countries. This is what is known as 'most-favoured nation' treatment (MFN). It is provided for in Article I of the GATT which states in part 'any advantage, favour, privilege or immunity by any contracting party to any product originating in or destined for any other country shall be accorded immediately and unconditionally to the like product originating in or destined for the territories of all other contracting parties'.

In ordinary language, what this means is that if country 'A' reduces the import duty on a certain product imported from country 'B', the same reduction shall extend automatically and unconditionally to all other countries that are members of the GATT. These other members need not ask for, or apply to benefit from, the reduction accorded to the product imported from country 'B'. The same product imported from other countries enters the market of country 'A' under the same reduced import duty. Thus, the MFN principle ensures equality of treatment among all trading countries. It is not limited to customs duties but, in the words of GATT Article I, to 'charges of any kind, method of levying such duties and charges, all rules and formalities in connection with importation and exportation' (as well as to all internal measures).

Through the MFN obligations provided for in GATT Article I, all trading countries are assured of equal treatment in each other's market. But equality of treatment is not only among all trading countries, but is also between the imported and the like home-produced product. This is what is known as the 'national treatment' principle provided for in GATT Article III. It stipulates that once an imported product is cleared through the customs house of any country, it should be treated on a footing of equality with the like domestic product. Members of the GATT are thus required not to impose on imported products internal taxes and other internal charges in excess of those imposed on like domestic products. Moreover, they are required not to impose on imported products laws, regulations, and requirements which are less favourable than those imposed on like domestic products.

Rules of conduct

The second basic objective of the GATT is to lay down rules of conduct in international trade relations with the purpose of ensuring fair trade. The most important example of unfair trade is that related to dumping of products in the markets of other countries at prices less than those prevailing in the domestic market of the country in which these products originate. In the domestic market of 'A', for example, cement is sold at US $100 a ton. The cement is sent to be sold in the market of country 'B', at, say, US $80 a ton. Evidently, this is unfair competition between domestic and imported cement, which is condemned by GATT Article VI. Country 'B' is authorized in this case to impose anti-dumping duties on cement imported from country 'A' in an amount designed to offset the dumping margin, i.e. the difference between domestic and export price charged by country 'A'.

Unfair trade is not confined to dumping. Export products of country 'A' may be subsidized by its authorities with the purpose of reducing the price at which those products are sold in country 'B'. This is prohibited in GATT Articles VI and XVI. Country 'B' is authorized in this case to impose countervailing duties in an amount desired to offset the effect of export subsidies accorded by the authorities of country 'A'.

Liberalization of international trade

The third objective of the GATT is liberalization of the international flow of goods through reduction or elimination of tariffs and non-tariff barriers. This is perhaps the most well-known objective of the GATT. It is also the principal reason for which it is subject to criticism by developing countries. The GATT is simply regarded as the organization that strives to open up the markets of developing countries for the more competitive and more technologically advanced products from developed countries. In the view of those critics, the nascent industries of developing countries have no chance of withstanding such a competition. Development is thus nipped in the bud by a free trade ideology. Under the GATT, so the argument runs, developing countries are denied the instrument of protection used by developed countries when they were at the development stage.

This is, however, an oversimplification of the liberalization objective of the GATT. To be sure, the removal of trade barriers takes primacy of place in the overall activities of the GATT. But as the preceding analysis suggests, liberalization is not the only objective. More important is the fact that, according to the GATT, no country, developed or developing, is under obligation to reduce or remove its import duties. It may come as a surprise to know that, at the time the GATT was established, there was no provision requiring member countries to enter into negotiations for the purpose of reducing trade barriers. It was only in the 1955 Review of the GATT that Article XXVIII *bis* entitled 'Tariff Negotiations' was inserted. Moreover, Article XXVIII *bis* did not create an obligation on member countries to liberalize their trade. It merely declared the desirability of removing or reducing customs duties. In the words of Article XXVIII *bis*:

> The contracting parties recognize that customs duties often constitute serious obstacles to trade; thus negotiations on a reciprocal and mutually advantageous basis, directed to the substantial reduction of a general level

> of tariffs and other charges on imports and exports ... are of great importance to the expansion of international trade.
>
> The CONTRACTING PARTIES may therefore sponsor such negotiations from time to time.[1]

Clearly, the way Article XXVIII *bis* was drafted does not involve an obligation on the part of any member to reduce its import duties or to enter into negotiations with others for that purpose.

It is equally significant that Part I of the GATT is limited to Article I on 'General Most-Favoured-Nation Treatment' and Article II on 'Schedules of Concessions', whereas Article XXVIII *bis* on 'Tariff Negotiations' comes in Part III. The importance of the placement of different provisions of the GATT appears in Article XXX on 'Amendment'. Part I, where Articles I and II are located, cannot be amended except with the approval of all contracting parties. Other parts of the GATT on the other hand can be amended by the acceptance of two-thirds.

This is not to say that trade liberalization is not an important objective of the GATT. It is only to show that the commonly held view that the GATT, or WTO for that matter, forces developing countries to open up their markets before the highly competitive exports of developed countries is simply baseless.

Trade negotiations and tariff binding

The approach of the GATT to trade liberalization is based on an ingenious formula. The GATT founders were well aware that the right of member countries to tax imports at the border for protectionist or fiscal reasons is a sovereign right, which should not be impinged upon by membership in an international organization. At the time the GATT was created, as is the case now, no country was willing to yield this sovereign right by an *ex ante* obligation across the board. Given this fact and given the conviction of the GATT founders that free trade is good for everybody, the GATT approached trade liberalization through the mechanism of 'mutual advantage', not through the creation of an obligation on member countries. Country 'A' is an exporter of, say, glassware to 'B', 'C', and 'D'. But its exports to those countries are impeded by the

[1] Throughout the GATT, 'CONTRACTING PARTIES' is used to refer to the contracting parties acting jointly: see GATT Article XXV:1.

existence of high import duties on glassware. At the same time, country 'A' imports bicycles from 'B', 'C', and 'D'. It enters into negotiations with its trading partners with the purpose of reducing its own import duty on bicycles provided they reduce their import duties on glassware. Each party in these negotiations makes a judgment as to whether the benefits derived from mutual reduction of tariffs are roughly equal on both sides. If so, the two import duties are thereby reduced or eliminated. If not, another product (or products) may be thrown into the bargain alongside glassware or bicycles, in order to equalize the benefit. This is the process by which liberalization within the framework of the GATT comes about. No one is obliged to enter into such negotiations or to reduce its import duty. But the lure of advantage works as the driving force.

Once a tariff is reduced or eliminated in these negotiations, it is 'bound' at the level agreed upon and inscribed in the national schedule of concessions. By virtue of MFN treatment, reduction or elimination is not limited to trading partners with whom negotiations took place – it is immediately and conditionally extended to all other GATT members.

When a tariff is 'bound', the level agreed upon becomes 'binding' on the member who makes the concession of reduction or elimination. The member concerned can no longer raise the tariff unilaterally. It ceases to be an expression of sovereignty and becomes a subject of contractual relationship between the member making the concession and all the membership of the GATT. The term 'tariff binding' or 'bound tariff' does not occur in the GATT. But the concept itself is clearly contained in Article II. It states that import duties recorded in the schedule of concessions shall not be subject to other duties or charges of any kind in excess of those in the schedule.

In this connection it is important to keep in mind the following observations:

(1) The MFN principle applies to all tariffs or other charges whether or not they are bound.
(2) A tariff may be bound at the actual level in force at the time of negotiations or at a higher or lower level. This is a matter of negotiation. It may be asked, what is the value of binding a tariff at the actual level of application or at a higher level? The value is that it binds the member concerned not to raise that tariff above the negotiated level. Thus, all bindings are referred to as concessions, even if tariffs are bound at a higher level than that prevailing at the

time of negotiations. It goes without saying that members may not directly or indirectly raise a bound tariff, but they may lower it.

(3) Binding is a voluntary act, which is taken in the light of the national interest concerned. There is no obligation to bind tariffs at a certain level. Each country makes a judgment as to whether it is in its national interest to enter into tariff negotiations. For this reason the extent of tariff binding varies from one country to another. In fact, for a long time after the establishment of GATT, developing countries kept outside the 'binding' game. As a consequence, the number of tariff lines that were subject to binding was quite low. Gradually, however, they realized that this attitude is not exactly in line with their national interest. Now, practically all tariffs of the developed countries are bound and as much as 60 per cent on average in developing countries.

(4) Tariff binding normally takes place within the framework of rounds of multilateral trade negotiations which are open to all GATT members. During the first fifty years of its existence the GATT organized eight such rounds, including the Uruguay Round which resulted in the establishment of the World Trade Organization (WTO). These rounds are a kind of bazaar in which tariff concessions are exchanged among member countries. Each country that is interested in obtaining tariff concessions from its trading partners makes an 'offer' and a 'request'. The offer reflects the readiness of the country to reduce its own import duties on products of interest to its trading partners. The 'request' reflects its desire to see its trading partners responding by reducing their import duties on products of interest to the country in question. The value of the offer is supposed to be equivalent to the value of the request. There is a rule of thumb formula for measuring the respective values of offers and requests. This mechanism for tariff reduction explains the reason why concessions are made only in rounds of multilateral trade negotiations. Each country is in a position to have a comprehensive picture of concessions made by other member countries. On that basis it can adjust its own position to avoid making unnecessary concessions. The same mechanism explains also the phenomenon of 'free riders'. These are countries that make no concessions as long as they can benefit, through the operation of the MFN principle, from concessions made by other member countries. Most developing countries were classified as 'free riders', as they sat on the sidelines of negotiations waiting to reap the benefit

of concessions made by others. In that way, they avoided reducing their own import duties while benefiting from reductions made by others. There was something of a change in that position during the Uruguay Round under pressure from developed countries which urged developing countries to cease being 'free riders'.

(5) All tariff concessions made in the course of multilateral trade negotiations are recorded in the national schedule of concessions. By so doing, tariffs become bound at the level agreed upon with other member countries. Each country has its own schedule of concessions kept with the GATT and now with the WTO. These schedules can be consulted any time by any member country, in order to know the status of tariff binding. National schedules are part and parcel of each member country's obligations under the GATT. As stated in Article II, paragraph 7, they are an integral part of the GATT.[2]

(6) It may happen that circumstances change in such a way as to call for modification or withdrawal of a concession recorded in the national schedule. In such cases the country concerned cannot unilaterally modify or withdraw the concession. According to GATT Article XXVIII it has to obtain the agreement of the trading partners with which the concession was negotiated in the first place, as well as the agreement of other members determined by the totality of the GATT membership to have a 'substantial' or 'principal supplying' interest. To be released from a tariff binding, an equivalent concession on some other product or products has to be offered and accepted by the negotiating partners. If no agreement is reached, those partners are free to withdraw a concession equivalent in value to that which was modified or withdrawn.

Quantitative restrictions and non-tariff barriers

Tariffs are thus not prohibited by the GATT. They can be used by member countries for protectionist, fiscal, or balance of payments, or any other purpose deemed to be in their interest. The only constraint is that of binding as explained above. In this respect, tariffs are different from quantitative restrictions and other non-tariff barriers (NTBs)

[2] After conclusion of the Uruguay Round, this provision is supplemented by paragraph 1 of the Marrakesh Protocol to the General Agreement on Tariffs and Trade 1994, which deems a schedule annexed to the Protocol to be a schedule to the GATT 1994.

which are prohibited by virtue of GATT Article XI. In its first paragraph, Article XI provides:

> No prohibitions or restrictions other than duties, taxes or other charges, whether made effective through quotas, import or export licenses or other measures, shall be instituted or maintained by any contracting party ....

The reason for this distinction between tariff and non-tariff barriers is well known in economics. Both types distort the allocation of resources in the country imposing them. Tariffs, however, do not isolate the country in question from the world market. Any change in the world price of a given commodity is transmitted, under competitive conditions, to the domestic market in spite of the tariff. Changes in domestic prices in sympathy with world prices serve to alleviate the distorting effects of import duties. This is not the case with quotas which do isolate the domestic market from the world market. Once a quota is instituted, the price of the product concerned is governed by the interaction between supply and demand in the domestic market. Supply consists of what is locally produced, if any, plus the amount of quota. An upward or downward change in the world price of the product subject to quota has no bearing on the price prevailing in the domestic market. Such an isolation of the domestic market aggravates the distorting effect of quotas. No less important is the fact that the degree of protection is transparent in the case of tariffs, but not so with respect to quotas. A tariff of say, 20 per cent determines the degree of protection accorded to domestic producers. A quota, on the other hand, lacks transparency as to the degree of protection.

Article XI treats non-tariff barriers other than quotas in the same way quotas are treated. They are prohibited for being just as non-transparent as quotas, although they may not isolate the domestic market from the world market to the same degree. The list of NTBs is almost endless. They include any kind of measure taken by the importing country to impede access to its own market. This is illustrated by variable import levies, minimum import prices, discretionary import licensing, import deposits, foreign exchange control, voluntary export restraints, restrictive measures maintained by state-trading enterprises, and scores of other measures. In a recent study, UNCTAD identified a list of various types of NTBs running into hundreds.[3]

[3] UNCTAD, '*Quantification of Non-Tariff Measures*' (Geneva 2002), available online at http://192.91.247.38/tab/bluepubs.asp

The birth of the WTO

The creation of the World Trade Organization, which came into force on 1 January 1995, represented a quantum leap in terms of building up an open, rule-based international trading system. The WTO came about as the fruit of the longest round of multilateral trade negotiations, which lasted for almost seven years, from September 1986 to the end of December 1993. The Uruguay Round was the eighth round of negotiations organized by the GATT, but it exceeded all rounds before it, not only in length but also in coverage and ambition. The exceptional importance of the Uruguay Round can be gleaned from the following:

(1) The WTO was created as a fully-fledged international organization, thereby eliminating some of the shortcomings of the GATT. The new organization is endowed with a Ministerial Conference, which is the supreme body in the decision-making process, a General Council composed of all members, which carries out the functions of the organization in between meetings of the Ministerial Conference and sits as a dispute settlement body. It has various Councils in the different areas falling within its jurisdiction. According to Article III of the Marrakesh Agreement, the role of the WTO is to facilitate the implementation and administration and further the objectives of the Uruguay Round agreements, to provide the forum for negotiations, administer the Understanding on Rules and Procedures Governing the Settlement of Disputes (DSU) and the Trade Policy Review Mechanism, and to achieve greater coherence in global policy-making in cooperation with the IMF and the World Bank.
(2) Unlike the GATT, whose jurisdiction was strictly limited to international trade in goods, the WTO covers new areas such as trade in services, trade-related aspects of intellectual property (TRIPS), and trade policy review. By going into these areas, the GATT disciplines, such as the MFN principle, are no longer limited to treatment at the border but extend to matters pertaining to domestic law.
(3) The Uruguay Round succeeded in dealing with areas that, while falling within the jurisdiction of the GATT, were never effectively dealt with in the previous seven rounds of multilateral trade negotiations. These include two areas of particular interest to developing countries, namely, agriculture and international trade in textiles and clothing. The Agreement on Agriculture – one of the principal

achievements of the Uruguay Round – initiated a process of policy reform which tried to improve market access by converting non-tariff barriers to tariffs, with a reduction of 36 per cent to be implemented over a period of six years in the case of developed countries and by 24 per cent to be implemented over ten years for developing countries. Similarly, it significantly reduced subsidization to agricultural exports as well as domestic support to agricultural production. Equally important was the Agreement on Textiles and Clothing. Needless to say, textiles and clothing represent the backbone of exports by developing countries. But trade in these products was never subject to the GATT discipline. In view of the fact that it is a highly sensitive industry, employing hundreds of thousands in developed countries, it remained outside the successive rounds of negotiations affecting other manufactured products. Trade in these products was regulated since 1961 by sector specific arrangements, most recently the Multifibre Arrangement (MFA), which was renewed regularly once every five years. The MFA was one of the main sources of complaint of developing countries as it severely restricted access to the markets of developed countries through a system of export and import quotas, in stark violation of the GATT provisions. The Agreement on Textiles and Clothing succeeded in securing the support of developed countries for phasing out the restrictions that existed under the MFA in three stages over a period of ten years ending on 31 December 2004.

Settlement of disputes

Asserting the rights and obligations arising from the complex set of WTO treaties would be an exercise in futility, unless they were supported by an enforcement mechanism in case of dispute between different members. If this is true with respect to any international treaty, it is particularly so in the case of international trade relations. Countries vary a great deal in size, economic power, and in the extent of their domestic markets. In the absence of an enforcement mechanism, the big countries could bring their power to bear on the small countries, forcing them to renounce, or accept impairment, of their rights. This was one of the serious shortcomings of the GATT, under which disputes could not be referred to a formal dispute settlement process, and where any verdict could not be implemented, except with the consent of the party complained against.

The settlement of disputes under the GATT was based on two Articles: XXII and XXIII.

Article XXII speaks about the right of each party to seek consultation with another regarding any matter affecting the operation of the GATT. Article XXIII, entitled 'Nullification or Impairment', was the backbone of dispute settlement under the GATT. It provides that where any contracting party considers that any benefit accruing to it under the Agreement is being nullified or impaired by the action of another party, it may make written representations or proposals to the other contracting party with a view to the satisfactory adjustment of the matter. If no agreement is reached, the complaining party may refer the matter to the CONTRACTING PARTIES (i.e., to all membership of the GATT acting together). The CONTRACTING PARTIES, after investigation and consultation with all concerned, may, if they consider the matter to be serious enough, authorize the complaining party to suspend such concessions to the other party as they determine to be appropriate in the circumstances. The party against whom the complaint was brought may then comply or accept the suspension of concessions or, if it does not like such suspension, may give notice of its intention to withdraw from the GATT.

However, despite the modest and weak character of the system provided for in Article XXIII, the GATT managed over the years to provide a reasonable framework for settlement of disputes. But it remained, up to the establishment of the WTO in 1995, a voluntary system. The party which failed to carry out its obligations under the GATT, or acted in a manner that nullified or impaired a benefit legitimately expected by another party, could object to any unfavourable verdict. Its objection was sufficient to bury that verdict with no recourse. The implementation of any decision or verdict was contingent upon the consensus of all concerned, including the party which lost the case. Considering the voluntary character of the system under the GATT, it is in fact amazing that a large number of rulings and decisions were implemented with consensus. This was partly due to peer pressure and partly to the fact that all members have an interest in making the system function.

The establishment of the WTO brought with it a far superior system for the settlement of disputes. The Understanding on the Rules and Procedures Governing the Settlement of Disputes (DSU) was one of the greatest achievements of the Uruguay Round.

In the first place, the system shed its voluntary character. The party which is deemed to have nullified or impaired a benefit due to another party has no longer the right to stop a complaint or to reject a ruling or decision taken by a panel and confirmed by the newly established Appellate Body. Under the GATT, as pointed out, the implementation of a decision or a ruling taken in a dispute cannot be implemented except with the consensus of all concerned. Under the DSU such a decision has to be implemented except when there is a consensus not to do so. Stated differently, a single member under the GATT could abort such a decision. Under the DSU it takes the consensus of all members to abort a decision taken by the appropriate dispute settlement bodies.

Under the DSU, any complaint passes through five stages. The first stage is that of consultation (DSU Article 4). If no agreement is reached through the process of consultation, the aggrieved party may ask for the establishment of a panel composed of three or five experts in trade questions. Upon the request of the complaining party, a panel shall be established by the Dispute Settlement Body (DSB) unless it decides by consensus not to establish a panel (DSU Articles 6 to 16). The panel is required to finish its examination and issue its report within a period that does not exceed (as a general rule) six months. In cases of urgency, including those relating to perishable goods, the period for issuing the report is reduced to three months. Within sixty days after the date of circulation of a panel report to the members, the report will be adopted by a DSB meeting unless a party to the dispute notifies the DSB of its decision to appeal, or the DSB decides by consensus not to adopt the report.

The third stage is that of consideration of the panel report by the Appellate Body (DSU Article 17). The Appellate Body is composed of seven persons of recognized authority, with demonstrated expertise in law, international trade, and the subject matter of the agreements covered by the DSU. In considering any case referred to it, the Appellate Body is limited to issues of law covered in the panel report and legal interpretations developed by the panel. In other words, the Appellate Body considers only questions of law, not questions of fact, which are settled at the panel stage. As a general rule, the proceedings at the appellate stage must not exceed sixty days, from the date a party to the dispute notifies its decision to appeal, to the date the Appellate Body circulates its report. In no case must the proceedings exceed ninety days. The Appellate Body may uphold, modify, or reverse the legal findings and conclusions of the panel.

The fourth stage is that of consideration of the panel and Appellate Body reports by the DSB. According to paragraph 14 of DSU Article 17, an Appellate Body report shall be adopted by the DSB and unconditionally accepted by the parties to the dispute unless the DSB decides by consensus not to adopt the Appellate Body report within thirty days following its circulation to the members.[4]

The fifth and final stage is that of implementation (DSU Articles 21 and 22). Members are required to comply promptly with the recommendations and rulings of the DSB. The member concerned must inform the DSB, in a meeting held within thirty days after the date of adoption of the panel or Appellate Body report, of its intention in respect of implementation of the recommendations and rulings of the DSB. If it is impracticable to comply immediately with the recommendations and rulings, the member concerned will have a reasonable period of time in which to do so. The reasonable period of time will be that proposed by the member concerned and approved by the DSB, or, in the absence of such approval, a reasonable period of time mutually agreed by the parties, or, in the absence of such agreement, it will be a period of time determined through binding arbitration within ninety days after the date of adoption of the recommendations and rulings. In such an arbitration, a guideline for the arbitrator is that the reasonable period of time to implement panel or Appellate Body recommendations should not exceed fifteen months from the date of adoption of a panel or Appellate Body report. However, that time may be shorter or longer, depending upon the particular circumstances.

If the member concerned fails to bring the measure found to be inconsistent with a covered agreement into compliance within the reasonable period of time, such member must, if so requested, and no later than the expiry of the reasonable period of time, enter into negotiations with the complaining party, with a view to developing mutually acceptable compensation. If no satisfactory compensation has been agreed within twenty days after the date of expiry of the reasonable period of time, any party having invoked the dispute settlement procedures may request authorization from the DSB to suspend the application to the member concerned of concessions or other obligations as deemed appropriate. The level of the suspension of concessions or other obligations authorized by the DSB shall be equivalent to the level of the nullification or impairment that gave rise to the complaint in the first place.

4 A similar 'reverse consensus' rule applies to the adoption of panel reports under DSU Article 16.4.

From this description of the dispute settlement system under the DSU, it is clear that it is far more tight and effective than that which prevailed under the GATT. The stages of dispute settlement are well-defined and the periods to which each stage is subject are consistent with the need for a prompt resolution of the dispute.

Moreover, once the proceedings of dispute settlement are initiated, each stage leads automatically to the subsequent stage. The process cannot be delayed or suspended unless the parties to the dispute so decide in accordance with the provisions of the DSU.

Benefits and shortcomings

There is nothing in the preceding analysis to suggest that the GATT or the WTO impinges in any way on the development prospects of developing countries. On the contrary, there are reasons to believe that these countries derive substantial benefits from an open, rule-based international trading system. If we imagine a world without the GATT and WTO, the first losers would decidedly be developing countries. They are the weaker partners in dealing with developed countries. In support of this contention, it is enough to recall the position of developing countries in the international trading system prior to the establishment of the GATT. The state of affairs prevailing then could hardly be described as a 'system'. Most of them were subject to ruthless exploitation by their colonial masters. Discrimination among trading countries was the order of the day and the international flow of goods was severely restricted, except in the relationship between the metropolitan power and its colonies. While the principle of most-favoured nation treatment was not unknown, its application was subject to the pleasure of the big empires. It could be withdrawn at any time for political or short-term economic considerations. The concept of multilateralism was virtually absent and a good part of international trade was regulated by bilateral agreements.

The creation of the GATT was an important step in the direction of a rule-based trading system. From the viewpoint of developing countries, its most significant contribution was perhaps the improvement of access to the markets of developed countries. When the WTO came into being on 1 January 1995, the GATT had already organized eight successive rounds of multilateral trade negotiations. As a consequence, a good many barriers to trade had already been reduced or dismantled. This is particularly so with respect to trade in manufactured products.

It is estimated that import duties imposed by developed countries were reduced from an average of 40 per cent in 1948 to an average of some 6 per cent after the Uruguay Round. No less important is the fact that almost 100 per cent of reduced tariffs are bound. It is no exaggeration to say that tariffs are no longer a serious obstacle to trade. An important exception is trade in textiles and clothing which, as pointed out before, were subject to an elaborate system of export and import quotas. The same can be said with respect to trade in agricultural products which remained, until the creation of WTO, beyond the reach of the GATT discipline. It is also true that import duties imposed by some developed countries on labour-intensive products remain high. These are the so-called 'tariff peaks'. But a process of liberalization has already begun regarding trade in agricultural products as well as textiles and clothing, while tariff peaks are slated for elimination in the forthcoming rounds of trade negotiations.

The benefits from improved access were reinforced by benefits derived from discrimination in favour of developing countries. In this context, the establishment of the United Nations Conference on Trade and Development (UNCTAD) was an important landmark. It was established with the declared objective of taking into account the development needs of developing countries. The idea of treating developing countries on a footing of equality with developed countries in international trade was anathema to the founders of UNCTAD. According to Raul Prebisch, the spiritual father of UNCTAD, equality of treatment between unequals is itself inequality. As a result of this philosophy, UNCTAD instituted in the early 1970s the Generalized System of Preferences (GSP) with the aim of securing free access for manufactured and semi-manufactured products of developing countries in the markets of developed countries. The GSP was eventually accepted by virtually all developed countries. However, as an exception from MFN treatment it was not consistent with the GATT provisions. In 1971 the GATT contracting parties approved a waiver legitimizing this exception for a period of ten years ending in 1981. When this period was about to come to an end, the participants in the Tokyo Round of trade negotiations adopted a decision in 1979 on differential and more favourable treatment for developing countries, thereby putting the GSP on a permanent basis under the name of the 'Enabling Clause'.

The importance of the GSP for developing countries is a matter of opinion. The system suffers from some shortcomings which limit its value as a means of a better access to the markets of the granting countries. There can be no doubt, however, that it was a significant prop for the manufacturing sector of developing countries.

The trend towards special and differential treatment for developing countries gained momentum with the establishment of the WTO. This is reflected in the fact that practically all Uruguay Round agreements contain provisions for special treatment of developing countries. It is also noteworthy that wherever there is a transitional period it is longer, and wherever there is an obligation it is usually less onerous than that for developed countries. It is well recognized, however, that provisions on special and differential treatment contained in the agreements are inadequate given the development needs of developing countries, especially the least-developed among them. This was repeatedly emphasized in the Doha Ministerial Declaration in 2001:

> The majority of WTO Members are developing countries. We seek to place their needs and interests at the heart of the Work Programme adopted in this Declaration. Recalling the Preamble to the Marrakesh Agreement, we shall continue to make positive efforts designed to ensure that developing countries, and especially the least-developed among them, secure a share in the growth of world trade commensurate with the needs of their economic development. In this context, enhanced market access, balanced rules and well targeted, sustainably financed technical assistance and capacity-building programmes have important roles to play.

However, if an open, rule-based international trading system is so beneficial to developing countries, why is it that both the GATT and the WTO are subject to bitter criticism from many economists and politicians around the globe? There is not one single explanation for the phenomenon. At the time the GATT came into being in 1948, two factors militated against it from the viewpoint of developing countries. In the first place, it was seen as a creature of the rich industrial countries to further their own interests at the expense of developing countries. For this reason it was dubbed the 'rich man's club'. The rising importance of multinational corporations gave credence to this contention. In the second place, the GATT was to a very large extent an embodiment of the neoclassical economic model, according to which free trade based on comparative advantage, as well as markets and private enterprise, represent the most efficient and effective way for development. This view flew in the face of development theories prevailing at that time in most developing countries. Economists such as Raul Prebisch, Hans Singer,

Arthur Lewis, Gunnar Mydal, Walt Rostow, Paul Rosenstein-Rodan, as well as many others, emphasized the vital role of the state in promoting economic development, criticized the doctrine of comparative advantage, and denounced free trade and market-oriented strategies. Concepts such as secular deterioration in the terms of trade of developing countries, the 'unfair' distribution of trade benefits, the 'backwash effect' of free trade, the 'big push', and the need for balanced growth ran counter to the development model implicit in the GATT. Later on, particularly at the time the WTO was established, globalization was seen by many as the enemy of developing countries – witness the vehement demonstrations at Seattle, Geneva, and Bangkok on the occasion of the WTO and Group of Seven meetings. The WTO, more even than the IMF or the World Bank, is seen, rightly or wrongly, as the handmaiden of globalization and the big interest groups in the industrial countries.

There is now greater awareness of the need to convey an image of the WTO based on the reality of its principles and objectives, which are not as anti-development and anti-equity as they are made out to be.

8

North–South Issues of Foreign Direct Investments in the WTO: Is There a Middle-of-the-Road Approach?

MITSUO MATSUSHITA

Introduction

As yet there is no agreement on foreign direct investment (FDI)[1] in the WTO. As discussed later, however, the Ministerial Conference held in Doha in the autumn of 2001 adopted a resolution that there would be a negotiation on investment if consensus is achieved on the 'modalities' of negotiation. It is too premature to predict whether there will be such an agreement and, if there is, what shape this will take. However, globalization has progressed at an unprecedented speed in the past several decades and FDI has been one of the prime movers of globalization of the world economy. This necessitates some considerations for a comprehensive international agreement on FDI.

However, there is a sharp division of views with regard to the desirability of introducing a comprehensive agreement on FDI in the WTO. There are divergent views even among developed country members and among developing country members – one cannot easily draw a line between developed and developing country members and say that the former are for an FDI agreement and the latter are against it. Nevertheless, it is true that a sceptical sentiment on a comprehensive FDI agreement in the WTO is more prevalent among developing country members and, if the WTO is to incorporate an agreement on FDI in a future round, a compromise of the differing views of developed and developing country members must somehow be forged.

[1] The main focus of this chapter is on issues of foreign direct investment and so 'FDI' will be used unless otherwise specified.

A brief summary of past negotiations

In 1995, the OECD Ministerial Conference initiated a negotiation with a view to formulating a comprehensive and binding multilateral agreement on investment (known as the Multilateral Agreement on Investment, or MAI).[2] However, negotiating parties could not come to a conclusion by the deadline (1998) and the negotiation failed. The major issues were: whether or not (a) portfolio investment as well as FDI should be included within the scope of the agreement, (b) environmental and labour issues should be dealt with, (c) there should be a dispute settlement mechanism in which not only disputes between governments but also those between private parties and governments are dealt with, and (d) there should be exceptions to liberalization on the basis of, *inter alia*, maintaining public order, completing regional integration, and preserving identity of culture.

After the failure of the MAI, the arena for negotiation shifted to the WTO. Even during the Uruguay Round, there was a proposal by a group of developed countries to include rules of investment in the WTO Agreement on Trade-related Investment Measures (TRIMS Agreement). However, developing countries objected and the scope of the TRIMS Agreement was confined to trade-related investment measures. In the Singapore Ministerial Conference in 1996, the Working Group on the Relationship between Trade and Investment was established, and it has since turned out six reports in which it investigated issues related to trade and FDI. The last report was published in December 2002.[3]

In the Seattle Ministerial Conference (1999), a group of developed country members pressed the position that negotiations should begin to establish a multilateral framework of rules on FDI. On the other hand, developing country members argued that it was premature to initiate negotiations as to whether a comprehensive framework on investment should be introduced into the WTO regime. They argued that there were

[2] On the MAI, see the following: T. Clarke and M. Barlow, *MAI: The Multilateral Agreement on Investment and the Threat to Canadian Sovereignty* (Stoddart, Toronto, 1997); OECD, *Multilateral Agreement on Investment: Consolidated Text and Commentary* (OECD, Paris, 1997); OECD, *Main Features of the MAI* (OECD, Paris, 1997); OECD, *The Multilateral Agreement on Investment: Consolidated Text*, DAFFE/MAI/NM (98)2/REV1, 1998; OECD, *Commentary to Consolidated Text*, DAFFE/MAI/NM (98)4, 1998.

[3] Working Group on the Relationship between Trade and Investment, *Report*, WT/WGTI/6, 9 December 2002.

many unresolved issues and that the Working Group should continue to study advantages and disadvantages of FDI and the feasibility of introducing an international investment agreement on it. They insisted that the Working Group should take into consideration the needs of developing countries. However, the Seattle Ministerial Conference failed due to differences of views between developed and developing country members and this gave a 'temporary reprieve' to developing countries.

Agenda for FDI in the Doha Declaration

In the Doha WTO Ministerial Conference held in 2001, an agenda for negotiation of an agreement on FDI was adopted. Paragraphs 20, 21, and 22 of the Doha Ministerial Declaration,[4] adopted on 14 November 2001, constitute a section of the Declaration titled 'Relationship between Trade and Investment'.

Paragraph 20 states, in part, 'we agree that negotiations will take place after the Fifth Session of the Ministerial Conference on the basis of a decision to be taken, by explicit consensus, at that session on modalities of negotiations'. 'Modalities' are somewhat ambiguous and can include a variety of subject matters. Some substantive matters may be included in this category. The Fifth Session of the Ministerial Conference took place in September 2003 in Cancún, Mexico and, in that Ministerial Conference, the 'explicit consensus' required in order to begin this negotiation was not achieved.

Paragraph 21 emphasizes the importance of capacity building of, and technical assistance to, developing countries and the least developed countries in this area. It further notes the necessity of cooperation with other relevant intergovernmental organizations, including UNCTAD, and through appropriate regional and bilateral channels, to provide strengthened and adequately resourced assistance to respond to these needs.

Paragraph 22 states that the Working Group on the Relationship between Trade and Investment will focus on the clarification of some key issues. Such key issues include (i) scope and definition of FDI, (ii) transparency, (iii) non-discrimination, (iv) modalities for pre-establishment commitments along the lines of the GATS, (v) positive list approach, (vi) development provisions, (vii) exceptions and balance of payments, (viii) safeguards, (ix) consultation and the settlement of disputes between members. It also emphasizes the importance of the

[4] See www.wto.org

interests of home and host countries and due account for the development policies and objectives of host governments, as well as their right to regulate in the public interest. The special development, trade, and financial needs of developing and least developed countries are specifically listed as items to be considered. Lastly, the paragraph mentions that due regard should be paid to other relevant WTO provisions and existing bilateral and regional arrangements on investment.

Paragraph 22 points out a number of subjects. A 'positive list approach' is mentioned, which means that items listed in a positive list are subject to liberalization and not others. This suggests that paragraph 22 envisages a GATS-type approach, i.e., that of liberalizing only those sectors regarding which a member makes a commitment for liberalization. It also mentions 'development provisions'. This applies to developing country members and can include provisions providing for exceptions to the obligation to liberalize. These provisions are mentioned here in order to guarantee that interests of developing country members will be paid sufficient attention.

Division of views regarding the desirability of introducing an FDI agreement into the WTO regime

As stated earlier, the Cancun Ministerial Conference failed to initiate negotiations in the WTO with a view to concluding an agreement containing rules governing the relationship between trade and investment. However, this issue will come up again in the near future in upcoming trade negotiations under the WTO. It is, therefore, useful to investigate issues involved in the North/South relationship as it relates to FDI, in particular, the differences of views between developed and developing countries, and see if there is any middle-of-the-road approach.

Views of developed country members

It is to be noted that the views of developed country members are not unanimous on the desirability of introducing an FDI agreement into the WTO. The USA, for example, insists that any agreement on investment should include provision for portfolio investment whereas the EU and Japan would not go so far as to include such investment in a prospective agreement. By and large, however, there is commonality of views among developed country members with regard to the substance of an investment agreement. The core elements of those views are, *inter alia*:

(1) FDI should be generally free from governmental restrictions and controls and can be restricted only in exceptional circumstances.
(2) Liberalization of FDI increases inflow of foreign capital into host countries and this helps economic development of the host countries. In fact, this helps both home countries and host countries, regardless of whether they are developed or developing countries.
(3) FDI should be regulated by international rules.

Signatories of an FDI agreement should be bound by the terms of the agreement, violations of which should be brought to the dispute settlement process of the WTO.[5]

More specifically, the views of developed countries can be summarized as follows:[6]

(1) Foreign investors should be given the right to enter countries without conditions and regulations except for extraordinary circumstances.
(2) Foreign investors should be accorded national treatment and most-favoured nation treatment.
(3) Transparency in investment rules should be established.
(4) Performance requirements and local content requirements should be prohibited in principle.
(5) Control of mobility of funds into and out of the host country should be prohibited in principle.
(6) The definition of investment in an investment agreement should cover not only FDI but also such items as portfolio investment and extension of credit.[7]

[5] Views of developed and developing countries are summarized in reports of the Working Group on Trade and Investment (see *supra* n. 3).

[6] These views are shown in the OECD draft of the MAI and the EC paper proposing the agreement (see references cited *supra* n. 2). In 2002, the *Keidanren* (Federation of Japanese Business) published a report entitled *Requesting the Establishment of Rules on International Investment and of Suitable Conditions for Inward Direct Investment*. Views expressed in this report, which represent Japanese investors abroad, largely coincide with the above positions. Also, a survey conducted by JETRO (Japan External Trade Organization) in December 2001 of views of Japanese investors abroad reveals a similar result.

[7] As touched on earlier, there is diversity of views among developed countries on this matter. The USA is strong in urging that any investment, including portfolio investment, be included in the scope of an agreement. The EU and Japan would not go that far. However, the principal basis of their reluctance to include portfolio investment is that this would antagonize developing countries and would make negotiations difficult. Their reluctance does not reflect an opposition, in principle, to the inclusion of portfolio investment in an investment agreement.

(7) The rights of investors against expropriation should be strictly observed.
(8) Host countries should be prohibited from imposing conditions contrary to the principles incorporated into an investment agreement.
(9) Violations of an investment agreement should be subject to dispute settlement in the WTO.

On the whole, the above views emphasize the freedom of investment by investors with minimum restrictions. These views focus on the rights of investors and hold them above the rights of host countries to control their activities. As stated earlier, the premise of this view is that the freedom of investment without restrictions is a 'win-win game' for everyone – not only investors, but also host countries reap benefits from investment activities.

Views of developing countries

Developing countries do not necessarily speak in one voice on the issue of whether to introduce an investment agreement into the WTO. Countries such as India, Pakistan, Malaysia, and some other ASEAN countries are generally opposed to the introduction of such an agreement in the WTO. African countries and Caribbean countries are sceptical about such an introduction. Brazil and Egypt emphasize the importance of recognizing the role of development policy if such an agreement is introduced. The People's Republic of China, the largest receiver of FDI from abroad, has not expressed an explicit view, either pro or con, on this matter.[8] On the whole, developing countries' views stand on the notion that whether FDI benefits developing countries depends on a variety of factors and it is by no means a universal truth that developing countries gain economically or otherwise by accepting FDI without conditions. They argue that the loss of control and erosion of sovereignty caused by the imposition of international rules may cause

[8] See generally the Report of Trade and Investment, *supra* n. 3. See also UNCTAD, *Trade and Development Report* (United Nations, New York and Geneva, 1997); UNCTAD, *Trade and Development Report* (United Nations, New York and Geneva, 1998); UNCTAD, *Trade and Development Report* (United Nations, New York and Geneva, 1999); UNCTAD, *Industrial Countries Must Work Harder for Development if Globalization is to Deliver on its Promises* (UNCTAD/INF/2816, 1999); UNCTAD, *Report of the Secretary-General of UNCTAD to UNCTAD* (TD/380, Geneva, February 2000).

them disadvantages. Therefore, they argue that it should not be *a priori* assumed that, through the acceptance of FDI, developing countries can enjoy a 'win-win game'.

It should be stated that, generally, developing countries are not against the entry of FDI into their countries. In fact, many of them need FDI for their economic development and recognize the importance of introducing FDI into their economies. However, many developing countries feel that a hasty and indiscreet liberalization of FDI through binding international agreements may harm their national interests and that the governments of developing countries should be able to control and exercise surveillance of FDI activities. What underlies this attitude is a suspicion that unfettered activities of multinational corporations (most of which are of developed country origin) will subject developing countries to the arbitrary decisions of multinational corporations.

Articulate views on this issue are expressed by some writers such as Martin Khor[9] and L. Das.[10] Their views may probably be on the radical side of the scale among views of developing countries. However, they clearly point out problems and hazards to developing countries if an investment agreement is hastily introduced into the WTO and, therefore, are worthy of being taken into account.

Martin Khor states:[11]

(1) FDI generates positive and negative effects on the flow of foreign exchange. FDI brings in capital but also leads to a stream of outflows of profit and other investment income. This outflow increases through time as the stock of foreign capital rises.

(2) Too rapid a build-up of FDI could lead to denationalization, where the foreign share of the nation's wealth stock increases relative to the local share. To avoid any economic or social problems that this may cause, the rate of growth of domestic investment should exceed FDI growth.

9 M. Khor, *Globalization and the South* (Third World Network, Penang, 2000).

10 L. Das, *The WTO Agreement: Deficiencies, Imbalances and Required Changes* (Third World Network, Penang, 1998) and L. Das, *Suggestions for Improvements in the WTO Agreements* (Third World Network, Penang, 1999).

11 Khor, *Globalization and the South*, ch. 4 'Issues in Investment Liberalization'. See also Ghazali bin Atan, *The Effects of DFI on Trade, Balance of Payments and Growth in Developing Countries, and Appropriate Policy Approaches to DFI* (Third Word Network, Penang, 1996). The views of L. Das and Ghazali are essentially similar to those of M. Khor.

(3) For developing countries, except China, the recent FDI boom has consisted predominantly of mergers and acquisitions, its share of total FDI to developing countries being 72 per cent in 1988–91. Thus, much of FDI to developing countries is not in the form of 'greenfield investment', which creates new productive assets, but consists of the purchase of existing assets, especially through privatization and in the services sector.
(4) In Malaysia, the activities of foreign firms had a negative impact on both net transfers and the trade balance in the 1980s and early 1990s. In Thailand, FDI had a negative net impact on the trade balance in the late 1980s and early 1990s, on top of rising payments abroad for profits and royalties, and these features of FDI contributed to external imbalances that played an important role in the country's subsequent crisis.
(5) There are possible negative effects on the balance of payments due to increased imported inputs and profits remitted abroad.
(6) The high market power of multinationals can lead to monopoly pricing and its resulting overall inefficiency in resource allocation, an adverse impact on the competitive environment, and discouragement of development of technical know-how by local firms. Also, there may be problems of transfer pricing, which reduces tax revenue, and distortion of consumption patterns due to brand names of multinationals.
(7) If FDI constitutes a large component of total investment and involves loss of local control over strategic sectors, infrastructure, and natural resources, politico-strategic interests of a nation are at stake. Private decisions made abroad can impact the local economy and society and sometimes even the country's sovereignty may be at stake.
(8) In light of the above, governments of developing countries should adopt a selective policy towards FDI by determining the composition of capital inflows and should be able to manage these inflows, including FDI. In particular, these governments should adopt a selective policy with respect to specific projects, e.g., confining FDI to priority sectors, and observe prudence with respect to total FDI flows and stock to avoid more financial fragility. A global investment regime that takes away a developing country's ability to select 'right projects' from among FDI projects and exclude those which would hinder the growth of local firms in certain strategic sectors is harmful to the country's development and economic stability.

The above views are not necessarily against the introduction of FDI into developing countries. However, they argue that developing countries should have the right of 'self-determination' in regard to the selection of FDI. They argue that, given the possibility for uncertain and unpredictable consequences that might be brought about by uncontrolled inflow of FDI, governments of developing countries should be able to keep their rights to intervene, if necessary, and their freedom of taking actions should not be unduly restricted by an investment agreement.

Comments

Paragraph 22 of the Doha Ministerial Declaration lists eight items as subject matters for study by the Working Group on the Relationship between Trade and Investment. Although the Cancun Ministerial Conference failed to initiate negotiations on an investment agreement, these items still serve as useful guides for future negotiations. These items are: (i) scope and definition of investment, (ii) transparency, (iii) non-discrimination, (iv) modalities for pre-establishment commitments along the lines of the GATS, (v) positive list approach, (vi) development provisions, (vii) exceptions and balance of payments safeguards, and (viii) consultation and the settlement of disputes between members. In the following paragraphs, some selected topics from among the above list will be briefly discussed. Not all of the listed items need to be discussed, but there are several which will be controversial and focal points.

Scope and definition of investment

A question here is whether only FDI should be included or other forms of investment (such as portfolio investment) should be included in the scope of the agreement. In view of the currency crisis which began in 1997, some developing countries and especially some ASEAN countries will be extremely reluctant to introduce a wide concept into an investment agreement which covers portfolio investment. This would deprive developing country members of control of their currencies and arguably reduce the ability of governments of developing countries to cope with abrupt and excessive inflows and outflows of money.

In view of the above and also the fact that portfolio investment has different features as distinguished from FDI, an agreement on investment should be limited to matters closely related to FDI. However, there should be flexibility in defining FDI. In many instances of FDI, the parent companies enjoy only minority ownership of a subsidiary and yet act as the primary entity in control of that subsidiary. Therefore, the definition of ownership should cover minority ownership. One idea may be to rely on the IMF definition of FDI as an acquisition and ownership by a foreign entity of a domestic subsidiary of 10 per cent or more of outstanding stocks of the subsidiary.

Non-discrimination

This is a question of whether the principles of most-favoured nation treatment and national treatment should be introduced. In many instances, developing countries adopt development policies of promoting some sectors of the economy, some industries, or even some enterprises. For example, Malaysia has had a 'national car' project (Proton) and this consists of a joint venture of a Malaysian entity and Mitsubishi (a Japanese car company). In Indonesia, there was a national car project called 'Timor'. In the early stages of this project, the Indonesian government chose to create a joint venture between an Indonesian entity and a Korean car company (Kia) and give this joint venture favourable conditions. This led to claims filed with the DSB of the WTO by Japan, the EU, and the USA that this was a violation of GATT Article III (national treatment) and provisions of the TRIMS. This was held to be contrary to provisions of the WTO agreements[12] and, because of this and other reasons, eventually abandoned.

However, examples such as the above show that developing countries sometimes give preferential treatment to their national industries or companies, or to companies of a particular third country. For development purposes, this preferential treatment may be useful or even necessary. To incorporate the MFN principle and the national treatment principle, such as Articles I and III of the GATT 1994, into an investment agreement, and impose them uniformly on developing countries in FDI areas, seems to deprive them of the flexibility of policy choices. It may be useful to utilize the GATS model in which conditions can be attached to the MFN principle and the national treatment principle applies only when a member makes a commitment for it.

[12] See panel report, *Indonesia – Certain Measures Affecting the Automobile Industry*, WT/DS54/R, WT/DS55/R, WT/DS59/R, WT/DS64/R, 23 July 1998. Although not a case of a developing country, see also Appellate Body report, *Canada – Autos*.

Modalities for pre-establishment commitments along the lines of GATS

In many ways, the GATS and a prospective investment agreement share common features. Any FDI agreement should incorporate some features of the GATS. Pre-establishment commitments along the lines of GATS are probably the only choice. At the same time, the relationship between the GATS and an FDI agreement should be clarified. In fact, Mode 3 of the GATS provides for direct investment in the trade in services area. A question arises as to whether FDI in trade in services should be covered by an FDI agreement or the GATS. A related question is the relationship between the GATS and FDI with regard to adjacent areas. For example, production of goods in a host country is presumably covered by an FDI agreement and distribution and advertisement are covered by the GATS. There should be consistency between an FDI agreement and the GATS since an approval of production through FDI granted by a member under an FDI agreement may be made ineffective if the member is allowed to restrict distribution and advertisement of the product in question in accordance with the GATS.

Positive list approach

This is also a GATS-type approach. In this approach, a member is obligated to liberalize only those areas and subjects regarding which it has made a commitment to liberalize. This approach mitigates the concerns of developing country members mentioned earlier. A member need only liberalize those areas and subject matters where it feels confident that FDI in those areas will bring benefits to the country. However, a positive list approach should be premised on continual negotiations for liberalization in the future; otherwise, there would be a standstill of the status quo and no progress for liberalization is likely to be made.

Development provisions

As stated earlier, a concern of developing countries is that a sweeping FDI agreement may curtail the powers of governments to carry out their development and industrial policies. It is, therefore, useful to incorporate provisions which would declare that the rights of members to implement their development and industrial policies are recognized.

Developing country members should be allowed to exclude some sectors of economy for the purpose of achieving their development policy if there is sufficient reason for it. In such a case, a notification to the WTO should be made. In practice, however, many such development and industrial policies can be accomplished through a positive list approach, flexible application of the MFN and national treatment principles, and the use of exceptions.

Exceptions and balance of payments safeguards

Exceptions from the disciplines of an FDI agreement should be included in a similar way as Article XX of the GATT 1994. Members should be able to take measures which derogate from the obligations when necessary to protect some vital national interests. In order to determine what such national interests are, GATT Article XX may be a model. Items such as the protection of public order and morals and life and health of humans, animals, and plants, compliance with domestic laws and regulation, and the conservation of exhaustible natural resources, may provide justification for exceptions. Also, FDI-related provisions included in FTAs and Regional Trade Agreements (RTAs) should constitute an exception on certain conditions similar to GATT Article XXIV.[13]

Paragraph 21 of the Doha Ministerial Declaration mentions only balance of payments safeguards. Considering the experiences of some members during the Asian financial crisis, the inclusion of this safeguards provision is understandable. However, it seems that balance of payments safeguards are less crucial if the scope of an investment agreement is confined to FDI in a narrow sense than it would be if a wide variety of investment, including portfolio investments, were included.

Whether to include a provision for safeguards in a FDI agreement such as GATT Article XIX is an important issue to be considered although this item is not mentioned in the Doha Ministerial Declaration. One potential problem may be the definition of injury to a domestic industry. If, due to an inflow of FDI from abroad, a domestic industry which has lost competitiveness in the host country declines, there may be serious injury caused by such entry of FDI. However, in contrast to situations envisaged by GATT Article XIX, business entities established by the FDI maintain employment, pay local taxes, and

[13] See OECD Trade Committee, *The Relationship between Regional Trade Agreements and the Multilateral Trading System: Investment* (April 2000).

provide products and services. Even if a domestic industry is seriously injured, this does not automatically mean that there is loss in the national economy as long as the FDI keeps employment, pays taxes, and provides products and services. In any event, a positive list approach and a flexible application of MFN and national treatment principles, as discussed earlier, largely take care of the need to protect a domestic industry from the pressure of foreign competitors through FDI.

Potentially a more important issue seems to be that of a safety net. Foreign investors may provide basic infrastructures of the society in a developing country, such as a telecommunications network, water system, basic transportation and financial services. Foreign investors may decide to divest resources from this country due to the fact that there are more profitable markets elsewhere. Sudden divestitures may cause serious economic and social disruptions in that country. If it is a developed country, there are more resources to deal with this contingency. However, due to insufficient resources, a developing country may be more severely affected by these disruptions. Some provisions to deal with this type of situation seem worthy of consideration. Such provisions would include a consultation procedure for investors and the government of a developing country member and, in extreme cases, a temporary custodianship of the facility by the government.

Dispute settlement

Members of the WTO should be allowed to resort to the dispute settlement procedure provided by the DSU when a member deems that another member is not in compliance with provisions of an FDI agreement. In view of the fact that, in some bilateral and regional agreements as well as in public international law, the right to seek for compensation in connection with disputes involving FDI is provided for, it is worth considering whether the right to compensation should be incorporated in an FDI agreement.

Competition policy

Paragraphs 23–25 of the Doha Ministerial Declaration are devoted to competition policy.[14] Here, again, a negotiation will be initiated if an

[14] With regard to competition policy issues at the WTO, see M. Matsushita, 'Basic Principles of the WTO and the Role of Competition Policy' (2002) 3 (4) *Journal of World Investment* 567; M. Matsushita, T. J. Schoenbaum, and P. Mavroidis, *The World Trade Organization: Law, Practice and Policy* (Oxford University Press, 2003), pp. 539–88.

explicit consensus is achieved on modalities of negotiation and, at the time of writing this chapter, it is not certain whether a negotiation will be initiated. Regardless of the outcome of this negotiation, it is submitted here that competition policy has a close link to the issues of FDI and this is especially important for developing countries. As examined earlier, developing countries are concerned that their countries' economic and social welfare may be subjected to the whims of large multinational corporations. If so, it is worthwhile thinking about introducing competition policy into an FDI agreement whereby abuses of dominant positions of multinational corporations can be controlled. In Article 40 of the TRIPs Agreement, it is provided that members are authorized to enact domestic legislation to deal with restrictive business practices involved in intellectual property licensing agreements. Likewise it makes sense to incorporate in an FDI agreement the power of members to adopt a measure to counter abusive conduct of multinational corporations.

If the WTO is successful in introducing an agreement on competition policy, the task of controlling abusive conduct of multinationals should be left to that agreement. However, it is not certain whether such an agreement will be achieved. Nor is it clear what the details of this agreement will be if it is agreed upon. Here it is submitted that an FDI agreement is not complete unless supplemented by competition policy and this is especially important for developing countries.

Conclusion

The above is not an exhaustive and comprehensive list of the subject matters to be considered when negotiating FDI at the WTO. The above discussions have focused mainly on items about which the positions of developed country members and developing country members are likely to differ, and where compromises are necessary. Some more items may be added when a negotiation begins, such as transparency of governmental process, intellectual property, free movement of personnel, labour rights, and social security issues, which may vitally affect FDI. However, these are outside the scope of this chapter and studies must be made on those subjects by other experts.

9

The Participation of Developing Countries in WTO Dispute Settlement and the Role of the Advisory Centre on WTO Law

LEO PALMA

My first opportunity to meet Justice Florentino Feliciano was when he was first appointed as a Member of the Appellate Body of the World Trade Organization, and I gave him a lift. Contemporary music was playing on my car radio. I asked him if he preferred to listen to another type of music. He asked me if, by any chance, I had Gregorian chants. It was my lucky day.

As a Filipino and as a member of the Philippine bar, I had known of Justice Florentino Feliciano before I had the opportunity to meet him. When I started my career as an apprentice in a law firm in the Philippines, Justice Feliciano was a partner in another law firm bearing his name. My mentors in the law firm were his former associates in that other law firm. They spoke of 'Toy' in hushed tones, almost bordering on reverence. Many years later, I had the opportunity to meet Justice Feliciano face to face and to get to know him more. I then realized why my mentors spoke of him in that manner.

Etched in stone in the main hall of the law school in the Philippines where Justice Feliciano obtained his first degree in law are the following words:

> The business of a law school is not sufficiently described when you merely say that it is to teach law or to make lawyers. It is to teach law in the grand manner and to make great lawyers.

Passion for the rule of law is an essential attribute of a great lawyer. In this, and in many other attributes, Justice Feliciano is a great lawyer.

The rule of law can truly flourish only if those who are its subjects render themselves capable of asserting and enforcing their rights. In a book dedicated to Justice Feliciano, it is therefore appropriate to cite how some developing countries – with the indispensable support and cooperation of certain developed countries – have rendered themselves more capable of asserting and enforcing their rights under the rules-based multilateral trading system.

Advisory Centre on WTO Law

History records the pursuit of international relations by governments oblivious to ethical or shared concerns. *Realpolitik* exacerbates the intrinsic disadvantages of the weak and entrenches the privileged position of the strong. The rule of law is the antithesis of *realpolitik*, to the extent that law is a reflection or manifestation of ethical or shared concerns.

The Marrakesh Agreement Establishing the World Trade Organization ('the WTO Agreement') is the result of the continuing effort of states to establish the rule of law in international economic relations. Aside from the promulgation of comprehensive substantive rules governing those relations, the WTO Agreement also established binding third party adjudication as an alternative means to settle disputes. The combination of substantive rules and binding third party adjudication is an indispensable first step towards the establishment of the rule of law in international economic relations and tends to level the playing field:

> It has often been said that the WTO dispute settlement system provides an opportunity for economically weak smaller countries to challenge trade measures taken by more economically powerful Members ... This system works to the advantage of Members, but it especially gives security to the weaker Members who often, in the past, lacked the political or economic clout to enforce their rights to protect their interests. In the WTO right perseveres over might.[1]

However, the establishment of substantive rules and of a dispute settlement system to settle disputes on those rules does not in itself necessarily entrench the rule of law:

> Rules do not enforce themselves. In all societies, national as well as international, the asymmetries in the organization and political influence of interest groups favour the progressive erosion of liberal rules through a political protection trap: concentrated producer interests can reap important 'protection rents' from trade restrictions, trade distortions and political lobbying, and tend to be well organized and politically

[1] J. Lacarte-Muró and P. Gappah, 'Developing Countries and the WTO Legal and Dispute Settlement System: A View from the Bench' (2000) *Journal of International Economic Law* 395.

> influential. Periodically elected governments depend on political support and may benefit from granting import protection and export subsidies in exchange for political assistance from 'rent-seeking' interest groups.[2]

The resolution of disputes under the WTO dispute settlement system – as in any other dispute settlement system – entails resources, both human and financial. On numerous occasions, developing countries have expressed the challenges confronting them in this regard. For example, the African Group in the WTO has stated that:

> Developing-country Members will need supplementary resources and means to be provided to develop both the institutional and human capacity for using the [dispute settlement system] ... It needs to be clearly recognized that every decent legal system ensures that parties that would not be able to exercise their rights in the judicial system for financial constraints are provided means to do so.[3]

State legal assistance for the benefit of those who do not have the resources to protect their rights or defend their interests has been recognized as a legal right by some domestic courts, which have taken the view that the provision of legal aid should be read together with the right to equal protection of the law.[4]

In the same manner, the Understanding on Rules and Procedures Governing the Settlement of Disputes (DSU) recognizes the need to provide legal assistance to developing countries. DSU Article 27.2 provides:

> there may also be a need to provide additional legal advice and assistance in respect of dispute settlement to developing country Members. To this end, the Secretariat shall make available a qualified legal expert from the WTO technical cooperation services to any developing country Member

[2] E. U. Petersmann, 'Preface' in *The GATT/WTO Dispute Settlement System: International Law, International Organizations and Dispute Settlement* (Kluwer Law International, 1997), p. xiii.

[3] See the submission Negotiations on the Dispute Settlement Mechanism Understanding, Proposal by the African Group, TN/DS/W/15, 25 September 2002, paragraph 3.

[4] See, e.g., *Airey* v. *Ireland* (1979) where the European Court of Human Rights declared a right to counsel in civil cases based on the 'fair hearing' guarantee of the European Convention on Human Rights and Fundamental Freedoms; *New Brunswick* v. *JG* (1999) where the Supreme Court of Canada declared constitutional the right to counsel in civil cases relating to child custody; and *Nkuzi Development Association* v. *Legal Aid Board* (2001), where the Land Claims Court of South Africa declared that the right to a 'fair hearing' in the South African Constitution requires government to provide indigents with free counsel in proceedings under the Land Tenure Act.

> which so requests. This expert shall assist the developing country Member in a manner ensuring the continued impartiality of the Secretariat.

While the need to provide legal advice and assistance to developing countries in respect of dispute settlement is recognized, the limitation is that it shall be made 'in a manner ensuring the continued impartiality of the Secretariat'. This is a critical limitation. However, this must necessarily be so, as an international secretariat must be neutral and must serve the interests of the organization as a whole, and not that of the individual members. DSU Article 27.2 is but a reflection of Article VI:2 of the WTO Agreement, which provides:

> The responsibilities of the Director-General and the staff of the Secretariat shall be exclusively international in character. In the discharge of their duties, the Director-General and the Staff shall not seek or accept instructions from any government or any other authority external to the WTO.

Given the challenges confronting developing countries in relation to their ability to pursue their rights and defend their interests under the WTO dispute settlement system, in 1998, at the initiative of three Geneva-based delegates of Colombia, the Netherlands, and the United Kingdom, a small group consisting of twelve to fourteen delegates of countries at various levels of development started to discuss those challenges and the possible means of addressing them. As a result, in December 1999, in the wings of the WTO Third (Seattle) Ministerial Conference, representatives of nine developed countries[5] and twenty developing countries/customs territories[6] signed the Agreement Establishing the Advisory Centre on WTO Law ('the Agreement'). The signing ceremony was held in the presence of representatives of thirty-seven least developed countries.

The Agreement calls for the establishment of the Advisory Centre on WTO Law as an independent intergovernmental organization. The Preamble to the Agreement succinctly explains the reasons for the establishment of the Centre:

[5] Canada, Denmark, Finland, Ireland, Italy, the Netherlands, Norway, Sweden, and the United Kingdom.

[6] Bolivia, Colombia, Dominican Republic, Ecuador, Egypt, Guatemala, Honduras, Hong Kong China, Kenya, Nicaragua, Pakistan, Panama, Paraguay, Peru, Philippines, Thailand, Tunisia, Uruguay, Venezuela, and Zimbabwe. As used hereinafter, the term 'developing countries' includes countries and customs territories.

- the WTO Agreement created a complex legal system and elaborate procedures for the settlement of disputes;
- developing countries, in particular the least developed among them, and countries with economies in transition have limited expertise in WTO law and the management of complex trade disputes, and their ability to acquire such experience is subject to severe financial and institutional constraints;
- a proper balance of rights and obligations under the WTO Agreement can only be maintained if all WTO members have a full understanding of their rights and obligations thereunder and an equal opportunity to resort to the WTO dispute settlement procedures;
- the credibility and acceptability of the WTO dispute settlement procedures can be ensured only if all WTO members can effectively participate in it;
- therefore, there is a need to establish a source of legal training, expertise, and advice on WTO law readily accessible to developing countries, in particular the least developed among them, and countries with economies in transition.

Accordingly, the purpose of the Centre is to 'provide legal training, support and advice on WTO law and dispute settlement proceedings to developing countries, in particular to the least developed among them, and to countries with economies in transition'.[7] To achieve this purpose, the Centre has the following specific mandates:

- to provide legal advice on WTO law;
- to provide support to parties and third parties in WTO dispute settlement proceedings;
- to train government officials in WTO law through seminars on WTO law and jurisprudence, internships, and other appropriate means; and
- to perform such other functions assigned to it by the General Assembly.

The Agreement was open for signature up to 31 March 2000. Prior to that deadline, India and Latvia also became signatories to the Agreement.[8] The Agreement entered into force on 15 July 2001, and

[7] Agreement Establishing the Advisory Centre on WTO Law Article 2.1.

[8] As explained in a subsequent part of this chapter, subsequent to 31 March 2000, any WTO member or any state or separate customs territory in the process of acceding to the WTO may still become a member of the Centre by acceding to the Agreement.

Table 9.1: *Annex II members by category*

Category	*World Trade Share*	*GNP per capita*
A	> = 1.5% or	high income countries
B	> = 0.15% and < 1.5% or	upper middle income countries
C	< 0.15%	

the Advisory Centre on WTO Law ('the Centre') became operational on 17 July 2001.

The Centre has two general categories of members: (i) developed countries (hereafter referred to as 'Annex I members') and (ii) developing countries and countries with economies in transition, including separate customs territories (hereafter collectively referred to as 'Annex II members'). Annex II members are in turn classified into Category A, B, and C members, on the basis of their share of world trade with an upward correction reflecting their per capita income, as indicated in Table 9.1.

While the Centre is an intergovernmental organization in form, it could be said that in substance, it is like any other law firm, except for the following:

- its practice is confined to WTO law;
- in addition to providing legal advice and support in WTO dispute settlement proceedings – services that are likewise provided by other law firms – its mandate includes the training of government officials;
- it provides services exclusively to developing countries and countries with economies in transition, including separate customs territories.[9]

Moreover, the Centre provides legal advice and training for free to Annex II members and to least developed countries. Free legal advice is subject to a maximum number of hours fixed by the Management Board. To date, however, the Management Board has not fixed the maximum number of hours of free legal advice. By all indications, it would seem that the Management Board is unlikely to do so, at least within the immediate future.

[9] While the Centre has developed country members, those members are not entitled to the services of the Centre.

Table 9.2: *Centre charging rates per hour*

Members	*Rate per hour (CHF)*
Category A	324
Category B	243
Category C	162
Least developed countries	40

In respect of support in WTO dispute settlement proceedings, the Centre charges graduated subsidized rates to Annex II members and to least developed countries, depending on their level of development. Annex IV to the Agreement provides the rates per hour that the Centre respectively charges. These rates were all originally denominated in US dollars (US$). However, pursuant to the Decision on Currency Conversion adopted by the General Assembly of the Centre on 25 April 2002, these rates have been converted into Swiss francs (CHF) at the rate of exchange prevailing in May 2002, as specified in the United Nations Operational Rates of Exchange. This rate was determined to be CHF1.62:US$1.00. Applying the decision, the rates per hour that the Centre charges for support in WTO dispute settlement proceedings are shown in Table 9.2.

The rate per hour is only one factor affecting the fees charged by the Centre. Another factor is the number of hours billed. Under the Billing Policy of the Centre[10] established by the Management Board, as a general rule, the number of hours that the Centre can charge for each specific step in the dispute settlement process is limited to a range of a maximum number of hours, depending on the complexity of the case. The ranges are summarized in Table 9.3.

Applying the respective rates per hour to the foregoing maximum ranges, the estimated fees chargeable by the Centre are as follows shown in Table 9.4.

Thus, depending on the level of development of the country concerned and the complexity of the dispute, the fees charged by the Centre for services rendered from the panels to the Appellate Body stages ranges from CHF10,280[11] to CHF 228,744.[12]

[10] As revised by the Management Board on 26 March 2004.
[11] Least developed country, in a dispute of 'low' complexity.
[12] Category A member, in a dispute of 'high' complexity.

Table 9.3: *Summary of time budget for legal assistance to the complainant in a WTO dispute settlement proceeding*

	Degree of complexity		
Stage	*Low*	*Medium*	*High*
Panel (including consultations)	186	336	538
Appellate Body	71	108	168
Total	257	444	706

Table 9.4: *Estimated fees (in CHF) chargeable by the Centre*

	Degree of complexity		
Entity availing of the services/stage	*Low*	*Medium*	*High*
Category A Member			
Panel	60,264	108,864	174,312
Appellate Body	23,004	34,992	54,432
Total, Panel and Appellate Body	83,268	143,856	228,744
Category B Member			
Panel	45,198	81,648	130,734
Appellate Body	17,253	26,244	40,824
Total, Panel and Appellate Body	62,451	107,892	171,558
Category C Member			
Total Panel process	30,132	54,432	87,156
Appellate Body	11,502	17,496	27,216
Total, Panel and Appellate Body	41,634	71,928	114,372
Least developed country			
Panel	7,440	13,440	21,520
Appellate Body	2,840	4,320	6,720
Total, Panel and Appellate Body	10,280	17,760	28,240

Based on experience, the time actually spent by the Centre in providing services far exceeds the number of hours prescribed under the Billing Policy. But this is deliberate, as the Centre was not established for the purpose of generating income from the exercise of the legal profession, but to be of service to members entitled to its services and to least developed countries. Thus, not only are the rates subsidized, the number of hours is likewise subsidized.

It must be noted that least developed countries need not be members of the Centre to obtain the benefit of free legal advice and training and subsidized rates in WTO dispute settlement proceedings.

In case of a dispute between two members or a member and a least developed country, there would be a conflict of interest, and the Centre cannot provide direct support to both parties. In this situation, the Centre may provide support directly only to one party. To ensure that the other party is adequately represented, upon request, and subject to the rules promulgated by the Management Board, the Centre may hire an external legal counsel to represent that other party. The Centre pays the fees charged by the external legal counsel, and the party represented by the external legal counsel pays the Centre at the rates the Centre would have charged had the Centre provided support directly to that party.

The Centre also has a Technical Expertise Trust Fund. In some disputes, expertise of a technical or scientific nature may be required or necessary. Through this fund, the Centre subsidizes a portion of the cost of expertise. For Category A members, the subsidy is 20 per cent; for Category B members, 40 per cent; for Category C members, 60 per cent, and for least developed countries, 90 per cent.

Thus far, the Centre has held two training courses for Geneva-based government officials. These courses are held once a week during the period October – April. The first course, held in 2002–3, was on WTO dispute settlement procedures. The second course, held in 2003–4, was on WTO jurisprudence.

The management structure of the Centre consists of three levels: the General Assembly, the Management Board, and the Executive Director.

The General Assembly is composed of representatives of all members. Its principal functions are to:

- evaluate the performance of the Centre;
- elect the Management Board;
- adopt regulations on the basis of proposals of the Management Board;
- adopt the annual budget on the basis of proposals of the Management Board.

The Management Board consists of (i) three nominees of each of the groups classified as Category A, B, and C members, (ii) two nominees of developed country members, (iii) a representative of the least developed countries, and (iv) the Executive Director, serving in an *ex officio* capacity. Members of the Management Board serve in their personal capacity and are selected on the basis of their professional qualifications in the field of WTO law or international trade relations and development. The principal functions of the Management Board are to:

- take the decisions necessary to ensure the efficient and effective operation of the Centre;
- prepare the annual budget for the Centre for approval by the General Assembly;
- decide on appeals by members to whom legal support in a dispute settlement proceeding has been denied;
- supervise the administration of the Centre's Endowment Fund;
- appoint an External Auditor; and
- appoint the Executive Director in consultation with members.

The Executive Director manages the day-to-day operations of the Centre, including the hiring of the staff in accordance with staff regulations adopted by the General Assembly. The Executive Director reports to the Management Board.

To finance the operations of the Centre, two funds were established: (i) Multiyear Contributions and (ii) the Endowment Fund. During the first five years of operations of the Centre (from 2001–5), the Centre's operations are financed solely by Multiyear Contributions made by the following developed country members: Canada, Ireland, the Netherlands, Norway, Sweden, and the United Kingdom.

As originally conceived, starting in 2006, the Centre's operations will be financed by (i) income from investments of the Endowment Fund and (ii) fees for services rendered. All income for services rendered during the first five years of operations form part of the Endowment Fund. The following developed country members have contributed to the Endowment Fund: Denmark, Finland, Ireland, Italy, the Netherlands, Norway, and Sweden. In addition, all developing country members have likewise made contributions to the Endowment Fund.

Article 16 of the Agreement provides that any member of the WTO and any state or separate customs territory in the process of acceding to the WTO may become a member of the Centre by acceding to the Agreement on terms and conditions agreed between it and the Centre. Accessions are effected by an instrument of accession approved by the General Assembly. With respect to developing countries, the instrument of accession may be approved by the General Assembly only upon the advice of the Management Board that the accession 'would cause neither financial nor operational problems for the Centre'.[13]

While the terms and conditions for accession are dependent on the agreement between the Centre and the acceding member, based on the accessions thus far approved, the following are the terms and conditions that the General Assembly are expected to impose:

(a) for developed countries, a contribution of at least CHF1,620,000 either to (i) the Endowment Fund or (ii) Multiyear Contributions;
(b) for developing countries, a contribution of the following amounts to the Endowment Fund:

   (i) Category A member = CHF 486,000
   (ii) Category B member = CHF 162,000
   (iii) Category C member = CHF 81,000

A developing country member has the option to pay its contribution to the Endowment Fund in four equal annual instalments. Contributions to the Endowment Fund are one-time contributions. There are no annual dues or other recurring obligations associated with membership, as such.

Today, the Centre has the members shown in Table 9.5.[14]

The organizational, financial, and management structures of the Centre were designed to strike a balance between the need for members to retain overall control of the Centre and the autonomy necessary to enable the Centre to pursue its activities, considering the nature of its mandate. Had the Centre been organized and funded exclusively by developed country members to provide the services that it is meant to provide, the Centre would have been just another channel for foreign aid provided by developed countries.

Thus, with the exception of least developed countries, those who wish to avail of the services of the Centre that are provided for free or at subsidized costs must first become members of the Centre and make a contribution to the Endowment Fund. Membership in the Centre gives them a voice in the General Assembly, equal to that of any other member. In this context, the Centre is a genuine partnership between developed and developing countries. Members retain overall control through the General Assembly.

[13] Agreement Establishing the Advisory Centre Article 16.
[14] As of 31 May 2004.

Table 9.5: *Members of the Centre*

Developed countries/ economies in transition/territories	*Developing countries/ countries with separate customs*
Canada	Bolivia
Denmark	Chinese Taipei
Finland	Colombia
Ireland	Dominican Republic
Italy	Ecuador
Netherlands	Egypt
Norway	El Salvador[a]
Sweden	Guatemala
United Kingdom	Honduras
	Hong Kong China
	India
	Indonesia
	Jordan
	Kenya
	Latvia
	Mauritius
	Nicaragua
	Oman
	Pakistan
	Panama
	Paraguay
	Peru
	Philippines
	Thailand
	Tunisia
	Turkey
	Uruguay
	Venezuela

[a] In the process of depositing its instrument of ratification.

Since contributions are fixed in advance, and at amounts intended ultimately to ensure the financial self-sufficiency of the Centre, decisions on the annual budget of the Centre are not influenced by considerations regarding the contribution of each member as a consequence of the adoption of a particular budget level.

The establishment of the Centre has engendered expectations. In this regard, the following views have been expressed:

> The Advisory Centre represents a major advance for developing countries. In regularly participating in WTO litigation, the Advisory Centre will gain significant WTO expertise that individual developing countries cannot acquire cost-effectively on their own. The Centre eventually could provide services to developing countries in a manner somewhat analogous to the way in which the European Commission's legal services division assists EC member states. It could develop a reservoir of WTO expertise into which developing countries could tap as need. By working on WTO cases with the Centre's lawyers, national officials can develop their own internal resources.[15]

> [The Centre] . . . has created a precedent that will be difficult to ignore for other international bodies. First, unlike the trust funds created for the ICJ and the ITLOS, and other forms of legal aid, it concentrates on providing human resources, not cash, to defray litigation costs. Second, it is an independent organ, external to the organization and its judicial body, thus reinforcing its credibility as an impartial player. Third, it brings together developing countries and developed countries into a partnership, rather than leaving the financial support of the endeavour to gratuitous contributions by developed countries. Finally, it is partially sustained by user-pays fees, which help reduce waste and unnecessary litigation, and it reinforces the commitment of the parties to the case.[16]

The Centre has thus far provided legal support in fifteen WTO dispute settlement proceedings and has likewise provided legal advice on various non-dispute related matters. By all indications, and based on the increasing demand for its services, the Centre is fulfilling its mandate. But the practice of law is a day-to-day challenge.

[15] G. Shaffer and V. Mosoti, 'EC Sardines: A New Model for Collaboration in Dispute Settlement?' (2002) 6(7) *Bridges* (a publication of the International Centre for Trade and Sustainable Development) (October).

[16] C. Romano, 'International Justice and Developing Countries: A Qualitative Analysis' (2002) 1(2) *Law and Practice of International Courts and Tribunals* 565.

10

Reform of the WTO Dispute Settlement System: What to Expect from the Doha Development Round?

PETER VAN DEN BOSSCHE

Introduction

The WTO dispute settlement system has been operational for almost nine years now. In that period it has arguably been the most prolific of all state-to-state dispute settlement systems. Since 1 January 1995, 302 disputes have been brought to the WTO system for resolution.[1] That is more than were brought to the GATT, the WTO's predecessor, in the forty-seven years between 1948 and 1995. In almost one-quarter of the disputes brought to the WTO system, the parties were able to reach an amicable solution through consultations, or the dispute was resolved otherwise without recourse to adjudication. In other disputes, parties have resorted to adjudication and, to date, such adjudication procedures have been completed in more than seventy-three disputes.[2]

Some of the disputes dealt with by the WTO dispute settlement system have triggered considerable controversy and public debate and have attracted much media attention. This has been the case, for example, for disputes on national legislation or other measures for the protection of public health or the environment, such as:

This chapter is based on a lecture delivered in November 2003 at a conference on 'The WTO and New Agendas in the 21st Century', organized in Taipei, Taiwan, by Chung-Hua Institution for Economic Research and Shu-Te University. The assistance of Carol Ní Ghiollarnáth is gratefully acknowledged. Unless otherwise indicated, this contribution takes account of events until 2 November 2003.

[1] i.e., the number of requests for consultations notified to the Dispute Settlement Body (DSB) on 2 November 2003. See www.WorldTradeLaw.net visited on 2 November 2003.

[2] i.e., the number of disputes in which panel and/or Appellate Body reports have been adopted by the DSB. See www.wto.org, *Update of WTO Dispute Settlement Cases*, WT/DS/OV/16, 17 October 2003, p. ii.

- the *EC – Hormones* dispute on the European Union's import ban on meat from cattle treated with growth hormones;[3]
- the *US – Shrimp* dispute on the American import ban on shrimp harvested with nets that killed sea turtles;[4]
- the *EC – Asbestos* dispute on a French ban on asbestos and asbestos-containing products;[5]
- the *EC – Biotech Products* dispute on measures affecting the approval and marketing of genetically modified products in the European Union;[6] and
- the *EC – Bananas III* dispute on the European Union's preferential import regime for bananas which was, for many years, headline news.[7]

Florentino Feliciano was one of the 'original' seven members of the Appellate Body. In the six years that he served in the WTO's highest judicial organ, he sat in twenty-one appeals, including the appeals in *EC – Hormones*, *US – Shrimp*, and *EC – Asbestos*. He also served as an arbitrator three times, under Article 21.3(c) of the Dispute Settlement Understanding (DSU), to determine the reasonable period of time to implement the recommendations and rulings of adopted dispute settlement reports. Working for – or as he used to say 'working with' – him on these appeals and arbitrations has been a highlight in my professional life. In this chapter in his honour, I will first briefly recall the basic features of the WTO dispute settlement system that was, and is, so dear to Toy Feliciano. Subsequently, I will examine the functioning of the dispute settlement system to date. As indicated by its title, however, the focus of this chapter is on the current negotiations on the further improvement of the system in the context of the Doha Development Round.

[3] Appellate Body Report, *European Communities – Measures Concerning Meat and Meat Products (Hormones)*, WT/DS26/AB/R, 13 February 1998, complaints by the USA (DS26) and Canada (DS48).

[4] Appellate Body Report, *United States – Import Prohibition of Certain Shrimp and Shrimp Products*, WT/DS58/AB/R, 20 May 1996, complaint by India, Malaysia, Pakistan, and Thailand.

[5] Appellate Body Report, *European Communities – Measures Affecting Asbestos and Asbestos-Containing Products*, WT/DS135/AB/R, 5 April 2001, complaint by Canada.

[6] Appellate Body Report, *European Communities – Measures Affecting the Approval and Marketing of Biotech Products* (not yet reported), complaint by the USA (DS291), Canada (DS292), and Argentina (DS293).

[7] Appellate Body Report, *European Communities – Regime for the Importation, Sale and Distribution of Bananas (EC – Bananas III)*, WT/DS27/AB/R, 25 September 1997, complaint by Ecuador, Guatemala, Honduras, Mexico, and the USA (DS27).

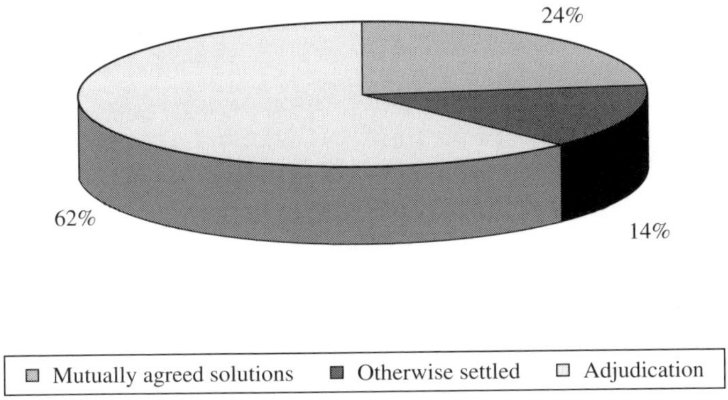

Figure 10.1: Success of consultations – totals 1995–2003[a]

[a] See www.wto.org, 'Update of WTO Dispute Settlement Cases', WT/DS/OV/14, 30 June 2003, p. ii.

Basic features of the WTO dispute settlement system

The prime object and purpose of the WTO dispute settlement system is the prompt settlement of disputes through multilateral proceedings. The system prefers to resolve a dispute through consultations rather than adjudication.

The WTO dispute settlement system serves to preserve the rights and obligations of members under the covered agreements, and to clarify the existing provisions of those agreements.[8] The system may not, however, add to or diminish the rights and obligations of the WTO members.[9]

The jurisdiction of the WTO dispute settlement system is very broad in scope, covering disputes arising under the WTO Agreement, the DSU, all multilateral agreements on trade in goods, the GATS, and the TRIPS Agreement.[10] Furthermore, the jurisdiction of the WTO dispute settlement system is compulsory, exclusive, and contentious in nature.[11]

Access to the WTO dispute settlement system is limited to WTO members. A WTO member can use the system when it claims that a

[8] DSU Article 3.2. [9] DSU Articles 3.2 and 19.2.

[10] Covered agreements as per DSU Appendix 1.

[11] See DSU Articles 23.1 and 23.2 (on compulsory and exclusive jurisdiction), Panel Report, *United States – Section 301 Trade Act*, WT/DS152/R, 27 January 2000, paragraph 7.43 (on exclusive jurisdiction) and Appellate Body Report, *United States – Measures Affecting Imports of Woven Wool Shirts and Blouses from India*, WT/DS33/AB/R, 23 May 1997, p. 340 (on contentious jurisdiction).

benefit accruing under one of the covered agreements is nullified or impaired.[12] A complainant will almost always argue that the respondent violated a provision of WTO law (violation complaint). If the violation is shown, there is a presumption of nullification or impairment of a benefit.[13]

Non-governmental organizations (NGOs), industry associations, and individuals have no access to the WTO dispute settlement system. However, the Appellate Body has ruled in a series of controversial reports that panels and the Appellate Body have the right to accept and consider *amicus curiae* briefs submitted by those entities.[14]

The WTO dispute settlement process entails four major steps: consultations, the panel proceedings, appellate review proceedings, and implementation and enforcement of the recommendations and rulings. The WTO dispute settlement process is subject to strict time limits.[15]

Panels and the Appellate Body interpret provisions of the covered agreements in accordance with the ordinary meaning of the words of the provision taken in their context and in the light of the object and purpose of the agreement involved.[16] If necessary and appropriate, panels and the Appellate Body have recourse to supplementary means of interpretation. The burden of proof in WTO dispute settlement proceedings is on the party, the complainant or the respondent, that asserts the affirmative of a particular claim or defence.[17]

The WTO dispute settlement proceedings are characterized by their confidentiality. Written submissions by the parties are confidential.[18] Panel meetings or the oral hearing of the Appellate Body take place behind closed doors. The Rules of Conduct require panelists and Appellate Body members to be independent and impartial, to avoid direct or indirect conflicts of interest, and to respect the confidentiality of proceedings.[19]

[12] Appellate Body Report, *US – Shrimp*, paragraph 101. [13] DSU Article 3.8.

[14] See Appellate Body Report, *US – Shrimp*, paragraphs 104–6; and Appellate Body Report, *United States – Imposition of Countervailing Duties on Certain Hot-rolled Lead and Bismuth Carbon Steel Products Originating in the UK*, WT/DS138/AB/R, 10 May 2000, paragraph 39.

[15] DSU Articles 12.8, 12.9, and 17.5.

[16] DSU Article 3.2, which has been interpreted to refer to Article 31 of the Vienna Convention on the Law of Treaties.

[17] Appellate Body Report, *US – Wool Shirts and Blouses*, p. 335.

[18] See DSU Articles 17.10, 18.2, and Appendix 3, paragraph 3. Note, however, that a party may make its own submissions to the panel and the Appellate Body available to the public. A number of WTO members, including the USA, Canada, New Zealand, and the European Communities, do this as a matter of course.

[19] WT/DSB/RC/1, 11 December 1996.

The DSU provides for three types of remedy for breach of WTO law: one final remedy, namely the withdrawal (or amendment) of the WTO inconsistent measure; and two temporary remedies, namely compensation or suspension of concessions or other obligations (commonly referred to as 'retaliation').[20] Compliance with the recommendations or rulings of the DSB must be immediate, or if that is impracticable, within a 'reasonable period of time'.[21] Retaliation measures (usually in the form of a drastic increase in custom duties on strategically selected products) put economic and political pressure on members to withdraw or amend their WTO inconsistent measures. However, doubts exist as to the effectiveness of retaliation as a temporary remedy for breach of WTO law.

In recognition of the difficulties developing country members may encounter when they are involved in WTO dispute settlement, the DSU contains some special rules for developing country members.[22] Most of these rules are, however, of limited significance. Effective legal assistance to developing country members in dispute settlement proceedings is given by the Geneva-based Advisory Centre on WTO Law (ACWL), an independent, international organization that operates as a law firm.[23]

The WTO dispute settlement system offers an opportunity for economically weak countries to challenge trade measures taken by economically stronger countries. The system works to the advantage of all members, but it especially gives security to the weaker members who, in the past, often lacked the political or economic clout to enforce their rights and to protect their interests.[24] As a result of the dispute settlement system, right prevails over might in the WTO.

WTO dispute settlement from 1995 to 2003

The WTO dispute settlement system became operational when the WTO Agreement entered into force on 1 January 1995. In the period of more than eight years since January 1995, the WTO dispute settlement system has been much and widely used and its 'output' in terms of the number of dispute settlement reports has been remarkable.

[20] DSU Articles 3.7 and 22. [21] DSU Articles 21.1 and 21.3.
[22] DSU Articles 3.12, 4.10, 8.10, 12.10, 12.11, 24 and 27.
[23] For up-to-date information on ACWL, see www.acwl.ch
[24] J. Lacarte and P. Gappah, 'Developing Countries and the WTO Legal and Dispute Settlement System' (2000) *Journal of International Economic Law* 400.

Disputes

To illustrate the use made of the WTO dispute settlement system to date, this section examines:

- the number of disputes brought to the WTO;
- the identity of the WTO members acting as complainant or respondent; and
- the agreements at issue in the disputes brought to the WTO.

Number of disputes

Between January 1995 and October 2003, a period of eight and a half years, WTO members have brought 302 disputes to the WTO for resolution under the multilateral rules and procedures of the DSU.[25] The WTO dispute settlement system is undoubtedly one of the most used international dispute settlement systems. With the exceptions of 1997 (higher) and 2001 (lower), the number of disputes brought to the WTO in any given year has been fairly stable. Roughly speaking, anywhere from thirty to forty disputes are annually brought to the WTO.

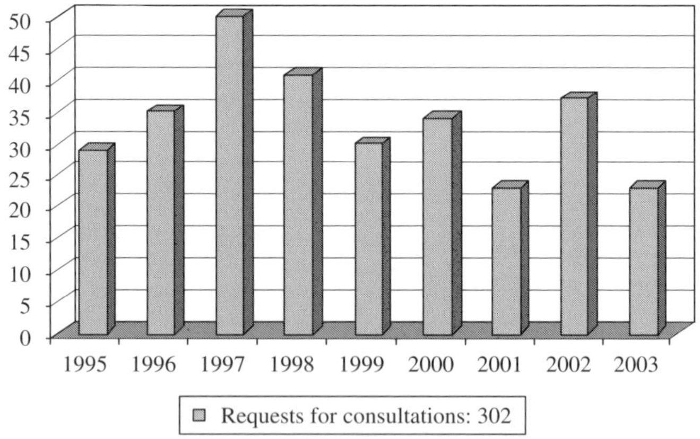

Figure 10.2: Requests for consultations – trend 1995–2003[a]
[a] See www.WorldTradeLaw.net visited on 2 November 2003.

[25] See www.WorldTradeLaw.net visited on 2 November 2003. This number refers to the number of requests for consultations notified to the DSB.

Complainants and respondents

Unlike the old GATT dispute settlement system, which was scantly used by developing country members, the WTO dispute settlement system has been used by developed and developing country members alike. In fact, in 1995, 2000, 2001, 2002 and up to November 2003, developing country members (i.e., upper[26] and lower middle income countries[27] and low income countries)[28] brought more disputes to the WTO than the developed country members (i.e., high income countries).[29]

Taken over the whole period from 1995 to 2003, high income countries have been the most prolific users of the WTO dispute settlement system. In 61 per cent of all disputes, high income countries, such as the USA or the European Communities, were the complainant. In view of their share of world trade, this is not surprising. However, in 39 per cent of all disputes, developing country members, and in particular, upper middle income countries (22 per cent), were complainants. The USA has been the single most active complainant (in seventy-five disputes), followed by the European Communities (in sixty-two disputes), Canada (in twenty-four disputes), and Brazil (in twenty-two disputes). To date, Chinese Taipei, China, and Hong Kong China were each complainants in one

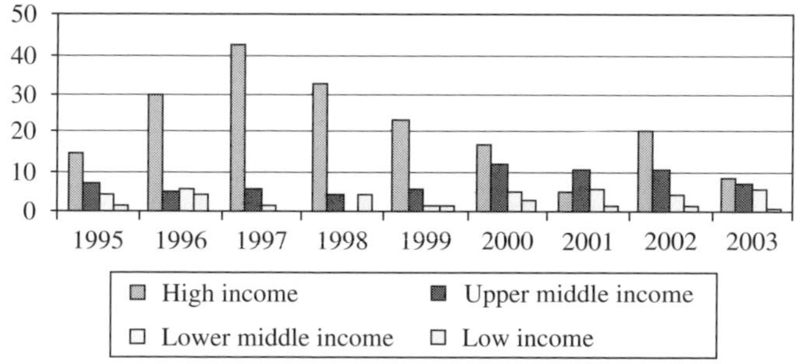

Figure 10.3: Complainants per income category – trend 1995–2003[a]
[a] See www.WorldTradeLaw.net visited on 2 November 2003.

[26] Upper middle income countries are, e.g., Argentina, Brazil, Mexico, Poland, and Slovakia.
[27] Lower middle income countries are, e.g., China, Colombia, Philippines, Romania, and Turkey.
[28] Low income countries are, e.g., India, Indonesia, Nicaragua, and Pakistan.
[29] High income countries are, e.g., USA, European Communities, Canada, Japan, Chinese Taipei, and Hong Kong China.

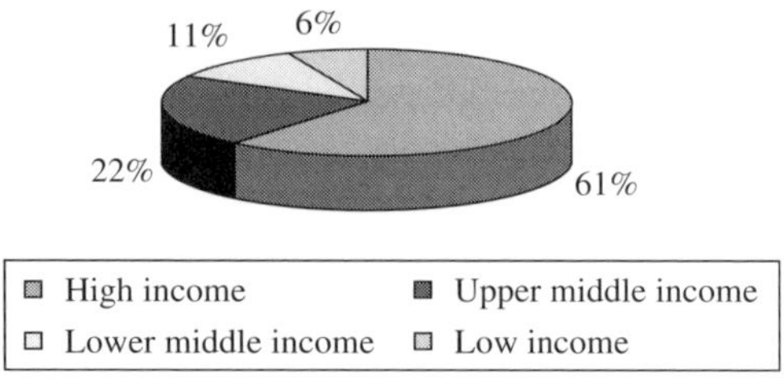

Figure 10.4: Complainants per income category – totals 1995–2003[a]
[a] See www.WorldTradeLaw.net visited on 2 November 2003.

dispute only.[30] It is remarkable that India, a low income country, has been a complainant in fifteen disputes. Low income countries were complainants in a total of twenty disputes. Least developed country members have not yet brought any dispute to the WTO to date.[31]

Thus far, 62 per cent of all disputes have related, or relate, to measures of developed country members; 38 per cent have related, or relate, to measures of developing country members. Cases brought against measures of developing country members have often been brought by other developing country members. Small developing country members have brought cases, and have won cases, against large developed country members. A classic example of this is *United States – Restrictions on Imports of Cotton and Man-Made Fibre Underwear*, WT/DS24/AB/R, 25 February 1997, a complaint by Costa Rica. The USA was the single most important respondent (in eighty-one disputes), followed by the European Communities (in forty-seven disputes), India (in fourteen disputes), Japan (in thirteen disputes), and Canada, Korea, and Brazil (in twelve disputes each). To date, there has been no case against a measure of a least developed country member.[32] Also Chinese Taipei, China, and Hong Kong China have never been respondents to date.

[30] Chinese Taipei and China are complainants in *United States – Definitive Safeguard Measures on Imports of Certain Steel Products*, WT/DS248/AB/R, 10 December 2003, WT/DS274 (complaint by Chinese Taipei) and WT/DS252 (complaint by China). Hong Kong China was a complainant in *Turkey – Textiles*, WT/DS29.

[31] For the data, see www.WorldTradeLaw.net visited on 2 November 2003.

[32] See www.WorldTradeLaw.net visited on 2 November 2003. Note that a number of these disputes concern the same measure, e.g., *India – Quantitative Restriction on Imports of Agriculture, Textiles and Industrial Products* (*India – Quantitative Restrictions*), WT/DS90/AB/R, 22 September 1999, which is counted six times (complaints by the EC (DS96), Switzerland (DS94), New Zealand (DS93), Canada (DS92), Australia (DS91), and USA (DS90).

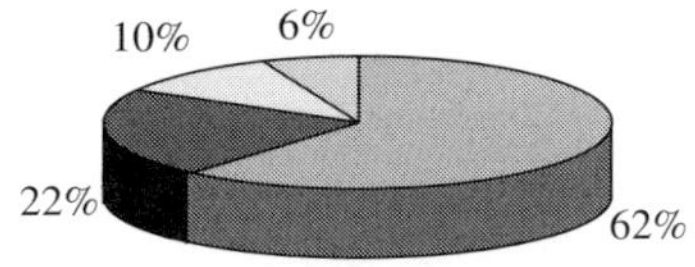

Figure 10.5: Respondents per income category – totals 1995–2003[a]
[a] See www.WorldTradeLaw.net visited on 2 November 2003.

WTO agreements at issue in disputes

While a number of disputes concern limited economic interests, other disputes raise important and politically sensitive issues relating to the conflict between trade liberalization and the protection of public health or the protection of the environment, or the conflict between liberalized trade and economic development or survival. The disputes brought to the WTO to date have concerned all the covered agreements. There has been dispute settlement on a very broad scope of rights and obligations. However, in 39 per cent of all disputes, the complainant argued that the respondent had violated a provision of the GATT 1994. The GATT 1994 was, and is, by far the most invoked covered agreement. In 10 per cent of disputes, the complainant argued a violation of the Anti-dumping Agreement and in 9 per cent a violation of the Agreement on Agriculture, and also in 9 per cent a violation of the SCM Agreement. The number of disputes in which a violation of the GATS or the TRIPS Agreement was argued has been relatively low to date.

Reports and arbitral awards

In the period from January 1995 to November 2003, panels and the Appellate Body circulated ninety-three and fifty-five reports respectively.[33] Panel reports, in particular, tend to be quite voluminous. Furthermore, the WTO dispute settlement system also produced a number of arbitration

[33] See www.WorldTradeLaw.net visited on 2 November 2003. Not included are four panel reports in cases where a mutually agreed solution was reached. Also not included is the Appellate Body report in *India – Measures Affecting the Automotive Sector (India – Autos)*, WT/DS146/AB/R, 5 April 2002, in which the appeal was withdrawn.

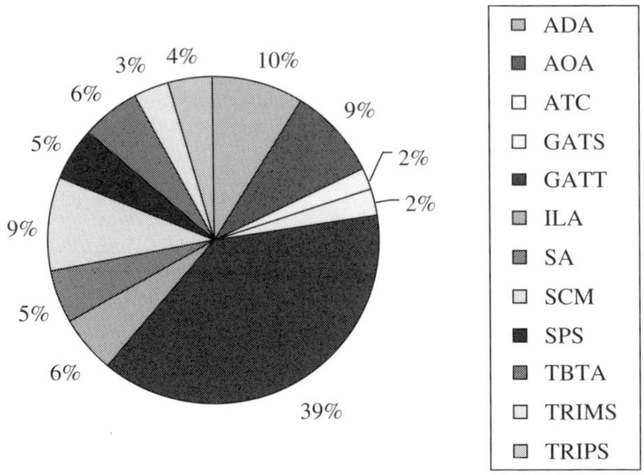

Figure 10.6: WTO agreements at issue – totals 1995–2003[a]

[a] See www.WorldTradeLaw.net visited on 18 July 2003. Covered agreements under which less than five disputes under the Agreement on Government Procurement.

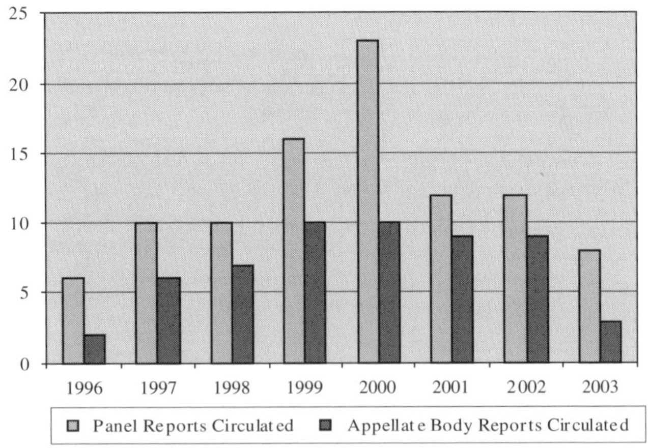

Figure 10.7: Number of reports – trend 1995–2003[a]

[a] For the data, see www.WorldTradeLaw.net visited on 2 November 2003.

awards.[34] When compared with the 'output' of the International Court of Justice or the International Tribunal on the Law of the Sea, the WTO dispute settlement system has been remarkably 'industrious'.

The number of panel reports peaked in 2000 (with twenty-three reports), an exceptional year partly reflecting the high number of requests for consultations in 1997. The number of panel reports has dropped considerably since 2001 and is now around twelve per year. The number of Appellate Body reports peaked in 1999 and 2000 (with ten reports) but has remained at approximately that level since then.

Proposals for the reform of WTO dispute settlement

The WTO system for resolving trade disputes between WTO members has been, in many respects, a remarkable success. However, the current system can undoubtedly be further improved. This section first briefly discusses past and current attempts to amend the dispute settlement system, from the DSU review (1998–9) to the current negotiations on the DSU in the context of the Doha Development Round. It then examines a number of key proposals of members for institutional, procedural, and systemic changes to the DSU currently under negotiation. This section concludes with an analysis of the main challenge to the WTO dispute settlement system, i.e., the imbalance in terms of effectiveness and impact between the political, rule-making bodies and processes, on the one hand, and the quasi-judicial, dispute settlement bodies and process of the WTO, on the other hand.

From DSU review to DSU negotiations

DSU review and beyond

As agreed at the time of the adoption of the WTO Agreement in 1994, the WTO members reviewed the DSU in 1998 and 1999.[35] While at the start of

[34] Sixteen arbitration awards under DSU Article 21.3(c) on the reasonable period of time for implementation, not including the award in *United States – Definitive Safeguards Measures on Imports of Circular Welded Carbon Quality Line Pipe from Korea (US – Line Pipe)*, WT/DS202/17, 26 July 2002, in which the parties reached an agreement on the reasonable period of time for implementation; seven arbitration decisions under DSU Article 22.6 on the suspension of concessions or other obligations; and one arbitration award under DSU Article 25. See www.WorldTradeLaw.net visited on 2 November 2003.

[35] Decision on the Application and Review of the Understanding on Rules and Procedures Governing the Settlement of Disputes, reproduced in *The Legal Texts: The Results of the Uruguay Round of Multilateral Trade Negotiations* (Cambridge University Press, 1999), p. 465.

this review, members expressed the view that the dispute settlement system was working satisfactorily, they nevertheless made a large number of proposals and suggestions for further improvement of the system. After January 1999, most members were convinced that – if anything – the review should address and resolve the 'sequencing' issue concerning the relationship between DSU Articles 21.5 and 22, a serious systemic problem that had then just surfaced. However, despite the best efforts of members, the DSU review was concluded in July 1999 without agreement on any amendment to the DSU. Discussions on amendments to the DSU continued on an informal basis in the run-up to the Seattle Session of the Ministerial Conference in December 1999. These discussions resulted in a proposal for reform to the Ministerial Conference by a group of developed country and developing country members, including the European Communities but without the USA.[36] While addressing also a number of minor technical issues, this proposal focused primarily on resolving the 'sequencing' issue. At the Seattle Session of the Ministerial Conference, agreement on this proposal might have been possible, but fell victim to the overall failure of that session.[37]

Doha Development Round and DSU negotiations

In 2000 and 2001, informal efforts outside the DSB to reach agreement on amendments to the DSU were continued. These efforts resulted in October 2001 in a revised proposal for amending the DSU tabled by a group of fourteen WTO members, 'chaired' by Japan but not including the European Communities or the USA.[38] This proposal again focused on the 'sequencing' issue but also addressed the time-frames of panel proceedings, third party rights, and the 'carousel' retaliation issue. However, members failed to reach agreement on this proposal.

In November 2001, members decided, at the Doha Session of the Ministerial Conference, to open formal negotiations on the DSU in January 2002.[39] These negotiations, based on the work on DSU reform

[36] See WT/MIN(99)/8.

[37] The only issue of disagreement left was the 'carousel' retaliation issue.

[38] Proposal to Amend Certain Provisions of the Understanding on Rules and Procedures Governing the Settlement of Disputes (DSU) pursuant to Article X of the Marrakesh Agreement Establishing the World Trade Organization, Submission by Bolivia, Canada, Chile, Colombia, Costa Rica, Ecuador, Japan, Korea, New Zealand, Norway, Peru, Switzerland, Uruguay and Venezuela for Examination and Further Consideration by the General Council, WT/GC/W/410/Rev.1, 26 October 2001.

[39] Ministerial Declaration adopted 14 November 2001, WT/MIN(01)/DEC/1, 20 November 2001, paragraph 30.

done so far as well as on any additional proposals by members, are currently still under way.[40] The Doha Ministerial Declaration clearly states that the negotiations on the DSU will not be part of the single undertaking, i.e., that they will not be tied to the overall success or failure of the other negotiations mandated by the Ministerial Declaration. As the improvement of the dispute settlement system is in the interest of all members, it was considered inappropriate to make the DSU negotiations part of the give and take of the overall negotiations. The desire to keep the DSU negotiations 'separate' from the rest of the Doha Development Round is also reflected in the time-frame for the DSU negotiations. Unlike the Doha Development Round, which is to be concluded in January 2005, the deadline for the DSU negotiations was initially set at May 2003.[41]

The negotiations on the DSU were conducted by the Special Session of the DSB, established for that purpose by the Trade Negotiations Committee on 1 February 2002. Between February 2002 and May 2003, the Special Session of the DSB met formally thirteen times to carry out negotiations on the DSU. In addition, it also met many times informally. While the prevailing view of members was that 'the DSU has generally functioned well to date', in total forty-two proposals for clarifications and amendments to the DSU were submitted.[42] These proposals touched on almost all DSU provisions, and were submitted by developed country as well as developing country members. Unsurprisingly, the major users of the dispute settlement system, such as the USA, the European Communities, Canada, India, and Brazil, all tabled proposals for reform. Of these proposals, the proposal by the European Communities was undoubtedly the most elaborate and far-reaching. Surprisingly, however, members that have not used the dispute settlement system to date also tabled proposals for reform. Note in this respect, the proposal by the African Group, the proposal by the Group of Least-Developed Country Members ('the LDC Group'), and the proposals by Jordan and Kenya. Also noteworthy are the proposals for reform submitted by the 'new' members, China and Chinese Taipei.

Due to the large number and the complexity of the proposals for reform, it took until the end of March 2003 merely to complete an initial

[40] Members have been asked, however, to resubmit any proposals they may have made in the past and they still want to be considered.

[41] Ministerial Declaration, WT/MIN(01)/DEC/1, 20 November 2001, paragraph 30.

[42] Special Session of the Dispute Settlement Body, *Report by the Chairman to the Trade Negotiations Committee*, TN/DS/9, 6 June 2003, paragraph 3.

review of the proposals.[43] The Chairman of the Special Session of the DSB, Ambassador Péter Balás, subsequently put forward draft legal texts in April 2003.[44] This work eventually culminated in the so-called 'Chairman's Text', issued on 16 May 2003.[45]

The Chairman's Text contained proposals for reform on a significant number of issues, including:

- the extension of third party rights;
- improved conditions for members seeking to be joined in consultations;
- the introduction of remand and interim review in appellate review proceedings;
- the 'sequencing' issue and other problems concerning the suspension of concessions or other obligations;
- the enhancement of compensation as a temporary remedy for breach of WTO law;
- the strengthening of notification requirements for mutually agreed solutions; and
- the strengthening of special and differential treatment for developing country members.[46]

In the absence of a sufficiently high level of support, other proposals by members were not included in the Chairman's Text. These 'rejected' proposals included proposals on:

- accelerated procedures for certain disputes;
- a list of permanent panelists or a permanent panel body;
- increased control by members over panel and Appellate Body reports;
- the treatment of *amicus curiae* briefs;
- collective retaliation and monetary compensation.

During the intensive discussions on the Chairman's Text at the end of May 2003, members generally welcomed this document. However, in spite of a number of amendments, they were eventually unable to agree

[43] The WTO Secretariat made a very useful compilation of the proposals made by the members. This compilation is contained in Job(03)/10/Rev.3.

[44] The draft legal texts were contained in the so-called 'Framework Document', which can be found in Job(03)/69/Rev.2.

[45] The Chairman's Text can be found in Job(03)/91.

[46] Special Session of the Dispute Settlement Body, *Report by the Chairman to the Trade Negotiations Committee*, TN/DS/9, 6 June 2003, paragraph 5.

to the proposals for reform it contained.[47] Certain members had conceptual problems with some of these proposals or objected to the fact that other proposals had been excluded from the Chairman's Text.[48]

Members were thus unable to meet the May 2003 deadline for the DSU negotiations provided for in the Doha Ministerial Declaration. While there was general recognition of the need for the Special Session of the DSB to continue its work, members were divided over whether further work should build on the Chairman's Text only *or* on other proposals by members as well. At its meeting on 24 July 2003 the General Council, acknowledging the fact that members needed more time to conclude the negotiations on the DSU, agreed to extend the negotiating mandate of the Special Session of the DSB by one year, to May 2004.[49] In May 2004, there was, however, still no agreement on the amendment of the DSU and in July 2004 the General Council decided once more to extend the negotiating mandate of the Special Session of the DSB.[50]

Proposals for DSU reform

Among the proposals for DSU reform currently on the negotiating table, one must distinguish between proposals with respect to:

- the institutions of WTO dispute settlement;
- the proceedings of WTO dispute settlement; and
- systemic issues, such as transparency of WTO dispute settlement, the *amicus curiae* brief issue, and special and differential rights for developing country members.

This section will briefly discuss the most significant of these proposals. Some of these proposals were included in the Chairman's Text, indicating a wide support among members. Other proposals discussed below were not included in the Chairman's Text but nevertheless deserve attention as these proposals indicate how the WTO dispute settlement system may develop in the future.

47 The amended version of the Chairman's Text can be found in Special Session of the Dispute Settlement Body, *Report by the Chairman to the Trade Negotiations Committee*, TN/DS/9, 6 June 2003, Annex.

48 *Ibid.* at paragraphs 10 and 11.

49 On 16 and 17 October 2003, the Special Session of the DSB met for the first time since May 2003 to continue the negotiations on the reform of the DSU. See TN/DS/W/59, 14 October 2003.

50 See General Council, Doha Work Programme, WT/L/579, 2 August 2004, paragraph 1(f).

Key proposals with respect to the institutions of WTO dispute settlement

A far-reaching proposal not included in the Chairman's Text is the proposal by the European Communities to move from the current system of ad hoc panelists to a system of permanent panelists.[51] According to the European Communities such change will lead to faster procedures and increase the quality of the panel reports. In the opinion of the European Communities, there is currently a growing quantitative discrepancy between the need for panelists and the availability of qualified ad hoc panelists. Not only is the number of disputes much higher than under the old GATT, the actual conduct of a dispute settlement procedure has become much more sophisticated than before and has substantially increased the workload of panelists. Also, the substance of the cases, both from a factual and a legal point of view, has become significantly more complex. For the European Communities, it is, therefore, necessary to introduce a system of permanent panelists. Under the proposal by the European Communities, panels would be composed of individuals included on a roster of permanent panelists established by the DSB.[52] The panelists would be appointed by the Director-General on a random basis within five days from the establishment of the panel. The parties may agree, however, at the time of the establishment of the panel, that the panel may include two individuals from outside the roster with particular expertise on the subject matter of the dispute. The chairman of the panel must always be an individual included in the roster of permanent panelists. If, within ten days of the establishment of the panel, the parties have not agreed on the panelists from outside the roster or the Director-General has not been requested to nominate such panelists from outside the roster, the panelists would be drawn from the roster by the Director-General on a random basis. Under the proposal of the European Communities, the DSB would include persons on the roster for six-year terms, non-renewable. The roster would be broadly representative of membership in the WTO. This radical proposal, which if adopted would constitute another significant step in the process of 'judicialization' of WTO dispute settlement, has

[51] Communication from the European Union, TN/DS/W/1, 13 March 2002, p. 3, and Communication from the European Union, TN/DS/W/38, 23 January 2003, p. 3.

[52] The number of panelists is for the DSB to decide but the European Communities has suggested a number ranging from sixteen to twenty-five panelists.

received little open support to date. One concern of the members is the additional budgetary cost of a roster of permanent panelists. There currently seems to be more support for a less radical proposal by Thailand for a 'roster of panel chairs' comprised of individuals who may be appointed as chair of a panel by lot.[53] However, this proposal was not included in the Chairman's Text.

With regard to the Appellate Body, and in particular, to ensure the capability of the Appellate Body to meet its workload, the European Communities has suggested the DSB should be given the power to modify, when necessary, the number of Appellate Body members, now set at seven by DSU Article 17.1.[54] This proposal has been included in the 'Chairman's Text'.[55] The European Communities as well as India have proposed to appoint Appellate Body members for a non-renewable term of six years rather than a renewable term of four years.[56] However, this proposal has not been included in the Chairman's Text.

Key proposals with respect to the proceedings of WTO dispute settlement

A number of members, including the European Communities, have proposed that the parties to a dispute would have the authority to extend the time limits set forth in the DSU by mutual agreement.[57] This proposal, which is clearly intended to give members more control over dispute settlement proceedings again, is included in the Chairman's Text. Proposals by Australia and China for accelerated time-frames for disputes on safeguard measures and anti-dumping actions are not included.[58]

[53] Communication from Thailand, TN/DS/W/ 31, 22 January 2003, p. 2.

[54] Communication from the European Union, TN/DS/W/1, 13 March 2002, p. 12. According to the European Communities, it would also appear 'desirable' – in view of the volume of the workload of the Appellate Body and on the basis of past experience – to convert the mandate of the Appellate Body members into a full-time appointment. *Ibid.* at p. 8.

[55] Note that Thailand proposed to increase the number of the Appellate Body members by at least two to four persons (Communication from Thailand, TN/DS/W/2, 20 March 2002, p. 1).

[56] Proposal on DSU by Cuba, Honduras, India, Malaysia, Pakistan, Sri Lanka, Tanzania, and Zimbabwe, TN/DS/W/18, 7 October 2002, pp. 4–5; Communication from the European Union, TN/DS/W/1, 23 January 2003, p. 5.

[57] Communication from the European Union, TN/DS/W/1, 13 March 2002, p. 1.

[58] Communication from Australia, TN/DS/W/49, 17 February 2003, p. 1 and Communication from China, TN/DS/W/29, 22 January 2003, p. 2.

With respect to consultations, the European Communities, Japan, and China have proposed to reduce the minimum period for consultations from sixty days to thirty.[59] However, this proposal did not receive sufficient support to be included in the Chairman's Text. The LDC Group has proposed that in disputes involving least developed country members it should be possible to hold consultations in the capital of that member, rather than in Geneva. This proposal has been included in the Chairman's Text. Jamaica, Costa Rica, and Chinese Taipei have all submitted proposals to facilitate members joining consultations between other members.[60] The Chairman's Text includes, in this respect, wording that is largely based on the proposal by Chinese Taipei. Finally, Jordan and the European Communities have proposed that a request for consultations shall be deemed to have been withdrawn by the complainant if that party has not submitted a panel request within twelve or eighteen months after the request for consultations.[61] The proposal for a time limit on consultations of eighteen months has been included in the Chairman's Text.

With respect to the panel proceedings, Japan and the European Communities have proposed that the DSB establish a panel by reverse consensus at the meeting at which the panel request first appears as an item on the DSB's agenda.[62] Currently, the DSB can only establish a panel by reverse consensus at the meeting at which the request appears on the agenda for the second time. This proposal was included in the Chairman's Text. However, reflecting a proposal by China, the Chairman's Text provides that in cases against developing country members the establishment of the panel will be postponed to the next DSB meeting if the developing country member so requests.[63] Costa Rica and the African Group have proposed a significant extension of the

[59] Communication from the European Union, TN/DS/W/1, 13 March 2002, p. 9; Proposal by Japan, TN/DS/W/32, 22 January 2003, p. 9; Communication from China (Revision), TN/DS/W/51/Rev.1, 13 March 2003, p. 1.

[60] Communication from Jamaica, TN/DS/W/21, 10 October 2002, p. 2; Communication from the Separate Customs Territory of Taiwan, Penghu, Kinmen, and Matsu, TN/DS/W/25, 27 November 2002, p. 3; Communication from Costa Rica, TN/DS/W/12, 24 July 2002, p. 2.

[61] Communication from Jordan, TN/DS/W/43, 28 January 2003, p. 10; Communication from the European Union, TN/DS/W/1, 13 March 2002, p. 12, and Communication from the European Union, TN/DS/W/38, 23 January 2003, p. 27.

[62] Communication from the European Union, TN/DS/W/1, 13 March 2002, p. 5, and Communication from the European Union, TN/DS/W/38, 23 January 2003, p. 4.

[63] Communication from China (Revision), TN/DS/W/51/Rev.1, 13 March 2003, p. 1.

rights of third parties in panel proceedings.[64] The Chairman's Text contains a proposal for allowing third parties to participate in all substantive panel meetings and to receive a copy of all written submissions of the parties to the panel. The Chairman's Text also took up the proposal that non-confidential summaries of submissions, currently contemplated by DSU Article 18.2, but subject to no timing requirements, be required no later than fifteen days following a request. This proposal was taken up in the Chairman's Text. Not included in the Chairman's Text was a proposal by Mexico for an interim relief procedure in case the measure at issue in a dispute is causing or threatening to cause harm which would be difficult to repair.[65]

With respect to appellate review proceedings, the USA and Chile have proposed, in a joint proposal, to introduce interim review in appellate review proceedings.[66] They also proposed that the time-frame for appellate review be extended from a maximum ninety days to a maximum 120 days.[67] Both proposals are reflected in the Chairman's Text. The European Communities submitted a proposal to introduce a remand procedure, under which any party can request, within ten days after the adoption of the Appellate Body report, the DSB to remand to the original panel those issues on which the Appellate Body could not rule.[68] The Chairman's Text incorporates, to a large degree, this proposal of the European Communities. A proposal of Jordan to give the Appellate Body itself remand authority was not retained.[69]

The LDC Group and the African Group have proposed that in panel and Appellate Body reports, each panellist and each Appellate Body member shall deliver a fully-reasoned separate opinion on the issues and make findings stating clearly the party which has prevailed.[70] The majority opinion shall be the decision of the panel or the Appellate

[64] Communication from Costa Rica, TN/DS/W/12, 24 July 2002; Proposal by the African Group, TN/DS/W/15, 25 September 2002, p. 4.

[65] Proposal by Mexico, TN/DS/W/23, p. 4.

[66] Textual Contribution by Chile and USA, TN/DS/W/52, 14 March 2003, p. 1.

[67] Textual Contribution by Chile and USA, TN/DS/W/52, 14 March 2003, p. 1.

[68] Communication from the European Communities, TN/DS/W/38, 23 January 2003, p. 6.

[69] Communication from Jordan, TN/DS/W/43, 28 January 2003, p. 6. In May 2003, however, Jordan replaced its proposal to grant the Appellate Body remand authority with a proposal to provide a remand procedure similar to the remand procedure proposed by the European Communities (Communication from Jordan, TN/DS/W/56, 19 May 2003, p. 2).

[70] Proposal by the African Group, TN/DS/W/15, 25 September 2002, p. 11, and Proposal by the LDC Group, TN/DS/W/17, 9 October 2003, p. 5.

Body. These proposals are not reflected in the Chairman's Text. The same is true for a proposal by Chile and the USA that the DSB may by consensus decide *not* to adopt a specific finding of the panel or the Appellate Body or not to adopt the basic rationale behind a specific finding.

With respect to the implementation and enforcement of recommendations and rulings, the European Communities and Japan have proposed the inclusion of an Article 21 *bis* on 'Determination of Compliance'.[71] According to this proposed Article 21 *bis*, disputes on the existence or WTO consistency of implementing measures will be heard by a compliance panel consisting of the members of the original panel. While the procedure set forth in Article 21 *bis* reflects, to a large extent, the current practice under Article 21.5, it elaborates and clarifies the latter provision considerably. The European Communities and Japan have also proposed the amendment of DSU Article 22. According to the amended DSU Article 22, the complainant may only request from the DSB authorization to retaliate *after* the compliance panel or the Appellate Body finds that the respondent has failed to bring the measures found to be WTO inconsistent into compliance with the WTO Agreement. Both proposals (on Article 21 *bis* and on Article 22) have been included in the Chairman's Text. If adopted, the amended Article 22 would resolve the 'sequencing' issue in an unambiguous manner.

The European Communities and Japan have also proposed a procedure for the termination of retaliation measures. According to this proposed procedure, it is for the member who is subject to retaliation measures, to request the DSB for the termination of the authorization to retaliate on the grounds that it has taken the necessary WTO consistent measures.[72] This proposal on a termination procedure is included in the Chairman's Text. A proposal by Mexico to allow members to transfer, i.e., to sell, the right to suspend concessions or other obligations has not been retained in the Chairman's Text. The same is true for proposals by the African Group and the LDC Group for collective retaliation, i.e., the suspension of concessions or other obligations by all members, rather than only by the complainant(s) in the dispute.[73] Other proposals on, for example, the withdrawal of membership rights or compulsory

[71] Communication from Japan, TN/DS/W/22, 28 October 2002, p. 4, and Communication from the European Communities, TN/DS/W/38, 23 January 2003, p. 27.

[72] Communication from Japan, TN/DS/W/22, 28 October 2002, p. 6, and Communication from the European Communities, TN/DS/W/38, 23 January 2003, p. 7.

[73] Proposal by the African Group, TN/DS/W/15, 15 September 2002, p. 3, and Proposal by the LDC Group, TN/DS/W/17, 9 October 2003, p. 4.

monetary compensation in case of failure to implement, were not discussed in the latter part of the negotiations.

Key proposals with respect to systemic issues

With respect to the transparency of the WTO dispute settlement system, the European Communities and Canada have submitted a proposal to allow panel meetings and Appellate Body hearings to be opened to the public (if the parties to the dispute agree).[74] These proposals are not included in the Chairman's Text.

With respect to the *amicus curiae* brief issue, the African Group and India have proposed language that would explicitly prohibit panels and the Appellate Body to accept and consider unsolicited information and advice.[75] The European Communities has made a detailed proposal to give panels and the Appellate Body the right to accept and consider unsolicited information and advice provided that this information or advice is directly relevant to the factual and legal issues under consideration.[76] None of the proposals on *amicus curiae* briefs was retained in the Chairman's Text.

Finally, with respect to special and differential treatment for developing country members, a number of specific proposals have been made to 'strengthen' DSU provisions relating to special attention given to the needs of developing country members by replacing 'should' by 'shall'. Most of these proposals have been taken up in the Chairman's Text. Also, proposals to strengthen the rights of developing country members regarding the prolongation of consultations, composition of panels and the timetable for panel proceedings, panel reports, and assistance by the WTO Secretariat were all included in the Chairman's Text. This is also the case for the proposal to make it possible for panels and the Appellate Body to award – upon request – an amount for litigation costs.[77] Not included in the Chairman's Text, however, are:

[74] Communication from the European Communities, TN/DS/W/1, 13 March 2003, p. 6, and Communication from Canada, TN/DS/W/41, 24 January 2003, p. 5.

[75] Proposal by the African Group, TN/DS/W/15, 15 September 2002, p. 5, and Proposal on DSU by India and others, TN/DS/W/18, 7 October 2002, p. 2.

[76] Communication from the European Communities, TN/DS/W/1, 13 March 2002, p. 11. Note that the European Communities in fact proposes to include in the DSU a procedure very similar to the Additional Procedure adopted by the Appellate Body in *EC – Asbestos*.

[77] While this proposal does not exclude that panels and the Appellate Body would award litigation costs to developed country members, it is clearly intended to facilitate the use of the dispute settlement system by developing country members. See, in this respect, the Communication from China, TN/DS/W/29, 22 January 2003, pp. 1–2.

- a proposal by the African Group to establish a WTO Fund on Dispute Settlement to provide financial assistance so as to facilitate the effective utilization of the WTO dispute settlement system by developing and least developed country members;[78] and
- a proposal by China to require that developed country members exercise due restraint in cases against developing country members and limit the number of cases brought against any particular developing country member to a maximum of two in one calendar year.[79]

Conclusion

To date, the negotiations of the reform of the WTO dispute settlement system have not yet led to any agreement on the amendment of the DSU. The proposals for amendment contained in the Chairman's Text are proposals on which a large group of members can agree and which will most likely be part of the agreement on the amendment of the DSU eventually reached. Many of these proposals are to be welcomed as they will strengthen the WTO dispute settlement system. This is the case, for example, for the proposed amendments to DSU Articles 21 and 22 resolving the 'sequencing issue', the proposal for extending the rights of third parties, the proposal allowing for a faster establishment of panels, the proposal introducing a remand procedure, and the proposal strengthening provisions for special and differential treatment of developing country members. Other proposals contained in the Chairman's Text, such as the introduction of 'interim review' in the appellate review procedure, are, in my opinion, less fortunate as they go against the process of 'judicialization' of WTO dispute settlement. A large number of DSU reform proposals, made by members, were not included in the Chairman's Text. With regard to a number of proposals, the exclusion is to be applauded. This is the case, for example, for the proposal to require each panelist and each Appellate Body member to deliver a fully-reasoned separate opinion on all issues in a dispute. Such a development would severely limit the ability of panels and the Appellate Body to contribute to the development of WTO law. With respect to other proposals not included in the Chairman's Text, it should be noted that their time has not come yet. This is the case, for example, for the proposal regarding

[78] Proposal by the African Group, TN/DS/W/15, 25 September 2002, p. 2.
[79] Communication from China, TN/DS/W/29, 22 January 2003, p. 1.

permanent, instead of ad hoc, panelists and the proposal to open hearings of panels and the Appellate Body to the public. If the WTO dispute settlement system wants to retain its current effectiveness and credibility, the system will have to be amended along the lines of these proposals.

While the WTO dispute settlement system is definitely still open to improvement, it currently already constitutes an effective and efficient system for the peaceful resolution of disputes. It brings a degree of security and predictability in international trade to all its members and their citizens. According to Peter Sutherland, a former WTO Director-General and now Chairman of BP and Goldman Sachs International, the WTO dispute settlement system is 'the greatest advance in multilateral governance since Bretton Woods'.[80] However, there is a genuine danger that members might overburden, and thus undermine, the dispute settlement system as a result of their inability to agree on (clearer) rules governing politically sensitive issues concerning international trade. Since 1995, the WTO dispute settlement system has been severely put to the test by politically sensitive disputes over issues touching on public health (*EC – Hormones* and *EC – Asbestos*), environmental protection (*US – Gasoline* and *US – Shrimp*), cultural identity (*Canada – Periodicals*), taxation (*US – FSC*), and foreign and development policy (*US – Havana Club* and *EC – Bananas III*). So far, the WTO dispute settlement system has performed well in handling these and other sensitive disputes. However, the task may steadily become more difficult as the WTO is drawn more deeply into politically controversial issues. Some observers fear the system may soon be overwhelmed. Claude Barfield of the Washington-based American Enterprise Institute has stirred keen debate in the international trade policy community by suggesting that the WTO dispute settlement system is 'substantively and politically unsustainable'. Barfield suggests governments may only continue to obey its rulings if its powers are curbed.[81] While disagreeing with Barfield's prescription, others have also warned WTO members against relying too heavily on adjudication, instead of negotiated solutions, to settle disputes. Claus-Dieter Ehlermann, former chairman of the Appellate Body, has noted that:

80 As quoted by Guy de Jonquières, 'Rules to Fight By', *Financial Times*, 24 March 2002.

81 Claude Barfield, *Free Trade, Sovereignty, Democracy: The Future of the World Trade Organisation* (AEI Press, 2001), p. 245.

the system is threatened by 'dangerous imbalances' between the WTO's highly efficient judicial function and far less impressive rule-making record.

To preserve the effectiveness and efficiency of the WTO dispute settlement system, members will need to improve the ability of the political institutions of the WTO to address the major issues confronting the multilateral trading system.

11

Interpretation and Application of WTO Rules: Florentino Feliciano and the First Seven

LUIZ OLAVO BAPTISTA

In this chapter I try to look with the eyes of a historian at the first years of the Appellate Body.[1] Specifically, I will examine how the rules on interpretation applicable to WTO law were implemented, and further developed, in the first cases before the Appellate Body. I will also examine the drafting of the Working Procedures for Appellate Review ('Working Procedures'). As decisions in specific appeals, the rules on interpretation and the Working Procedures were the result of the 'collective thinking' and of intense discussions among all seven Appellate Body members leading to a consensus view.

The first members of the Appellate Body were appointed by the Dispute Settlement Body of the WTO in November 1995. Florentino Feliciano was one of the seven.[2] As he is the person to whom we render homage in this book, I feel that some words about him in particular are appropriate before I broach the general subject of this chapter. Who is Florentino Feliciano? Who is the man behind the portrait drawn by the biographical note appearing on the WTO website? What events and facts shaped his personality? How did this personality affect the 'collective thinking' of the Appellate Body?

I knew of Florentino Feliciano and his life through his writings, although I did not have the privilege of meeting him until I took up my function of Appellate Body member. I now have the pleasure of meeting him frequently

[1] I am not supporting nor dissenting from the opinions expressed by other Appellate Body members. These opinions apply to the cases in which they were expressed and to the specific circumstances thereof.

[2] James Bacchus of the USA (1995–2003), Christopher Beeby of New Zealand (1995–2000), Professor Claus-Dieter Ehlermann of Germany (1995–2001), Dr Said El-Naggar of Egypt (1995–2000), Justice Florentino Feliciano of the Philippines (1995–2001), Julio Lacarte Muró of Uruguay (1995–2001), Professor Mitsuo Matsushita of Japan (1995–2000).

at the Institute for Commercial Practices and at the Commission on Arbitration at the International Chamber of Commerce.

I first heard of Florentino Feliciano at the end of the 1970s, when, as President of the São Paulo Bar Association, I organized a World Law Congress in São Paulo with the World Jurists Association. This organization, created by the Washington lawyer Charles Rhine, had as its objective the attainment of world peace through the rule of law. At the time the number of totalitarian governments worldwide was large. Brazil, as well as the Philippines, were at that point in time among the countries under dictatorship and suffered the severe repercussions thereof. Many lawyers revolted against this state of affairs and fought in their own field – the courts – for the peaceful restoration of freedom through the use of reason and law. Florentino Feliciano, President of the World Jurists Association, was one such lawyer.

Later, as Justice at the Supreme Court of the Philippines, he was recognized for his landmark decisions in the area of human rights and his courageous efforts to give back deprived human beings their freedom and rights. However, in spite of his ideals, while serving on the Supreme Court, he never made what is called in the USA 'creative jurisprudence'. He never rewrote the law or created it to suit his ideas. He did, as he should, interpret the words in their context and applied the rules in a reasonable way, as everyone in his country recognizes. Fidelity to the ideal of law and comprehension of the duties of a judge are traits of Justice Feliciano's life, and his independent and honourable conduct responds to traits inherent in his character. Thus, he fits what the WTO members consider to be the right profile of an Appellate Body member.

When Appellate Body members are sworn in they take a solemn oath, and that is why, in the selection process, in addition to the interviews carried out by a group of persons in accordance with the rules, many WTO representatives like to interview the candidates personally to evaluate their personality. Being honourable, or independent, are traits of character, in addition to being qualities of certain actions. Impartiality stems from honour and independence. To act conscientiously, also, is something that some people can do and others cannot, as it demands that things are done with careful attention. However, in the expectations of the WTO members when they created the Appellate Body, infallibility was not among them, and nowhere in the rules is this required of the Appellate Body or its members.

The negotiators of the WTO agreements realized that the application of intricate rules to complex factual situations would give rise to disputes on the correct legal interpretation. Courts are needed to resolve such disputes. The negotiators were also aware that man is neither perfect nor infallible. When designing the Appellate Body, they wisely and prudently decided that the Appellate Body should be composed of 'persons of recognized authority, with demonstrated expertise in law, international trade and the subject matter of the covered agreements generally'.[3] It was also agreed that Appellate Body membership should be 'broadly representative of membership in the WTO'.[4] As a result, the Appellate Body members have different professional and cultural backgrounds. Thus, the members envisaged avoiding as long as possible the margin of error induced by personal idiosyncrasies or human failure, or resulting from memories of one's professional practices, knowledge, or national cultural bias, by putting together people from various origins and diversified professional experiences. Following the same direction, the members also agreed that the opinions of the Appellate Body should be anonymous, so as to favour ample discussion, examination of different angles of the issues being decided, and avoidance of the creation of 'stars'. These carefully crafted rules were directed at ensuring that the Appellate Body decisions would be the right ones for all WTO members regarding their agreements, having in view the limits of human nature, and they would be complemented by the qualities demanded of the people chosen to serve on the Appellate Body.

But these were not all of the measures taken in that careful planning. So as to avoid the Appellate Body members incurring the temptation to become legislators, to which many courts of justice have succumbed at one time or another, the authors of the Treaty specified in Article 3.2 of the DSU a directive, the purpose of the dispute settlement system:

> providing security and predictability to the multilateral trading system. The Members recognize that it serves to preserve the rights and obligations of Members under the covered agreements, and to clarify the existing provisions of those agreements in accordance with customary rules of interpretation of public international law. Recommendations and rulings of the DSB cannot add to or diminish the rights and obligations provided in the covered agreements.[5]

Thus, the authors of the WTO Agreement established the limits for interpretation. One thus not only imagines, but also knows, that the

[3] Understanding on Rules and Procedures Governing the Settlement of Disputes (DSU) Article 17.3.

[4] DSU Article 17.3. [5] DSU Article 3.2.

Appellate Body will not always reason exactly as each party would like them to do, or that it will always arrive at the results that trade experts might expect.

An interpreter of law is someone who tries to explain what other people have drafted. He does not and should not create new rules. The interpreter does not have the right to say more or less than what is said in the text he is interpreting, and which is not his will but that of the author of the rules.[6] The word 'interpretation' is used both for translation and for legal interpretation. And both words are subject to the good faith duty to be as faithful as possible to the writing and thinking of the drafter.[7] That is why the Italians, in the phrase '*traduttore traditore*', made a witty criticism of some translators' sins. It could also be seen as an admonition to interpreters of the law, regarding the fidelity they must have to the meaning of the words in their context.

WTO dispute cases were not the only challenge for the first seven members of the Appellate Body. As they were inaugurating a brand new institution in which people had put high hopes, they had to build its reputation, set its ethical standards, establish adequate Working Procedures, all the while working on the appeals put at their door. The patterns that govern Appellate Body behaviour were shaped by the Working Procedures, which are at the same time ample and rigorous, complementing well the rules set out in the DSU and rendering them operational and effective.

The Working Procedures contain many important institutional provisions that reflect decisions made by the first seven. These rules start by addressing the Appellate Body members, establishing that they 'shall abide by the terms and conditions of the DSU, these Rules and any decisions of the DSB affecting the Appellate Body'(Rule 2(1)).

Independence and ethical rigour were contemplated in the following paragraphs of the same rule:

> (2) During his/her term, a Member shall not accept any employment nor pursue any professional activity that is inconsistent with his/her duties and responsibilities. (3) A Member shall exercise his/her office without accepting or seeking instructions from any international, governmental, or non-governmental organization or any private source.[8]

6 J. F. Rezek, *Direito dos Tratados* (Forense, Rio de Janeiro, 1984), p. 445.
7 W. G. Friedmann, O. J. Lissitzyn, and R. C. Pugh, *International Law* (West Publishing Co., Saint Paul, 1969), p. 389; Rezek, *Direito dos Tratados*, p. 454.
8 Working Procedures Rule 2(2), (3).

Rule 4 stresses the need for the members of the Appellate Body to stay abreast of 'dispute settlement activities and other activities of the WTO' and for them to convene on a regular basis to discuss matters with each other. It also promotes consensus decision-making but permits matters to be decided by a majority vote.

Rule 4 is titled 'Collegiality' and may have been the most innovative and important rule crafted by the original seven. A key provision in this rule states that:

> the division responsible for deciding each appeal shall exchange views with the other Members before the division finalizes the appellate report for circulation to the WTO Members.[9]

But the reach of this rule is broader, as it also assures the aid and the consensus of the members who are not on the Division, and yet who contribute to complete and perfect the work done by the Division. Thus, the procedures provided for in Rule 4 have played a key role in achieving consistent application of rules by the Appellate Body, and this will serve as a guarantee of legal certainty for WTO members on that issue.

Turning now to the issue of the interpretation of the agreements, one can see the development of a deliberative judicial method in the decisions in which Florentino Feliciano participated in the Division. One of the first cases was *EC – Hormones*,[10] where the Appellate Body said:

> We cannot lightly assume that sovereign states intended to impose upon themselves the more onerous, rather than the less burdensome, obligation by mandating *conformity* of *compliance with* such standards, guidelines and recommendations. To sustain such an assumption and to warrant such a far-reaching interpretation, treaty language far more specific and compelling than that found in Article 3 of the *SPS Agreement* would be necessary.[11]

There, one finds the first mention of interpretation, where the Appellate Body decided that it was reading the text of the rule having in mind 'that sovereign states [should not be assumed to] impose upon themselves the more onerous, rather than the less burdensome, obligation' whenever they sign a treaty. In other words, it was said that the

[9] Working Procedures Rule 4(3).

[10] Appellate Body Report, *European Communities – Measures Concerning Meat and Meat Products (Hormones)*, WT/DS26/AB/R and WT/DS48/AB/R, 13 February 1998.

[11] Appellate Body Report, *EC – Hormones*, paragraph 165 (original italics).

interpretation should not be extensive, but rather restrictive. In the same *EC – Hormones* case, the first seven also said that:

> [t]he fundamental rule of treaty interpretation requires a treaty interpreter to read and interpret the words actually used by the agreement under examination, not words the interpreter may feel should have been used.[12]

This statement points to the limits of interpretation and reflects a literal approach to that exercise. This is why the first seven resorted many times to dictionaries to find the exact meaning of each expression used.

Another case before the Appellate Body demonstrated the importance of Article 31 of the Vienna Convention on the Law of Treaties[13] to WTO dispute settlement. In *Argentina – Textiles and Apparel*, the Vienna Convention appears. The panel had relied heavily on what it characterized as 'past GATT practice', without undertaking much analysis of the ordinary meaning of the terms from GATT 1994 that were at issue.[14] In Article 31 of the Vienna Convention, however, there is the reference to 'the object and purpose', which commentators on the Vienna Convention say should be looked for in the words that have been written and in the limits of the treaty, rather then elsewhere.[15] In some other cases, the Vienna Convention is also mentioned, such as in *Canada – Measures Affecting the Export of Civilian Aircraft*,[16] in which it was stated that '[t]hese principles, set out in part in the Vienna Convention on the Law of Treaties, require that a treaty be interpreted in accordance with the ordinary meaning of its terms, in their context and in the light of its object and purpose'.[17] In *European Communities – Anti-dumping Measures on Imports of Cotton-type Bed-linen from India*,[18] the Appellate Body decided: 'In this case, the Panel explicitly recognized that it was to interpret the Anti-Dumping Agreement in accordance with the customary rules of interpretation of public international law

12 Appellate Body Report, *EC – Hormones*, paragraph 181.

13 Done at Vienna, 23 May 1969, 1155 UNTS 33; 8 ILM 679.

14 See Appellate Body Report, *Argentina – Measures Affecting Imports of Footwear, Textiles, Apparel and other Items*, WT/DS56/AB/R, 22 April 1998, paragraph 42.

15 N. Montgomery, *As Convenções de Viena sobre direito dos tratados* (NICIN /Livraria do advogado, Porto Alegre, 1999), pp. 101–32; P. Reuter, *Introduction au Droit des Traites* (3rd edn, PUF, Paris, 1995), p. 87; Rezek, *Direito dos Tratados*, p. 452.

16 Appellate Body Report, *Canada – Measures Affecting the Export of Civilian Aircraft*, WT/DS70/AB/R, 20 August 1999.

17 *Ibid.* at paragraph 7.

18 Appellate Body Report, *European Communities – Anti-dumping Duties on Imports of Cotton-type Bed-linen from India*, WT/DS141/AB/R, 12 March 2001.

as set out in the Vienna Convention'.[19] The same opinion was expressed in *European Communities – Measures Affecting Importation of Certain Poultry Products*, where the Appellate Body Report states that 'the only rules which may be applied in interpreting the meaning of a concession are the general rules of treaty interpretation set out in the Vienna Convention'.[20] In *United States – Standards for Reformulated and Conventional Gasoline*, the first seven said that the general rule of interpretation 'forms part of the customary rules of interpretation of public international law'.[21] Further on in this decision it was said that 'the Appellate Body considers that the basic international law rule of treaty interpretation, discussed earlier, [is] that terms of a treaty are to be given their ordinary meaning, in context'.[22] In *United States – Anti-dumping Measures on Certain Hot-rolled Steel Products from Japan*, it was mentioned that 'the panel shall interpret the relevant provisions of the Agreement in accordance with customary rules of interpretation of public international law'.[23] Also in *Mexico – Anti-dumping Investigation of High-fructose Corn Syrup from the United States*, the same position is expressed.[24]

The first seven understood that the sources of law for their decisions should be the WTO agreements, and that other sources of law were not to be applied. For example, in *European Communities – Measures Affecting Asbestos and Asbestos-Containing Products*, it was said that the provisions of the GATT 1994 should be interpreted on their own and that '[t]he scope and meaning of Article III:4 should not be broadened or restricted beyond what is required by the normal customary international law rules of treaty interpretation'.[25]

The principle of effectiveness appears in the *Korea – Dairy* case where the decision, taken with the participation of Florentino Feliciano who was on the Division, said that:

[19] Panel Report, WT/DS141/R, 12 March 2001, paragraph 6.46.

[20] Appellate Body Report, *European Communities – Measures Affecting Importation of Certain Poultry Products*, WT/DS69/AB/R, 23 July 1998, paragraph 82 (emphasis added).

[21] Appellate Body Report, *United States – Standards for Reformulated and Conventional Gasoline*, WT/DS2/AB/R, 20 May 1996, p. 17.

[22] *Ibid.* at p. 20.

[23] Appellate Body Report, *United States – Anti-dumping Measures on Certain Hot-rolled Steel Products from Japan*, WT/DS184/AB/R, 23 August 2001, paragraph 50, (ii).

[24] Appellate Body Report, *Mexico – Anti-dumping Investigation of High-fructose Corn Syrup from the United States – Recourse to Article 21.5 of the DSU by the United States*, WT/DS132/AB/RW, 21 November 2001, paragraph 129, (ii).

[25] Appellate Body Report, *European Communities – Measures Affecting Asbestos and Asbestos-Containing Products*, WT/DS135/AB/R, 5 April 2001, paragraph 115.

> in the light of the interpretive principle of effectiveness, it is the *duty* of any treaty interpreter to 'read all applicable provisions of a treaty in a way that gives meaning to *all* of them, harmoniously'. An important corollary of this principle is that a treaty should be interpreted as a whole, and, in particular, its sections and parts should be read as a whole. Article II:2 of the WTO Agreement expressly manifests the intention of the Uruguay Round negotiators that the provisions of the WTO Agreement and the Multilateral Trade Agreements included in its Annexes 1, 2 and 3 must be read as a whole.[26]

In these cases, we see how the first seven understood and effected treaty interpretation. First, they said that sovereign states should not be assumed to impose upon themselves the more onerous, rather than the less burdensome, obligation whenever they sign a treaty, and following this reasoning they made literal and restrictive interpretations. Having in mind that 'treaty interpretation requires a treaty interpreter to read and interpret the words actually used by the agreement', they started using dictionaries and looked for the meaning of the words in their context. Furthermore, the first seven said one should look at all the applicable provisions of a treaty; and that such reading should be made 'in the light of the object and purpose of the GATT 1994, in accordance with the general rules of treaty interpretation set out in Article 31 of the Vienna Convention'. They also included as one of the instruments of the interpreter the principle of effectiveness, which the first seven found should 'include an appropriate reading of this "inseparable package of rights and disciplines" [and] must, accordingly, be one that gives meaning to *all* the relevant provisions'. An important corollary of this principle is that a treaty should be interpreted as a whole, and, in particular, its sections and parts should be read as a whole. Article II: 2 of the *WTO Agreement* expressly manifests the intention of the Uruguay Round negotiators that the provisions of the *WTO Agreement* and the Multilateral Trade Agreements included in its Annexes 1, 2 and 3 must be read as a whole.

Speaking of the intention of the negotiators, anyone spending time with Uruguay Round negotiators may occasionally hear a concern that a holding rendered by the Appellate Body is inconsistent with what the drafters had intended. 'But, I was not thinking this or that when I negotiated this treaty', it is said. The possibility of such supposed divergence can be explained by

[26] Appellate Body Report, *Korea – Definitive Safeguard Measure on Imports of Certain Dairy Products*, WT/DS98/AB/R, 12 January 2000, paragraph 81 (emphasis added).

the fact that the role of the treaty interpreter is not to look for the will of one of the parties or the intended will of one of the parties, but the consensual will of all the parties, which stems from the text they agreed to and upon which the agreement was built.

Having lived by the Working Procedures myself, and after reviewing and rereading these cases to examine how the first seven Appellate Body members (without regard to their conclusions) effected interpretation, it seems clear to me that all the members of the Divisions whose reports were mentioned here have done their duty 'honourably, independently, impartially, conscientiously, and in accordance with the law of the World Trade Organization'. That was what had been asked of them.

12

Dispute Settlement in the WTO: On the Trail of a Court

HÉLÈNE RUIZ FABRI

Introduction

Is the dispute settlement mechanism of the World Trade Organization (WTO) a court? It is easy to imagine the first members of the Appellate Body asking themselves this question and contemplating their degree of latitude and discretion. International economic law is traditionally considered not to be amenable to the judicial settlement of disputes, and this might even be considered one of its distinguishing features.[1] From this standpoint, the advent of a genuine court would indicate a process of evolution and indeed its consecration as 'real' law (expounded and sanctioned by a judge). It would also support and validate the thesis of rejection of the 'clinical isolation' of WTO law, particularly as the hypothesis of movement towards a judicial system is not specific to the settlement of trade disputes but applies to international law as a whole.[2] Thus, there may be a sort of dialectic according to which the settlement of trade disputes is affected by this general trend insofar as it participates in and nourishes that trend. The approach is all the more tempting in that 'judicialization' has its own intrinsic value. Indeed, it is often viewed as a remedy for the traditional ailments or primitiveness of international law.[3]

[1] For an account of the traditional approach to this debate, see P. Weil, 'Le droit international économique, mythe ou réalité?' in SFDI, *Aspects du droit international économique* (Pedone, Paris, 1972), pp. 3–34 and 105–17. On the specificity of the settlement of economic disputes, see in particular G. Malinverni, *Le règlement des différends dans les organisations économiques internationales* (Sijthoff, 1974).

[2] See SFDI, *La juridictionnalisation du droit international* (Pedone, Paris, 2003).

[3] M. Virally, 'Sur la prétendue "primitivité" du droit international' in *Le droit international en devenir: essais écrits au fil des ans* (PUF, 1990), p. 91; J. Combacau, *Le droit international: bric-à-brac ou système?* (Arch. Phil. Dr., 1986), p. 85.

Although the dispute settlement mechanism may, in the course of only a few years, have developed a judicial structure and in so doing displayed a readiness to model itself on the jurisprudence of other international courts, especially in terms of procedure,[4] various analysts prefer to use the convenient term 'quasi-judicial'. Is that 'quasi' really necessary? It raises the question of why one might wish to pass off as judicial something which in reality is not, or alternatively why one should hesitate to describe as judicial something which obviously is. It presupposes the consideration of a number of criteria. Not all of these necessarily have the same demonstrative value, particularly as neither the notion of a court nor the identification criteria can be considered invariable, either in themselves or in their interrelationships. The notion has an historical reality which calls for relativism in the analysis.

Whether a court is defined as a 'body which settles a dispute by a binding decision ... rendered in application of the law',[5] or as a 'body responsible for stating the law (*jurisdictio*) in a binding manner (*imperium*)',[6] the fundamental question is whether this is in fact what is going on within the framework of the dispute settlement mechanism. The approach I have chosen is to consider the mechanism in its totality, both chronologically and organically. On the one hand, it is a question of incorporating, in addition to the phase leading to the decision, the surveillance of its implementation, on the assumption that a 'broad conception of *imperium* (covering) both the bindingness and the enforceability of the judicial decision'[7] will give a clearer picture of the judicial nature of the system in the case of the WTO. At the same time, there is a need to go beyond the relative diversity of the bodies which make up the dispute settlement mechanism, by postulating that it is against the yardstick of the mechanism viewed as a whole and as a unity that its judicial parameters can be measured.[8] It turns out that the mechanism and its *modus operandi* have almost all the characteristics of a court. This may be deduced by analysing not only a number of criteria generally

[4] P. Shahrjerdri and V. Tomkiewicz, 'Le procès équitable dans l'espace normatif de l'OMC' in H. Ruiz Fabri (ed.), *Procès équitable et enchevêtrement des espaces normatifs* (Editions de la Société de législation comparée, 2003).

[5] C. Santulli, 'Qu'est-ce qu'une juridiction internationale?' (AFDI, 2000), p. 61.

[6] H. Ascensio, 'La notion de juridiction internationale en question' in SFDI, *La juridictionnalisation du droit international* (Pedone, Paris, 2003), p. 163.

[7] *Ibid.*

[8] Clearly, the standpoint is different, but I am thinking here of the method used by the European Court of Human Rights to verify a fair trial, which is applied on the scale of the procedure as a whole.

associated with the notion of a court, in the absence of which the case would be much harder to make, in particular the concept of *jurisdictio*, but also the *imperium*, although the difficulties of characterizing the dispute settlement mechanism in this way should not be ignored.

Jurisdiction

In general, there are three criteria (organic, formal, and material) which must all be satisfied if a body is to be described as a court.

First, the organic criterion relates to the judicial status of the body responsible for settling the dispute and is generally interpreted as the requirement that it be both independent and impartial. As far as WTO dispute settlement is concerned, it is a question of determining how to treat the Dispute Settlement Body (DSB), insofar as it is the DSB which takes the decision that makes the solution of the dispute binding. The complete formality of this intervention (virtually automatic adoption) suggests that the influence of the DSB on the judicial status may be discounted and justifies concentrating exclusively on the Appellate Body and the panels when examining the relevant criterion, in the belief that the conclusions reached will hold true for the whole of the dispute settlement mechanism. However, it should not be assumed that taking this approach precludes the possibility of considering that, as a political organ, the DSB is incapable of performing a judicial function. Nevertheless, such a mingling now tends to be analysed as residual primitiveness or an inconsistency which as far as possible should be removed[9] and the criterion of independence and impartiality forms, at the very least, an integral part of the objective perception of the court ('justice must not only be done, it must also be seen to be done'). On the other hand, however, the criterion of independence and impartiality has become so intimately bound up with the image of the judge and the virtues ascribed to the tasks he performs that there is a tendency to extend the requirement to bodies with other missions in the hope of seeing them benefit from the same legitimacy. Thus, the organic criterion alone is not enough to authorize a conclusion and should be treated with caution.

[9] Thus, the fact that, when the European system for the protection of human rights was reformed by Protocol No. 11, the Committee of Ministers was deprived of its previous powers of adjudication which were thereafter reserved for the court alone, was regarded as progress. See F. Sudre, *Droit international et européen des droits de l'homme* (6th edn., PUF, 2003), pp. 498–502.

However this may be, the development of permanent courts has structured this criterion of independence and impartiality by imposing a number of statutory conditions, which an examination of the rules governing the composition of panels and the Appellate Body, their selection procedures, and the standing of their members, suggests that the dispute settlement mechanism has met. The 'judicial tendency' discernible in the Dispute Settlement Understanding (DSU), especially in the case of the standing Appellate Body, is asserting itself in the case of panels as well. The fact that members can still choose their 'judges' of first instance is not 'anti-judicial'.[10] Moreover, in this particular case, the third party element is exclusive since citizens of the parties to the dispute cannot be appointed. This condition does not apply to the Appellate Body but the selection procedure, which calls for a membership broadly representative of that in the WTO (DSU Article 17.3), may be viewed as 'an adaptation of the principle of impartiality to the context of international society'.[11] The presence of a national of a state party in the Division responsible for a particular case would be merely a coincidence[12] and not a manifestation of the institution of the ad hoc judge which, as distinct from other international courts, does not exist at the WTO. Furthermore, in the absence of exclusion based on nationality, the DSU prohibits participation in the consideration of 'any disputes that would create a direct or indirect conflict of interest'.[13] To this should be added the qualifications required of both panel and Appellate Body members and the conditions of independence,[14] impartiality,[15] and 'conduct', such as the obligation to respect the confidentiality of documents and deliberations.[16] Finally, collective independence and impartiality are both reinforced by the ban on *ex parte* communications. These various obligations, contained in the DSU, are supplemented by the Rules of Conduct for the Understanding on Rules and Procedures Governing the Settlement of Disputes[17] whose very existence shows that members have been much more concerned about the organic than the

[10] On the contrary, it is a characteristic of arbitration, one of the two main ways of judicially settling intergovernmental disputes.

[11] Ascensio, 'La notion de juridiction', p. 170. This type of approach is common to courts which do not have one judge per state party.

[12] Since the members of the examining Divisions serve in rotation, which does not normally allow members to choose their 'judges'.

[13] DSU Article 17.3. [14] DSU Articles 8.2, 8.9, and 17.3. [15] DSU Article 11.

[16] DSU Articles 14.1 for panels, 17.10 for the Appellate Body, and 18.2 for submissions by parties.

[17] Decision adopted by the DSB on 11 December 1996, WT/DSB/RC/1.

procedural aspects, with the result that the Appellate Body and panels may be regarded as satisfying the criteria of independence and impartiality generally imposed on courts and tribunals.

Secondly, the formal criterion relates to the judicial status of the procedure. The strengthening of the procedural safeguards began long before the establishment of the new dispute settlement mechanism since it was observable even during the GATT period.[18] Nevertheless, the judicial option is clearly confirmed in the form of a 'right to due process' in which it is doubtless possible to discern, in a minor mode, the equivalent at intergovernmental level of the principle of a fair trial.[19]

The principles of equality of the parties and equality of arms and, indeed, the rule that both parties shall be heard and the obligation to give the grounds for a judgment, embodied in the fair trial model, are also demanded by the principle of sovereign equality. In fact, the procedure is meant to provide parties with strictly equal rights of representation, a 'fundamental tenet'[20] requiring that a party be provided with an opportunity to respond to claims made against it,[21] while the operation of the system of evidence prohibits a panel from seeking the advice of experts where a party has failed to establish a *prima facie* case based on specific legal claims.[22] The obligation to give reasons (for a judgment) is clearly stipulated in the DSU (Article 12.7), as it is in most, if not all the statutes of the international courts. This does not prevent the settlement bodies from applying the principle of judicial economy, which is taken to mean that, although they must deal with all the claims necessary to settle a dispute, they do not have to deal with more claims than necessary.[23] Thus, the obligation to set out a rationale should not be

[18] V. Coussirat-Coustère and P. M. Eisemann, 'La procédure devant les juridictions internationales permanentes' in SFDI, *La juridiction internationale permanente* (Pedone, Paris, 1987), p. 105; T. Flory, 'Les accords du Tokyo Round du GATT et la réforme des procédures de règlement des différends dans le système commercial interétatique' (1982) *RGDIP* 240.

[19] See the above-mentioned analysis by Shahjerdri and Tomkiewicz, *Le procès équitable*. See also S. Guinchard *et al.*, *Droit processuel* (3rd edn., Dalloz, 2005), pp. 869–912.

[20] See Appellate Body Report, *Australia – Measures Affecting Importation of Salmon*, WT/DS18/AB/R, 6 November 1998, paragraph 278.

[21] Some consider it necessary to go one step further and make the proceedings public. See D. Palmeter, 'The Need for Due Process in WTO Proceedings' (1997) 1 *Journal of World Trade* 51.

[22] In this connection, see Appellate Body Report, *Japan – Measures Affecting Agricultural Products*, WT/DS76/AB/R, 19 March 1999, paragraph 129.

[23] See Appellate Body Report, *United States – Safeguard Measures on Imports of Fresh, Chilled or Frozen Lamb Meat from New Zealand and Australia*, WT/DS177/AB/R, 16 May 2001, paragraph 194.

confused with an obligation to consider every plea or argument. However this may be, compliance with the obligation on the part of panels is subject to the scrutiny of the Appellate Body, although, in practice, the latter has generally swept the matter swiftly aside, without deeming it 'necessary, or desirable to attempt to define the scope' of the obligation,[24] which is perfectly understandable from a pragmatic point of view, since the reports are already so long and the grounds so detailed.[25] Among other things, the anticipation of a possible appeal encourages such fastidiousness, just as it encourages greater rigour in the legal reasoning.[26]

The element of dispatch embodied in the procedure also enables the WTO to meet the reasonable time-frame requirement much more easily than some other courts.[27] In fact, the pressure becomes particularly intense as soon as predetermined time limits are imposed. Ultimately, only the question of transparency may be seen to pose a problem, inasmuch as the WTO settlement procedure is explicitly confidential (DSU Articles 14 and 17.10). However, this confidentiality is the deliberate choice of the members who are also the litigants, and a majority of them continue to cling to it. Accordingly, although the object of holding proceedings in public is primarily to protect against the secret, and hence potentially arbitrary, administration of justice, including where the rights and interests of third parties are concerned, it is essentially from this latter standpoint (taking third parties to include private individuals) that the question is actually being posed, as evidenced by the way in which it is being debated within the context of the post-Doha review of the dispute settlement rules. This stems from a demand for transparency aimed at the organization as a whole, as a means of allaying the mistrust it arouses among the public, concerning not only its objectives but also the means it uses to achieve them. It is under this latter heading, in particular, that dispute settlement is involved. Thus, in

[24] See Appellate Body Report, *Korea – Taxes on Alcoholic Beverages II*, WT/DS75/AB/R, 17 February 1999.

[25] The same tendency can be observed in most international courts which, apart from the nature of the litigants, probably has to do with the fact that the courts are composed of judges from different legal traditions whose views have to be reconciled.

[26] Incidentally, the interim review phase (DSU Article 15) provides an opportunity for the future 'winner' to suggest to the panel ways of strengthening or improving the legal reasoning on which its conclusions are based.

[27] DSU Article 3.3 explicitly links the prompt settlement of disputes with the maintenance of a 'proper balance' between the rights and obligations of members.

relation to the problem of the judicial nature of the system, the question is mainly one of legitimacy.

At the same time, the affirmation of the right to due process is linked with the goal of effective dispute settlement and their point of intersection lies in the development of the functional autonomy of the dispute settlement bodies. Apart from a few procedural rules contained in the DSU and the standing Rules of Procedure of the Appellate Body,[28] the procedure depends on ad hoc decisions, with panels even being allowed to depart from the Working Procedures set out in Appendix 3 to the DSU provided they consult the parties. Although the Appellate Body has agreed to examine the preliminary rulings made by panels, its own are last instance. The status of all these preliminary procedural rulings is special but imprecise. Their citation and justification in the final report of the body making them nevertheless leads to the conclusion that they are incorporated in that report as findings of law. This, at least, is the interpretation that could justify the willingness of the Appellate Body to examine them, within the context of a global (and all encompassing) interpretation of its mission under DSU Article 17.13 to 'uphold, modify or reverse the legal findings and conclusions of the panel'.

The jurisprudence is entirely oriented towards the search for a balance between the need to provide procedural safeguards and the need to avoid an overemphasis on procedure that would undermine the effectiveness of the mechanism, with procedural objections becoming a means of evading the settlement of the underlying dispute. A way out of this classical dilemma can be found by affirming the autonomy of the settlement bodies in matters of procedure, while making the procedure more inquisitorial (as spectacularly apparent, for example, in the oral proceedings before the Appellate Body). The linking of this autonomy with the goal of effective dispute settlement is an expression not only of an organic need but also of a concern for pragmatism. It leads to the acceptance of, and even a demand for, a procedure with 'sufficient flexibility'. Though subjectively it might seem inconsistent with a judicial approach, this is prescribed by the DSU itself, which calls for both high quality and no undue delay in the settlement of disputes (DSU Article 12.2). In this connection, the Appellate Body, while heedful of

[28] Working Procedures for Appellate Review, adopted on 15 February 1996, as amended, WT/AB/WP/3, 28 February 1997, WT/AB/WP/4, 24 January 2002, and WT/AB/WP/5, 19 December 2002. The above-mentioned Rules of Conduct are incorporated in an annex.

the rules of procedure and in particular the question of balance, also resorts to the principle of good faith to counteract the temptation to pursue courtroom strategies that involve introducing certain procedural arguments only if the case is going badly, sometimes very late in the day.[29] The proliferation of these procedural questions explains the sympathy sometimes expressed for the adoption of standard rules of procedure for the panel phase.[30] The issue is one of those being discussed as part of the post-Doha review. In any event, it would be desirable for the rules adopted by panels at the beginning of the proceedings to be made public, which they are not at present.[31]

All this is tending to restrict the grip of the parties on the procedure. Procedural decisions are admittedly 'interlocutory rulings',[32] which must be taken in accordance with due process[33] or 'in consultation with the parties'.[34] However, this is not resulting in a 'bilateralization' of the procedure.[35] The fact that the parties may agree on a rule of procedure does not oblige the panel or the Appellate Body itself to adopt it. The power to make procedural decisions is a discretionary power, with the Appellate Body doing no more than ensuring that it has not been abused.[36] This discretion

[29] In particular, it noted that the principle of good faith requires the responding member to draw attention to procedural deficiencies 'seasonably and promptly' so that corrections can be made, stressing that 'the procedural rules . . . are designed to promote, not the development of litigation techniques, but simply the fair, prompt and effective resolution of trade disputes'. See *United States – Tax Treatment for 'Foreign Sales Corporations'*, WT/DS108/AB/R, 20 March 2000, paragraph 166.

[30] See, e.g., Appellate Body Report, *India – Patent Protection for Pharmaceutical and Agricultural Chemical Products*, WT/DS50/AB/R, 16 January 1998, paragraph 95.

[31] P. Monnier, 'Working Procedures before Panels, the Appellate Body and Other Adjudicating Bodies of the WTO' in *The Law and Practice of International Courts and Tribunals: A Practitioner's Review* (Kluwer, 2002), vol. 1, p. 481.

[32] See Appellate Body Report, *Canada – Measures Affecting the Export of Civilian Aircraft*, WT/DS70/AB/R, 20 August 1999, paragraph 195.

[33] See Appellate Body Report, *European Communities – Measures Concerning Meat and Meat Products (Hormones)*, WT/DS26/AB/R, 13 February 1998, paragraph 154.

[34] *Ibid.* at paragraphs 148 and 152, note 138.

[35] See Canada – *Aircraft*, in which the Appellate Body refused to adopt additional procedures relating to confidential information, despite a joint request by Brazil and Canada.

[36] Thus, the panel is perfectly at liberty to request the opinion of individual experts and draw up rules for consulting them. See Appellate Body Report, *EC – Hormones*, paragraph 148, or Appellate Body Report, *Argentina – Measures Affecting Imports of Footwear, Textiles, Apparel and Other Items*, WT/DS56/AB/R, 22 April 1998, or Appellate Body Report, *Australia – Salmon*. Similarly, panels also have discretion to set time limits for the submission of evidence. See Appellate Body Report, *United States – Measures Affecting Imports of Woven Wool Shirts and Blouses from India*, WT/DS33/AB/R,

is not alien to the judicial system and cannot be assumed to render the label 'judicial' inappropriate.

Thirdly, the material criterion relates to the subject matter of the task assigned to the body, in this case the settlement of disputes by application of the law, which actually comprises two requirements: settling disputes and doing so in accordance with the law in force.

The dispute settlement mechanism is explicitly reserved for the settlement of intergovernmental disputes. However, a certain ambiguity may result from the 'non-contentious' approach recommended by the DSU (Article 3.10). The question is what is meant here by 'contentious', i.e., whether it is synonymous with conflict, in which case the aim is to rule out a conflictual approach to dispute settlement, or whether it is intended to characterize a category of cases insofar as they can be submitted to a judge. Support for the first interpretation can be derived from the fact that in other contexts practice accepts that the judicial function may be exercised in non-contentious cases.[37] It follows that the term 'judicial' (*jurisdictio*) does not in itself imply the existence of a trial but designates the function that consists in stating the law. However, in this particular case, even though the DSU calls for the parties to take a non-conflictual approach to the dispute, the configuration of the dispute settlement process nevertheless corresponds quite closely to what is traditionally regarded as contentious. Hence, it is probably the special nature of the litigants that, to a large extent, explains the recommendation of a non-contentious approach and leads to its being seen, above all, as a rhetorical precaution, in conjunction with the essentially non-judicial nature of an international society not accustomed to using procedures even where they exist.[38] This pragmatic message addressed to members is consistent with the overall conception of the system, with everything being done to make effectiveness prevail over sensitivities or mere power relationships by removing any opportunity for blocking the proceedings that governments may previously have had. The Appellate Body has pushed this logic to the limit. Thus, it has appealed to DSU

23 May 1997, paragraph 80. They can even accept evidence submitted after the deadline initially fixed for submission. See Appellate Body Report, *Australia – Salmon*, paragraph 272.

[37] Reference is often made to the example of a criminal trial where justice is certainly administered although, strictly speaking, there is no contentious proceeding between two opposing parties, or to the case in which the law calls for the intervention of a judge to confirm an agreement or transaction between two parties so as to make it enforceable.

[38] Although the situation appears to be changing slightly, as illustrated, for example, by the additional burdens being placed on the ICJ.

Article 3 and, in particular, to the requirement not to consider recourse to dispute settlement as a 'contentious act' and to engage in procedures in good faith, in order to reinforce the affirmation of a 'fundamental right' to dispute settlement and justify an inquisitorial interpretation of the DSU.[39] Thus understood, the exclusion of a contentious approach is unconnected with the judicial nature of the function to be performed, which resides in the fact that the activity consists in settling disputes in accordance with the law in force.

The second possible interpretation raises the question of whether disputes are really the issue and whether the purpose of the mechanism is in fact to settle them. From a strictly nominalistic point of view, the answer is yes, since the creators of the mechanism explicitly earmarked it for the 'settlement of disputes'. In any event, and *a priori*, there seems to be no denying that the situation in which one member requests another to amend or withdraw a measure it considers to be inconsistent with WTO law and the other member refuses to accede to that request constitutes a dispute, defined as 'a disagreement on a point of law or fact, a conflict of legal views or of interests between two persons',[40] it being noted that 'disagreements, objections ... only constitute a dispute if they arise in connection with a complaint made by one State against another which the latter refuses to allow'.[41] As far as the approach taken by panels and the Appellate Body is concerned, it consists in asking whether the measure in question is inconsistent with WTO law, as one member claims and the other denies, and requiring that it be withdrawn or amended, if the answer is yes.

It might be objected that, even though two or more particular members may confront each other during the proceeding and even though this inter-subjective configuration may appear to have all the characteristics of a dispute, the duty of the DSB is not really to undertake 'a legal

[39] Thus, in Appellate Body Report, *Canada – Aircraft*, it rejected the Canadian refusal to provide information requested by the panel. Its main argument in support of the normative conditional ('should' in DSU Article 13.1) was systemic and cited the principle of effectiveness. It based itself on the fundamental logic of the pairing right/obligation, considering that the panel could not have a 'right' to seek information (as stated in Article 13.1) if there was not a corresponding obligation to respond. According to the Appellate Body, any other interpretation would allow a party to thwart the panel's powers and prevent it from ascertaining the facts and hence settling the dispute: Appellate Body Report *Canada – Aircraft*, paragraph 187 *et seq*.

[40] PICJ, *Mavrommatis Palestine Concessions (Greece* v. *UK)*, 30 August 1924, Series A, No. 2, 11.

[41] J. Combacau and S. Sur, *Droit international public* (6th edn., Montchrestien, 2004), p. 552.

evaluation of the claims of the parties. It is only to say whatever may be necessary for the implementation of the agreements, the legal assessment of the claims not being part of its functions.'[42] These functions consist in preserving members' rights and obligations and clarifying the provisions at issue. Regardless of what legal form they may take, these are 'executive administrative functions'. One argument that could be made in favour of this approach is the non-requirement of a legal interest in bringing proceedings as a condition of admissibility (the plaintiff does not have to prove that he has a direct or even legitimate personal interest to protect), together with the absence of any consideration for injury. Although, admittedly, an adverse impact is presumed as soon as a breach of the rules has been proved (DSU Article 3.8), the proceedings are not intended to make good any injury as such, since the injury is considered to have been incurred only from the moment at which an infringement was found and only if the measure has not been brought into conformity.[43] From this standpoint, the system operates in preventive mode and has no other purpose than to verify, and thereby facilitate, the proper discharge of treaty obligations. However, this approach fails to take into account the existence of a multitude of bodies having nothing to do with dispute settlement whose function is explicitly to oversee the proper implementation of the agreements, since each of the agreements that make up WTO law has its own administrative organ. Moreover, the situation regarding legal interest and injury is open to a different interpretation.

Admittedly, in *EC – Bananas*, the Appellate Body found no trace of a legal interest requirement[44] either in the DSU or in the form of a general principle that applied where the texts were silent. Nevertheless, it also

[42] Santulli, 'Q'est-ce qu'une juridiction internationale?' 81.

[43] From this standpoint, there is even a certain consistency in that the mechanism has no urgent case procedures of the provisional measure type. See H. Ruiz Fabri, 'L'absence de procédures d'urgence' in H. Ruiz Fabri and J.-M. Sorel (eds.), *Le contentieux de l'urgence et l'urgence dans le contentieux devant les juridictions internationales: regards croisés* (Pedone, Paris, 2003), p. 162.

[44] Inasmuch as the DSU requires third parties or a member wishing to join in consultations to have a substantial trade interest, the European Community had concluded that *a fortiori* a complainant should have a legal interest, which led it to deny the USA the possibility of being a complaining party in this case (paragraph 17). However, the Appellate Body rejected this interpretation. See Appellate Body Report, *European Communities – Importation, Sale and Distribution of Bananas*, WT/DS27/AB/R, 25 September 1997, paragraph 132.

noted that this did not settle the question of standing and that certain provisions gave guidance on how standing should be determined.[45] Thus, GATT Article XXIII:1 extends dispute settlement to the case in which 'any contracting party [considers] that any benefit accruing to it directly or indirectly under this Agreement is being nullified or impaired or that the attainment of any objective of the Agreement is being impeded'. The Appellate Body considered that this provision 'is consistent with' DSU Article 3.7 according to which 'before bringing a case, a Member shall exercise its judgment as to whether action under these procedures would be fruitful'; the Appellate Body then concluded that, although the texts call for great discipline, members have broad discretion in deciding whether to bring a case.[46] And although, in *EC – Bananas III*, the Appellate Body appeared to take an interest in the way in which a member assesses its situation,[47] it also noted that the discipline required was a 'largely self-regulating' obligation, so that a member bringing an action should be presumed to have duly examined its potential fruitfulness.[48] Theoretically, this presumption may be questioned. In practice, however, it is virtually impossible to rebut, owing to the extremely comprehensive way in which the direct or indirect nullification or impairment of benefits is conceived, since, in its determination, not only trade volumes but also prospective competitive relations can be taken into account. From this standpoint, the presumption is a reasonable one. It reveals a very open system. Such a degree of openness is rarely to be found in national systems within which, for obvious practical reasons, it may be necessary, on the contrary, to devise ways of restricting access to the courts, which explains, in particular, the importance attached to legal interest. On the other hand, in international law in general and in the WTO system in particular, this openness poses no problems, given the small number of potential litigants. It does not prevent that system from being described as judicial – far from it.

[45] See Appellate Body Report, *EC – Bananas III*, paragraph 133.

[46] *Ibid.*, at paragraph 135.

[47] *Ibid.*, at paragraph 136. In this particular instance, the Appellate Body said it was satisfied that the USA was justified in bringing its claims and referred, in particular, to 'a potential export interest' by the USA as a basis for acknowledging its right to bring a case.

[48] A panel does not have to consider this assessment nor question it on its own authority. See Panel Report, *Mexico – Corn Syrup (Article 21.5 – US)*, WT/DS132/AB/R, 21 November 2001, paragraph 74.

The same applies to the role of injury. There will be a direction to withdraw or amend the measure at issue as soon as an infringement of WTO law has been established. Does this mean that the complainant's right to what he is claiming will not be verified because ultimately that is not the real object of the exercise or, in other words, that a finding of inconsistency could be made even though the complainant was not entitled to what the defendant had refused him? The DSU appears to rule out such a conclusion since it states that 'in cases where there is an infringement of a covered agreement, the action is considered *prima facie* to constitute a case of nullification or impairment' (Article 3.8). The establishment of an infringement therefore reduces to showing that the complainant was right to consider that one of his benefits had been nullified or impaired. Admittedly, here again, we are faced with reasoning by presumption since the DSU stipulates that 'there is normally a presumption that a breach of the rules has an adverse impact on other Members parties to that covered agreement, and in such cases, it shall be up to the Member against whom the complaint has been brought to rebut the charge'. The precise subject of the rebuttal – the infringement of the law or injury – is not made clear, but the main point is whether it is enough to show that the measure in question is not causing any injury in order to validate it. This is possible in theory but infeasible in practice. *EC – Bananas* was one of those 'exceptional' cases in which rebuttal could be envisaged since the USA, not being a banana exporter, could not claim to have suffered commercial injury as a result of the organization of the European market. However, the idea of nullification or impairment of benefits already mentioned in connection with legal interest (the Appellate Body says that it is in fact a question of taking the same elements into account) makes it possible to envisage injury even in these circumstances, so that the rebuttal debate can be usefully conducted only in terms of the law, in order to deny the alleged inconsistency. Clearly, it is possible to question the precise role of injury, since it is not verified. However, this verification is not necessary, not because it would reveal a fiction but because, on the contrary, there is no point in proving the obvious. The presumption reveals the pragmatism. Moreover, the Appellate Body has noted that increasing interdependence could give members a greater interest in compliance with the rules, since any non-compliance could affect them directly or indirectly.[49] To the extent that it

[49] 'We ... agree with the Panel's statement that "with the increased interdependence of the global economy, ... Members have a greater stake in enforcing WTO rules than in the past since any deviation from the negotiated balance of rights and obligations is

incorporates expectations of competitive relations, this conception of injury might appear to give the proceedings a declaratory slant, since instead of concerning the effect of the legal rule the complaint concerns only its presuppositions. However, this does not preclude us from seeing in this the exercise of a judicial function. The underlying principle arouses mistrust because of the anticipative element, but no legal system can reject it completely inasmuch as it enables another trial in aggravated circumstances to be avoided. In any event, the system remains in balance because these presumptions in favour of the complainant are offset by another presumption in favour of the defendant. Thus, the defendant is presumed to be fulfilling his obligations in good faith as long as no evidence to the contrary has been adduced and it is only once such evidence has been adduced that injury is deemed to have been established, which may explain why it is only from that moment on that, if the slate is not wiped clean by bringing the measure into conformity, compensation may be envisaged.

The second requirement associated with the material criterion – ruling in accordance with the law in force – also appears to be satisfied, both in principle and in practice. DSU Articles 3.4 and 3.7 call for a solution consistent with WTO law and it is possible to speak of a solution based in law irrespective of the question of the 'quality' of that law, that is to say, whether substantively it is weakly or strongly binding, precise or imprecise, or possibly characterized by lacunae. These latter characteristics are more related with the extent of the discretion allowed to whoever states the law. Moreover, even though the settlement bodies do their best to avoid *obiter dicta*, the effect of the operation of the dispute settlement mechanism is to reinforce the prescriptiveness of the covered agreements[50] inasmuch as it serves not only 'to preserve the rights and obligations of Members under the covered agreements' but also 'to clarify the existing provisions of those agreements in accordance with customary rules of interpretation of public international law' (Article 3.2). It is therefore indeed an issue of law.[51] The fact that the mission of the settlement bodies is to rule not in terms

more likely than ever to affect them, directly or indirectly"': see Appellate Body Report, *EC – Bananas III*, paragraph 136.

50 The appeal procedure further reinforces this aspect since it is exclusively devoted to the consideration of points of law.

51 The fact that the mechanism can be used for cases of non-violation does not discredit the analysis, inasmuch as the procedure is then modified to operate as a conciliation process.

of the whole of international law but only in accordance with WTO law, albeit including all the external rules that it incorporates by reference,[52] does not prevent us from considering that mission as being to state the law and establish the status of the disputed measure in relation to that law. It means only that the dispute settlement mechanism corresponds to a specialized 'court'[53] which, however, claims not to operate in 'clinical isolation'.[54] Nor does the highly technical nature of the rules applied compromise per se the judicial basis of the function performed.

The requirement that solutions must be consistent with the Agreements (Article 3.5) and must not add to or diminish the rights and obligations of members in no way prevents their being viewed as *jurisdictio*. It simultaneously expresses a prohibition on according any normative power to the settlement body, the exercise of which might disturb the balance derived from the negotiations which at the same time constitutes the law as it stands, and a prohibition on any compromise settlement which, while reconciling the parties, would not be consistent with the general rules they have accepted and the commitments they have made in their schedules of concessions (which cannot be modified at their convenience on a bilateral basis). The second of these prohibitions simply refers to the application and hence the statement of the law. As for the first, it might appear to be associated with a conception of the judge as a 'mouthpiece for the law', reasoning by mere syllogisms. It could simply be objected that this conception is scarcely realistic and, moreover, that it has now been abandoned in those systems of internal law which may have adopted it. In addition, it may appear to conflict with the explicit bestowal of powers of interpretation. The contradiction becomes less apparent if these powers of interpretation are reduced to the status of a mere directive.[55] However this may be, it is the scope of the judicial power rather than its principle which is ultimately at issue.

[52] For example, external law or sources of rules mentioned in the Agreement on Trade-Related Intellectual Property Rights or the Agreement on the Application of Sanitary and Phytosanitary Measures.

[53] It is only indirectly, that is to say through interpretation, that other rules of international law can be taken into account.

[54] See Appellate Body Report, *United States – Standards for Reformulated and Conventional Gasoline*, WT/DS2/AB/R, 20 May 1996, p. 17; see also, G. Marceau, 'A Call for Coherence in International Law: Praises for the Prohibition Against "Clinical Isolation" in WTO Dispute Settlement' (1999) 5 *Journal of World Trade* 87.

[55] The authentic power of interpretation remains in the hands of the plenary political bodies, which could use it to overthrow a 'judicial' interpretation which did not suit them. This is something they have never yet done and, in practice, it seems hardly likely that they would act in this way.

Thus, the criteria for deeming the dispute settlement mechanism to be a court responsible for settling disputes by stating the law may, without too much difficulty, be considered to have been met. However, the case for a judicial system is not yet complete and it remains to examine the final decision, taken at the end of the proceedings when not only the obligation to enforce it but also the manner of its enforcement make their formal appearance, all within the context of a broad conception of *imperium*.

Imperium

The classical approach would lead only to a consideration of the bindingness of the decision. Taking the question of its enforceability into account allows us to adopt a rather more systemic approach, embracing the significance and effects of the phase in which the measure is brought into conformity, which has no equivalent at the international level. This detour through enforcement to establish the existence of a court may seem rather curious; however, it provides a means of determining whether the originality of the dispute settlement mechanism in this respect confirms that we are not really in a judicial environment or, on the contrary, expresses an unusual firmness of intention to ensure the execution of judgments.

Leaving aside certain decisions resulting from arbitration, dispute settlement mechanism decisions are made binding by the DSB's adoption of the panel report, as amended by the Appellate Body report if there has been an appeal. Insofar as it is traditional to associate the bindingness of the decision taken with the element of proclamation of the legal truth in order to define the judicial function, and to speak in connection with the former of the force of *res judicata*, it seems logical, if we are to carry the analysis through to its conclusion, to examine whether the bindingness of DSB decisions can indeed be ascribed to the force of *res judicata* and hence investigate its nature and scope.

The fact that the term *res judicata* is not used is not in itself an obstacle to its being employed, but in this particular case the analysis is complicated by the separation of the body which proclaims the legal truth from the body which formally takes the decision.[56] No matter how explicit or

[56] The *res judicata* argument has already been made before a panel and the way in which the panel dealt with it, circumventing it without settling it, shows at least that the issue cannot be resolved merely by finding that the body which takes the decision is political.

implicit the references to it in the DSU may be,[57] the acquisition of binding effect presupposes that the formality of adoption by the DSB has been completed. By virtue of the characteristics of the decision procedure, this adoption is automatic,[58] so that a binding settlement based in law may be regarded as guaranteed as soon as the procedure is initiated. This corresponds closely to the judicial case, subject to the reservation that the decision is formally taken by a political body. However, it may be worth recalling that 'the bindingness generally considered inherent in the notion of a judgement, at least in its "*res judicata*" aspect, is entirely external to the activity consisting in stating the law' and that it 'is attributable to the delegation of part of the *imperium* to the body responsible for stating the law'.[59] This delegation is difficult to discern in the WTO mechanism, because of the above-mentioned organic disjunction. However, this is only a problem if it is desired to give the nature of the body precedence over that of the function, not if it is accepted that a political body can perform or contribute to a judicial function.

Irrespective of the issue of *res judicata*, the authority in question is relative, that is to say, limited to the parties to the dispute. Panel and Appellate Body reports adopted by the DSB do not constitute subsequent practice as contemplated in Article 31.3.b of the Vienna Convention on the Law of Treaties and the interpretations they contain cannot be regarded as binding on all members, even though in practice they undoubtedly shape their behaviour.[60] This position, which would conflict with the express devolution of authentic powers of interpretation to the Ministerial Conference or the

See Panel Report, *India – Measures Affecting the Automotive Sector*, WT/DS146/AB/R, 5 April 2002, paragraph 7.59.

57 According to DSU Article 17.14, an Appellate Body report shall be adopted by the DSB and 'unconditionally accepted by the parties to the dispute' and, although no such clarification is provided concerning panel reports, the existence of this binding effect can be inferred from both DSU Article 3.7 and the terms of Article 21.1 according to which 'prompt compliance with recommendations or rulings of the DSB is essential'. This provision has been interpreted by the arbitrators called upon to rule on the implementation period as establishing a principle of immediate execution, which presupposes that the recommendations are binding.

58 Subject to inclusion on the agenda.

59 Ascensio, 'La notion de juridiction', p. 178.

60 The previous decisions concerning Article 3.4 of the Anti-dumping Agreement offer a good example. See Appellate Body Report, *Thailand – Anti-dumping Duties on H-Beams from Poland*, WT/DS122/AB/R, 5 April 2001. Whatever the criticisms that may be made of an interpretation that adds to the investigative burden on national administrations, members nevertheless align themselves on its requirements.

General Council, has been rejected by the Appellate Body.[61] In the DSU itself the binding effects of adopted reports are considered only in relation to the parties to the dispute and translated into a duty of implementation on their part when the recommendations of the DSB so require. Finally, a further argument can be derived from the situation of third parties, which are not bound by the recommendations.

With regard to enforceability, it might be argued that, although it is always possible, for reasons of efficiency, to invest a court with powers relating to enforcement, these powers are external to the judicial function and examining them would therefore contribute nothing to the characterization of a system as judicial. However, there is something to be learnt from the compliance phase and the legal and institutional surveillance system incorporated in the dispute settlement mechanism, which appears to set it apart from the usual model of an international court.

On the one hand, the compliance phase throws light on the configuration of the initial phase and includes several procedures which lead back to the judicial bodies.[62] The careful regulation of the compliance phase is doubtless associated with the fact that the injury, since it is not made good, should at least be ended as quickly as possible. In this respect, it is significant that the principle is immediate execution and, failing that, priority for negotiations between the parties concerning both the time limits for implementation and possible compensation. Moreover, if the parties cannot agree on implementation, they have at their disposal several procedures which take them back to the judicial bodies (in particular, those of DSU Articles 21.5 and 22.6). The place occupied by *jurisdictio* at the very heart of a phase corresponding *a priori* exclusively to *imperium* helps to give that phase substantive coherence relative to the law stated in the initial phase, thereby endowing the latter with a special force.

On the other hand, this phase, though original as compared with the other international courts, does not make WTO dispute settlement so very different from the usual model. The general diagnosis of lack

[61] GATT period reports, even if adopted, cannot be described as subsequent practice of the parties to the Treaty since they have no binding effect outside the circle of the parties to the dispute and, moreover, do not constitute an authentic and definitive interpretation. See Appellate Body Report, *Japan – Taxes on Alcoholic Beverages II*, WT/DS8/AB/R, 1 November 1996, paragraph 16.

[62] H. Ruiz Fabri, 'Le contentieux de l'exécution dans le règlement des différends de l'OMC' (2000) 2 *JDI* 605.

of enforceability of decisions of the international courts[63] is linked with the finding that the beneficiary of the decision lacks access to means of enforcement whose effectiveness is, in principle, guaranteed. Nevertheless, coercion is not inconceivable under the international system.[64] It is merely that it is generally associated with intergovernmental countermeasures and much less frequently with centralized and/or institutionalized mechanisms. Although WTO dispute settlement makes unprecedented provision for enforcement, the various remedies of the compliance phase, while intended to facilitate implementation and allowing the 'judge' to offer guidance,[65] do not enforce implementation in themselves. More generally, the compliance phase is only comparable with an attempt to enforce implementation to the extent that the monitoring of the situation by the DSB puts pressure on the member concerned.[66] Otherwise everything still ends, in the case of persistent non-implementation, in countermeasures taken by the initial complainant or complainants, though their utilization is governed, from the procedural viewpoint, by the need for prior multilateral authorization and, from the substantive viewpoint, by the principle of equivalence (the observance of which can be verified). Thus, the system has a compensatory rather than a punitive purpose. Accordingly, a member which fails to implement continues to benefit from a presumption of good faith – a mere fiction against all the evidence? No doubt, but a functional fiction since, without it, the system would not stand the strain, at least as far as its procedures for maintaining balance are

[63] This (characteristic) can be viewed as corresponding to part of the *imperium* that has not been delegated to the court, the term *imperium* being used here to designate the power to issue orders in respect of persons present in some area, in this case a normative area.

[64] On the other hand, the lack of enforceability of decisions of the international courts in internal law is well established, the preference being for a wholly dualistic approach. Although the principle may well be debatable, the approach itself corresponds closely to the general situation of WTO law.

[65] DSU Article 19 provides that 'in addition to its recommendations, the panel or Appellate Body may suggest ways in which the Member concerned could implement the recommendations'. However, in practice, apart from the field of subsidies which has its own special regime, there appears to be reluctance on the part of panels and the Appellate Body which prefer, even when requested to make such suggestions, not to do so and to cite the traditional freedom of choice of means enjoyed by governments. See Panel Report, *United States – DRAMs* (not yet reported), paragraph 7.4 and Award of the Arbitrator, *EC – Bananas III*, paragraph 38.

[66] The issue normally remains on the DSB's agenda until implementation is complete, and the member concerned must submit a status report prior to each meeting of the DSB.

concerned, as it is already clear that, even in its present configuration, the compliance phase is far from having demonstrated its efficacy.[67] Many of the authorized countermeasures are never actually applied. Here again, this retrospectively illuminates the way in which injury is treated from the initial phase onwards, inasmuch as implementing countermeasures is a much less complicated affair than establishing a system of compensation (consider, for example, the calculation of the compensation, the form it should take, the procedures for awarding it, etc.). There is a logic in this (which could of course be challenged) in that the system eliminates the compensation dimension even though it does not eliminate the injury.[68] Again, this does not prevent us from concluding that the system is judicial.

Conclusion

Despite the conviction that the dispute settlement mechanism does in fact have all the characteristics of a court, there remains the question of the reluctance to describe it as such, which leads people to prefer to use the term 'quasi-judicial'. The crux of the matter seems to be the role of the DSB. This is indicative of a problem of balance of powers within the WTO system and hence of a problem of legitimacy.

Even though, theoretically, it might be argued that the political nature of the DSB does not prevent the DSB from participating in the performance of a judicial function and does not preclude the mechanism, viewed in its totality, from being described as judicial, this political intervention nevertheless continues to be viewed as an obstacle to, or rather a bulwark against, such a description. There lies its importance since, while formal from the standpoint of the decision, this intervention is functional from the standpoint of the system. Even though adoption

[67] P. Monnier, 'Système de rétorsions de l'Organisation mondiale du commerce: les Membres de l'OMC jouent-ils aux échecs comme des billes ou jouent-ils aux billes comme des nuls?'(2003) *International Law Forum du Droit International* 47.

[68] The problem arose, e.g., in Panel Report, *Australia – Subsidies Provided to Producers and Exporters of Automotive Leather (Article 21.5 – US)*, WT/DS126/RW, 11 February 2000, where the issue of the repayment of subsidies improperly received was considered. See also, H. Ascensio, 'La portée temporelle des décisions de l'ORD: quelles conséquences pour les bénéficiaires de l'aide considérée comme illicite?' in J.-M. Thouvenin (ed.), *Le contrôle des aides publiques à l'industrie aéronautique civile: le point sur les réglementations communautaire et internationale* (PUF, Paris, 2000), p. 165; Ruiz Fabri, 'Le contentieux de l'exécution'.

may never be in doubt,[69] the phase leading up to adoption nevertheless provides an opportunity for members to engage in a debate, which can be particularly interesting if one focuses – as judges generally do – on the question of the 'social acceptability' of the solution. Moreover, this debate may seem all the more necessary in that the WTO's institutional and decision-making structure is so out of balance. The political decision does not have the importance it should. Thus, certain mechanisms, such as the various committees for administering the Agreements, which should function as 'political filters'[70] and keep dispute settlement within bounds, do not really work.[71] But this is only one of the effects of preserving, with the notable exception of dispute settlement, the old mode of decision-taking, namely, consensus, even though the WTO Charter opened up the option of multiple recourse to voting.[72] Consensus, though good enough for a 'club' such as the GATT, acts as a blocking mechanism in an organization on the scale of the WTO. In these circumstances, the intervention of the DSB provides a strategic opportunity for discussing and criticizing the decisions of the 'judge'. The opportunity should therefore not be missed, at pain of endowing that judge with extreme powers. These powers are in fact even greater

[69] Particularly as every attempt to introduce qualifications has so far been firmly rejected. See Appellate Body Report, *India – Autos*, where India's attempt to obtain separate treatment for different parts of the report in terms of adoption, and hence to accommodate selective adoption, met with the firm refusal of the other members, in particular the European Community.

[70] C.-D. Ehlermann, *Some Personal Experiences as Member of the Appellate Body of the WTO* (Robert Schuman Center Policy Paper 02/9), p. 38.

[71] Thus, the Appellate Body Report, *Turkey – Restriction on Imports of Textile and Clothing Products*, WT/DS34/AB/R, 19 November 1999, brought out the disadvantages associated with the non-functioning of the Committee on Regional Trade Agreements. The same applies to the Committee on Balance of Payments Restrictions as illustrated by the Appellate Body Report, *India – Quantitative Restrictions on Imports of Agricultural, Textile and Industrial Products*, WT/DS90/AB/R, 22 September 1999.

[72] The situation is ambiguous. Thus, according to WTO Charter Article IX paragraph 1, 'The WTO shall continue the practice of decision-making by consensus followed under the GATT 1947 (the body concerned shall be deemed to have decided by consensus on a matter submitted for its consideration, if no Member, present at the meeting when the decision is taken, formally objects to the proposed decision). Except as otherwise provided, where a decision cannot be arrived at by consensus, the matter at issue shall be decided by voting. . . . Decisions of the Ministerial Conference and the General Council shall be taken by a majority of the votes cast, unless otherwise provided in this Agreement or in the relevant Multilateral Trade Agreement (Decisions by the General Council when convened as the Dispute Settlement Body shall be taken only in accordance with the provisions of paragraph 4 of Article 2 of the Dispute Settlement Understanding)'.

than those conferred by most internal systems. In the latter, politics retains (at least relatively speaking) the right to have the last word, by resorting to the ratification of decisions (when possible) or to legislative or indeed constitutional reform. Admittedly, this is theoretically also possible in the WTO,[73] except that to 'reverse' a previous decision there must be unanimity (since this is what consensus implies) and that applies both to the adoption of a decision on interpretation and to a reform of the law, the latter being even more difficult in that it involves an amendment[74] or renegotiation of the Agreements.

Through a backlash effect, this situation prevents the judge from asserting himself too openly. In a way, he is caught on the horns of a dilemma. On the one hand, unlike the political bodies, he is obliged to deal with the cases brought before him (as required by DSU Article 3.2) and therefore cannot evade taking a decision on the pretext that it would be politically sensitive. On the other hand, the mere fact of deciding proportionally increases the risk of adding to what already exists and making choices of a political nature, and hence directly conjuring up the spectre of 'government by judges' (note that it is not the judge's making of political choices that shocks, since it would be saintly and even contrary to the nature of the law if he were not to). In these circumstances, the judges are reduced to self-limitation. This is discernible, in particular, in the customary, highly casuistical approach to dispute settlement and the tendency of the reports to 'overjustify'.[75] The power to state the law must therefore be handled with caution. This is all the more true in that, although anyone may aspire to state the law, not everyone can expect not to have that statement treated merely as a subjective opinion concerning the law as it stands. To identify those genuinely entitled to act in this capacity, it is necessary to proceed upstream, beyond *jurisdictio*, to identify the authorizing entity and hence detect 'the presence of a community governed by the rule of law "behind" the court', since 'it is this community that provides the basis for the legitimacy of the institution and invests it with the

[73] According to Article IX paragraph 2, 'the Ministerial Conference and the General Council shall have the exclusive authority to adopt interpretations of this Agreement and of the Multilateral Trade Agreements ... The decision to adopt an interpretation shall be taken by a three-fourths majority of the Members. This paragraph shall not be used in a manner that would undermine the amendment provisions in Article X'.

[74] The procedure for which is singularly complicated. See Article X of the WTO Charter.

[75] Ehlermann, *Some Personal Experiences*, p. 36.

"public" element contained in the idea of legal obligation'.[76] It remains to be seen whether the WTO can be regarded as a community governed by the rule of law. It is not the least of the merits of the initial members of the Appellate Body, foremost among them Justice Feliciano, to have given it a decisive push in that direction.

[76] Ascensio, 'La notion de juridiction', p. 180.

13

A Proposal to Introduce an Advocate General's Position into WTO Dispute Settlement

A. L. C. DE MESTRAL AND M. AUERBACH-ZIOGAS

Introduction

Thanks to the legal statesmanship of members of the World Trade Organisation (WTO) Appellate Body and to support of WTO members, the legal procedures established under the Understanding on Rules and Procedures Governing the Settlement of Disputes (DSU) have enjoyed very considerable success. But the DSU remains a work in progress. Much can still be done to develop and refine this process. A host of issues, some reflecting policy choices, some more strictly legal, remain to be resolved. By no means have all the concerns of negotiators in 1994 been answered. Some have proven to be well-founded, and new problems have arisen which challenge both the procedures and the rules of the DSU. As a contribution to the search for solutions, this chapter proposes the creation of a new position attached to the DSU process – that of the Advocate General.

The Advocate General (AG) would participate in WTO dispute settlement procedures. A roster of Advocates General should be created to serve both panels and the Appellate Body. Given the nature of the function, the roster should be composed exclusively of jurists, knowledgeable in WTO procedure and law, and would be selected by the Dispute Settlement Body (DSB). An AG would be designated to follow each dispute. His or her principal function would be to participate in the dispute settlement procedures from the point that a panel is constituted to the point that the Appellate Body has rendered its decision. The AG would receive a copy of party submissions and *amicus curiae* briefs submitted to the panel for consideration. Subsequent to the completion of written party presentations and submissions to the panel, and prior to the panel's oral deliberations, the AG would be responsible for submitting to the panel an 'AG's Report' which articulates the legal and policy issues posed by the case. The AG's Report could also advise the panel regarding which of the *amicus* briefs ought to be consulted, and evaluate the factual evidence and the legal arguments expressed in the selected briefs. The AG's Report would be strictly non-binding, although the panel members would be encouraged to consider the AG's Report carefully prior to releasing the panel report. The AG's Report would be released to the public with the release of the panel report.

In the event that the panel report is appealed by one or more of the parties, the AG would continue to be involved with the dispute at the Appellate Body level. At the conclusion of Appellate Body written proceedings, the AG would be responsible for submitting to the Appellate Body a new report which re-evaluates the legal and policy issues posed by the case. Once again, the AG's Report could advise the Appellate Body regarding which of the *amicus* briefs to the Appellate Body ought to be consulted, and evaluate the legal and policy arguments expressed in the selected briefs. In the AG's Report to the Appellate Body, the AG has the additional task of remarking upon any shift in the parties' legal positions that may not be apparent from the complete record of the panel proceeding, transmitted to the Appellate Body under Rule 25 of the Working Procedures for Appellate Review.[1] The AG's Reports would also be released to the public with the release of the Appellate Body report. Similarly, the AG would be called upon to participate in any subsequent enforcement proceedings arising out of a panel or Appellate Body decision. It is hoped that the AG could contribute to the DSU procedures in the same highly positive way that Advocates General contribute to the work of the European Court of Justice (ECJ) and the Court of First Instance (CFI), and to the work of many other civil and administrative courts.

Implementation of the proposal

Model for the Advocate General

The ECJ and CFI, and the WTO panels and Appellate Body, are tribunals in intergovernmental organizations that deliver single consensus-based opinions.[2] Nevertheless, the institution of the AG cannot be

[1] WTO, Working Procedures for Appellate Review, WT/AB/WP/4, 24 January 2002, Article 25.1.

[2] A. Arnull *et al.*, *Wyatt and Dashwoods' European Union Law* (Sweet and Maxwell, London, 2000), p. 205.

transplanted wholesale from EC law. The role of the AG, in both the ECJ and the CFI, is strongly related to the provision of legal reasoning. A putative AG position in the WTO might not be concerned, to the same extent, with legal reasoning. Many of the concerns of non-governmental organizations (NGOs) in trade law issues are based on factual rather than legal assessments. For this reason the AG should not be restricted to considering the legal arguments made by NGOs. Despite superficial similarities between the WTO dispute settlement process, and the ECJ and CFI, certain fundamentals relating to the EC AG must be changed for application in the WTO.

The concept of the AG, although best known internationally as an aspect of ECJ practice, finds its origins in continental European civil and administrative tribunals. In the French Conseil d'Etat and the Cour de Cassation the Avocat Général is concerned to provide broad law and policy advice to courts whose formal decisions are rendered in very spare language, but which are frequently based on wide-ranging reflection upon the impact of a decision upon the legal system as well as upon a surprisingly open consideration of broader policy considerations.[3]

Although the proposal of the AG role has precedent in international legal literature, commentators suggesting such a position have failed to engage the details of how an AG would work under the DSU. This is unfortunate given that the efficacy of such a role depends largely on the details. It is therefore instructive to turn to the ECJ and CFI AG positions as a model. The AG role present in ECJ and some CFI proceedings derives loosely from the judge-rapporteur of French legal tradition, although the iteration of the AG role in EC law has undergone such change that it can be said to be novel in its own right.

Lasok states that 'in both the ECJ and the CFI, the advocate general assigned to a case assists the court by making a reasoned submission on the case in open court, acting with complete impartiality and independence but he does not participate in the deliberations between the judges that lead up to the making of the judgment'.[4] More specifically, the AG: (1) may present an oral opinion before the open court[5] with the option of submitting a written opinion reserved for judges and may

[3] See generally M. Lasser, 'Trois palais; deux styles?' in N. Kasirer (ed.), *Le droit civil, avant tout un style?* (Ed. Thémis, Montréal, 2003), pp. 1–38.

[4] K. P. E. Lasok, *The European Court of Justice* (2nd edn, London, Butterworths, 1994), p. 21.

[5] ECJ Rules of Procedure Article 59.1; CFI Rules of Procedure Article 61.

recommend to the court a particular conclusion on them; (2) may recommend further investigation; (3) may recommend that the case be referred to the full court or a larger chamber; or (4) may recommend that the oral procedure be re-opened.[6] Lasok notes that 'the court does not sit on appeal from the advocate general and in consequence the parties are not invited to comment on what he has said. The opinion is intended for the court, not the parties, which is why it is not formally served on them'.[7] The court is therefore not bound to follow the opinion of the AG, and is exclusively competent for appraising his judgment. Nevertheless, 'in the majority of cases, the judgment and its rationale follow the Advocate General's Opinion fairly closely'.[8] Furthermore, the court often refers expressly to the AG's Opinion without elaborating, and the Opinion is published alongside the judgment in European Court Reports so that it may be cited as authority in future cases, or in the legal literature.[9]

It is true that the 'duties of the Advocate General before the CFI are described in identical terms to those of the Advocate General before the ECJ'.[10] The differing roles of the two courts result in two functionally different conceptions of the AG, however, even if AGs in both courts theoretically have nearly identical duties. While AGs in the ECJ are taken from a pool of AGs assigned to the ECJ, and are mandatory in every case, AGs in CFI proceedings are appointed from the pool of CFI judges and are only called upon to serve on rare occasions. This difference was explained in the ECJ proposal for the creation of the CFI court: the proposal advised against the recourse to AGs in ordinary cases because 'the fundamental role of the Advocates General at the ECJ, that of assisting the ECJ in the development of Community law, was not indispensable in the CFI'.[11] In a compromise between this position and that of the Commission, AGs were designated only for certain CFI cases, to be determined on the basis of the CFI Rules of Procedure.[12]

AGs are, therefore, mandatory when the CFI sits in plenary session,[13] and absent in regular Chambers sessions, except where 'it is considered

[6] Lasok, *European Court of Justice*, p. 87. [7] *Ibid.* at pp. 87–8.
[8] Arnull, *Wyatt and Dashwood*, p. 196. [9] *Ibid.*
[10] T. Millet, *The Court of First Instance of the European Communities* (Butterworths, London, 1990), p. 16.
[11] *Ibid.* at p. 15.
[12] Council Decision of 24 October 1988 establishing a Court of First Instance of the European Communities, 88/591/ECSC, EEC, Euratom.
[13] See CFI Rules of Procedure Article 17.

that the legal difficulty or the factual complexity of the case so requires'.[14] The former situation rarely occurs because it is very rare for the CFI to sit in plenary session.[15] In the latter situation, parties may request the appointment of an AG, but it is up to the chamber to pass the recommendation on, and it is up to the court in plenary session actually to appoint an AG.[16] Despite the mention in the CFI Rules of Procedure that AGs might be appointed when 'the factual complexity of the case so requires', this has not been shown to be the primary motivator. Bo Vesterdorf, who has since been appointed President of the CFI, noted in an article published in 1992 that after two years of operation of the CFI, the AG had only been appointed outside of plenary session four times out of 317 cases.[17] In each of those four cases, an AG was appointed because there were legal questions of great importance to be answered, and 'no unambiguous case law on the matters raised'.[18] AGs in the CFI, at least until 1992, therefore seem to have been more concerned with legal determinations than fact-gathering or policy concerns external to the management of EC law.

Form of implementation

The method by which the proposal might be implemented must be discussed as a preliminary matter. Depending upon the method of implementation, the nature of the AG position might differ. Upon examination of the relevant agreements, namely the Agreement Establishing the World Trade Organization ('the WTO Agreement'), Annex 2 to the WTO Agreement entitled the Understanding on Rules and Procedures Governing the Settlement of Disputes (DSU), and the Working Procedures for Appellate Review, it appears that there are four methods by which the proposal might be implemented.

First, the proposal might be implemented by amending the DSU to include the creation of a roster of Advocates General. This method would allow the introduction of the proposal in its totality and would ensure the greatest degree of legitimacy. It is also the most demanding method of introducing the proposal. Under WTO Agreement Article X:8

[14] CFI Rules of Procedure Article 18. [15] Arnull, *Wyatt and Dashwood*, p. 205.

[16] Lasok, *European Court of Justice*, p. 31.

[17] B. Vesterdorf, 'The Court of First Instance of the European Communities after Two Full Years in Operation' (1992) 29 *CML Rev.* 897 at 905.

[18] *Ibid.* at 906–12.

unanimity among the members of the WTO is required for any amendment of the DSU.[19] This would, in effect, give all members of the WTO a veto over every detail of the AG position. Implementation of the proposal through amendment would therefore dramatically lessen the likelihood of early implementation in its entirety, and probably the likelihood of its implementation altogether.

Secondly, the proposal might be introduced by amendment to the Working Procedures for the panel, and for the Appellate Body. The Panel Working Procedures are contained in Appendix 3 to the DSU, and it would therefore appear that amendment to these Procedures would carry the same unanimity requirement as a direct amendment to the text of the DSU. The goal of drafters of the DSU in subjecting the Working Procedures to such a rigorous amendment requirement is unclear. A method of avoiding the unanimity requirement might be found in Article 11 of the Panel Working Procedures,[20] which subjects the panel to 'any additional procedures specific to the Panel'. The Chairperson of the DSB might draft 'additional procedures' within the meaning of Article 11 that would implement the AG position in all its particulars. Although the Chairperson would certainly be expected to consult the members in drafting such a position, this would not incorporate a unanimity requirement.

The amendment of the Working Procedures for Appellate Review is far more straightforward. DSU Article 17.9 states that 'working procedures shall be drawn up by the Appellate Body in consultation with the Chairman of the DSB and the Director-General, and communicated to the Members for their information'.[21] Once again, this amendment mechanism avoids the unanimity requirement of DSU amendments. It should be noted, however, that the DSB has committed itself to offer members a chance to comment on any amendments and will 'request

[19] Agreement Establishing the World Trade Organization, 15 April 1994, 33 ILM 1144, Article X:8 ('Any Member of the WTO may initiate a proposal to amend the provisions of the Multilateral Trade Agreements in Annexes 2 and 3 by submitting such proposal to the Ministerial Conference. The decision to approve amendments to the Multilateral Trade Agreement in Annex 2 shall be made by consensus and these amendments shall take effect for all Members upon approval by the Ministerial Conference. Decisions to approve amendments to the Multilateral Trade Agreement in Annex 3 shall take effect for all Members upon approval by the Ministerial Conference').

[20] Agreement Establishing the World Trade Organization, Annex 2: Understanding on Rules and Procedures Governing the Settlement of Disputes, 15 April 1994, 33 ILM 112, Appendix 3.

[21] DSU Article 17.9. See Working Procedures for Appellate Review Article 32.2.

the Appellate Body to take them into account'.[22] Nothing suggests that reception of conflicting comments by different members, some supporting amendments and some opposing them, would compel the Appellate Body into inaction. Indeed, the contrast between the successful amendments to the Working Procedures for Appellate Review in January 2002,[23] and the Doha Round proposed amendments to the DSU which linger unimplemented, suggests the greater flexibility of the former method.

Thirdly, both panels and the Appellate Body have the authority to adopt ad hoc changes to the Working Procedures. DSU Article 12.1 states that 'Panels shall follow the Working Procedures in Appendix 3 unless the Panel decides otherwise after consulting the parties to the dispute'.[24] This provision gives panels broad control of their procedures on a case-by-case basis, with the caveat that the procedures contained in the text of the DSU itself cannot be deviated from. It might be argued that the invitation of an Advocate General to participate in a panel proceeding is not precluded by the DSU text. The only restriction for the types of ad hoc procedures that panels may adopt is in DSU Article 12.2, which requires that 'Panel procedures should provide sufficient flexibility so as to ensure high-quality Panel reports, while not unduly delaying the Panel process'.[25] The AG position would arguably enhance the proceedings. Given the fact that panel members are drawn from a roster, and not a standing body, however, it seems unlikely that any panel would use the discretion granted in the DSU to implement something as complicated as the proposal. Remuneration of a person whose role is not envisaged by the DSU would also present problems.

Similarly, the Appellate Body can adopt ad hoc procedures under Article 16.1 of the Working Procedures for Appellate Review, which states:

> In the interests of fairness and orderly procedure in the conduct of an appeal, where a procedural question arises that is not covered by these Rules, a division may adopt an appropriate procedure for the purposes of that appeal only, provided that it is not inconsistent with the DSU, the other covered agreements and these Rules. Where such a procedure is

[22] WTO Dispute Settlement Body, Additional Procedures for Consultations between the Chairperson of the DSB and WTO Members in relation to Amendments to the Working Procedures for Appellate Review, WT/DSB/31, 19 December 2002.

[23] See Working Procedures for Appellate Review, *supra* n. 1.

[24] DSU Article 12.1. [25] DSU Article 12.2.

> adopted, the Division shall immediately notify the participants and third participants in the appeal as well as the other Members of the Appellate Body.[26]

Despite the broad discretion granted to the Appellate Body in this provision, past attempts to exercise this discretion have caused considerable unease among WTO members. In the Appellate Body hearing of *EC – Asbestos*, the Appellate Body submitted a detailed set of requirements for the submission of *amicus* briefs, under its Article 16.1 ad hoc authority, which was posted on the WTO website.[27] Despite the sitting members' careful consultation of the parties and third parties to the case, as well as the four other members of the Appellate Body, the issuance of additional procedures under Article 16.1 sparked immediate reaction from certain DSB members, particularly among developing countries.[28]

All but one of the DSB members speaking at a special session of the WTO General Council, called by Egypt in response to the procedures released by the Appellate Body, criticized the Appellate Body for exceeding its mandate under Article 16.1 and for usurping General Council authority under Article V:2 of the WTO Agreement to 'make arrangements for consultation and cooperation with non-governmental organizations concerned with matters related to those of the WTO'.[29] Summing up the members' objections, the Chair of the special meeting concluded that 'the Appellate Body should exercise extreme caution in future cases until Members have considered what rules are needed'.[30] Possibly in response to this negative reaction, the Appellate Body rejected some seventeen *amicus* briefs submitted for consideration in *EC – Asbestos*.[31] Although one cannot be certain regarding the Appellate Body's motivations, at least one of the delegates was confident that the special session of the General Council had had its desired effect.[32]

26 Working Procedures for Appellate Review Article 16.1.

27 See Appellate Body Report, *European Communities – Measures Affecting Asbestos and Asbestos – Containing Products*, WT/DS135/AB/R, 5 April 2001, paragraphs 50–1.

28 See D. B. Hollis, 'Private Actors in Public International Law: Amicus Curiae and the Case for the Retention of State Sovereignty' (2002) 25 *BC Int'l and Comp. L Rev.* 235 at 251–6.

29 See *ibid.* at 252–3 (citing WTO General Council, Minutes of WTO General Council Meeting, WT/GC/M/60, 22 November 2000).

30 *Ibid.* at 253 (citing WTO General Council Minutes at paragraph 120).

31 Appellate Body Report, *EC – Asbestos*, paragraphs 55–7.

32 See Steve Charnovitz, 'Opening the WTO to Nongovernmental Interests' (2000) 24 *Fordham Int'l LJ* 173 at 189.

The WTO members' reactions at the General Council special meeting, although without strict legal significance, must be considered carefully given the absence of any mechanism for direct review of Appellate Body reports, save unanimous opposition to the report among members.[33] Members objected to the substantive import of the ostensibly procedural guidelines set out by the Appellate Body.[34] Still, the members' objections did not seem to be aimed at the content of the procedures per se, so much as the Appellate Body's earlier decisions in such cases as *US – Lead and Bismuth II*[35] and *US – Shrimp*[36] to allow the consultation of unsolicited *amicus* briefs at all. The guidelines released by the Appellate Body under Article 16.1 were not the central issue in the ensuing controversy. The guidelines, though drawing additional NGO attention to the possibility of submitting *amicus* briefs, merely sparked indignation at a controversial decision that had already been made by the Appellate Body. By adopting this approach, one does not have to infer limitations on the scope of Article 16.1 from the members' opposition to the *amicus* brief guidelines issued in *EC – Asbestos*, and the Appellate Body's subsequent backing down. However, given that one of the elements of the proposal is a mechanism by which *amicus* briefs might be effectively presented to panels and the Appellate Body, implementation of the proposal through Article 16.1 would run the obvious risk of re-igniting the hostile reaction encountered during the *EC – Asbestos* proceedings.

Fourth, and lastly, the proposal might be implemented through the provisions allowing the Secretariat to provide legal support to panel and Appellate Body. The Secretariat is obliged to assist 'panels, especially on the legal, historical and procedural aspects of the matters dealt with' in DSU Article 27.1.[37] Furthermore, DSU Article 17.7 states that 'The Appellate Body shall be provided with appropriate administrative and legal support as it requires'.[38] Although Article 17.7 does not stipulate which organ of the WTO is responsible for providing this support, one

[33] See DSU, *supra* note 22, Article 17.14.

[34] See, e.g., Hollis, 'Private Actors', 254 (citing in note 85 Canadian views noting that issues surrounding participation 'could not be characterized as exclusively procedural').

[35] Appellate Body Report, *United States – Imposition of Countervailing Duties on Certain Hot-rolled Lead and Bismuth Carbon Steel Products Originating in the UK II*, WT/DS 138/AB/R, 7 June 2000.

[36] Appellate Body Report, *United States – Import Prohibition of Certain Shrimp and Shrimp Products*, WT/DS58/AB/R, 6 November 1998.

[37] DSU Article 27.1. [38] DSU Article 17.7.

must assume that there is an implicit reference to the Secretariat, since it is the only relevant bureaucracy. The Secretariat could partially fulfil both of these mandates by formalizing its commitment of support in the creation of an office of the AG. Such a move would not interfere with the role of the AG as a means of distancing the Secretariat from panel proceedings as long as the Secretariat provided for selection of the AG by independent means, in effect delegating nomination to other elements of the WTO.[39]

Advantages to be derived from the presence of an Advocate General

A number of advantages could be derived from implementation of this proposal. Foremost would be the strengthening of the fidelity of the DSU process to law. The AG could play a role in ensuring that systemic issues, such as the integrity of the WTO Agreements, are put to panels and the Appellate Body in a manner that reflects the coherence of the DSU legal system, as well as analysing the issues raised by new legal questions. An AG is ideally situated to ventilate issues pertaining to difficult factual, procedural, and legal matters. The presence of an AG could contribute to the development of a workable mechanism for the introduction of *amicus* briefs, as well as ensuring that the Secretariat maintain a proper distance from panel proceedings. The AG could also contribute to the improvement of continuity of the file as considered by the panel and subsequently by the Appellate Body. Finally, it is hoped that the AG could promote the popular legitimacy of WTO dispute settlement. The introduction of an AG position, or AG-like position, has been previously suggested in the context of many of these issues, although it does not appear that any commentator has previously undertaken a detailed analysis of what the AG position might look like, and how it might be implemented.

The Advocate General and fidelity to law: defending the integrity of the WTO agreements

The principal role to be played by the AG before panels and the Appellate Body would be the same as that played before other tribunals: to ensure fidelity to law. However scrupulous the lawyers representing the parties may be and however well-versed in the law of the GATT/WTO, their mandate is to win their case. Furthermore, they are usually

[39] This goal of the proposal is explained below, see *infra* text at n. 61.

lawyers in the permanent employ of their respective governments and thus strongly concerned to reflect a national interest. Even in those rare situations where both parties agree as to a matter of law this does not ensure that the position they adopt jointly will be faithful to the letter and the spirit of the law which the panel or the Appellate Body is required to apply in the particular case. It must often happen that the interests of neither party are best served by scrupulous adherence to the text of the WTO Agreement in question. More generally, as in any pleading, the quality of the arguments of the parties can have a determining influence. This is all the more true in international litigation where the parties frame the ambit of the dispute. But while the parties must be free to frame the dispute, they should not be free to determine its outcome.

The presence of an AG before panels and the Appellate Body would reinforce fidelity to law in that the AG could address systemic issues such as the extent to which certain matters are settled and where other matters are not settled or may be ripe for change or new analysis. Where legal matters are before a panel for the first time, the memorandum of the AG would allow for a wider-ranging analysis of issues and options available. The AG could also address issues of common concern to the general membership of the WTO, something which is not always done, even in cases attracting a large number of interveners. The AG might also be able to address issues of fact in a more dispassionate fashion than either party to the dispute, or to deal openly with procedural matters that are not well resolved by the text of the WTO agreement under consideration.

The Advocate General and continuity between the panel and Appellate Body

Upon appeal, the Advocate General who has presented a report at the panel hearing should also participate in proceedings before the Appellate Body in the same case. At the subsequent hearing, the report submitted by the AG might contain information regarding any shift in the parties' argument that might not be apparent from the 'full record' which the panel is obliged to transmit to the Appellate Body under Article 25 of the Working Procedures for Appellate Review.[40] The Appellate Body will benefit from the point of view of an individual

[40] Working Procedures for Appellate Review Article 25: '(1) Upon the filing of a Notice of Appeal, the Director-General of the WTO shall transmit forthwith to the Appellate

who has dealt with the dispute from the initial stages of the formal dispute, and who was privy to the tenor of the discussions at panel level that may not be evident on the face of the written submissions. This additional information may be useful in assessing parties' claims, particularly with respect to the intended benefits of a discriminatory domestic trade restriction for which an Article XX exception is claimed.

The Advocate General and specialization of panellists and Appellate Body members

The Advocate General position might also be used as a means to introduce certain kinds of expertise into panel deliberations regarding specialized matters. The composition of panels is often rather homogenous, with reference in Article 8.1 only being made to diplomats, civil servants, and academics.[41] Trebilcock and Howse note the regrettable omission of mention of other categories of persons bringing additional expertise: activists, businessmen, environmentalists, experts in medical and sanitary matters, and other individuals who might bring specialized knowledge of the matter under dispute.[42] The Members of the Appellate Body almost have to be generalists by necessity, given the few members of the Body and the immense diversity of 'linkage'[43] issues which may arise.

Body the complete record of the panel proceeding. (2) The complete record of the panel proceeding includes, but is not limited to:

(i) written submissions, rebuttal submissions, and supporting evidence attached thereto by the parties to the dispute and the third parties;
(ii) written arguments submitted at the panel meetings with the parties to the dispute and the third parties, the recordings of such panel meetings, and any written answers to questions posed at such panel meetings;
(iii) the correspondence relating to the panel dispute between the panel or the WTO Secretariat and the parties to the dispute or the third parties; and
(iv) any other documentation submitted to the panel.'

41 DSU Article 8.1 ('Panels shall be composed of well-qualified governmental and/or non-governmental individuals, including persons who have served on or presented a case to a panel, served as a representative of a Member or of a contracting party to GATT 1947 or as a representative to the Council or Committee of any covered agreement or its predecessor agreement, or in the Secretariat, taught or published on international trade law or policy, or served as a senior trade policy official of a Member').

42 M. J. Trebilcock and R. Howse, *The Regulation of International Trade* (2nd edn, Routledge, New York, 2001), p. 64.

43 See J. E. Alvarez, 'How Not to Link: Institutional Conundrums of an Expanded Trade Regime' (2001) 7 *SPG Widener L Symp. J* 1.

In the context of environmental matters, Steve Charnovitz, inspired by the Advocates General who serve before the ECJ, has proposed the position of an 'Environmental Advocate' 'to speak for 'the environment' in WTO environmental disputes [and] work with NGOs and scientists to produce a report discussing the significance of the environmental treaty or law challenged in the WTO dispute resolution procedure'.[44] Similarly, the AG proposal here discussed could be brought to bear on the specialization issue by choosing Advocates General active and knowledgeable in the areas typically under dispute under the DSU. Although the AG position here proposed would not be conceived as an advocate for the environment, or any other specific cause, where the AG has an extended familiarity with the issue under consideration, the panel's ability to best make an 'objective assessment' only stands to benefit from the nomination of a person with specialized experience. The benefits of specialized experience might be obtained either by selection of candidates having experience in areas which frequently give rise to controversy, such as trade and environment issues or international standard setting or, if this proves difficult, recourse might be allowed to ad hoc nominations of similar persons.

The Advocate General and *Amicus* briefs

In *US – Shrimp*, the Appellate Body found that 'attaching a brief or other material to the submission of either appellant or appellee, no matter how or where such material may have originated, renders that material at least *prima facie* an integral part of that participant's submission'.[45] The Appellate Body in that case ruled that a 'panel has the discretionary authority either to accept and consider or to reject information and advice submitted to it, *whether requested by a panel or not*'.[46] The Appellate Body also accepted three *amicus* briefs appended to the USA's submission, after receiving confirmation from the USA that it agreed with the arguments made in the *amicus* submissions, to the extent those arguments 'concur with' the USA's own arguments.[47] In *US – Lead and Bismuth II*, the Appellate Body confirmed its own authority to receive *amicus* submissions, which it based on DSU

[44] Steve Charnovitz, 'Participation of Nongovernmental Organizations in the World Trade Organization' (1996)17 *U Pa. J Int'l Econ. L* 331 at 356.

[45] Appellate Body Report, *United States – Import Prohibition of Certain Shrimp and Shrimp Products*, WT/DS58/AB/R, 6 November 1998, paragraph 89.

[46] *Ibid.* at paragraph 108 (original emphasis).

[47] Appellate Body Report, *US – Shrimp*, paragraphs 90–1.

Article 17.9.[48] Finally in *EC – Asbestos*, the Appellate Body drafted a series of guidelines for that dispute only, under Article 16.1 of the Working Procedures for Appellate Review, which might be construed as actively seeking *amicus* briefs.[49] Despite the controversy which attended this action, and the Appellate Body's subsequent unwillingness to consult unsolicited *amicus* briefs, both the panels and the Appellate Body appear to retain their legal capacity to admit *amicus* briefs under the prevailing interpretation of the WTO conventions.[50] The current situation is therefore one where practice does not reflect law: unsolicited *amicus* briefs are theoretically admissible, but there are strong political pressures to ignore them.

***Amicus* briefs and procedural concerns** Introduction of the AG position would provide a middle ground by which the *amicus* brief debate might be resolved. From the procedural perspective, the introduction of an AG would ensure that the WTO would in fact be equipped to receive *amicus* briefs in a timely fashion and that the briefs would receive appropriate attention. This would alleviate one fear of outside groups who have no means of knowing what happens to briefs once they are dispatched to the WTO. The fact of designating the AG to perform this function would be a potent symbol to the outside world that the WTO is listening to the concerns of interest groups.

One of the major fears of developing countries motivating opposition to the admissibility of *amicus* briefs appears to be that better funded NGOs might compete with and eclipse governmental submissions to the adjudicatory body.[51] The introduction of an AG figure might allay such concerns by acting as a primary, or possibly even exclusive, method of transmission for the content of *amicus* briefs. This would reinforce the impression that party submissions were of primary importance, and unsolicited submissions only of secondary or tertiary importance, to the resolution of the dispute. Softening the opposition of developing countries to the submission of *amicus* briefs would be advantageous because it would allow the incorporation of such briefs to match in practice the

[48] Appellate Body Report, *US – Lead and Bismuth II*, paragraphs 36–42.
[49] See *supra* text at n. 10.
[50] See, e.g., Appellate Body Report, *US – Shrimp (Article 21.5 – Malaysia)*, paragraph 78 (where the Appellate Body did not admit an unsolicited *amicus* brief, but gave no hint that it was legally unable to do so: 'In rendering our decision in this appeal, we have not found it necessary to take into account the brief submitted by Professor Howse').
[51] See Charnovitz, 'Opening the WTO', 210–12.

legal capacities for admission confirmed by the Appellate Body. *Amicus* briefs are desirable contributions to WTO dispute settlement proceedings because, first, they may contain information and arguments which ought to be considered for the panel to make an 'objective assessment', and secondly, because they provide a feasible means by which NGOs can contribute to WTO dispute settlement.

***Amicus* briefs and the duty to make an objective assessment** DSU Article 11 requires panels to make 'an objective assessment of the matter before it'.[52] DSU Article 13.1 gives panels 'the right to seek information and technical advice from any individual or body which it deems appropriate'.[53] Confirming this investigatory function, DSU Article 13.2 allows panels the ability to 'seek information from any relevant source and [to] consult experts to obtain their opinion on certain aspects of the matter'.[54] These provisions provide a clear basis for panels to consult sources outside the membership of the WTO. Furthermore, the Appellate Body in *EC – Hormones* found that disregard of the evidence implies 'not simply an error of judgment in the appreciation of evidence but rather an egregious error that calls into question the good faith of a panel'.[55] The excluding of evidence on the legal ground of non-relevancy is a decision of law reviewable by the Appellate Body.[56] All these factors combine to shape a dispute settlement institution that is concerned with more than finding the most compelling side of a bilateral dispute. WTO panels attempt to determine whether a party to the dispute is objectively in breach of its treaty obligations. Arguably, the participation of an AG in the process of reaching an objective assessment would enhance the process and ensure that all factors are weighed in as objective a fashion as possible.

The obligation of WTO panels to make an objective assessment is entirely consistent with the fact that panel reports have repercussions beyond the affairs of the two or more parties implicated in the dispute. This is confirmed in DSU Article 3.8: 'there is normally a presumption that a breach of the rules has an adverse impact on other Members parties to that covered agreement'.[57] If other members are adversely affected by a breach of rules, those members have an interest in the outcome, even if they did not instigate or involve themselves in the

[52] DSU Article 11. [53] DSU Article 13.1. [54] DSU Article 13.2.
[55] Appellate Body Report, *EC – Hormones*, paragraph 133.
[56] *Ibid.* at paragraph 143. [57] DSU Article 3.8.

dispute settlement process. In a more theoretical sense, all parties to an agreement have an interest in having situations that constitute breach of obligations clearly and consistently determined because this enhances the effectiveness of the agreement. Finally, although reports of the DSB may not 'add to or diminish the rights and obligations provided in the covered agreements',[58] the Appellate Body has stated that reports 'are often considered by subsequent panels. They create legitimate expectations among WTO Members, and, therefore, should be taken into account where they are relevant to any dispute.'[59] It is clear that although past reports may not be binding, panel and particularly Appellate Body reports have some degree of influence on future legal determinations.[60] Reports have attenuated consequences for all members who are party to a given agreement, and it is therefore correct that a broad interpretation be given to the panel's obligation to make 'an objective assessment of the matter before it'. All this would suggest that the AG can voice a variety of systemic concerns and speak to the interests of the whole membership of the WTO collectivity.

The diversity of opinions encouraged by the admission of unsolicited *amicus* briefs is consistent with the panel's mission, broadly speaking, to make an objective assessment of the matter before it. Conversely, a bar on the admissibility of *amicus* briefs, be it either as the result of a legal determination of incapacity to admit, or a consequence of political pressures, runs contrary to the panel's obligation to make an objective assessment. Were the panel's determinations constrained to matters of pure law, one might argue that under the doctrine of *curia novit legem*, unsolicited private party legal briefs are superfluous. The panel's determinations often involve matters of policy. For example, the panel's determination that American import restrictions on foreign shrimp were 'related to' the 'conservation of exhaustible natural resources' within the meaning of Article XX:g of the GATT 1994 in *US – Shrimp* cannot be characterized as a determination of pure law. There was a question of where the correct balance between regulation of environmental concerns and national barriers to trade should be set, and this determination was based on sophisticated factual determinations. In

[58] DSU Article 3.2.

[59] Appellate Body Report, *Japan – Taxes on Alcoholic Beverages II*, WT/DS8/AB/R, 1 November 1996, paragraph 15.

[60] See, e.g., D. Palmeter and P. C. Mavroidis, 'The WTO Legal System: Sources of Law' (1998) 92 *AJIL* 398 at 413.

these scenarios, unsolicited *amicus* briefs serve a useful complementary function to the panel's investigatory functions under DSU Article 13. By weighing and presenting what appear to be the most pertinent points in various briefs, the AG would be able to perform a most valuable service which currently does not fall within the responsibility of any WTO officer.

***Amicus* briefs and NGO participation** Unsolicited *amicus* briefs also provide a mechanism by which NGOs can be granted some degree of participation in WTO dispute settlement. Steve Charnovitz points out that 'drawing on the expertise of NGOs is a hallmark of . . . intergovernmental organizations and institutions'.[61] Charnovitz then goes on to quote from a programme of action implemented by the United Nations Conference on Environment and Development (UNCED):

> all intergovernmental organizations and forums should, in consultation with non-governmental organizations, take measures to: . . . enhance existing or, where they do not exist, establish mechanisms and procedures within each agency to draw on the expertise and views of non-governmental organizations in policy and programme design, implementation and evaluation; [and] . . . [p]rovide access for non-governmental organizations to accurate and timely data and information to promote the effectiveness of their programmes and activities.[62]

Indeed, there is a broad consensus among international law experts that NGO participation in the deliberations of governmental organizations is both common and useful. Participation of NGOs in the world trade system is, in fact, a tradition that can be traced through a series of proposed trade agreements: Article 87.2 of the ITO Charter provided that 'the Organization may make suitable arrangements for consultation and co-operation with nongovernmental organizations concerned with matters within the scope of this Charter'.[63] This language was incorporated into the draft text for an agreement regarding the proposed Multilateral Trade Organization (MTO).[64]

[61] Charnovitz, 'Participation of NGOs', 335.

[62] Agenda 21, UN Doc.A/CONF.151/26 (1993), Article 27.9.

[63] ITO Charter Article 87.2, reprinted in US Department of State, *Havana Charter for an International Trade Organization* (1948), p. 110.

[64] The draft text for the MTO would have authorized: 'suitable arrangements for consultation and cooperation with non-governmental organizations concerned with matters within the scope of the MTO'. Draft of Final Act Embodying the Results of the

In the WTO Agreement this language evolved somewhat into Article V:2: 'The General Council may make appropriate arrangements for consultation and cooperation with non-governmental organizations concerned with matters related to those of the WTO.'[65] The WTO General Council implemented this provision in July 1996 with the approval of Guidelines for Arrangements on Relations with Non-Governmental Organizations.[66] The Guidelines, although they encourage the WTO Secretariat and members to consult NGOs independently, conclude:

> As a result of extensive discussions, there is currently a broadly held view that it would not be possible for NGOs to be directly involved in the work of the WTO or its meetings. Closer consultation and cooperation with NGOs can also be met constructively through appropriate processes at the national level where lies primary responsibility for taking into account the different elements of public interest which are brought to bear on trade policy-making.[67]

The implementation of Article V:2 of the WTO Agreement has occurred with little impact on WTO functioning, and no impact whatsoever on the deliberations of the DSB. NGOs' participation is largely limited to submitting briefs to their host governments to be appended to those governments' briefs, given the current chill regarding the admission of unsolicited *amicus* briefs. The Advocate General proposal would re-invigorate the option of unsolicited *amicus* briefs through providing a compromise admission method acceptable to developing countries.

Restriction of NGO involvement to the submission of briefs to the government parties ignores the realities of international NGOs that have no 'host' government to represent their concerns. Governments may choose not to transmit the concerns or collected evidence of an NGO for strategic or political reasons.[68] It is not sufficient to rely on state parties to the DSB to funnel NGO concerns. The idea of NGO participation in WTO processes has, appropriately, been a consideration since the

Uruguay Round of Multilateral Trade Negotiations, MTN.TNC/W/FA, 20 December 1991, p. 93.

65 WTO Agreement Article V:2.

66 Guidelines for Arrangements on Relations with Non-Governmental Organizations, Decision adopted by the General Council on 18 July 1996, WT/L/162, 23 July 1996.

67 *Ibid.* at paragraph 6.

68 Charnovitz, 'Participation of NGOs', 353 ('A government might not want to repeat an NGO point if doing so could undermine the government in another WTO case or in domestic litigation').

beginning of the modern international trade regime and the failure to implement this idea effectively has undermined the WTO's value and popular legitimacy.

Allowing NGOs powers of intervention commensurate to those allowed to states under the WTO is not an appropriate solution to the problem posed by the current exclusion of NGOs. Jonathan Fried argues this point convincingly:

> Private actors, whether corporate or non-governmental, might normally be expected to espouse their own interest: a corporation will pursue its market access concerns without regard to social consequences of so doing; an NGO will pursue its concerns, say, regarding the environment, potentially without regard to economic considerations.[69]

In addition to status at public international law denied to NGOs, governments presumptively defend all interests of their peoples, whereas NGOs focus on the limited mandate for which they were created to advance. However, there is substantial middle ground between limiting NGOs' input into WTO dispute resolution to the discretion of trade ministers, and arguing for the granting of full rights of intervention to private parties. A compromise that would allow NGOs meaningful input would be a mechanism by which *amicus* briefs might be submitted and considered. The Advocate General proposal provides such a mechanism.

The Advocate General: a means of protecting the integrity of the Secretariat's involvement in dispute settlement

Some legal commentators have proposed the introduction of a position modelled on the Advocate General as a means of reducing direct Secretariat involvement in the substantive determinations of WTO panels. Hudec stated in 1992, prior to the introduction of the modern WTO dispute settlement system, that 'GATT will not be ready for an appellate tribunal until . . . the GATT is ready to establish an Advocate General's office to represent the longer term interests of GATT in tribunal proceedings'.[70] A. F. Lowenfeld expressed a similar concern in an article published in 1994:

[69] J. Fried, 'Globalization and International Law: Some Thoughts for States and Citizens' (1997) 23 *Queen's LJ* 259.

[70] R. E. Hudec, 'The Judicialization of GATT Dispute Settlement' in M. M. Hart and D. P. Steger (eds.), *In Whose Interest?* (Centre for Trade Policy and Law, Ottawa, 1992), p. 30.

> The Understanding contemplates that the secretariat will continue to assist Panels 'especially on the legal, historical and procedural aspects of the matters dealt with' (Art. 27.1). Nothing is said about the secretariat's role in the appellate process, and I think it is important that there be no such role. The drafters of the Understanding on Dispute Settlement might have drawn on the model of the European Court of Justice, which relies on Advocates General, a high-level group of friends of the court independent of the Commission and of the litigants. Typically, the Advocates General have provided more thorough scholarship and more closely reasoned analysis than are evident in the decisions of the Court of Justice.[71]

Ragosta also expresses concern that the degree of Secretariat involvement in panel reports is troubling, and proposes the development of a standing judiciary of panel judges similar to that created for the Appellate Body.[72] Ragosta also notes that others have proposed the position of Advocate General as an alternative solution.

Concerns regarding Secretariat involvement stem from the many functions of the Secretariat in constituting and supporting the panel. Under DSU Article 8, panels are composed of three panellists nominated by the Secretariat from its rosters,[73] whose nominations can only be opposed by the parties for 'compelling reasons'.[74] The Secretariat is also responsible for assisting panels, 'especially on the legal, historical and procedural aspects of the matters dealt with'.[75] Finally, the Secretariat may also 'provide additional legal advice and assistance in respect of dispute settlement to developing country Members'.[76] Ragosta notes that this concentration of tasks is troublesome, especially considering that Secretariat staff are often from the states which are parties to the dispute.[77] That the Secretariat has been able to perform these functions for close to fifty years is a tribute to the tact, professionalism, and impartiality of its staff. The role played by the GATT/WTO Secretariat in dispute settlement is virtually without parallel in contemporary international law. It is a function that should be protected and defended. Arguably, a proposal which might take the Secretariat out of the

[71] A. F. Lowenfeld, 'Remedies Along with Rights: Institutional Reform in the New GATT' (1994) 88 *American Journal of International Law* 477 at 484.

[72] A. Ragosta, 'Unmasking the WTO: Access to the DSB System – Can the WTO DSB Live up to the Moniker "World Trade Court"?' 31 *Law and Policy in International Business* 739 at 761–2.

[73] See DSU Articles 8.3 and 8.6. [74] DSU Article 8.6. [75] DSU Article 27.1.

[76] DSU Article 27.2. [77] Ragosta, 'Unmasking the WTO', 760.

limelight would function to the advantage of all participants in WTO disputes.

Although the Advocate General's role as it is conceived here is not primarily concerned with representing the interests of the WTO as an institution, it is suggested that the Advocate General could serve as a 'middleman' to provide independent support for the panel process. Furthermore, because the Advocate General is responsible for articulating the balance of policy concerns, this official might fill the role of representing 'the long term interests of GATT (WTO) in tribunal proceedings' as Hudec suggests. As a result of the Advocate General's responsibility to convey the policy-related arguments contained in *amicus* briefs, such an official would attempt to determine an appropriate balance between the extra-trade concerns that are likely to be represented in *amicus* briefs, and the interests of the WTO institution. In this manner, the Advocate General would be neither a partisan figure, nor indeed an advocate for or against trade, but rather, similarly to the ECJ's Advocate General, someone 'who speaks only for the public interest'.[78] This development would, if only in appearance, introduce some degree of separation between the Secretariat and the panel, as well as articulating an interest which the Secretariat can hardly defend without appearing to take sides.

The Advocate General and the popular legitimacy of WTO dispute resolution

Finally, the facilitation of admitting unsolicited *amicus* briefs, the somewhat greater separation of panels from the Secretariat, and the introduction of a specialized judicial figure can all be said to have the ancillary benefit of improving the popular legitimacy of WTO dispute resolution. The World Wildlife Foundation, in arguing for the 'installation of a counsel to Panels or Appellate Body' which resembled, in many respects, the AG position here discussed, suggested that such a reform 'would make that service more independent, accountable, and open to the public, so that it can strengthen the legitimacy of the decisions made under the WTO dispute settlement system'.[79] The popular protests which culminated in the havoc that greeted the WTO Ministerial Conference in Seattle in 1999 are more productively accommodated

[78] T.C. Hartley, *The Foundations of European Community Law* (4th edn, Oxford University Press, 1998), p. 55.

[79] 'Environmental Group Urges Reform of WTO Dispute Settlement Process', (1999) 16 *Int'l Trade Rep. (BNA)* 1362 (18 August).

through compromise than ignored. Although the AG proposal would only answer some of the concerns of those who claim that the WTO system suffers from a 'democratic deficit',[80] and for most of these would probably not go far enough, it may constitute a move in the right direction.

[80] Charnovitz, 'Opening the WTO', 173–4.

14

Arbitration at the WTO: A *Terra Incognita* to be Further Explored

LAURENCE BOISSON DE CHAZOURNES

Introduction

There is no doubt that the WTO dispute settlement system, set out in the 1994 Understanding on Rules and Procedures Governing the Settlement of Disputes (DSU), is 'unique',[1] first, because of its compulsory jurisdiction covering any dispute between WTO members,[2] and secondly, because of surveillance and implementation procedures put in place when a decision has been adopted. Another feature, not often highlighted but wisely noted by Florentino Feliciano and Peter Van den Bossche, is that the WTO provides 'for a multitude of dispute settlement procedures'.

Articles 4 to 20 of the DSU set out in great detail the 'mainstream procedures' which rest on consultations, the possibility of establishing a panel, and recourse to the Appellate Body. However, parties to a dispute can agree to resort to other means of dispute settlement, of a more diplomatic nature, such as good offices, conciliation, and mediation.[3] Parties can also resort to arbitration.

The author would like to thank Pieter Jan Kuijper for his very insightful comments and Makane Moïse Mbengue for his invaluable help in preparing this chapter.

1 F. P. Feliciano and P. L. H. Van den Bossche, 'The Dispute Settlement System of the World Trade Organization: Institutions, Process and Practice' in N. M. Blokker and H. G. Schermers (eds.), Proliferation of International Organizations (Kluwer Law International, The Hague, 2001), p. 298.

2 Although some of the WTO agreements provide for special and additional rules and procedures 'designed to deal with the particularities of dispute settlement relating to obligations arising under a specific covered agreement': *ibid.* at pp. 303–4.

3 See DSU Article 5.6. Thus far, there has been only one case of mediation through the Director-General of the WTO. See General Council – Request for Mediation by the Philippines, Thailand and the European Communities – Joint Communication from the European Communities, Thailand and the Philippines, WT/GC//71, 3 August 2003.

Among the alternative means to the WTO mainstream dispute settlement procedures, arbitration is worth taking into account.[4] Indeed, it stands as a judicial 'alternative means of dispute settlement'.[5] In the context of the DSU, arbitration appears as a stand-alone procedure through Article 25. It can also be seen as a procedure complementing WTO mainstream dispute settlement procedures with respect to specific issues (DSU Articles 21.3 and 22.6).

All dispute settlement procedures, be they mainstream or alternative, are rooted in the DSU. The DSU is the *lex generalis*, providing substantial and procedural directions to the various types of arbitration that can be initiated at the WTO. Thus, these arbitrations will be imbued with three characteristics underlying the WTO dispute settlement system, i.e., predictability, balance, and confidentiality.

The notions of predictability and balance rest on DSU Article 3.2, which states that 'The dispute settlement system of the WTO is a central element in providing security and predictability to the multilateral trading system'. Member states have attempted to circumscribe as much as possible the discretionary power of dispute settlement bodies in their interpretation of WTO agreements provisions, so as to maintain them within the limits set by the agreements.[6]

The predictability notion is associated with the principle of judicial economy. DSU Article 3.7 specifies that 'The aim of the dispute settlement mechanism is to secure a positive solution to a dispute. A solution mutually acceptable to the parties to a dispute and consistent with the covered agreements is clearly to be preferred.' In *US –Wool Shirts and Blouses*, the Appellate Body declared that '[g]iven the explicit aim of dispute settlement that permeates the DSU, we do not consider that Article 3.2 of the DSU is meant to encourage either panels

[4] 'The concept of arbitration has a long history in international trade, having been identified as a means for settling disputes in the 1947 Havana Charter. However, the idea was not explicitly imported into the GATT 1947, with the result that Contracting Parties failed to make use of this mechanism throughout most of the GATT years. The possibility of resolving disputes through arbitration first appeared explicitly in the 1989 Improvements, but this did not lead to frequent use of the mechanism.' See V. Hughes, 'Arbitration within the WTO' in F. Ortino and E. U. Petersmann (eds.), *The WTO Dispute Settlement System, 1995–2003* (Kluwer Law International, 2004), p. 85.

[5] See DSU Article 25.1.

[6] L. Boisson de Chazournes and M. M. Mbengue, 'Le rôle des organes de règlement des différends dans le développement du droit: à propos des OGM' in *Le commerce international des OGM* (J. Bourrinet and S. Maljean-Dubois, La documentation française, collection 'Monde européen et international', 2002), pp. 177–212.

or the Appellate Body to "make law" by clarifying existing provisions of the WTO Agreement outside the context of resolving a particular dispute'.[7] For instance, a panel must only deal with the necessary allegations to solve the issue at stake in a dispute.[8] These rules impose themselves on arbitrators as well; their powers cannot conceivably go beyond those of panels or the Appellate Body.

Predictability may have another meaning within the framework of arbitration. It implies that arbitrators have been granted access to all necessary information before they deliver their final decision, in order to secure the efficiency of the principle *audiet alteram partem*. In *EC – Bananas III (Ecuador) (Article 22.6 – EC)*, as the consequence of a plea for a prejudicial decision articulated by Ecuador, the arbitrators, in the context of a procedure under DSU Article 22.6, had considered that DSU Article 22.7 provides that:

> 'the parties shall accept the arbitrator's decision as final and shall not seek a second arbitration' ... it is inappropriate to give a ruling on the admissibility or relevance of certain information at this early stage of the proceeding ... in past arbitration cases, arbitrators have developed their own methodology for calculating the level of nullification or impairment as appropriate and have requested additional information from the parties until they were in a position to make a final ruling. However, the arbitrators have decided, in light of the concerns regarding due process, to extend the deadline for the submission of rebuttals for both parties ... This should give both parties adequate time to respond to the factual information and legal arguments submitted by the other party.[9]

[7] Appellate Body Report, *United States – Measures Affecting Imports of Woven-Wool Shirts and Blouses from India*, WT/DS33/AB/R, 23 May 1997, p. 19, paragraph VI. The Appellate Body specified that Article IX of the WTO Agreement provides that the Ministerial Conference and the General Council have the 'exclusive authority' to adopt interpretations of the WTO Agreement and the Multilateral Trade Agreements. This is expressly recognized in DSU Article 3.9. About the exclusive nature of the power of the two mentioned bodies, see Appellate Body Report, *Japan – Taxes on Alcoholic Beverages II*, WT/DS8/AB/R, 1 November 1996, p. 15; Appellate Body Report, *United States – Import Measures on Certain EC Products*, WT/DS165/AB/R, 10 January 2001, paragraph 92.

[8] Appellate Body Report, *Australia – Measures Affecting Importation of Salmon*, WT/DS18/AB/R, 6 November 1998, paragraph 110. See also Appellate Body Report, *Brazil – Measures Affecting Desiccated Coconut*, WT/DS22/AB/R, 20 March 1997, paragraph 293.

[9] Appellate Body Report, *European Communities – Importation, Sale and Distribution of Bananas III*, WT/DS27/AB/R, 25 September 1997, (Ecuador) (Article 22.6 – EC), paragraph 18.

The notion of balance derives from the warning contained in the DSU that dispute settlement bodies should not increase or diminish the rights of WTO member states. This principle is clearly laid down in DSU Articles 3.2 and 19.2. Article 3.2 provides that '[t]he Members recognize that [the dispute settlement system] serves to preserve the rights and obligations of Members under the covered agreements'. As for DSU Article 19.2, it establishes that 'in their findings and recommendations, the panel and Appellate Body cannot add to or diminish the rights and obligations provided in the covered agreements'. These rules apply *mutatis mutandis* to the different arbitration procedures set by the DSU. This being said, there is a fine line between respecting the balance by not increasing or diminishing the rights of member states and by developing international law.

Confidentiality is an omnipresent principle of the DSU for all proceedings foreseen for dispute settlement among member states of the WTO. This is even more the case in certain procedures such as anti-dumping, subsidies and safeguards, where information from business operators plays a role. *Brazil – Aircraft (Article 22.6 – Brazil)*[10] provides an example where the issue of business confidentiality was at stake. During the proceedings, Brazil had emphasized the confidential character of certain documents it had entrusted to the arbitrators. Considering the severe problems that might be caused by divulging certain commercial or financial information, and the fact that an objective evaluation of facts often depends on an appropriate protection of the confidential information, the arbitrators decided in this case to establish two versions of their report. The first version included the details of the calculation and all the information taken into account. It was delivered to the parties only, on a confidential basis. The most sensitive information – from a commercial point of view – was omitted in the second version, which was distributed to the member states of the WTO.[11] The arbitrators thought they had respected their obligations as defined in the DSU,

[10] Appellate Body Report, *Brazil – Aircraft* (*Article 22.6 – Brazil*) (not yet reported), paragraphs 2.13–2.14.

[11] The text of the version handed to the member states of the WTO was identical to that of the confidential version given to the parties, except for the information the arbitrators considered as confidential, with respect to the parties' observations.

while preserving the confidential character of certain information, for which the parties had requested that status.[12]

This being said, arbitration at the WTO is coloured with a certain sense of identity, which manifests itself through its role in the WTO multilateral surveillance system. Multilateral surveillance is one of the distinctive features of the dispute settlement system at the WTO. It lies at the origin of the effectiveness and of the efficiency of the dispute settlement bodies' jurisdiction as a whole. Arbitration is summoned at different stages of the multilateral surveillance process.

A first type of arbitration at the WTO is found in the supervision and application phase, following the adoption by the Dispute Settlement Body (DSB) of panel and/or Appellate Body reports and recommendations. The supervision and application proceedings establish that during a meeting of the DSB held within the thirty days following the date of the report or its adoption, the losing party shall have to make known its intentions concerning the application of the recommendations adopted by the DSB (DSU Article 21.3). If the concerned party cannot possibly comply immediately, it will be granted a reasonable period of time to this effect.[13] The reasonable period of time may be the period of time

[12] It is true that confidentiality remains one of the distinctive traits of all arbitration proceedings. In an ICSID dispute, *Metalclad* v. *Mexico*, the arbitral tribunal considered that 'There remains nonetheless a question as to whether there exists any general principle of confidentiality that would operate to prohibit public discussion of the arbitration proceedings by either party. Neither the NAFTA nor the ICSID (Additional Facility) Rules contain any express restriction on the freedom of the parties in this respect. Though it is frequently said that one of the reasons for recourse to arbitration is to avoid publicity, unless the agreement between the parties incorporates such a limitation, each of them is still free to speak publicly of the arbitration. It may be observed that no such limitation is written into such major arbitral texts as the UNCITRAL Rules or the draft Articles on Arbitration adopted by the International Law Commission . . . The above having been said, it still appears to the Arbitral Tribunal that it would be of advantage to the orderly unfolding of the arbitral process and conducive to the maintenance of working relations between the Parties if during the proceedings they were both to limit public discussion of the case to a minimum, subject only to any externally imposed obligation of disclosure by which either of them may be legally bound'. (2001) XXVI *Yearbook of International Commercial Arbitration* 103.

[13] See P. Monnier, 'The Time to Comply with an Adverse WTO Ruling: Promptness within Reason' (2001) 35(5) *Journal of World Trade*, 825: 'The time period for compliance is the eye in the cyclone of the WTO Dispute Settlement Mechanism . . . If the concept of compliance period relies mainly on the "Reasonable Period of Time" set forth in Article 21.3 of the DSU, the concept of "without delay" provided for prohibited subsidy cases should not be forgotten. In both cases, the basic principle is immediate compliance. For example, Article 21.1 of the DSU prescribes that "Prompt compliance

suggested by the member concerned with the DSB's approbation (DSU Article 21.3(a)), or the period of time agreed to by the parties in the forty-five days following the report's adoption (DSU Article 21.3(b)), that is to say a period of time determined by arbitration in the ninety days following the report's adoption (DSU Article 21.3(c)). When the reasonable period of time has been determined by arbitration, the arbitrator should work with the principle that the reasonable period of time for applying the panel's or the Appellate Body's recommendations should not be longer than fifteen months, starting from the date of the adoption of the panel or Appellate Body report. Nevertheless, this duration may be shorter or longer, according to the circumstances of the particular case (DSU Article 21.3(c)). The span between the date at which a panel has been established by the DSB and the date of the reasonable period of time's determination must not be longer than fifteen months, unless the parties to the dispute decide otherwise. In cases where either the panel or the Appellate Body will have extended the time for examining a case, the extra period of time granted will be added to the fifteen months. Nevertheless, unless the parties to the dispute agree that exceptional circumstances exist, the overall period of time must not exceed eighteen months (DSU Article 21.4).

When there is a disagreement about the compatibility of measures taken to conform to the DSB recommendations with a WTO agreement, a party can have recourse to the procedures of the DSU (Article 21.5). If, in the reasonable period of time, the concerned state does not transform the measure found incompatible with a WTO agreement into a conforming one, this state must, if asked to do so, lend itself to negotiations, with a view to finding mutually acceptable compensation (DSU Article 22.2). The complaining state may ask the DSB for the authorization to withhold concessions and other obligations if no other satisfying compensation has been agreed to in the twenty days following the date on which the reasonable time limit has expired. The DSB must grant this authorization within a time-frame of thirty days, starting from the expiry of the reasonable period of time, unless it decides by consensus

with recommendations or rulings of the DSB is essential in order to ensure effective resolution of disputes to the benefit of all Members" . . . But this "zero delay" standard looked probably unrealistic to the negotiators of the WTO agreements who installed safety-valves such as "Reasonable Period of Time" in the DSU or "time-period within which the measure must be withdrawn" in part II of the Agreement on Subsidies and Countervailing Measures (ASCM).'

to reject the requirement. The DSU imposes certain limitations to the fields to which countermeasures should apply.[14]

A second type of arbitration at the WTO comes up at this point. The level of suspension of concessions or other obligations authorized by the DSB must be equivalent to the level of nullification or impairment (DSU Article 22.4). In case of disagreement concerning the equivalence of the level of nullification or impairment with that of countermeasures, an arbitral award may be requested (DSU Article 22 paragraphs 5, 6, and 7). This arbitration will be conducted by the initial panel if its members are available, or by an arbitrator appointed by the Director-General, and it will be completed in the sixty days following the date when the reasonable time limit will have expired. Concessions or other obligations will not be suspended during the arbitration (DSU Article 22.6). During the performance of their task, arbitrators will not examine the nature of concessions, or other obligations, that are the objects of countermeasures, but they will determine whether the level of the requested suspension is equivalent to the level of nullification or impairment. The arbitrator may also determine whether the requested suspension of concessions or other obligations is authorized in accordance with the relevant WTO agreement.[15]

DSU Article 25 establishes a third type of arbitral award, which may cover the fields of arbitration proceedings foreseen in Articles 21.3(c) and 22.6, or supplement the proceedings of a panel or the Appellate Body to settle the dispute. Thus, it is related to the multilateral surveillance system, although from a systemic perspective.

[14] The DSU specifies that compensation and countermeasures are only temporary measures, to which one can have recourse if the recommendations and decisions are not applied in a reasonable period of time. To this end, multilateral commercial agreements have been grouped into three distinct agreements: the GATT 1994 (to which other multilateral commercial agreements on goods trade have been added), the General Agreement on Trade in Services (GATS), and the Agreement on Trade-Related Aspects of Intellectual Property Rights (TRIPS). The general principle is that the plaintiff party should first seek to withhold concessions or other obligations in the same sector as the one in which an annulment or reduction of advantages has been ascertained. If it is impossible or inefficient to do so in the same sector, withholding concessions or other obligations will be possible in other sectors, invoking the same agreement. If this solution is not possible and circumstances are severe enough, the plaintiff party may seek to withhold concessions or other obligations invoking another WTO Agreement (see DSU Article 22).

[15] See Ch. M. Valles and B. P. McGivern, 'The Right to Retaliate under the WTO Agreement: The "Sequencing" Problem' (2003) 34(2) *Journal of World Trade* 63.

The arbitrators' decisions are not subject to adoption by the DSB, contrary to the panels' and the Appellate Body's reports; the DSB simply 'takes note' of their content. In the case of arbitration under DSU Article 25, awards are notified to the DSB. This neither lessens in any way the binding character of arbitral awards, nor their judicial effect of '*autorité de la chose jugée*'. This is demonstrated by DSU Article 21.3(c), establishing *expressis verbis* that the reasonable period of time will be determined through 'binding arbitration'. DSU Article 22.7 – with respect to arbitration under Article 22.6 – stipulates that '[t]he parties shall accept the arbitrator's decision as final and the parties concerned shall not seek a second arbitration'. Article 25 puts forward the parties' consent to the award, insisting specifically on the fact that '[t]he parties to the proceeding shall agree to abide by the arbitration award'.

Arbitration as a complementary means of dispute settlement

Arbitration under Article 21.3(c) as a 'residual' means of dispute settlement

The meaning of DSU Article 21.3(c) must be elucidated within its context. The latter includes, first, the introductory text to Article 21.3, acknowledging that the issue of a 'reasonable period of time' for enforcement is involved only 'if it is impracticable [for a Member] to comply immediately' with the recommendations and rulings. Secondly, there is DSU Article 21.1, underlining that '[p]rompt compliance with recommendations or rulings of the DSB is essential in order to ensure effective resolution of disputes to the benefit of all Members'. Thirdly, there is DSU Article 3.3, acknowledging that '[t]he prompt settlement of situations ... is essential to the effective functioning of the WTO and the maintenance of a proper balance between the rights and obligations of Members'. Thus, the DSU underlines explicitly the importance of prompt conformity.

The arbitrator's warrant in accordance with DSU Article 21.3(c) consists exclusively of determining the 'reasonable period of time' for enactment. It does not enable the arbitrator to propose or determine ways or means to ensure it.[16] Article 21.3(c) aims at ensuring the conformity with, or the application of, a decision made by the DSB.

[16] Award of the Arbitrator, *Australia – Measures Affecting Importation of Salmon*, WT/DS18/9, 23 February 1999, paragraph 35.

The purpose of Article 21 is to render the measure, that is deemed incompatible with the obligations of a state member of the WTO in accordance with specific provisions of a WTO agreement, compatible with these same provisions. DSU Article 3.7 underlines that 'the first objective of the dispute settlement mechanism is usually to secure the withdrawal of [a measure inconsistent with WTO rules]'. Moreover, the DSU indicates that it is possible to have recourse to compensation only if 'the immediate withdrawal of the measure is impracticable', and then solely 'as a temporary measure pending the withdrawal of the measure which is inconsistent with [a WTO agreement]'. Suspending concessions or other obligations is explicitly designated as a last resort measure, subject to DSB authorization. It also remains a 'temporary' corrective measure, authorized in accordance with DSU Article 22.8 only in order to achieve the removal of the non-conforming measure, or the reaching of a 'mutually satisfactory solution'.

Determination of the reasonable time for applying the DSB recommendations and rulings depends on the factual, juridical, and structural circumstances faced by the state to which the non-conformity or violation of a WTO agreement is imputed.

Arbitration in accordance with DSU Article 21.3(c) aims at setting the reasonable period of time for enacting a panel's or the Appellate Body's recommendations. The notion of 'reasonable' period of time is not easy to define legally. The Appellate Body, in *US – Hot-rolled Steel*, attempted to draw a definition for 'reasonable' within the context of the Anti-dumping Agreement. The Appellate Body indicated that the term 'reasonable':

> implies a degree of flexibility that involves consideration of all of the circumstances of a particular case. What is 'reasonable' in one set of circumstances may prove to be less than 'reasonable' in different circumstances. This suggests that what constitutes a reasonable period or a reasonable time . . . should be defined on a case-by-case basis, in the light of the specific circumstances of each investigation . . . In sum, a 'reasonable period' must be interpreted consistently with the notions of flexibility and balance that are inherent in the concept of 'reasonableness', and in a manner that allows for account to be taken of the particular circumstances of each case.[17]

[17] Appellate Body Report, *United States – Anti-dumping Measures on Certain Hot-rolled Steel Products from Japan*, WT/DS184/AB/R, 23 August 2001, paragraphs 84 and 85.

In the absence of a mutually agreed solution, the primary objective is usually the immediate withdrawal of the measure deemed incompatible with one of the WTO agreements. Indeed, DSU Article 21.1 states the general principle according to which '[p]rompt compliance with recommendations or rulings of the DSB is essential in order to ensure effective resolution of disputes to the benefit of all Members'. This obligation is specified in DSU Article 21.3, which provides that 'if it is impracticable to comply immediately with the recommendations and rulings, the Member concerned shall have a reasonable period of time in which to do so'. WTO member states must thus seek to conform 'immediately' to the DSB recommendations and rulings. The state concerned has the right to a reasonable period of time for implementation only if it is materially impossible for it to proceed to immediate withdrawal. Thus, having recourse to the reasonable period of time is a second best solution.

In determining the reasonable period of time, the arbitrator must work on the principle that this time should not exceed fifteen months beginning from the date of adoption of the panel's and/or Appellate Body's report. The reasonable period of time may be shorter or longer, depending on the circumstances. It is clear from the text of DSU Article 21.3(c) that the fifteen months' time-frame, introduced as a basic principle, is merely an indication. As it has been said in *Australia – Salmon*, it does not mean 'that the arbitrator is obliged to grant fifteen months in all cases'.[18] Article 21.3(c) clearly leaves the possibility open to settle on a period lesser or greater than fifteen months for applying the DSB recommendations and rulings.

Determining the reasonable period of time for implementation may also be dependent on a state's specific situation. Arbitration rulings have kept in mind the fact that DSU Article 21.2 'usefully enjoins, *inter alia*, an arbitrator functioning under Article 21.3(c) to be generally mindful of the great difficulties that a developing country Member may, in a particular case, face as it proceeds to implement the recommendations and rulings of the DSB'.[19] In *Argentina – Hides and Leather*,[20] Argentina had considered that its economic interests as a developing country and its financial solvency with the IMF were at stake. Argentina required

[18] Award of the Arbitrator, *Australia – Salmon*, paragraph 30.

[19] Award of the Arbitrator, *Chile – Taxes on Alcoholic Beverages*, WT/DS87/15, 23 May 2000, paragraph 45.

[20] Award of the Arbitrator, *Argentina – Hides and Leather*, WT/DS155/10, 31 August 2001, paragraph 51.

from the arbitrators that they take into account its 'interest' in benefiting from a longer period of time allowing it progressively to enforce DSB recommendations and rulings. The arbitrator acknowledged that by virtue of DSU Article 21.2, together with Article 21.3(c), he could take into account, in an appropriate way, the circumstances surrounding a developing country member of the WTO facing severe economic and financial problems and having to conform to DSB recommendations and rulings. In the arbitration concerning *Chile – Alcoholic Beverages*, it has been said that, 'although cast in quite general terms, because Article 21.2 is in the DSU, it is not simply to be disregarded'. In *Indonesia – Autos*, the arbitrator took into account, as 'particular circumstances', Indonesia's status as a developing country and the fact that the country was then 'in a dire economic and financial situation' and that its economy was 'near collapse'.[21] The arbitrator thus granted substantial additional time to the 'normal' necessary time to achieve the internal process for elaborating the domestic regulation. A point to be noted is that the arbitrator's assessment of a situation is enshrined in the limits of his or her jurisdiction.

Arbitration under Article 21.3(c) does not allow the arbitrator to modify the conclusions of a panel or of the Appellate Body. This principle was recalled in *Australia – Salmon*.[22] In other words, when a state is in the situation of violating a WTO agreement, and this situation has been qualified as such by a panel and/or the Appellate Body, the relevant state cannot take advantage of it to obtain a longer reasonable period of time. This is an application of the maxim 'no one can profit from his or her own turpitude' (*nemo suam turpitudinem allegans auditur*) within the context of Article 21.3(c). Good faith remains an important principle in the evaluation of the notion of 'reasonable period of time'. *Australia – Salmon* provides an illustration of this principle. In this case, the Appellate Body had concluded unequivocally that the measure at issue was a prohibition against the importation of fresh, chilled, or frozen Canadian salmon. It also noticed unequivocally that this prohibition against importation was incompatible with Articles 5:1, 2:2, 5:5 and 2:3 of the Agreement on the Application of Sanitary and Phytosanitary Measures ('the SPS Agreement'). Hence, it was naturally difficult for the arbitrator to accept the opinion according to which, to

[21] Award of the Arbitrator, *Indonesia – Certain Measures Affecting the Automobile Industry*, WT/DS54/15, 7 December 1998, paragraph 24.

[22] Award of the Arbitrator, *Australia – Salmon*, paragraph 34.

determine the reasonable period of time, it should be necessary to take into account the time needed to conduct risk assessments in order to demonstrate the compatibility of the prohibition against importation, as the prohibition had already been found to be incompatible with the provisions of the SPS Agreement.[23]

This leads to the conclusion that there is an underlying 'subordination' of an Article 21.3(c) arbitration to the panel and the Appellate Body. The arbitrator comes across as the 'executive arm' of a panel or of the Appellate Body, endowed with the capacity to act so that the rulings and recommendations can be enforced as quickly as possible in order to correct commercial damage. It is within this context that arbitrators have insisted on specifying that the suggestion of ways and means to ensure enforcement is not part of their mandate. The choice of the means of enforcement remains the prerogative of the concerned state. As the arbitrator said in *EC – Hormones*: 'An implementing Member, therefore, has a measure of discretion in choosing the means of implementation, as long as the means chosen are consistent with the recommendations and rulings of the DSB and with the [WTO] Agreements'.[24]

Arbitration under Article 22.6

DSU Article 21.5 on 'Implementation of Recommendations and Rulings' (panel and Appellate Body) and Article 22.6 ('Arbitration') may be entangled. *Brazil – Aircraft* is illustrative here again. Brazil had appealed to the Appellate Body with respect to certain observations made by the Article 21.5 panel at the same time that it requested arbitration under DSU Article 22.6. For the arbitrators, the Appellate Body's ruling could have had an effect on the measure, such that Brazil could have been considered as having put its legislation in conformity with its WTO obligations. The proper functioning of the proceedings demanded that the parties be able to formulate observations on the content of the Appellate Body's report.[25] As a consequence, the arbitrators adopted a calendar that, in their opinion, respected the gist of both

[23] *Ibid.*

[24] Award of the Arbitrator, *European Communities – Measures Concerning Meat and Meat Products (Hormones)*, WT/DS26/15, 29 May 1998, paragraph 38.

[25] In this aspect, the arbitrators agreed with the arbitrators' declaration in *EC – Bananas III (US) (Article 22.6 – EC)*, paragraph 2.12: 'given that our own decisions cannot be appealed, we considered it imperative to achieve the greatest degree of clarity possible with a view to avoiding future disagreements between the parties. Reaching this

DSU Articles 21 and 22 and the aim of arbitration in accordance with DSU Article 22.6, without illegally delaying the ruling's publication. In this specific case, the arbitrators established a calendar planning for the Appellate Body report's publication. One should note at this point the existence of a sort of hierarchy between arbitrations and Article 21.5 proceedings, that is, proceedings requiring a panel and the Appellate Body.

It is interesting to notice that DSU Article 22.6 allows arbitrators to develop their own procedures.[26] For instance, third parties' rights to intervene have been recognized in the arbitration proceedings under Article 22.6 pertaining to *EC – Hormones*,[27] then rejected in *EC – Bananas III (US) (Article 22.6 – EC)*.[28] In the ruling on *EC – Hormones*, the arbitrators considered that the DSU provisions pertaining to panel proceedings, which are referred to by way of analogy in the arbitrators' work proceedings, endowed arbitrators with the discretionary power to decide on procedural issues remaining not covered by the DSU (Article 12.1).[29] Given the fact that the DSU does not deal with the

objective required the parties to have more time to submit to us the information necessary for us to complete our tasks'.

[26] See *Brazil – Aircraft (Article 22.6 – Brazil)*, paragraphs 3.4 and 3.5. See also Award of the Arbitrator, *EC – Hormones (US) (Article 22.6 – EC)*, paragraph 12. Arbitrators sometimes go to the extreme, comparing for instance their warrant with that of the panels: 'There is, however, a difference between our task here and the task given to a panel. In the event we decide that the US proposal is not WTO consistent, i.e. that the suggested amount is too high, we should not end our examination the way panels do, namely by requesting the DSB to recommend that the measure be brought into conformity with WTO obligations. Following the approach of the arbitrators in the *Bananas* case – where the proposed amount of US$520 million was reduced to US$191.4 million – we would be called upon to go further. In pursuit of the basic DSU objectives of prompt and positive settlement of disputes, we would have to estimate the level of suspension we consider to be equivalent to the impairment suffered. This is the essential task and responsibility conferred on the arbitrators in order to settle the dispute. In our view, such approach is implicitly called for in Article 22.7.' *Ibid*. See P. Monnier about this question, 'Working Procedures before Panels: The Appellate Body and Other Adjudicating Bodies of the WTO' (2002) 1(3) *Law and Practice of International Courts and Tribunals* 514.

[27] Award of the Arbitrator, *Brazil – Aircraft*, paragraph 7.

[28] Award of the Arbitrator, *EC – Bananas III (US) (Article 22.6 – EC)*, paragraph 2.8.

[29] About this, see the note at Appellate Body Report, *European Communities – Measures Concerning Meat and Meat Products (Hormones)*, WT/DS26/AB/R, 13 February 1998, n. 138, 'the DSU, and in particular its Appendix 3, leave panels a margin of discretion to deal, always in accordance with due process, with specific situations that may arise in a particular case and that are not explicitly regulated. Within this context, an appellant requesting the Appellate Body to reverse a panel's ruling on matters of procedure must demonstrate the prejudice generated by such regal ruling'.

issue of the participation of third parties in arbitration proceedings, arbitrators are thus responsible for granting or refusing this prerogative.

Nevertheless, arbitrators sometimes practise self-limitation of their powers. For instance, they have generally deemed that DSU Article 6.2 applies *de lege ferenda* to the arbitration procedure of Article 22.6. According to the well-established practice concerning dispute settlement under Article 6.2,[30] panels and the Appellate Body have systematically ruled that a measure questioned by a complainant cannot be considered as included in a panel's remit if it is not clearly identified in the request for establishment of the panel. In disputes concerning Article 6.2, in which a plaintiff party was intent on maintaining the possibility of later completing the initial list of measures included in the request for the panel's establishment (for instance, by using the phrase 'including, but not exclusively, the listed measures'), it has been held that the panel's remit was limited to the specifically identified measures. Thus, the scope of the arbitrators' powers under Article 22.6 is limited to the sector(s) and/or to the agreement(s) for which suspension is specifically requested to the DSB.[31]

It is relevant to point out that the DSU itself remains vague about certain aspects of arbitrators' scope of powers deriving from Article 22.6. DSU Article 22.7 enables arbitrators to examine the allegations concerning the principles and procedures stated in Article 22.3 in its entirety, while Article 22.6 seems to limit the arbitrators' ability if a request to allow the suspension of concessions is presented in virtue of Article 22.3(b) or (c).[32] At this point, the arbitrators have stated that there is no

[30] See Appellate Body Report, *European Communities – Customs Classification of Certain Computer Equipment*, WT/DS62/AB/R, 22 June 1998, paragraphs 64–73; Appellate Body Report, *EC – Bananas III*, paragraphs 141–3; Appellate Body Report, *Korea – Definitive Safeguard Measures on Imports of Certain Dairy Products*, WT/DS98/AB/R, 12 January 2000, paragraphs 114–31, quoting prior reports about the interpretation of DSU Article 6.2; Panel Report, *Japan – Measures Affecting Consumer Photographic Film and Paper*, WT/DS44/R, 22 April 1998, paragraphs 10.8–10.10 and 10.15–10.19; Appellate Body Report, *Australia – Salmon*, paragraphs 90–105.

[31] Appellate Body Report, *EC – Bananas III (Ecuador) (Article 22.6 – EC)*, paragraphs 28–9.

[32] Refer particularly to DSU Article 22.3(a), (b), and (c): 'In considering what concessions or other obligations to suspend, the complaining party shall apply the following principles and procedures: (a) the general principle is that the complaining party should first seek to suspend concessions or other obligations with respect to the same sector(s) as that in which the panel or Appellate Body has found a violation or other nullification or impairment; (b) if that party considers that it is not practicable or effective to suspend concessions or other obligations

contradiction between paragraphs 6 and 7 of Article 22, and that these provisions can be read harmoniously together. For the arbitrators, the fundamental raison d'être of these provisions is to ensure that the suspension of concessions or other obligations between sectors or agreements (excluding those sectors or agreements for which a panel or the Appellate Body has notified violations) remains an exception and does not become the rule. For DSU Article 22.3 to be fully implemented, the arbitrators' power to examine on demand whether the principles or procedures in paragraphs (b) and (c) have been followed implies that the arbitrators have the competence to examine whether a requirement presented in virtue of paragraph (a) should have been made, wholly or partly, according to paragraphs (b) or (c). If the arbitrators were deprived of this implicit power, principles and procedures contained in Article 22.3 could easily be bent. Indeed, if there was no sort of test whatsoever for authorization requirements to suspend concessions presented in virtue of paragraph (a), members could be tempted to invoke this paragraph always so as to skip the multilateral surveillance system to which the intersector suspension of concessions or other obligations is submitted, and the rules in other paragraphs of Article 22.3 could simply become obsolete.[33]

Arbitration as an 'alternative' and 'autonomous' means of dispute settlement at the WTO

Arbitration appears in the DSU as an 'expeditious' procedure and 'as an alternative means of dispute settlement'.[34] Until now, only in one

with respect to the same sector(s), it may seek to suspend concessions or other obligations in other sectors under the same agreement; (c) if that party considers that it is not practicable or effective to suspend concessions or other obligations with respect to other sectors under the same agreement, and that the circumstances are serious enough, it may seek to suspend concessions or other obligations under another covered agreement'.

33 Appellate Body Report, *EC – Bananas III (US) (Article 22.6 – EC)*, paragraphs 3.5 and 3.7.

34 Article 25 states that: '1. Expeditious arbitration within the WTO as an alternative means of dispute settlement can facilitate the solution of certain disputes that concern issues that are clearly defined by both parties. 2. Except as otherwise provided in this Understanding, resort to arbitration shall be subject to mutual agreement of the parties which shall agree on the procedures to be followed. Agreements to resort to arbitration shall be notified to all Members sufficiently in advance of the actual commencement of the arbitration process. 3. Other Members may become party to an arbitration proceeding only upon the

instance, *US – Section 110(5) Copyright Act (Article 25.3)*,[35]was an arbitration procedure based on DSU Article 25 put in place. Moreover, it was the first case in which a WTO dispute settlement body was required to determine the level of nullification or impairment following a failure to comply with obligations deriving from the Agreement on Trade-Related Aspects of Intellectual Property Rights (TRIPS).[36] It is also noteworthy that this arbitration presented great resemblance in its object with an arbitration to be led under DSU Article 22.6.

The arbitrator as the judge of the 'competence of the competence'

The only recourse to arbitration under DSU Article 25[37] naturally raised the question of the arbitrators' competence. Whereas the DSB establishes panels or directs issues towards arbitration bodies, Article 25 sets a different procedure. Parties to a dispute can choose to resort to arbitration and must solely notify to the DSB their decision to have recourse to arbitration. No decision from the DSB is necessary for a question that must be submitted to an Article 25 arbitration. In the absence of multilateral and institutional control over the procedure, the arbitrators themselves have to ensure that it is applied in conformity with the rules and procedures of the WTO dispute settlement system.[38] As reminded by the Appellate Body in *US – 1916 Act*,[39] there exists a widely accepted rule according to which an international court has the competence to examine the question of its own competence.[40]

agreement of the parties which have agreed to have recourse to arbitration. The parties to the proceeding shall agree to abide by the arbitration award. Arbitration awards shall be notified to the DSB and the Council or Committee of any relevant agreement where any Member may raise any point relating thereto. 4. Articles 21 and 22 of this Understanding shall apply mutatis mutandis to arbitration awards.'

35 *US – Section 110(5) Copyright Act (Article 25.3)*.

36 The lessons to draw from practice are thus inscribed within a limited frame.

37 The arbitrators were reminded that arbitration was rarely used within the framework of the GATT 1947.

38 In particular, the arbitrators have deemed that the arbitration procedure at stake should not be enacted so as to distort the provisions in DSU Article 22.6.

39 See Appellate Body Report, *United States – Anti-dumping Act of 1916*, WT/DS136/AB/R, 26 September 2000, paragraph 54, note on p. 30.

40 This point of view is corroborated by Article 21 of the Optional Rules for Arbitration Involving International Organizations and States. See Permanent Court of Arbitration, Optional Rules for Arbitration Involving International Organizations and States, effective 1 July 1996, The Hague, Netherlands.

In *US – Section 110(5) Copyright Act (Article 25.3)*, the arbitrators deemed that this principle also applies to arbitration courts. They insisted on pointing out the reasons why they deemed it necessary to take cognizance of the dispute presented to them. The arbitration proceedings had been initiated to examine a specific question resulting from the enactment of the decisions and recommendations adopted by the DSB on the basis of the panel report in *US – Section 110(5) Copyright Act*. The arbitrators' remit was to determine the level of annulment or reduction of advantages for the European Community resulting from the provisions in Article 110(5) (B) in the USA's law on copyright.

DSU Article 25.2 states that recourse to arbitration is subordinated to parties' mutual agreement on procedures to be undertaken, except for a contrary provision of the DSU.[41] Article 25 does not specify that having recourse to arbitration is excluded when the issue is to determine the level of nullification or impairment undergone by a member state of the WTO. On the contrary, the terms of Article 25.1, referring to 'the solution of certain disputes that concern issues that are clearly defined by both parties', may allow one to think that Article 25 should be interpreted as an arbitration mechanism to which member states of the WTO may have recourse every time they deem it necessary. Moreover, it is relevant to note that DSU Article 22.2 mentions the 'negotiations with any party having invoked the dispute settlement procedures, with a view to developing mutually acceptable compensation'.[42] According to the arbitrators in the above-mentioned dispute, nothing in the wording of this provision seems to forbid considering arbitration as a means for achieving a mutually acceptable compensation.

In addition, the nature of arbitration allows it to contribute to the swift settlement of a dispute between WTO member states, as required in DSU Article 3.2. Indeed, it may facilitate the resolution of a dispute in the context of a negotiation of compensation, thus opening the way for implementation, while avoiding the suspension of concessions or other obligations. In the arbitrators' logic:

[41] See P. Monnier, 'Working Procedures before Panels, the Appellate Body and Other Adjudicating Bodies of the WTO' (2002) 1(3) *Law and Practice of International Courts and Tribunals* 512. According to the author, 'Article 25 arbitration is probably the most diplomatic procedure among WTO adjudicating bodies since it was designed as " an alternative means of dispute settlement" '.

[42] Appellate Body Report, *US – 1916 Act*, paragraph 2.4.

> In general, recourse to arbitration under Article 25 strengthens the dispute resolution system by complementing negotiation under Article 22.2. The possibility for the parties to a dispute to seek arbitration in relation to the negotiation of compensation operates to increase the effectiveness of that option under Article 22.2. Incidentally ... compensation, is always to be preferred to countermeasures of any sort, since it enhances trade instead of restricting or diverting it ... such an application of Article 25 does not, at least in the case at hand, affect the rights of other Members under the DSU.[43]

Considering the object of arbitration requested by parties, and the fact that other states' rights within the framework of the DSU should not be affected by the USA's and European Communities' decision to have recourse to arbitration according to Article 25, the arbitrators thought that while waiting for an ulterior interpretation provided by the member states of the WTO, they had to declare themselves able to determine the level of the European Communities' advantages that were nullified or impaired.[44]

Arbitration under Article 25: an autonomous 'means' of dispute settlement and an autonomous 'procedure' in the DSU?

The DSU remains vague on the issue of the autonomy of arbitration under Article 25. First, it is stipulated that an agreement on the recourse to arbitration will be notified to all WTO member states quite a long time before the effective starting of the arbitration proceedings. Does this mean that member states could question the arbitration agreement's validity? Could this agreement be annulled or declared in non-conformity if it were to include provisions contrary to the WTO agreements? At this level, what is the role of the multilateral surveillance system? Moreover, one is entitled to wonder whether procedures provided for in an arbitration

[43] *Ibid.*, paragraph 2.6.

[44] It is interesting to note the arbitrators' 'profession of faith' in this case (*Ibid.*, see footnote 30): 'The Arbitrators' recognition of their jurisdiction in this case is not a unilateral extension of WTO jurisdiction, since it is dependent on the agreement of the parties to a dispute to have recourse to Article 25 of the DSU. This decision is without prejudice to the DSU compatibility of the decision of the parties to accept this award as the level of nullification or impairment for the purpose of any further proceedings under Article 22 of the DSU in relation to this case. It is also without prejudice to any interpretation of the provisions of Articles 22 and 25 of the DSU by the Ministerial Conference or the General Council.'

agreement are *lato sensu* 'additional or special procedures' covered by the terms of DSU Article 1.2.[45] In *Guatemala – Cement I*,[46] the Appellate Body asserted that the special or additional rules and procedures of DSU Article 1.2 fitted together with the generally applicable rules and procedures of the DSU to form 'a comprehensive, integrated dispute settlement system'.[47] These special or additional rules and procedures will prevail over the provisions of the DSU to the extent that there is a difference between the two sets of provisions. If there is no difference, the rules and proceedings of the DSU apply jointly to the special or additional provisions of the WTO agreement. It should be noted that a special or additional rule or procedure prevails over a DSU provision when application of the former implies the latter's violation, i.e., in case of conflict between the two provisions.[48]

Thus, it seems that, according to DSU Article 1.2, the procedures to be followed in an arbitration under Article 25 – set by a mutual agreement between the parties to a dispute – are not 'additional or special procedures' that could prevail, and *a fortiori* depart from, the procedures set by the DSU. Indeed, Article 1.2 lays down a restrictive list of the WTO agreements containing these 'additional or special' procedures. Arbitration agreements – which are not 'covered agreements' as defined by the DSU – are not mentioned in it. What is more, DSU Article 25.2 creates the possibility for the parties to agree on procedures to follow 'except as otherwise provided in the DSU'. Hence, it would be difficult to

[45] 'The rules and procedures of this Understanding shall apply subject to such special or additional rules and procedures on dispute settlement contained in the covered agreements as are identified in Appendix 2 to this Understanding. To the extent that there is a difference between the rules and procedures of this Understanding and the special or additional rules and procedures set forth in Appendix 2, the special or additional rules and procedures in Appendix 2 shall prevail. In disputes involving rules and procedures under more than one covered agreement, if there is a conflict between special or additional rules and procedures of such agreements under review, and where the parties to the dispute cannot agree on rules and procedures within 20 days of the establishment of the panel, the Chairman of the Dispute Settlement Body provided for in paragraph 1 of Article 2 (referred to in this Understanding as the "DSB"), in consultation with the parties to the dispute, shall determine the rules and procedures to be followed within 10 days after a request by either Member. The Chairman shall be guided by the principle that special or additional rules and procedures should be used where possible, and the rules and procedures set out in this Understanding should be used to the extent necessary to avoid conflict.'

[46] Appellate Body Report, *Guatemala – Cement I*. See also Appellate Body Report, *Brazil – Measures Affecting Desiccated Coconut*, WT/DS22/AB/R, 20 March 1999, p. 15.

[47] Appellate Body Report, *Guatemala – Cement I*, paragraph 66.

[48] *Ibid.*, paragraph 65.

confer a *lex specialis* status on arbitration agreements, effectively severing them from the DSU and its rules and procedures.

Article 25 merely provides that the arbitration award will be 'notified' to the DSB and to the Council or Committee of any relevant agreement. Contrary to the panel's and the Appellate Body's reports, the arbitration award rendered in virtue of Article 25 does not require an adoption procedure by the DSB. An original aspect must be noticed: the arbitration report must be notified to a Council or Committee of any relevant agreement. For instance, it will be notified to the TRIPS Council if the award concerned issues related to the TRIPS.

Prima facie, the parties to the arbitration procedure must 'agree' to conform to the award. Article 25 does not set specific procedures and substantial rules to warrant the respect of the award. Nevertheless, it provides that DSU Articles 21 and 22 will apply *mutatis mutandis* to the awards.[49] This is a token of effective implementation of the arbitral awards delivered according to DSU Article 25 as they may benefit from the multilateral surveillance system machinery. However, it can be seen also as an indication that the negotiators wanted to privilege dispute settlement through panels and the Appellate Body, rather than by an ad hoc arbitration procedure, since the enactment of the ruling issued by an arbitration procedure under Article 25 is rooted in the general procedure of dispute settlement.

Last, the enigma of the relevant law to be applied within the framework of DSU Article 25 needs to be addressed. Is it possible to conceive that states parties to an arbitration procedure could decide by a common agreement to determine the applicable law to their dispute outside of the WTO agreements? This hypothesis is probably unsustainable. DSU Article 3.2 underlines *expressis verbis* that:

> The dispute settlement system of the WTO is a central element in providing security and predictability to the multilateral trading system. The Members recognize that it serves to preserve the rights and obligations of Members under the covered agreements, and to clarify the existing provisions of those agreements in accordance with customary rules of interpretation of public international law. Recommendations and

[49] See V. Hughes who considers that 'the words "*mutatis mutandis*" suggest that an arbitration award duly notified pursuant to Article 25.3 would be equivalent of the recommendations and rulings referred to in Articles 21 and 22', Hughes, 'Arbitration within the WTO.'

rulings of the DSB cannot add to or diminish the rights and obligations provided in the covered agreements.

Although this provision *a priori* addresses the WTO dispute settlement bodies, it seems to imply *in extenso* that the states parties to a WTO dispute are limited in their choice of the applicable law. Where states derogate from the 'WTO law' in an arbitration agreement, it would be quite plausible that the arbitrator(s) should decide to determine the legality of the agreement setting their powers in the light of the DSU. In this area, however, practice at the WTO does not yet exist.

Conclusion

Although the WTO Agreement provides 'for a multitude of dispute settlement procedures',[50] one cannot but note that the so-called 'mainstream procedures', i.e., consultations, the possibility of establishing a panel, and recourse to the Appellate Body, play a key role in practice for resolving disputes. Arbitration is foreseen in different ways in the DSU, one of them being arbitration as an alternative means of dispute settlement. It is hoped that in the future the latter contributes more forcefully to preventing and avoiding trade disputes.

A careful analysis of the arbitration procedures in the WTO reveals that alternative dispute settlement procedures such as arbitration cannot be considered as fully autonomous within the WTO. They are enshrined in the DSU and must conform to certain principles and rules. Some arbitration procedures have been heavily moulded against this background. The procedure stemming from DSU Article 25 has been granted more autonomy (one can think of the freedom of the parties to choose the arbitrators and to some extent, the procedural rules), but draws many of its '*lettres de noblesse*' from the DSU.

50 Feliciano and Van den Bossche, 'Dispute Settlement System', p. 304.

15

The Challenges to the Legitimacy of the WTO

DEBRA P. STEGER

Introduction

The World Trade Organization (WTO) faces two major challenges to its legitimacy and credibility as an international organization. The first is to make its internal decision-making system more transparent and inclusive, especially for the developing and least developed countries (which now represent the majority of its 147 members). This is the challenge of 'internal legitimacy'. The second is to respond to external critics – mainly non-governmental organizations (NGOs) and non-state actors – who maintain that the WTO is a closed, non-democratic, bureaucratic, supranational entity. This is the issue of 'external legitimacy'.

The external legitimacy challenge arises, in part, because the WTO administers a complex set of agreements that reach deeply into subjects formerly the exclusive province of national and subnational levels of government, for example, intellectual property, health and safety standards, regulation of services, and subsidies. In addition, the dispute settlement system, with its compulsory jurisdiction and binding decisions, more closely resembles domestic judicial systems than the normal, voluntary, international arbitration mechanisms.

With respect to the issue of internal legitimacy, the difficulty with the decision-making procedures in the WTO does not result from defects in the rules, per se, but rather from the inflexible determination of WTO members to take all decisions by consensus. Changing the decision-making rules is not likely to change the attitudes of WTO members. Moreover, it would increase the perceptions of developing countries that they are not included in the important decision-making processes.

However, the WTO has become a very complex enterprise and needs a smaller body than the General Council to address the many administrative, procedural, and house-keeping issues that arise, as well as to help set priorities and provide direction for the system. In my view, a representative management board could be made to work in a way that would be inclusive of all WTO members.

With respect to the issue of external legitimacy, the dispute settlement system has become the focus of attention since 1995. Whereas the political and legislative bodies of the WTO have been viewed as weak and incapable of taking decisions, the dispute settlement system is viewed by most members and observers as being extremely effective.

There is a growing perception in Washington, especially among lawyers representing American industries in anti-dumping, countervail, and safeguards investigations, that WTO panels and the Appellate Body have been 'overreaching' and legislating in recent cases.[1] The allegation is that the adjudicative bodies have disregarded the intent of the negotiators in the WTO agreements and have created new rights and obligations contrary to the provisions of the Dispute Settlement Understanding (DSU). In doing so, it is argued, the dispute settlement bodies 'undermine the legitimacy of the WTO's agreements, the WTO and its dispute settlement system, and future negotiations on trade'.[2] The imbalance that has emerged between the judicial and legislative branches of the WTO, some have argued, is a 'formidable constitutional flaw'.[3] It is against this background that the USA and Chile tabled a proposal in the negotiations on the DSU in Geneva aimed at 'improving flexibility and Member control in WTO dispute settlement'.[4]

Is the WTO constitutionally flawed? Have the judicial bodies exceeded their authority under the WTO Agreement and 'legislated', thereby creating new rights and obligations for members and threatening the legitimacy of the WTO? I will argue that panels and the Appellate

[1] See John Greenwald, 'WTO Dispute Settlement: An Exercise in Trade Law Legislation?', James P. Durling, 'Deference, by Only When Due: WTO Review of Anti-Dumping Measures', and Richard O. Cunningham and Troy H. Cribb, 'A Review of WTO Dispute Settlement of US Anti-Dumping and Countervailing Duty Measures' (2003) 6(1) *Journal of International Economic Law* 113 at 125, 155. See also Paul C. Rosenthal and Jeffrey S. Beckington, 'Dispute Settlement before the World Trade Organization in Antidumping, Countervailing and Safeguard Actions: Effective Interpretation or Unauthorized Legislation?', speech delivered at a conference presented by the Trade and Customs Law Committee of the International Bar Association, 'Developments in WTO Law', Geneva, Switzerland, 20–21 March 2003.

[2] See *ibid.* at p. 1.

[3] Claude E. Barfield, *Free Trade, Sovereignty, Democracy: The Future of the World Trade Organization* (AEI Press, 2001), p. 1.

[4] Contribution by Chile and the USA, Negotiations on Improvements and Clarifications of the Dispute Settlement Understanding on Improving Flexibility and Member Control in WTO Dispute Settlement, TN/DS/W/52, 14 March 2003.

Body have not been 'legislating' contrary to the intent of negotiators, but rather have been 'clarifying' the existing provisions of the WTO Agreement in accordance with the customary rules of interpretation of public international law as they are obliged to do under the DSU.[5] In other words, they have simply been doing their jobs.

WTO dispute settlement has two tracks, diplomatic and judicial. The diplomatic track includes consultations, mediation, conciliation, and arbitration mechanisms, including the good offices of the Director-General. A significant percentage of WTO cases settle early in this diplomatic phase.[6] When a case is referred to a panel, it moves into the judicial track.[7]

The current panel and Appellate Body process in the WTO is thus a hybrid between the 'diplomatic' and the 'judicial' models. Rather than injecting more 'flexibility and member control' into the panel and Appellate Body processes as some have proposed, the legitimacy challenges facing the WTO would best be met by improving the diplomatic process while at the same time taking measures to further 'judicialize' or 'professionalize' the panel system, improve the rules and procedures for compliance with WTO rulings, and enhance transparency and understanding of the system by opening up panel and Appellate Body hearings to the public.

The following section discusses the issue of legitimacy in conceptual terms. Subsequently, the issues of legitimacy raised by the functioning of the dispute settlement mechanism and of the WTO's rule-making institutions are addressed in turn. The final section draws some conclusions.

What is 'Legitimacy'?

The issue of legitimacy is, as noted by J. H. H. Weiler, an inveterate observer of the evolution of the European Community, 'part of the

[5] Under Understanding on Rules and Procedures Governing the Settlement of Disputes (DSU) Article 3.2 and Agreement on Implementation of Article VI of the General Agreement on Tariffs and Trade 1994 ('the Antidumping Agreement') Article 17.6.

[6] Marc L. Busch and Eric Reinhardt, 'The Evolution of GATT/WTO Dispute Settlement' in John Curtis and Dan Ciuriak (eds.), *Trade Policy Review 2003* (Public Works and Government Services Canada, 2003), p. 143.

[7] Interestingly, Busch and Reinhardt maintain that, after a panel has been established and a case has moved into the formal judicial process, the chances for settlement are greatly diminished. This is not surprising. In fact, it demonstrates that the parties realize that, at that point, they have entrusted the dispute to an independent, impartial tribunal to be determined on the basis of the law. *Ibid.*

standard vocabulary of court watching'.[8] In the last few years, it has also become a hot topic for WTO watchers. Although many commentators have written about the so-called 'crisis of legitimacy' in the WTO, few have defined the term with any precision.[9]

Robert Keohane and Joseph Nye Jr. equate 'legitimacy' with notions of democracy and accountability. They state that 'in the contemporary world, democratic norms are increasingly applied to international institutions as a test of their legitimacy'. Although Keohane and Nye recognize that domestic models of democracy do not apply to international organizations (in particular, because there is neither a coherent world polity nor are there institutional arrangements linking the public to those governing these organizations), they recommend that formal political channels be established between international organizations and constituencies within civil society.[10]

Robert E. Hudec has questioned whether the WTO *is* an institution of governance, separate from the governments which comprise it.[11] He maintains that the WTO is, first and foremost, an international organization and, as such, definitions of legitimacy applied to it cannot be the same as definitions applied to national governments. Grounding discussions of legitimacy in relation to the WTO in notions of democracy, in his view, is fundamentally flawed.

Thomas M. Franck, in his book, *The Power of Legitimacy Among Nations*, searches for the properties of 'legitimacy' as it applies to international systems of rules.[12] He defines 'legitimacy' in this context as:

[8] J. H. H. Weiler, 'The Rule of Lawyers and the Ethos of Diplomats: Reflections on the Internal and External Legitimacy of WTO Dispute Settlement' (2001) 35(2) *Journal of World Trade* 191 at 193.

[9] See Robert Howse and Kalypso Nicolaidis, 'Legitimacy and Global Governance: Why Constitutionalizing the WTO is a Step Too Far' (with comments by Steve Charnovitz and Gary N. Horlick); Robert O. Keohane and Joseph S. Nye Jr., 'The Club Model of Multilateral Cooperation and Problems of Democratic Legitimacy' (with comments by Robert E. Hudec and Daniel C. Esty); and Frieder Roessler, 'Are the Judicial Organs of the WTO Overburdened?' (with comments by William J. Davey) in R. B. Porter, P. Sauvé, A. Subramanian, and A. B. Zampetti (eds.), *Efficiency, Equity, Legitimacy: The Multilateral Trading System at the Millennium* (Brookings, 2001), pp. 227–333.

[10] *Ibid.* at pp. 290–1.

[11] Comment by Robert E. Hudec in Porter, Sauvé, Subramanian, and Zampetti, *Efficiency, Equity, Legitimacy*, pp. 295–300 at p. 298.

[12] Thomas M. Franck, *The Power of Legitimacy Among Nations* (Oxford University Press, 1990). For an excellent review of Franck's seminal work, see José E. Alvarez, 'The Quest for Legitimacy: An Examination of the Power of Legitimacy Among Nations by Thomas M. Franck' (1991) 24 *New York University Journal of International Law and Politics* 199.

> 'a property of a rule or rule-making institution which itself exerts a pull toward compliance on those addressed normatively[13] because those addressed believe that the rule or institution has come into being and operates in accordance with generally accepted principles of right process.'[14]

In developing his hypothesis, Franck defines and examines four indicators of legitimacy applicable in 'the community of states': determinacy, symbolic validation, coherence, and adherence. His hypothesis asserts that 'to the extent a rule, or rule process, exhibits these four properties it will exert a strong pull on states to comply. To the extent these properties are not present, the institution will be easier to ignore and the rule easier to avoid by a state tempted to pursue its short-term self-interest.'[15]

Franck's indicators of determinacy, symbolic validation, coherence, and adherence provide a framework for assessing the legitimacy of the WTO as an international system of rules. By using these indicators, we can examine the extent to which the WTO legal system exerts a 'compliance pull' on its members. We can examine the inputs into the WTO rule-making and dispute settlement processes to assess whether due process and fairness (i.e., 'right process') are applied in making and interpreting the rules. And we can analyse the outputs of the system, by assessing the quality and coherence of the dispute settlement decisions interpreting the rules.

The WTO dispute settlement system, which has pulls both towards greater diplomacy and judicialization, can be analysed to determine whether it is effective in contributing to the legitimacy of the WTO as an international system of rules.

The dispute settlement system

The 'diplomatic' v. the 'judicial' model

There has long been a tension between the 'diplomatic' and the 'judicial' features of GATT/WTO dispute settlement.[16] Even during the GATT era,

[13] 'Those addressed', Franck states, could include 'nations, international organizations, leadership elites, and, on occasion, multinational corporations and the global populace'. Franck, *Power of Legitimacy*, p. 16.

[14] *Ibid.* at p. 24. [15] *Ibid.* at p. 49.

[16] I have previously referred to this as a 'balance' between the pragmatic and the legalistic, but if it is a balance, it is a delicate one. Debra P. Steger and Susan M. Hainsworth, 'World Trade Organization Dispute Settlement: The First Three Years' (1998) 1(2) *Journal of International Economic Law* 199; see also Robert E. Hudec, *Enforcing International Trade Law: The Evolution of the Modern GATT Legal System*

multilateral dispute settlement was evolving towards a judicialized model. The reforms to the DSU agreed in the Uruguay Round accelerated this trend.

A major problem in the GATT system had been that reports or decisions of panels had to be adopted by a consensus decision of the Contracting Parties in order to become legally effective. However, a party could block the adoption of a panel report. The DSU reforms addressed this problem by providing that reports of panels and the Appellate Body were to be automatically 'adopted' by the Dispute Settlement Body (DSB) unless there were 'reverse consensus' decisions against adoption. The DSB could also authorize suspension of concessions for failure to implement the rulings of a panel or the Appellate Body more or less 'automatically', unless there was a 'reverse consensus'.

The establishment of the Appellate Body was intended by Uruguay Round negotiators as part of the *quid pro quo* for automatic adoption of panel reports – in effect, it was to safeguard against the occasional 'wrong' decision of panels.[17] The Appellate Body is comprised of seven persons, appointed by consensus by the members of the WTO, on the basis of their qualifications and taking into account the overall geographic representation and diversity of legal systems within the WTO membership. All but one of the seven incumbent members of the Appellate Body are legally-trained jurists with distinguished backgrounds in public international law or international economic law. Their qualifications are very similar to those of judges appointed to other international tribunals.

While the DSU reforms, especially the establishment of the Appellate Body, have driven the system more dynamically towards a judicialized model of dispute settlement, elements of the diplomatic model remain. These diplomatic elements make the dispute settlement system more acceptable to WTO members, and thus contribute to its 'internal' legitimacy. However, these same diplomatic elements raise questions about the transparency and accountability of the WTO dispute settlement system to the outside world, and therefore detract from its 'external' legitimacy.

There is a struggle for legitimacy within the WTO, and the dispute settlement system has become the battleground. There are conflicting pulls on the system. From *within*, member governments perceive the

(Butterworths, 1993), pp. 11–15; J. H. Jackson, *Restructuring the GATT System* (Royal Institute of International Affairs, 1990), pp. 59–68.

[17] Debra P. Steger, 'The Appellate Body and its Contribution to WTO Dispute Settlement' in D. Kennedy and J. Southwick (eds.), *The Political Economy of International Trade Law: Essays in Honour of Robert E. Hudec* (Cambridge University Press, 2002), pp. 482–95 at 483.

dispute settlement system as essentially diplomatic and want to keep it that way so as to enhance their control over it. From *outside*, NGOs and representatives of civil society maintain that the system must become more open and transparent, and must provide rights of participation for non-state 'stakeholders' as well as WTO members.[18]

The 'diplomatic' vestiges remaining in the panel system

Several vestiges of the 'diplomatic' model of dispute settlement remain in the panel system in the WTO. They endure because most WTO members put a high priority on retaining control and authority over the system (both in terms of inputs and outputs).[19] Two of the most important diplomatic features are the selection and *modus operandi* of panels and the confidentiality or secrecy of dispute settlement proceedings.

Panels are selected by the agreement of the parties to the dispute, based on nominations made by the WTO Secretariat, and can be composed of government officials or non-governmental individuals.[20] The overwhelming majority of panelists selected to serve since 1995 have been government officials, often working with delegations in Geneva. When the parties cannot agree on the three persons to sit on a panel, the Director-General of the WTO may appoint the panel.[21] This is occurring in an increasing number of cases, because the parties cannot always agree on the composition of panels.

The function of panels, as set forth in DSU Article 11, illustrates the tension between the 'judicial' and 'diplomatic' approaches. On the one

[18] For an excellent debate on who are the 'stakeholders' in the WTO, and who should have standing in WTO dispute settlement, see Philip M. Nichols, 'Extension of Standing in the World Trade Organization' (1996) 17 *University of Pennsylvania Journal of International Economic Law* 310; Richard Shell, 'The Trade Stakeholders Model and Participation by Nonstate Parties in the World Trade Organization' (1996) 17 *University of Pennsylvania Journal of International Economic Law* 370; Steve Charnovitz, 'Participation of Nongovernmental Organizations in the World Trade Organization' (1996) 17 *University of Pennsylvania Journal of International Economic Law* 339; Philip M. Nichols, 'Realism, Liberalism, Values, and the World Trade Organization' (1996) 17 *University of Pennsylvania Journal of International Economic Law* 859.

[19] The recent proposal by Chile and the USA in the Doha Round DSU negotiations underlines this desire to 'control' even the judicial aspects of the dispute settlement system. See *supra* n. 4.

[20] DSU Article 8. [21] DSU Article 8.7.

hand Article 11 requires a panel to 'make an objective assessment of the matter before it, including an objective assessment of the facts of the case and the applicability of and conformity with the relevant covered agreements'. On the other hand, this same Article states that panels 'should consult regularly with the parties to the dispute and give them adequate opportunity to develop a mutually satisfactory solution'.[22] In order to assist them in carrying out their functions, panels are provided with a sparse set of working procedures in an appendix to the DSU, and are instructed that they may devise additional procedures that 'provide sufficient flexibility as to ensure high-quality panel reports, while not unduly delaying the panel process'.[23] While the DSU provides only that a panel must 'consult' with the parties to the dispute when it wishes to adopt additional procedures, panels have been reluctant, on their own, to adopt procedures without the agreement of the parties. This has led the WTO Secretariat to develop a model set of Working Procedures, which most panels now adopt. However, these Procedures deal mostly with issues such as time-frames for filing submissions, holding meetings, and responding to questions. They do not deal with the more difficult and contentious issues, such as admissibility of *amicus curiae* briefs or procedures for preliminary rulings and injunctions.

The continuing selection of panelists on an ad hoc basis from the pool of Geneva-based government officials contributes to the 'internal' legitimacy of the dispute settlement system because it gives WTO member governments the perception of control over panel proceedings. Parties to the dispute can select those whom they want to sit on a particular case (more particularly, they can reject suggestions made by the Secretariat). The parties can determine the panel's procedures. They can present the facts as they see them, and they are given an opportunity to comment on the panel's description and assessment of the facts. Finally, the parties can comment on a panel's conclusions and legal reasoning even before the final panel report has been circulated and made public.

The ad hoc nature of the panel system, the background and qualifications of persons typically appointed as panelists, the lack of consistency and coherence in panel procedures from case to case, and the inconsistency in the quality of the legal reasoning of panels, all contribute to a perception by the outside world of a closed system run by bureaucrats and government trade policy officials.

[22] DSU Article 11. [23] DSU Article 12.2.

Confidentiality or secrecy is a hallmark of WTO dispute settlement which is explicitly required in the DSU: panel deliberations, Appellate Body proceedings, submissions of parties and third parties to a dispute, as well as information provided to a panel by outside individuals or bodies, are required to be kept confidential.[24] This emphasis on confidentiality is a vestige of diplomatic dispute settlement. Governments have traditionally maintained that the strict rules on confidentiality in the DSU were designed to give the parties flexibility to resolve disputes through negotiation.

There are important counterarguments. Under the GATT, there was a perception that disputes were of interest only to the parties to the dispute. However, this perception is changing within the WTO. A growing number of WTO disputes involve multiple parties and third parties. Also, it has become commonplace for WTO members who are not parties or third parties in a dispute to express their views in DSB meetings relating to that dispute.

Although many members of the WTO remain deeply committed to the principles of confidentiality in dispute settlement, the current rules work against the interests of members of the WTO who are not parties or third parties to a dispute but who may face similar legal issues in other cases.

The rules protecting the confidentiality of documents and proceedings in the DSU undermine the internal legitimacy of the dispute settlement system because they deny WTO members who are not parties to the disputes the opportunity to know what is being argued in particular cases. Furthermore, within civil society, these rules breed distrust and misunderstanding of the WTO dispute settlement system. Nothing works against the external legitimacy of the WTO dispute settlement system as powerfully as its lack of transparency. Opening up the system would not only eradicate the perceptions of closed, secretive proceedings, but would also improve public understanding of the system.

The 'judicial' features

The combined effect of introducing compulsory adjudication, automatic adoption of panel and Appellate Body reports, and automatic authorization of retaliation in cases of non-compliance, has been to give

[24] DSU Articles 13.1, 14.1, 17.10, 18.2 and Appendix 3, paragraph 3.

the WTO dispute settlement system some degree of predictability and to make the findings and conclusions of panels legally binding.

Some commentators, however, have argued that the DSU reforms gave an inordinate amount of power to the 'judicial' branch of the WTO, resulting in an imbalance of power vis-à-vis the 'legislative' branch.[25] They maintain that the Appellate Body has 'overreached' its constitutional authority in the DSU in several cases, arguing that its decisions have filled gaps in the legal framework left by the Uruguay Round negotiators. The result, according to this argument, is that the Appellate Body has 'legislated' and thereby modified the rights and obligations of members contrary to the rules of the DSU.

Are these commentators correct? Has the Appellate Body exceeded its authority and created difficulties for the internal legitimacy of the WTO? Has it contributed to, or detracted from, the external legitimacy of the WTO?

To answer these questions, we turn to Professor Franck's indicators of legitimacy. With respect to the indicator of 'determinacy', not all WTO rules are models of textual clarity. Indeed, some of the language in the 500 or so pages of the text of the WTO Agreement is deliberately vague, reflecting a lack of agreement among the negotiators. That being said, one of the purposes of dispute settlement as stated in DSU Article 3.2 is 'to *clarify* the existing provisions of those agreements in accordance with customary rules of interpretation of public international law'. It is common for treaties, and even constitutions, to contain rules that have a certain degree of ambiguity because of unresolved disagreements or uncertainties.[26] Such vagueness is not necessarily a problem; it may leave room for a rule to evolve flexibly through interpretation and application by a process of clarification recognized as legitimate by those to whom the rules are addressed.[27] Franck suggests that courts are a credible process of clarification, but not the only such process. Whether a 'clarifying process' is successful in transforming an 'indeterminate' rule into a 'determinate' one depends upon such factors of

[25] See Frieder Roessler, 'Are the Judicial Organs of the World Trade Organization Overburdened?' in Porter, Sauvé, Subramanian, and Zampetti, *Efficiency, Equity, Legitimacy*, pp. 308–28; Frieder Roessler, 'The Institutional Balance between the Judicial and the Political Organs of the WTO' in M. Bronckers and R. Quick (eds.), *New Directions in International Economic Law: Essays in Honour of John H. Jackson* (Kluwer, 2000), pp. 325–45.

[26] Franck, *Power of Legitimacy*, p. 53. [27] *Ibid.* at p. 61.

legitimacy '*as who* is doing the interpreting, their *pedigree* or authority to interpret, and the *coherence* of the principles the interpreters apply'.[28]

The Appellate Body, in its very first case, *US – Gasoline*, set forth the interpretative approach that it was to follow in subsequent cases. In that case, the Appellate Body stated that the 'general rule of interpretation' set forth in Article 31 of the Vienna Convention on the Law of Treaties is a rule of customary international law that is to be followed in interpreting and applying the provisions of the WTO Agreement. DSU Article 3.2, the Appellate Body noted, recognizes that the WTO rules are 'not to be read in clinical isolation from public international law'.[29]

Rather than 'legislating' to fill in gaps in the WTO's legal rules, the Appellate Body has consistently applied an internationally agreed set of rules to interpret the provisions of the WTO Agreement. In so doing, it has developed a coherent approach to interpretation, in accordance with accepted principles of international law, and has required that panels follow the same method. Thus, the Appellate Body has adopted a 'right process' for interpreting and clarifying the sometimes 'indeterminate' rules in the WTO Agreement.

With respect to the factor of 'symbolic validation', which features of the WTO's judicial bodies might be said to correspond to Franck's concepts of 'rituals' and 'pedigree'? In relation to 'pedigree', the Appellate Body is a relatively new judicial institution and did not come endowed with an established reputation. It had to develop, through its first cases, its own credibility and legitimacy as an international tribunal.

As Franck has observed, *who* decides is an important factor in determining the legitimacy of a clarifying judicial process. The original seven members of the Appellate Body were all highly respected jurists with impeccable credentials – senior judges, high ranking diplomats, lawyers, and law professors, with extensive backgrounds in public international law or international economic law generally – the very type of persons who would be appointed to the International Court of Justice or other international tribunals. In more recent appointments, the DSB has followed the same pattern, selecting senior jurists, law professors, and judges with backgrounds in public international law. There is no doubt that the selection of

[28] *Ibid.*

[29] Appellate Body Report, *United States – Standards for Reformulated and Conventional Gasoline*, WT/DS2/AB/R, 20 May 1996, p. 17.

persons with these impressive credentials has made a major difference in the quality, style and content of the decisions of the Appellate Body.

Scanning for 'rituals', one might examine the procedures adopted by the Appellate Body. Before the first appeal was filed, the members of the Appellate Body developed and adopted their own detailed rules of procedure, dealing with internal matters relating to the functioning of the Appellate Body as well as the appellate review process. One of the most important rules provided for 'collegiality' in the Appellate Body's decision-making. In practice, while the DSU requires that three Appellate Body members hear and decide a particular appeal, all seven members of the Appellate Body convene in Geneva to discuss and provide guidance on each case. This practice has done much to ensure coherence and consistency of the Appellate Body's rulings on questions of legal interpretation as well as on matters of practice and procedure.

Another 'ritual' that has helped to establish the Appellate Body as a respected, judicial institution is the swearing-in ceremony for new members. The first such ceremony, held in 1995, was a small, closed affair, attended by the Director-General, his Deputies, the Chairs of the General Council, the DSB, and the Councils for Trade in Goods, Trade in Services, and Trade-related Intellectual Property, members of the Appellate Body and their staff. The second such ceremony was conducted in a similar manner, with only the Chairs of the General Council, the DSB, and the Councils for Trade in Goods, Trade in Services, and Trade-related Property representing the WTO membership; however, a large reception was held after the ceremony to which the general WTO membership was invited. In 2001, the ceremony swearing in three new members and bidding farewell to three retiring members was held in a formal meeting of the General Council, with the WTO members in attendance. The progressive development of this ritual indicates recognition of the growing respect and esteem held by WTO members for the Appellate Body.

Another important ritual is the Appellate Body oral hearing. Unlike panel meetings with the parties, Appellate Body hearings are conducted in a highly judicial manner. After the parties and third parties have made their opening arguments, the members of the Appellate Body engage in intensive, detailed questioning of the parties and third parties until all the legal issues in the case have been thoroughly examined. While this is often gruelling for the parties' counsel, this 'face-to-face' interrogation on the issues of law in the case is critical to the Appellate Body's understanding and appreciation of the appeal. This procedure has a ritualistic quality that has worked to establish the credibility and reputation of the Appellate Body as an impartial and independent judicial institution.[30]

With respect to Franck's indicator of 'coherence', in its early jurisprudence, the Appellate Body established a rigorous approach to treaty interpretation, based on the general principles of interpretation set forth in the Vienna Convention as required by DSU Article 3.2. It also drew guidance from time to time, where appropriate, from the practice of other international tribunals and public international law generally. Moreover, the Appellate Body developed a comprehensive set of rulings on matters of judicial practice and procedure, dealing with such issues as standing, burden of proof, treatment of evidence and experts, standard of review, jurisdiction of panels, rights of third parties, right to be represented by counsel, and treatment of *amicus curiae* briefs.

In making some of its procedural rulings, particularly with respect to the right to representation by private counsel and the admissibility of *amicus* briefs, the Appellate Body has been criticized by many WTO members and some commentators, who maintain that these procedural gaps in the DSU can only be filled by the members of the WTO acting in their legislative capacity, and not by the 'judicial' bodies of the WTO through the development of case law.[31] Whether or not they agree with individual rulings of the Appellate Body on these matters, legal scholars generally concur that the Appellate Body has behaved, in general, like a prudent, conservative court, motivated by general principles of natural justice, due process, and fairness, taking pains to demonstrate its motivations and legal reasoning in its published decisions.[32]

[30] One Ambassador for a third party in *European Communities – Importation, Sale and Distribution of Bananas III*, WT/DS27/AB/R, 25 September 1997, took the opportunity to comment to the Appellate Body Division hearing that case that he wished the rest of the WTO worked as effectively and efficiently as the Appellate Body in that hearing.

[31] Barfield, *Free Trade*, pp. 50–3.

[32] See William J. Davey, 'Has the WTO Dispute Settlement System Exceeded Its Authority?' and Robert Howse, 'The Most Dangerous Branch? WTO Appellate Body Jurisprudence, on the Nature and Limits of the Judicial Power' in Thomas Cottier and Petros Mavroidis (eds.), *The Role of the Judge: Lessons for the WTO* (Kluwer, 2003); Robert Howse, 'Adjudicative Legitimacy and Treaty Interpretation in International Trade Law: The Early Years of WTO Jurisprudence' in J. H. H. Weiler (ed.), *The EU, the WTO and the NAFTA: Towards a Common Law of International Trade* (Oxford University Press, 2000), p. 35; John H. Jackson, 'Dispute Settlement and the WTO: Emerging Problems' (1998) 1 *Journal of International Economic Law* 329; Robert E. Hudec, 'The New WTO Dispute Settlement Procedure: An Overview of the First Three Years' (1999) 8 *Minnesota Journal of Global Trade* 1; J. H. H. Weiler, 'The Rule of

On the issue of 'adherence', Professor Franck tells us: 'A rule has greater legitimacy if it is validated by having been made in accordance with secondary rules about rule-making'.[33] Although it is still early days in the history of the WTO dispute settlement system, there are some discernible trends beginning to emerge. The Appellate Body has developed a comprehensive and impressive set of rulings on practice and procedure in the appeals it has heard to date. These rulings, together with the many interpretative rulings made by the Appellate Body, weave together to make a fabric of secondary rules which help to build the foundation of a legitimate judicial institution out of the dispute settlement system of the WTO. This jurisprudence creates a permanent foundation, based on principles of natural justice, due process, and fairness – a 'right process' – for the WTO dispute settlement system.

The rule-making institutions

While the Appellate Body has been working purposefully towards establishing its credibility and legitimacy as an international tribunal, the same cannot be said of the WTO political/legislative bodies. The latter WTO bodies have been characterized as 'weak' by the key powers in the multilateral trading system.[34] European trade lawyer and scholar, Marco Bronckers, has stated that under the new WTO procedures for adopting definitive interpretations or amending provisions of the agreements, '[c]larifying rules is practically impossible' and '[a]dopting new rules is cumbersome'.[35]

The administrative structure and the decision-making apparatus of the WTO *is* complex.[36] The general rule on decision-making is that the

Lawyers and the Ethos of Dilplomats: Reflections on WTO Dispute Settlement' in Porter, Sauvé, Subramanian, and Zampetti, *Efficiency, Equity, Legitimacy*, pp. 334, 346.

33 Franck, *Power of Legitimacy*, p. 193.

34 See the speech by Pascal Lamy, European Trade Commissioner, referred to the German Council on Foreign Relations, Berlin, 27 November 2001, at http://europa.eu.int/comm/trade/speeches_articles/spla86_en.htm in note 1 herein.

35 Marco C. E. J. Bronckers, 'Better Rules for a New Millennium: A Warning against Undemocratic Developments in the WTO' (1999) 29(4) *Journal of International Economic Law* 547 at 551–2.

36 These organizational features of the WTO are set forth in the Marrakesh Agreement, which is a sort of 'mini-constitution' for the multilateral trading system. The Marrakesh Agreement was negotiated during the latter part of the Uruguay Round in the Institutions Group, chaired by Ambassador Julio Lacarte-Muró from Uruguay (who was the first Chairman of the Appellate Body). The history of this negotiation and the

WTO will 'continue the *practice* of decision-making by consensus followed under GATT 1947'.[37] When certain decisions cannot be arrived at by consensus,[38] the Marrakesh Agreement provides for a fallback to majority voting. However, for important decisions, such as adoption of a definitive interpretation of an agreement or approval of a waiver from obligations, the Ministerial Conference must first attempt to take the decision by consensus, and if this fails, the decision may be taken by a three-fourths majority of all the members of the WTO.[39] Decisions to propose amendments to the agreements must be initially attempted to be made by consensus. If, after ninety days, consensus has not been reached, the Ministerial Conference may take the decision by a two-thirds majority of the members.[40]

For most amendments, a decision by the Ministerial Conference to propose an amendment to the members is only the first step. Following this decision, members of the WTO must individually ratify and accept the amendment or the proposal for a new rule or agreement. Amendments will only take effect when they have been accepted by two-thirds of the members of the WTO (for most agreements).[41] Amendments of the DSU are effective upon a consensus decision of the Ministerial Conference approving the proposal to amend the agreement. It is not necessary for individual WTO members to ratify and accept amendments to the DSU, such amendments become effective

decision-making provisions of this agreement are described in Debra P. Steger, 'The World Trade Organization: A New Constitution for the Trading System' in M. Bronckers and R. Quick (eds.), *New Directions in International Economic Law* (Kluwer, 2000), pp. 135–53.

37 Marrakesh Agreement Article IX:1 (emphasis added). The term 'practice' is used to describe the way decisions were made in the GATT since the 1960s because consensus decision-making was not the rule – the rule under GATT Article XXV was majority voting – rather, it was the 'practice'. Marrakesh Agreement Article IX:1 enshrined this 'practice' and made it the 'rule' for the WTO.

38 'Consensus' does not mean 'unanimity'. A decision is 'deemed' to have been decided by consensus 'if no Member, present at the meeting when the decision is taken, formally objects to the proposed decision'. Marrakesh Agreement Article IX:1, note 1. The Rules of Procedure of the General Council (the highest political/legislative body in the WTO when the Ministerial Conference is not in session) and the other Councils require that a quorum of two-thirds of the members be present at any formal meeting; however, that does not always happen. Technically, therefore, a decision could be proposed for approval by consensus at a meeting with ninety-seven members represented in the room, and that decision would be taken unless one or more members formally objected to it.

39 Marrakesh Agreement Article IX, paragraphs 2 and 3.

40 Marrakesh Agreement Article X:1.

41 Marrakesh Agreement Article X, paragraphs 3, 4, and 5.

upon the consensus decision of the Ministerial Conference approving the amendment.[42]

On the face of it, the commentators *are* right – the WTO decision-making procedures *are* cumbersome and difficult. Here lies the paradox: the procedures are cumbersome because they are designed to be inclusive, to ensure that decisions are supported by all WTO members. However, consensus decision-making also allows one country, no matter what its size or relative power, to prevent a decision from being taken. Thus, individual members can, and do, 'hijack' the system from time to time, not always for rational reasons.

This has led the major powers to use informal techniques of 'consensus-building', involving groupings of countries (such as 'Green Room' meetings) which inevitably means that some countries are not included in the key planning and drafting stages of a particular decision. This solution can, however, lead to further problems: for example, at the Seattle Ministerial Meeting in 1999, a large group of developing countries threatened to walk out of the meeting because they claimed they were not included in the 'Green Room' meetings in which approximately sixty heads of delegation were involved. Moreover, even a proposal that has been subjected to a thorough informal 'consensus-building' process can meet with blocking tactics when a member attempts to put it on the agenda of a formal meeting for approval.[43]

Is there a 'constitutional defect' in the decision-making rules of the WTO? Can the rules be amended to make them more functional? How can developing countries be made to feel more included in the system?

To be fair, there has not been much experience with the new rules for adopting definitive interpretations and amendments since 1995. However, many important decisions have been taken, including decisions approving the accession of several new members to the WTO as well as decisions granting waivers from WTO obligations. Almost all of these decisions have been taken by consensus in the General Council

[42] Marrakesh Agreement Article X:8.

[43] For example, in 1999, before the Seattle Ministerial Meeting, an informal group of approximately fourteen countries met outside of the WTO to draft a proposed amendment to the DSU attempting to resolve some of the ambiguities in Articles 21.5 and 22 relating to implementation of rulings. The meetings of this informal group were open to any country that wished to participate. Although this group, chaired by Japan, attempted on several occasions to bring its draft amendment into a formal meeting of the DSB, this was blocked repeatedly by two developing country delegations (not because they were not included in the negotiation – they had indeed participated – but rather for strategic reasons not related to the text of that proposal).

after careful preparation in informal meetings of working parties open to participation by all WTO members. In only one case to date, the accession of Ecuador in 1995, was a decision taken by a vote, rather than by consensus.[44] A long struggle occurred in 1999 over the selection of a new Director-General because membership support was almost evenly divided between two candidates for the post. Eventually, that impasse was resolved when it was decided that the term would be split into two parts, with each candidate taking the post for a period of three years. However, while this issue was being settled, the WTO was nearly paralyzed for several months, which many observers believe contributed to the failure of the Seattle Ministerial Meeting.

Amending the decision-making rules of the WTO would be extremely difficult, if not impossible. All WTO members, from the major players to the least-developed countries, are wedded to the practice of decision-making by consensus. It is part of the *ethos* of the WTO. It would not be in the interests of the developing country members for the WTO to adopt weighted voting mechanisms such as those used in the International Monetary Fund and the World Bank. The Members of the WTO are strongly opposed to any such suggestion, and such a mechanism would not help to make the WTO more inclusive of developing countries.

One might ask: if it is so difficult to achieve consensus, why do members not use the voting procedures more often? Although the thresholds for decisions to adopt interpretations, waivers, or amendments are very high (three-fourths or two-thirds of the members), for many decisions, such as the election of a new Director-General, the 'fallback' would be to a simple majority vote. However, although the rules have always provided that decisions could be taken by a majority vote,[45] this has not been the practice in the GATT or in the WTO. Members seem to prefer to use the cumbersome and slow process of decision-making by consensus over the voting procedures allowed for in the rules.

[44] Article XII:2 of the Marrakesh Agreement stipulates that decisions on accession of new members are to be taken by a two-thirds majority vote of the Ministerial Conference, but, in practice, except for the accession of Ecuador, these decisions have been taken by consensus in meetings of the General Council.

[45] Article XXV of the GATT 1947 stipulated, as a general rule, that decisions of the Contracting Parties were to be taken by a majority vote (except for waivers and amendments that required a two-thirds majority). However, the practice, throughout most of GATT history, was for decisions to be taken by consensus.

The difficulty with the decision-making procedures in the WTO does not result from a 'constitutional defect' in the rules, but rather from the preferences and the practice of the members of the WTO. Changing the procedures for taking decisions is not likely to change the attitudes of WTO members. Furthermore, changing the decision-making rules would only exacerbate the problems of internal legitimacy within the WTO, because it would increase the perceptions of developing countries that they are not included in the decision-making process.

During the Uruguay Round, the USA put forward a proposal in the Functioning of the GATT System Group that a management board or committee, consisting of approximately eighteen members, should be established to set policy direction and assist in the management and administration of the system. That idea has resurfaced both among delegations in Geneva and in academic debate;[46] however, the developing countries remain opposed to any suggestion that would lead to some countries being excluded from any decision-making process.

Despite the objections of smaller and developing countries, a management board is essential and could be made to work in a way that would be inclusive of all WTO members. The WTO has become a complex enterprise – there are many administrative, procedural, and house-keeping decisions that could be made by a smaller body than the General Council. It is clear, particularly after the Seattle fiasco, that a smaller management body is needed to help set priorities and provide direction for the system. Informal groupings exist presently within the WTO. There is an African Group, made up of all the African countries in the WTO, which meets and develops coordinated positions on a regular basis. There is also an ASEAN Group, which meets regularly and takes coordinated positions in key WTO meetings. The Latin American countries have often acted in a coordinated fashion – they walked out *en masse* and blocked the Brussels Ministerial Meeting in 1990 over the contentious negotiations on agriculture. A management board or committee, structured so that it was truly representative of the WTO membership, could be made to work in a transparent and inclusive manner. It could also help to move proposals forward and to alleviate some of the

[46] Sylvia Ostry has long been a strong proponent of this idea. See, e.g., Sylvia Ostry, 'World Trade Organization: Institutional Design for Better Governance' in Porter, Sauvé, Subramanian, and Zampetti, *Efficiency, Equity, Legitimacy*, pp. 361–80; Barfield, *Free Trade*.

lengthy delays and paralysis caused by the existing cumbersome procedures.

Conclusion

In my view, the solution to the legitimacy crisis in the WTO lies not in turning back the clock and returning, as some have suggested, to a dispute settlement system grounded in diplomatic custom and practice, nor does it lie in encouraging greater 'flexibility and member control' over panel and Appellate Body proceedings. This sounds ominously like political interference with the judicial system. It is important that the independence and impartiality of the judicial bodies in the WTO not be diminished or undermined.

The key lies in recognizing that the WTO dispute settlement system has two tracks: 'diplomatic' and 'judicial'. A clear distinction must be made between the two.

WTO members should be encouraged to make more and better use of the alternative dispute resolution mechanisms available to them under the DSU. Improvements to the diplomatic dispute settlement mechanisms to make them more effective would increase recourse to them by WTO members and result in more cases being settled early.

At the same time, the independence, impartiality, and integrity of the judicial system should be maintained and defended against political interference. A softer, 'diplomatic' version of the judicial process is not in the interest of WTO members nor is it consistent with a rules-based international trading system. The judicial system should be strengthened and improved by 'professionalizing' the panel system, and giving it the attributes of a standing, independent tribunal based on the model of the Appellate Body. Transparency in panel and Appellate Body proceedings should also be guaranteed by making submissions of parties and third parties available to the public and by opening up panel and Appellate Body hearings to the public. At the same time, new rules for the protection of 'business confidential' information and workable procedures for admission of *amicus curiae* briefs should also be developed by WTO members.

The 'external' legitimacy problem of the WTO is a far greater threat to its continued viability than its 'internal' legitimacy difficulties. For that reason, the WTO must move, and be seen to move, decisively and purposefully in the direction of greater transparency and openness. There is simply no excuse, given the gravity and the importance of decisions being made by the WTO, for a dispute settlement system or a legislative system that operates in secret, behind closed doors. Governments will not lose control over the WTO if non-state actors are permitted access to information, to attend hearings and meetings as observers, and to submit *amicus curiae* briefs to panels and the Appellate Body. By making the WTO more transparent and accessible, it will be better understood and appreciated. This will help to enhance the legitimacy and credibility of the WTO as an international rules-based system.

16

The World Trade Organization after Cancún

GUIGUO WANG

Introduction

The Fifth WTO Ministerial Conference, which was held in Cancún, Mexico in September 2003, ended without any achievement. It was the second fruitless Ministerial Conference since the establishment of the WTO. So far as this aftermath is concerned, some may take it as a victory of the developing countries and thus feel cheerful and encouraged, while others consider it as a foreboding of the WTO's collapse and feel depressed and worried. Some developed countries declared that they would offset the aftermath of the Cancún Conference through bilateral free trade agreements.[1] So, why did the Cancún Conference fail? What are the effects of the failed Concun Conference upon the WTO, the developed countries, the developing countries, and economic globalization?

Issues and problems of the Cancún Conference

The Cancún Ministerial Conference was the follow-up of the Doha Round. Its main task was to carry out the Doha Declaration, which included the Singapore issues and the implementation of the Uruguay Round Agreements.[2] The Singapore issues include trade and investment, trade and competition, government procurement,[3] and trade

[1] Just at the close of the Cancún Conference (in fact the declaration of failure), Robert Zoellick, the trade representative of the USA, announced that the USA would negotiate bilateral trade agreements with other countries. He said that the USA had a long list of potential participants for bilateral trade agreements.

[2] The Fifth Ministerial Conference of the WTO organized a negotiation group on the following six issues: agriculture, 'Singapore' issues, non-agricultural market access (NAMA), development issues, cotton initiative, and other issues.

[3] It is related to the question of how to compel the developing countries to participate in government procurement agreements.

facilitation. The implementation of the Uruguay Round Agreements involves many issues, among which the notable ones include trade in services, agricultural trade, intellectual property protection, and dispute settlement. So far as agricultural trade is concerned, the Doha Ministerial Declaration aims at 'gradually reducing . . . with a view to phasing out, all forms of export subsidies, and substantial reductions in trade-distorting domestic support'.[4] In accordance with the aim of the negotiation, the Doha Ministerial Declaration required participants to submit their comprehensive draft schedules no later than 31 March 2003, including the provisions for special and differential treatment for the developing countries.[5] Agricultural subsidies in the USA and the EU are broad and complicated. Farmers exert great influence upon the domestic politics in those countries. It is therefore rather difficult for them to reach consensus on agricultural trade, especially on the special and differential treatment for the developing countries.

As capital exporters, the developed countries take a firm stand to support negotiations on the Singapore issues, such as trade and investment and government procurement.[6] However, most of the developing countries hold either an opposite or reserved view on these issues because they are afraid to follow the road of the Agreement on Trade-Related Intellectual Property Rights (TRIPS), which has significantly affected their domestic investment laws and policies.[7]

One of the results of the Uruguay Round is that the developed countries have committed to provide technical assistance for the developing countries.[8] However, since the establishment of the WTO, such commitment has remained mostly on paper, which has disappointed the developing countries greatly. For example, in regard to the laws on technical barriers to trade (TBT) and hygiene standards, the developing countries are in urgent need of technical assistance from the developed countries. In regard to the formulation and enactment of import

[4] Doha Ministerial Declaration, paragraph 13. [5] *Ibid.* at paragraph 14.

[6] It is this standpoint that led to the failure of the Multilateral Agreement on Investment (MAI). For the history and rules of the multinational investment agreement, see Guiguo Wang, *International Investment Law* (Peking University Press, 2001).

[7] Under the TRIPs, all WTO members, including developing countries, must adopt minimum standards in protecting intellectual property. This has imposed not only an obligation on the part of the developing countries in enacting laws in accordance with the TRIPs, but also the responsibility to enforce such laws effectively and efficiently.

[8] Such provisions can be found in a number of agreements of the WTO such as Article 25 of the General Agreement on Trade in Services (GATS), TRIPS Article 67, and Article 11 of the Agreement on Technical Barriers to Trade.

standards, apart from the aids on legislation, the developing countries need the developed countries to transfer related technologies as well. In addition, the Textile Agreement requires the developed countries to abolish import restrictions gradually within ten years. However, there is no explicit provision on the extent to which the market should be opened each year. As a result, the developed countries have adopted a strategy to delay the market opening in the first stage, hoping to implement their commitments at the second and final stage. All of these have constituted serious challenges to the implementation of the Uruguay Round Agreements.[9]

In regard to intellectual property protection, paragraph 6 of the Doha Ministerial Declaration acknowledges that, under the WTO rules, no member should be prevented from taking appropriate measures for the protection of human, animal or plant life or health, or of the environment, subject to the requirement that they are not applied in a manner which would constitute a means of arbitrary or unjustifiable discrimination between countries, or a disguised restriction on international trade. But does this provision apply only to the developing country members or all members? Combining paragraphs 6 and 1 to 4 together, it is obvious that the right to protect human, animal or plant life or health is established under the background of serious problems the developing countries confront. However, the authorization is applicable to all members. As a result of the authorization, each member could restrict the patent right in such ways as compulsory licensing and parallel importation for public health reasons. According to paragraph 6 of the Doha Ministerial Declaration, the EU and some non-governmental organizations suggested that members should have the right to allow local producers a licence to export medicines under patent protection to poor countries as an exception to TRIPS Article 30.[10] The reasoning was that, confronted with diseases that can infect people and be disseminated quickly and widely, such as AIDS and plague etc., patients in the developing countries could not afford the medicines produced in and exported from the developed countries. The prices of such medicines

[9] For the issues concerning the implementation of Doha Round Agreements, see Inaamul Haque, 'Doha Development Agenda: Recapturing the Momentum of Multilateralism and Developing Countries' (2002) 17 *American University International Law Review* 1097.

[10] Amir Attaran, 'The Doha Declaration on the TRIPs and Agreement on Public Health, Access to Pharmaceuticals, and Options under WTO Law' (2002) 12 *Fordham Intellectual Property, Media and Entertainment Law Journal* 859.

would decrease considerably if their production would not be protected by patent rights. A UN study reports, for example, that 150 mg of one HIV drug costs US$55 in India, where the drug does not enjoy patent protection, as compared with US$697 in Malaysia, US$703 in Indonesia, and US$817 in the Philippines, where the drug is patented.[11]

Apart from the legal issues, another problem that the developing countries confront is that even though the Doha Ministerial Declaration and the Declaration on the TRIPS Agreement and Public Health allow them to grant compulsory licences, these countries do not have the capacity to produce such medicines. According to TRIPS Article 31, any such use must be authorized predominantly for the domestic market of the member. The right-holder must also be paid an adequate remuneration.[12] It is generally accepted that the remuneration paid to the right-holder should link with the products manufactured. In other words, if relevant products are partly or wholly exported, the importing member should pay for the compulsory licence of the patent right.

On 16 December 2002, with a view to addressing the above difficulties for the least-developed countries, the Chairman of the Intellectual Property Council put forward a draft. This draft was passed by the Intellectual Property Council on 30 August 2003 as the Implementation of Paragraph 6 of the Doha Declaration on the TRIPS Agreement and Public Health ('the Implementation Decision'), which provides for exceptions for those members who are incapable of implementing the provisions concerning compulsory licensing under the TRIPS.

The Implementation Decision applies to those members which are completely incapable of making or lack effective capacity to make use of the compulsory licensing scheme. These members could import the pharmaceuticals that are manufactured through compulsory licensing to resolve the difficulties which arise from their lack of manufacturing capacity. They must, however, make a notification to the Council for

11 Alan O. Sykes, 'TRIPS, Pharmaceuticals, Developing Countries, and the Doha "Solution"' (2002) 3 *Chicago Journal of International Law* 47. Bearing in mind the seriousness and complexity of intellectual property, a declaration on the TRIPS and public health was passed in the Doha Round. It was declared that epidemics such as AIDS, tuberculosis, and plague have afflicted the public health of many developing and least-developed countries and that, therefore, it was necessary to use the TRIPS as a national and international initiative to resolve such problems.

12 TRIPS Article 31(6) and (8).

TRIPS of their intention to invoke the Implementation Decision and specify the names and expected quantities of the product(s) to be imported.[13] Those who are eligible to apply the Implementation Decision include the least-developed members and other members lacking or having insufficient manufacturing capacities in the pharmaceutical sector for the product(s) in question.[14] The application of the scheme is conditioned on the member's overall situation, national emergency, or other circumstances of extreme urgency or public non-commercial use. When the Implementation Decision is applied, TRIPS Article 31, which provides that the products manufactured through compulsory licensing should supply the domestic market of the member authorizing such use, is no longer applicable. In spite of the notification obligation, an eligible importing member should take reasonable measures to prevent improper use and re-exportation of the products that have actually been imported into their territories under this system.[15]

An exporting member is obligated to produce and export the products only for eligible importing members. The products concerned must be clearly identified as being produced under the system set out in the Implementation Decision through special packaging, colouring/shaping, labelling, or marking. Meanwhile, the licensee must post on a website information regarding the quantities being supplied to each destination and the distinguishing features of the relevant pharmaceutical product(s).

Under the system of the Implementation Decision, an exporting member should be paid an adequate remuneration pursuant to TRIPS Article 31(h) for compulsory licensing. Where a compulsory licence is granted for the same products in an eligible importing member, that member need not pay remuneration for the products imported.[16]

[13] The Implementation Decision itself has no provision that requires members who wish to invoke it to obtain prior approval of the Intellectual Property Council. However, according to the context of the Decision, such approval seems to be needed.

[14] Members, other than least-developed countries, that wish to apply the system of the Implementation Decision should establish before the Intellectual Property Council that they have insufficient or no manufacturing capacity for the relevant pharmaceutical product(s) in order to make use of the patent compulsory licensing system. Annex I to the Implementation Decision provides conditions for countries other than the least-developed members to use the system under the Implementation Decision.

[15] In this respect, the developed country members must provide, on request of the importing member, technical and financial cooperation in order to facilitate the implementation of relevant laws.

[16] Implementation Decision, paragraph 3.

Another effort made by the WTO was that on 3 September 2003, when the Council for Trade in Services held a special session and adopted a decision to boost least-developed countries' participation in services negotiations.[17] Generally speaking, the resolution allows the least-developed countries to make commitments compatible with their economic situations, and requires the developed countries to exercise restraint in their negotiation with the least-developed countries. On the whole, the developed countries should neither seek the removal of conditions which the least-developed countries may attach when making their markets accessible to foreign services suppliers, nor expect national treatment. Meanwhile, the developed countries should strengthen programmes to promote investment in the least-developed countries with a view to building up their domestic services capacity and enhancing their efficiency and export competitiveness.

It is obvious that the above-mentioned efforts of the WTO had laid a foundation for the Fifth Ministerial Conference to be held in Cancún, Mexico in September 2003. And that is why many people at the start of the Cancún Conference were optimistic.[18] However, the result of the Conference disappointed the international community. What are the reasons, then, for the failure of Cancún?

The failed Cancún Conference: reasons

There are a variety of views concerning the failure of the Cancún Ministerial Conference; however, none of them is considered to be a convincing one.[19] Nevertheless, it is beyond doubt that the serious disagreement on agricultural trade between the developed and the developing countries, especially serious disagreement on the agricultural subsidies of the developed countries, directly led to the failure of

[17] See 'WTO Members Agree on Ways to Boost LDC Participation in Services Negotiations' at www.wto.org/english/news-e/pres03-e/pr351-e.htm

[18] Anne O. Krueger, First Deputy Managing Director of IMF, said that a number of private meetings she had with individual delegates suggested a common desire to work constructively for a solution. Anne O. Krueger, 'Moving on from Cancún, Agricultural Trade and the Poor', Agricultural Trade Policy Workshop, 3 November 2003.

[19] The diplomats in Geneva tried not to use the word 'failure' to describe the result of the Cancún Conference and used word 'setback' instead. This was confirmed by Ambassador Shotaro Oshima of Japan to the WTO during his visit to the Law School of the City University of Hong Kong in late October 2003.

the Cancún Conference, because from the very beginning, the developing countries had insisted on progress in agricultural trade negotiation as a precondition for the negotiations in other fields. Developing countries deemed that immediate improvement of the agricultural trade system and the developed countries' reducing agricultural subsidies would be fatal to their interests.

Against the background of globalization, agricultural subsidies in the developed countries have substantially impaired and threatened the interests of the developing countries. Take Jamaica as an example: its unique natural situation makes it an ideal place for milk production. Vast amounts of grassland, plenty of water resources, and excellent cows, including a breed called 'the hope of Jamaica', have provided this island country, with a population of 2.5 million, good conditions for milk production. In addition, the local people have a habit of consuming milk and milk products. The annual consumption of milk products is around 0.14 million gallons.[20] However, subsidized milk powder from the EU is much cheaper. As a result, the milk products industry of Jamaica began importing milk powder from the EU, which then brought serious loss to the local farmers. In 1999, farmer Phyllis Marchs had to pour away more than 1,000 gallons of milk that could not be sold.[21] Needless to say, this was a considerable loss for a small farmer who makes a living by selling milk.

The same situation arises in other territories and sectors. The misery suffered by Mohammed Ali Indris in Ethiopia is another example. Five years ago, the annual income of Mohammed from selling coffee and corn was US$320, which was enough to cover the living expenses of the whole family. However, because of the competition from subsidized agricultural products, even if the sales volume had increased four times, Mohammed could not earn enough money to pay the family's expenses. As a result, he not only did not have money to send his children to school, he also had to sell his farm cattle to repay the loan lest he be sent to prison. Due to the lack of nutrition, the skin of Mohammed's children is very coarse.[22]

The Jamaican and Ethiopian experiences are shared by other developing countries which account for 80 per cent of the world's population.

[20] See Canadian Council for International Cooperation, *What Direction for Development? Focus on Agriculture*, document distributed by the Canadian Council for International Cooperation at the Fifth WTO Ministerial Conference.

[21] *Ibid.* [22] *Ibid.*

It was reported[23] that, before China's accession to the WTO, the Chinese government encouraged farmers to grow industrial crops by providing the latter with bank loans. Many farmers in Guangxi Autonomous Region hence engaged in growing sugar-cane and sugar production. Their living standards rose very quickly. Take a farmer, for example, who, at the initial stage, borrowed money from a bank to plant sugar-cane and started to produce sugar. By doing so, he was able to earn RMB2,500 annually and was full of hope. The WTO membership of China, however, led to an influx of subsidized imported sugar into the Chinese market, which resulted in a sharp decrease in sugar prices. This farmer's income decreased to less than RMB0.8 daily. With such a small amount of money, he could not cover his child's education fees, not to mention his original plan of reconstructing his house. Not only that, he had no money to repay the loan.

Most developing countries deem that farmers' problems have deteriorated due to economic globalization. Globalization and the establishment of the WTO have resulted in the influx of agricultural products with subsidies from the developed countries into the domestic markets of the developing countries, which links the agricultural subsidies in the developed countries directly with farmers' problems in the developing countries. This is so because as a general rule, the poorer a country, the more it depends on agriculture. For instance, food accounts for about 10 per cent of household expenditure in most developed countries, but more than 30 per cent in the vast majority of the developing countries.[24] That means the effect of the subsidized agricultural products from the developed countries on the income of the farmers of the developing countries has a direct bearing on the living standards of the latter.

Of course, the developed countries' agricultural subsidies have a long history. At least as early as 1947, when the GATT took effect, subsidies became one of the major issues of agricultural trade.[25] According to

23 This information was disclosed by a survey report of Oxfam Hong Kong published in a local newspaper during the Cancún Ministerial Conference. The report was prepared by surveyors of the Chinese Academy of Social Sciences and Chinese Agricultural Ministry. The author had an opportunity to discuss the issues in detail with the surveyors during the Cancún Conference in September 2003.

24 *Ibid.*

25 The difference lies in that, at that time, the interdependence among countries was limited, especially when there were high tariffs and non-tariff barriers as effective obstacles for market access and the dispute regarding agricultural subsidies was mainly between the USA and EU countries; while, at present, it is mainly between the developed and developing countries. One of the reasons is that the developed countries are financially capable of offering subsidies for agricultural products, while the developing

statistics, the total direct agricultural subsidies in the OECD countries averaged US$235 billion per year in 2000–2;[26] 80 per cent of grains and oilseeds are protected by subsidies.[27] As indicated in the research conducted by the OECD, those who substantially benefited from the agricultural subsidies are: farm household labour (10.4 per cent), farm household land (12.6 per cent), non-farming landowners (13.2 per cent), other input suppliers (36.7 per cent), and land resource costs (28.2 per cent).[28]

Apart from the grains subsidies, the subsidies to sugar and cotton in the developed countries are striking as well. For instance, the OECD countries' support for domestic sugar producers is roughly equal to the total sugar export value of the developing countries.[29] Moving to free trade in sugar would raise its price by close to 40 per cent, increase the sugar trade by 20 per cent, and generate around US$4.7 billion in welfare gains for the poor in the developing countries.[30]

In the cotton trade, which has raised heated debate, the subsidies in the developed countries are more significant. According to the statistics of the IMF, US$3.7 billion of subsidies are annually provided for cotton products, which is three times as large as the aid provided by the USA to Africa, and nearly one-fifth of the total value of the world cotton production.[31] Taking the EU and other countries' subsidies in cotton into account, it can be easily imagined to what extent the world cotton price has been distorted. In total, the IMF estimates that these

countries are incapable of competing with the subsidized agricultural products of the developed countries.

26 World Bank, *Market Access: Agricultural Policy Reform and Developing Countries* (10 September 2003).

27 However, it does not mean that all the farmers get a large amount of subsidies. It is reported that, generally, only a few large farms benefited from the subsidies. For instance, in the USA, the largest size group of farms, representing 5 per cent of all farms, received 20 per cent of government subsidies. See World Bank, *Domestic Support for Agriculture: Agricultural Policy Reform and Developing Countries* (10 September 2003).

28 OECD, *Agricultural Policies in OECD Countries: A Positive Reform Agenda* (June 2003), p. 3.

29 It has been estimated, for instance, that each of the 2,300 jobs saved in the American sugar industry through barriers to imports in the 1990s cost US$800,000 a year. It is not hard to imagine how expensive such subsidies are: Krueger, 'Moving on from Cancún', 3.

30 *Ibid.* at 4. For a general discussion on sugar subsidies of the EU and their effects on developing countries, see also Oxfam International, *Dumping on the World: How EU Sugar Policies Hurt Poor Countries* (Oxfam Briefing Paper 61, 2004).

31 Krueger, 'Moving on from Cancún', 4.

subsidies have depressed the world price by 20 per cent.[32] This was one of the reasons for the 'Cotton Initiative' of the Cancún Conference.[33]

The direct effect of agricultural subsidies in the developed countries is that, on the one hand, the products of the developed countries become more competitive to gain access to the markets of the developing countries; on the other hand, it is more difficult for the products of the developing countries to gain access to the developed country markets. Although an agricultural agreement was reached in the Uruguay Round, the barriers to market access for agricultural products are still substantial in different countries. The current average agricultural bound tariff is 60 per cent, which illustrates the degree of protectionism in agricultural trade. So far as the OECD countries are concerned, about 28 per cent of their domestic agricultural production is protected by import quotas.[34] The Uruguay Round brought agricultural trade into the multilateral discipline of the WTO, although some high levels of support and protection were left untouched. While there is no tariff imposed on most industrial products, the peak tariff on agricultural products is still as high as 200 per cent, which is really an irony for the WTO.[35] In addition, the tariff for agricultural products will increase along with the sophistication of the level of manufacturing, which aggravates the importing protection and adversely impacts the developing countries' interests of export.

There are several reasons for the above situation. In the first place, the tariff deduction method for agricultural products reached in the Uruguay Round makes it possible for the developed countries to maintain high tariffs on the sensitive agricultural products imported from developing countries. The Uruguay Round required members to commit to an average cut in tariffs rather than a cut in average tariffs. As a result, the developed countries can choose to reduce agricultural tariffs in the fields where tariff levels are already low and then easily meet the WTO's requirements. For example, if the original tariff for some product is 2 per cent, a 1 per cent cut represents a 50 per cent tariff reduction. But these fields are generally not sensitive agricultural

32 *Ibid.*

33 During his visit to the Hong Kong WTO Research Institute on 29 January 2004, Peter Thompson, Deputy Trade Representative of the European Union to the WTO, said that the EU was not prepared to re-open the negotiations on cotton.

34 World Bank, *Market Access.*

35 OECD, *Agricultural Policies in OECD Countries: A Positive Reform Agenda* (June 2003), p. 5.

products and, therefore, the tariff cuts would not have a substantial impact on the agricultural industry of the importing countries.[36]

Secondly, the bound tariff system on agricultural products is not reasonable. Superficially, both the developed and the developing countries have the same right to bind the importing tariffs. However, in practice, applied tariffs in the developing countries are always lower than the bound tariffs, while the applied tariffs of the developed countries are, as a general rule, higher than the bound tariffs.[37] This inequality *de facto* does not only have a direct adverse impact on the export of agricultural products of the developing countries but also creates a psychological obstacle to the negotiations at the Cancún Conference.

Thirdly, there are problems with the method under the WTO to calculate domestic subsidies. According to the Agreement on Agriculture, subsidies in general are grouped and represented by 'green box', 'blue box', and 'amber box'.[38] When calculating the aggregate of domestic support, WTO allows the blue box subsidies to be included, but in ascertaining the subsidy deduction, the blue box subsidies would not be taken into account. This will result in an overestimation of the domestic support and make it easier for the member concerned to satisfy the requirement of reduction in subsidies. Moreover, the aggregate support itself does not require the subsidy reduction in certain fields. There is also a tendency for the developed countries to try to avoid the important matters and dwell on the trivial issues to elude the obligation of reducing subsidies. As a result of the above maneuvers, it is possible that a member's subsidies in agriculture may increase constantly, while its aggregate domestic support decreases.

Fourthly, the peace clause of the Agreement on Agriculture prevents the developing countries from resorting to dispute settlement mechanisms of the WTO on issues concerning agricultural subsidies, provided those subsidies satisfy the requirements of the Agreement on Agriculture.[39] With the expiration of this clause at the end of 2003,

[36] At the moment, there is no international agreement on what constitutes sensitive products. As such, the issue is almost completely left to the discretion of the importing countries.

[37] A survey of the World Bank indicates that for some developing countries, the tariff overhang is five times more than the applied tariff, while the applied tariff of OECD countries is two times more than the bound tariff. See World Bank, *Market Access*.

[38] 'Green box' subsidies are not restricted; 'blue box' subsidies are for special circumstances; and 'amber box' subsidies should be reduced gradually. For details, see Guiguo Wang, *The Law of WTO* (Law Press, Beijing, 2003), ch. 7.

[39] For details, see Agreement on Agriculture Article 13.

this problem has officially ended. Taking into consideration the complexity of the subsidies provided by the developed countries in agriculture, it will take a long time for the developing countries to work out what subsidy is prohibited and what is not, not to mention taking such matters to the Dispute Settlement Body of the WTO.[40]

The Cancún Conference did not try to deal only with agricultural trade. Apart from agriculture, the developing countries and the developed countries also held different positions on the Singapore issues, as well as NAMA. As no progress was made in agriculture, no substantial negotiation was conducted on these other topics.

As well as the issue of agricultural trade, there are still many other reasons for the failure of the Cancún Conference. It is generally accepted that the following factors have contributed to the failure: the lack of transparency in the negotiation procedures; non-compliance with rules and principles; unpublicized appointment of facilitators; the lack of transparency in drafting the position papers; the timing for announcing the close of the Conference, etc.[41] The list could continue for another few pages, yet without an agreement.

The fundamental problem of agricultural trade is the agricultural subsidies of the developed countries. For the developed countries such as the USA, the EU and Japan, agricultural subsidies are the reflections of their domestic politics in the international context, and are impossible to repeal totally and immediately under present circumstances. It is also a critical issue for the developing countries whether the problem of agricultural subsidies of the developed countries can be resolved. The similar experiences, needs, and expectations of the developing countries made their negotiating stands similar at the Cancún Conference, which brought about a *de facto* negotiation alliance. Twenty-one members, including China, India, Brazil etc.,[42] allied together to stand in the same

[40] Even between the members which invented and have used such subsidies, such as the USA and the EU, there is hardly any agreement on what is a prohibited subsidy and what is a permissible subsidy. This illustrates the essential problems for negotiations on reduction of agricultural subsidies.

[41] One of the reasons for the Chairman of the Conference, the Commercial Minister of Mexico, to announce the closure of the Conference was that he had to go to Mexico City to participate in the celebration of the National Day that would be held the following day. However, at that time many delegations were ready for an extension of negotiations. In comparison, at the Doha Conference, the negotiations were extended for one day in order to complete the business.

[42] In the Cancún Conference, this negotiation group was called G21 and its spokesman was Brazil. Later on, there were other developing countries which took part in that

position and negotiate with the developed countries such as the USA and the EU. Such unity of the developing countries for the first time in the history of the WTO substantially boosted their strength in the negotiations and made them a match for the developed countries. Because of the vast gap between the standpoints of the two sides,[43] no agreement was reached on agricultural trade. As there was no compromise offered by either the developed countries or the developing countries on agriculture, no progress was made on other issues.[44] The Cancún Conference thus failed.

Impact of the failed Cancún Conference on the WTO

The failure of the Cancún Conference had a far-reaching effect on the WTO. Compared with the multilateral negotiations in the GATT era, the Cancún Conference was remarkably different for the developed countries which could no longer spread their full wings. Largely, it was because the developing countries such as China, India, and Brazil stood together to form a considerable force, the G21, at the Conference. To the developing countries, the failure of the Cancún Ministerial Conference can be seen as a success of their alliance. The developing countries in future negotiations may again adopt such an approach and negotiation strategy. In this regard, it can be said that the Cancún Conference changed the status of the developing countries in the WTO. Historically, the GATT was always regarded as a 'club of the rich', as only rich countries could exert substantial influence on it. The situation was not much different in the Uruguay Round. The direct consequence was that the agreements reached have not fully reflected the specific interests and conditions of the developing countries. The agricultural trade negotiations discussed above are an example. At the least, the failure of the Cancún Conference through the failure of the developing and developed countries to reach an agreement demonstrates the growing strength of the developing countries in the WTO system, which could not be felt during the Uruguay Round.

group. Some members such as the USA and the EU did not acknowledge the existence of the G21 and proposed bilateral negotiations in order to reach their respective goals.

43 The difference between the two sides was not whether to abolish agricultural subsidies, but rather as to the extent, scope, and timetable for abolition of such subsidies.

44 At the outset of the Cancún Conference, the developing countries considered that substantial progress on agricultural trade was a precondition for negotiation on other issues.

The failure of the Cancún Conference is also helpful in improving the system of the WTO. For a long time, the WTO has held itself out as 'rule-oriented' whilst the black-box operation is also an undeniable fact – 'Green Room' negotiations, the appointment of facilitators, and even how the position papers are drafted are just some examples.[45] It is quite certain that after the Cancún Conference, the voice of the developing countries in the WTO will be enhanced, and their special and different interests will be recognized more easily.

Some argue that the failure of the Cancún Conference was not necessarily a success for the developing countries, as they did not achieve anything; for instance no further reduction of market access barriers was made by the developed countries and no progress was made in connection with the implementation of the Doha Development Agenda. One may ask, however, if the developing countries had not allied at the Cancún Conference but taken individual initiatives in negotiations, would there have been a more favourable result for them? Of course, the failure of the Cancún Conference made it impossible for the developed and the developing countries to reach an agreement on the timetable of the Doha Development Agenda. However, the multilateral negotiations will not stop. Right after the Cancún Conference, the negotiations were resumed at the headquarters of the WTO in Geneva.[46]

The failure of the Cancún Conference made the developed countries such as the USA and the EU well aware of the difficulties of the multilateral negotiations within the WTO framework. As a result, they may accelerate the pace of bilateral negotiations or regional negotiations with the aim of establishing free trade areas (FTAs) so that what could not be achieved at the multilateral level may be achieved on a piecemeal basis. The proliferation of bilateral and regional arrangements will also exert influences upon the operation of the WTO system, making future negotiations more complicated, and differentiating the basic interests and standpoints of those developing countries involved in such bilateral and regional arrangements from others. The negotiating power of the developing countries will then be seriously weakened. The end result may be that the special needs and interests of the developing countries

[45] In some sense, the failure of the Cancún Conference is the result of the developing countries' distrust of the developed countries.

[46] After the Cancún Conference, representatives of the WTO members in Geneva restarted their negotiations. Although no agreement had been reached by the time of the completion of this chapter, it is obvious that no member thinks that the multilateral negotiations should not continue.

are not fully recognized and dealt with, or even neglected, through the process of globalization.

Without the failure of the Cancún Conference and the lack of consensus for the developing countries in the negotiation of agricultural trade, would there be less initiatives for bilateral and regional arrangements? In an era of intensified globalization, international trade and international politics connect closely with each other. Even with a success of Cancún, the developed countries such as the USA and the EU would still pursue the course of bilateral and regional agreements due to considerations of international politics and security.[47] The establishment of the FTA between the USA and Singapore and the plan to extend NAFTA to cover the entire Americas,[48] as well as the enlargement of the membership by the EU,[49] are all concerned with international politics. In fact, one can hardly believe that it is by coincidence that whilst the USA is engaged in southern expansion, the EU is working hard to move eastward. Without the failure of Cancún, neither the USA nor the EU would have implemented their regionalization plans as earnestly as they are doing now.

The above discussion notwithstanding, the failure of the Cancún Conference has helped change the tactics of FTA negotiations by the USA, the EU, and other developed countries. After the Cancún Conference, it is obvious that in negotiating FTAs, the developed countries will try to get what they did not achieve at Cancún by offering benefits to some developing countries, hoping that by doing so the developing countries will be divided in the multilateral negotiations.

Overall, the fruitless agricultural negotiation is the cause of the failure of the Cancún Conference. However, it is only superficial. A deeper

[47] Up to November 2003, there are 259 regional arrangements that had been notified to the WTO, in which 130 were notified after the establishment of the WTO in 1995. According to statistics of the WTO, there are still 70 regional arrangements in effect that have not been notified to the WTO. It is estimated that by 2005, regional arrangements will amount to 300. Certainly, this estimation by the WTO is rather conservative.

[48] On 20 November 2003, thirty-four countries, including the USA, Canada, and Brazil, discussed a draft of the agreement on establishing the American Free Trade Area proposed by the USA and Brazil. It is generally believed that the main obstacle for the USA in establishing a free trade area with Southern American countries is agricultural trade. Yet, as the USA is not as resistant as the EU in respect of agricultural subsidies, and the agricultural subsidy system of the USA is relatively simple compared with that of the EU, agricultural trade may not be a major obstacle for them to reach an agreement on an RTA.

[49] Starting from 1 May 2004, the EU membership was enlarged from the original fifteen to twenty-five, accounting for 25 per cent of world trade and GNP.

reason lies in the serious imbalance between the benefits that are a consequence of economic globalization, i.e., the fact that developing countries have not substantially benefited from it. It shows that economic globalization has entered into a structural adjustment after its high-speed development in the last few decades. The economic globalization of this stage is characterized by keen-edged conflicts among countries on such topics as international trade and investment. As a result, the international community must take a different approach in formulating the relationship among different members, particularly in its treatment of the developing countries. In the new stage of economic globalization, the special and different interests of the developing countries must be addressed sufficiently. In this regard, the concessions that the developed countries can make in agricultural trade could be taken as the 'water gauge'. So far as the current trend is concerned, the developed countries may gain some short-term benefits by entering into FTAs. In the end, however, the higher the level of economic globalization is, the more valuable market forces become. As market providers, the developing countries' negotiating power will increase gradually. Consequently, these countries will be capable of protecting their own interests. The completion of this process is the completion of the structural adjustment and therefore the beginning of an era of economic globalization which will lead to a more balanced development of the international community.

PART III

The Changing landscape of investment arbitration

17

The Reshaping of the International Law of Foreign Investment by Concordant Bilateral Investment Treaties

STEPHEN M. SCHWEBEL

Florentino Feliciano, in the course of his multifaceted and distinguished career as a scholar, practitioner, Justice of the Supreme Court of the Philippines, Member and Chairman of the Appellate Body of the World Trade Organization, judge of the Administrative Tribunal of the World Bank, and international arbitrator, has made his mark in more than one field of the law, national and international. His international imprint may be greatest on the law of international trade. A chapter in a collection in his honour in the allied area of international investment, another sphere in which his influence is considerable, is fitting.

What law governs the treatment of the investments by a national of one state in the territory of another state has long been in dispute. No less in dispute has been the question of the content of that governing law.

In the nineteenth century and the earlier decades of the twentieth, the Latin-American states espoused the Calvo Doctrine, subjecting foreigners and their investments exclusively to the law of the host state and excluding diplomatic intervention on their behalf. While efforts to promote this Doctrine by treaty, and through provisions of constitutional and domestic law, were ineffectual, the use of a 'Calvo Clause' in contracts with aliens became widespread. By the terms of the Calvo Clause, the alien contractor accepted the national law and courts of the host state as governing and renounced any right of diplomatic interposition by the state of which it was a national. The legality and effectiveness of the Calvo Clause remained in dispute between capital-exporting states and their nationals on the one hand, and the capital-importing states and their nationals on the other, for decades. The former generally denied that a national could validly renounce the state's right to intervene diplomatically on his behalf, whereas what nowadays are called 'developing states' generally affirmed the validity and effectiveness of such a renunciation.

Concurrently with the playing out of what might be seen as a kind of jurisdictional dispute were related differences over the content of the law governing foreign investment. Capital-exporting states maintained that there was a minimum standard of treatment of aliens and their property set by international law. Capital-importing states argued that the foreign investor was entitled to no more than equal treatment with the nationals of those states.

Among its many challenges to the establishment, the Russian Revolution of 1917 took the equal treatment doctrine to an early extreme. It deprived nationals and aliens alike of their property without compensation. Some two decades later, in famous exchanges between Secretary of State Hull and the Foreign Ministry of Mexico, turning on the nationalization of foreign investments in petroleum in Mexico, Mexico asserted that the foreign investor could ask for no more than could the national of Mexico, whereas the USA maintained that aliens were entitled to a minimum standard of treatment that could not necessarily be equated with national treatment. Hull set out the standard of 'prompt, adequate and effective compensation', a standard generally supported by predominant doctrine but not invariably sustained in practice. The post-Second World War years saw repeated departures from that standard.

Moreover, attempts to restate or rework the law for the most part divided the United Nations. While Resolution 1803 (XVII) of the United Nations General Assembly on Permanent Sovereignty over Natural Resources in 1962 brought together a large majority of the UN in recognition of the place of international law in the treatment of foreign investment, subsequent resolutions on that topic asserted the dominance of national law. So did General Assembly resolutions on the 'New International Economic Order' and the 'Charter of Economic Rights and Duties of States'. The latter resolution of 12 December 1974 provides in Article 2 that:

> Every State has and shall freely exercise full permanent sovereignty, including possession, use and disposal, over all its wealth, natural resources and economic activities.
>
> Each State has the right: ...
>
> (c) to nationalize, expropriate or transfer ownership of foreign property, in which case appropriate compensation should be paid by the State adopting such measures, taking into account its relevant laws and

> regulations and all circumstances that the State considers pertinent. In any case where the question of compensation gives rise to controversy, it shall be settled under the domestic law of the nationalizing State and by its tribunals, unless it is freely and mutually agreed by all States concerned that other peaceful means be sought on the basis of the sovereign equality of States and in accordance with the principle of free choice of means.[1]

Thus the Charter excluded international law and directed that only national law be taken into account. Major capital-exporting states voted against the Charter. As a General Assembly resolution not adopted as declaratory of international law, and as one whose terms were contested, it could neither make nor reflect international law. It nevertheless demonstrated that the majority of the states of the international community were not, collectively and as a whole, prepared to sustain the traditional rules of international law respecting the treatment and taking of foreign property.

The Charter was the high water mark of disregard of international law relating to foreign investment. But not long after 1974, the tide turned. Universal, multilateral agreement, expressed in a single international instrument, on which law governs foreign investment, and on the content of that law, remained unachievable, not only in the United Nations but through the OECD. But what is remarkable is that, in the last quarter of a century, more than 2,200 bilateral investment treaties (BITs) have been concluded.

These BITs were initially negotiated by European states such as Germany, Switzerland, United Kingdom, and the Netherlands, and subsequently by the USA and Japan, with developing countries. Today, they are found not only between the North and the South but with and between the states of the former Second and Third Worlds. Their universal reach is extraordinary, as are their provisions.

BITs specify in terms more explicit, detailed, and compelling than ever advanced under what was customary international law in the time of Cordell Hull, what may be described as an ideal law of international investment. They reflect the fact that states round the world seek to attract rather than repel foreign investment.

By the terms of these treaties, foreign investment is assured of fair and equitable treatment and full security and protection, as well as non-discrimination and management authority and control. The terms of contracts governing the investment are to be respected. In the event of a taking

[1] United Nations General Assembly Resolution 3281 (XXIX), 12 December 1974.

by the state of foreign investment, full compensation reflecting the fair market value of the investment will be paid. In case of dispute, the investor is authorized to pursue a binding international arbitral remedy against the host government. Diplomatic interposition is not debarred by the Calvo Doctrine; it is excluded by affording the foreign investor standing to invoke an international arbitral remedy without the uncertain and sometimes politicized diplomatic espousal of his own government.

As it was put in an international arbitral award of 14 March 2003:

> The requirement of compensation to be 'just' and representative of the 'genuine value of the investment affected' evokes the famous Hull formula which provided for the payment of prompt, adequate and effective compensation for the taking of foreign owned property. The formula was controversial. Capital exporting countries viewed it as an expression of customary international law. Developing countries and Communist States maintained that the foreign investor was entitled to no more compensation than that provided by the law of the host government however and whenever amended and applied. The controversy came to a head by the adoption by the General Assembly of the United Nations of the 'Charter of Economic Rights and Duties of States'. The major capital exporting states voted against the Charter. But in the end, the international community put aside this controversy, surmounting it by the conclusion of more than 2,200 bilateral (and a few multilateral) investment treaties. Today these treaties are truly universal in their reach and essential provisions. They concordantly provide for payment of 'just compensation', representing the 'genuine' or 'fair market' value of the property taken. Some treaties provide for prompt, adequate and effective compensation amounting to the fair market value of the investment expropriated immediately before the expropriation ... Others provide that compensation shall represent the equivalent of the investment affected. These concordant provisions are variations on an agreed, essential theme, namely, that when a state takes foreign property, full compensation must be paid.
>
> The possibility of payment of compensation determined by the law of the host State or by the circumstances of the host State has disappeared from contemporary international law as it is expressed in investment treaties in such extraordinary numbers, and with such concordant provisions, as to have reshaped the body of customary international law itself.[2]

[2] *CME Czech Republic BV* v. *Czech Republic*, Final Award, 14 March 2003, UNCITRAL Arbitration Tribunal; published in (2003/08) 15 *World Trade and Arbitration Materials* No. 4.

This Award proceeded to quote the NAFTA Award of 11 October 2002, in *Mondev International* v. *United States:*

> the vast number of bilateral and regional investment treaties (more than 2,000) almost uniformly provide for fair and equitable treatment of foreign investments and largely provide for full security and protection of investments. Investment treaties run between North and South, and East and West, and between States in these spheres inter se. On a remarkably widespread basis, States have repeatedly obliged themselves to accord foreign investment such treatment. In the Tribunal's view, such a body of concordant practice will necessarily have influenced the content of rules governing the treatment of foreign investment in current international law.[3]

The phenomenon of how and when provisions of treaties binding only the parties to those treaties may seep into general international law and thus bind the international community as a whole is subtle and elusive. It is nevertheless a process known to international law. It is a process of which some 2,200 bilateral investment treaties are the contemporary exemplar.

[3] *Mondev International Ltd* v. *United States*, ICSID Case No. ARB(AF) 99/2, 11 October 2002, (2003) 42 ILM 85.

18

ICSID Arbitration and the State's Increasingly Remote Consent: Apropos the *Maffezini* Case

BRIGITTE STERN

Introduction

Everyone knows that besides having been a member of the Appellate Body of the World Trade Organization's Dispute Settlement Mechanism, Florentino Feliciano also has extensive experience as an arbitrator in international investment and commercial disputes at the International Centre for Settlement of Investment Disputes (ICSID or 'the Centre') in Washington, at the International Chamber of Commerce (ICC) in Paris, and that he is on the Arbitrators Panel of the American Arbitration Association (AAA) in New York; hence the idea to reflect on the recent evolution of ICSID, in this homage to a person who has been so deeply involved in the evolution of international economic law. This contribution intends to give some general views of the overall dramatic changes in the role played, in this time of globalization, by the mechanism provided for by ICSID. This arbitral institution is designed specifically for arbitration between states – subjects of public international law, and investors – subjects of national laws. The Washington Convention on Settlement of Investment Disputes between States and Nationals of Other States, which entered into force on 14 October 1966 and created ICSID, can be considered as a success story. Today, new directions appear that will be presented in this contribution.

General background on consent to international arbitration

ICSID was created at a time when new states, just appearing on the international scene after decolonization, as well as Latin American states en bloc, were quite reluctant to submit their contractual disputes with a foreign investor to arbitration. In order to protect fully their sovereignty, they would rather have these difficulties submitted to their own national courts. Of course, foreign investors, whether private individuals or corporations, were in turn quite reluctant about this latter solution, fearing that the state would appear on the one hand as a contractor and on the other as a judge, in other words, that it would be 'judge and party', which is never a guarantee of fairness. The adoption of an international convention, under the auspices of the World Bank, seemed to be able to reconcile the conflicting interests of sovereign states and private investors. Private parties hoped that states would be induced to accept this new scheme because it was an international arbitral institution linked with the World Bank, and because it contained features respectful of the contracting states' sovereignty. States, indeed, had their sovereignty protected, because they were free to ratify or abstain from ratifying the Convention, and also, as we shall see later, because the rules governing the submission of a case to arbitration seemed also to be extremely respectful of their consent, which was to be explicitly given in writing. Interestingly enough, this analysis was put forward by the ICSID tribunal in *AMCO* v. *Indonesia:*

> ICSID arbitration is a method of settlement which corresponds to the interests, not only of the investors, but of the Contracting States as well, provided that by their adhesion to the Convention they have shown that they considered this method as being effectively in their interest, being also understood that *they keep full freedom to implement it or not, in respect of each particular investment agreement.*[1]

The first ICSID precedents concerned primarily difficulties raised by contractual relations between a state and a foreign investor, through what has come to be known as state contracts. But the picture today is completely different, and most of the cases are raised between an investor and a host state where no contractual nexus exists that embodies an arbitration clause between the investor and the host state, although many cases involve other types of legal or contractual relationships linking the investor and the host state. This has been christened with a very suggestive name by Jan Paulsson, as 'arbitration without privity'.[2] This evolution has been able to take place because of 'a growing

[1] *Amco Asia Corporation and others* v. *Republic of Indonesia*, Award on Jurisdiction, 25 September 1983 (1984) ILM 351, paragraph 23, at 368 (emphasis added).

[2] J. Paulsson, 'Arbitration Without Privity' (1995) *ICSID Review – Foreign Investment Law Journal* 232. See also A. El-Kosheri, 'ICSID Arbitration and Developing Countries' (1998) *ICSID Review – Foreign Investment Law Journal* 107.

acceptability of arbitration generally as a means of resolving disputes between States and foreign private parties', in the words of Antonio Parra, the Deputy Secretary-General of ICSID.[3] Or, in other words, because of what the then Secretary-General of the ICC Court of Arbitration, Horacio Grigera Naon, has called 'a Copernician change in the attitude of the host countries' described as follows:

> Since an integral part of the protective framework required by private investors and espoused by industrialized countries – such as the United States – includes access by the private investor to international commercial arbitration to resolve claims against the host country arising from its status as such or from the foreign investment, the new attitude of developing countries has also been evidenced through their acceptance to submit to binding arbitration should the private foreign investor opt for that means of dispute resolution to obtain redress for grievance.[4]

It is important to state at the outset that the submission – or even the consent to submission – of a case to an ICSID arbitration bars the state whose nationals are the private investors from granting them diplomatic protection. This was one of the provisions considered to be an incentive for the developing countries to ratify the ICSID Convention: if they accept an ICSID arbitration, they no longer have to fear the diplomatic protection of the investors by powerful states from the North,[5] where the investors usually come from.

In order for ICSID to have jurisdiction over a dispute, three well-known procedural conditions must be met, according to Article 25 of the Washington Convention:

- first, a condition *ratione personae*: the dispute must oppose a contracting state and a national of another contracting state;
- second, a condition *ratione materiae*: the dispute must be a legal one arising directly out of an investment;
- third, a condition *ratione voluntatis*, in other words, a condition relating to consent: the consent must be given by the two parties in writing.

[3] A. Parra, 'ICSID and New Trends in International Dispute Settlement', *News from ICSID* (Winter 1993), p. 8.

[4] H. Grigera Naon, 'The Settlement of Investment Disputes between States and Private Parties' (2000) *Journal of World Investment* 59.

[5] A good example is *Anglo-Iranian Co.* v. *Iran* [1952] ICJ Rep. 93, where Great Britain granted diplomatic protection to the British oil company which was nationalized by Mossadegh.

This contribution will focus on the third condition. One must bear in mind that ratification – necessarily in writing – of the Washington Convention cannot be considered as the required consent in writing from a state necessary in order to ground the jurisdiction of an ICSID tribunal. As the Preamble to the Convention states:

> No Contracting State shall by the mere fact of its ratification, acceptance or approval of this Convention and without its consent be deemed to be under an obligation to submit any particular dispute to conciliation or arbitration.

Concerning the jurisdiction *ratione voluntatis* based on a necessary consent in writing, it must be noted that the Report of the Executive Directors made at the time of the adoption of the Washington Convention stated that 'consent of the parties is the cornerstone of the jurisdiction of the Centre'. The act in which the parties agree to submit a future dispute to an ICSID arbitration was to be in writing, in order to avoid difficulties of proof and unnecessary discussions on the reality of the consent of both parties. What was probably intended in the Washington Convention was that the two parties enter into an arbitral clause or an arbitration agreement. However, in the above-mentioned Report, it was added that the consent need not be given in a single instrument:

> Nor does the Convention require that consent of both parties be expressed in a single instrument. Thus, a host State might in its investment promotion legislation offer to submit disputes arising out of certain classes of investments to the jurisdiction of the Centre, and the investor might give his consent by accepting the offer in writing.

This consent was traditionally given by the state's acceptance of an ICSID arbitration clause (*clause compromissoire*) included in a contract with a private investor, or through the signature of an ICSID arbitration agreement with such private party (*compromis d'arbitrage*).

However, the possibility left open by the comment of the Report of the Executive Directors is extensively used today by states in expressing their consent, and by ICSID tribunals dealing with jurisdictional issues. ICSID tribunals have found that not only national legislation but other types of commitment in writing by a state could be considered as a 'consent in writing' to submit an investment dispute to an ICSID arbitration. As far as consent in writing of the state is concerned, ICSID tribunals have thus adopted, some fifteen years ago, an innovative – although plausible in view of the text of the Washington Convention – interpretation, which gives a broad scope to ICSID tribunals' jurisdiction. At the same time, it gives a new dimension and meaning to arbitrations between an investor and a state.

In 1988, for the first time, a unilateral act – a law – of a state was found to contain the state's consent in writing. In the *Pyramids* case,[6] the reasoning of the ICSID tribunal relied upon three propositions to find jurisdiction:

(i) there was advance consent in writing to ICSID arbitration in the Egyptian Law No. 43 of 1974, dealing with international investments;
(ii) the consent of SPP (the investor) was given through the filing of the request;
(iii) these are the two necessary consents in writing, given in two different documents, which together create the necessary arbitration agreement.

This unprecedented approach spread rapidly, as appears from a reading of the arbitral award in the *Tradex Hellas* case, rendered a few years later by an ICSID tribunal:

> Starting with Article 25(1) of the ICSID, the Tribunal notes that, although consent by written agreement is the usual method of submission to ICSID jurisdiction, *it can now be considered as established and not requiring further reasoning* that such consent can also be effected *unilaterally* by a Contracting State in national laws, the consent becoming effective at the latest if and when the foreign investor files its claim with ICSID, making use of the respective national law ... The conclusion reached by the Tribunal is supported by the similar conclusion reached by another ICSID arbitral Tribunal in the case *SPP*.[7]

Very soon after the *Pyramids* case, in 1990, a bilateral investment treaty (BIT) was found to contain the state's consent in writing in *AAPL* v. *Sri Lanka*.[8] It is safe to say that it is now beyond doubt that a general reference to an ICSID arbitration in a BIT, or in a multilateral treaty on investment like NAFTA for that purpose, can be considered to

[6] ICSID Case No. ARB/84/3, Awards of 27 November 1985 and 14 April 1988 (1991) *Yearbook of Commercial Arbitration* 28.

[7] *Hellas SA* v. *Albania*, ICSID Case No. ARB/94/2, Award, 24 December 1996 (1999) *ICSID Review – Foreign Investment Law Journal* 186 (emphasis added).

[8] *Asian Agricultural Products Ltd* v. *Sri Lanka*, ICSID Case No. ARB/87/3, Award, 27 June 1990 (1991) *ICSID Review – Foreign Investment Law Journal* 514, with a commentary by N. G. Ziadé.

express the consent in writing required by Article 25 of the Washington Convention to give jurisdiction to ICSID.

These new perspectives have been described by many legal writers, such as Jacques Werner, who has declared: 'We enter the era of arbitration without contractual relationship';[9] or such as Antonio Parra, who in referring a few years ago to consent in internal laws, as well as in bilateral or multilateral treaties, concluded that we are faced with a revolution in our conception of arbitration: 'With the huge and still growing number of highly generalised consents by States, this puts the requirement of mutual consent in a new light, quite far removed from traditional contractual conceptions of arbitration'.[10] It is significant that what has emerged is what the dissenting arbitrator in the *SPP* case, El Mahdi, had criticized, when the very first step in that direction was made:

> The jurisdiction of the Centre does not and cannot exceed the limits traced by the Convention, allowing the Centre to become the Juge de Droit Commun of investment disputes on the assumption of a consent which does not exist in fact or in law.[11]

At the same time, others were welcoming this new trend, including Ahmed El Kosheri, who identified an opening up of 'unlimited opportunities for rendering ICSID arbitration the "natural judge" (*juge de droit commun*) in adjudicating investment disputes with the governmental authorities of the host State'.[12] To underscore the drastic change that occurred, it is worth looking back to the past. As stated by Antonio Parra, '[j]urisdiction in *all* of the cases brought to ICSID until about the mid-1980s was founded upon consents to arbitration recorded in the

[9] J. Werner, 'The Trade Explosion and Some Likely Effects on International Arbitration' (1997) *Journal of International Arbitration* 5.

[10] See A. Parra, 'Provisions on the Settlement of Investment Disputes in Modern Investment Laws, Bilateral Investment Treaties and Multilateral Instruments on Investment' (1997) *ICSID Review – Foreign Investment Law Journal* 287 and 'The Role of ICSID in the Settlement of Investment Disputes', *News from ICSID* (Winter 1999), p. 7. It is worth noticing that Antonio Parra had already welcomed what was coming in 1993, see Parra, 'ICSID and New Trends', where he states: 'The program for this panel discussion asks whether there is a trend towards granting private parties greater opportunities to participate in international procedures for the settlement of disputes with governments. From the vantage point of ICSID, it certainly seems that the answer to this question should be "yes"'.

[11] ICSID Reports (Grotius, Cambridge, 1993), p. 163.

[12] Statement made during the 87th Annual Meeting of the ASIL, April 1993, cited by Parra, 'ICSID and New Trends', 9.

traditional manner, by a clause in a single instrument such as an investment contract'.[13] Today, the overall picture has totally changed – only a minority of arbitration cases rests on a direct agreement between the two parties to the arbitration. It is worth noticing that the 'descent' of the *SPP* case based on a national law is quasi-non-existent – only a few cases – quite contrary to the proliferation of cases based on BITs, following the AAPL decision, or on NAFTA.

Maffezini v. *Spain*

Maffezini v. *Spain*[14] is illustrative of this trend, bringing it to its outer limits. In this case, a combination of two BITs were, by virtue of a most favoured nation (MFN) clause, considered as shaping the state's consent in writing. This case is one of the recent cases which, if followed, has the potential to extend endlessly the trend which I have called the 'marginalisation du consentement dans l'arbitrage international'.[15] This case concerned a claim raised by Mr Maffezini, an Argentinean national, arising from treatment by Spanish authorities, in connection with his investment in an enterprise for the production and distribution of chemical products in Galicia. What was at stake was, first, the BIT between Argentina and Spain and, secondly, the BIT between Chile and Spain. The reasoning of the tribunal was that the MFN clause contained in the Argentina–Spain BIT allowed a national of Argentina to benefit from the conditions surrounding consent to arbitration given by Spain in the Chile–Spain BIT. As a matter of fact, the Argentina–Spain BIT provided for a first step before a question could be submitted to international arbitration, which was that the dispute had first to be brought before the competent tribunal of the contracting state in whose territory the investment was made. This provision of Article X(2) of the BIT gave a clear shape to the consent of the two involved states to ICSID arbitration, requesting the exhaustion of some local remedies in Spain before resort could be made to international arbitration, in the following terms:

[13] Parra, 'ICSID and New Trends', 9 (emphasis added).

[14] *Emilio Augustín Maffezini* v. *Kingdom of Spain*, Case No. ARB/97/7, Decision of the Tribunal on Objections to Jurisdiction, 25 January 2000 (2001) *ICSID Review – Foreign Investment Law Journal* 212.

[15] See B. Stern, 'Un coup d'arrêt à la marginalisation du consentement dans l'arbitrage international (apropos de l'arrêt de la Cour d'appel de Paris du 1er juin 1999)' (2000) *Revue de l'arbitrage* 403.

1. Disputes which arise within the terms of this Agreement concerning an investment between an investor of one Contracting Party and the other Contracting Party shall, if possible, be settled amicably by the parties to the dispute.

2. If the dispute cannot thus be settled within six months following the date on which the dispute has been raised by either party, it shall be submitted to the competent tribunal of the Contracting Party in whose territory the investment was made.

3. The dispute may be submitted to international arbitration in any of the following circumstances:

(a) at the request of one of the parties to the dispute, if no decision has been rendered on the merits of the claim after the expiration of a period of eighteen months from the date on which the proceedings referred to in paragraph 2 of this Article have been initiated, or if such decision has been rendered, but the dispute between the parties continues;

(b) if both parties to the dispute agree thereto.

4. In the cases foreseen in paragraph 3, the disputes between the parties shall be submitted, unless the parties otherwise agree, either to international arbitration under the March 18, 1965 Convention on the Settlement of Investment Disputes Between States and Nationals of Other States or to an ad hoc arbitral tribunal established under the Arbitration Rules of the United Nations Commission on International Trade Law (UNCITRAL).

If after a period of three months following the submission of the dispute to arbitration by either party, there is no agreement to one of the above alternative procedures, the dispute shall be submitted to arbitration under the March 18, 1965 Convention on the Settlement of Investment Disputes Between States and Nationals of Other States, provided that both Contracting Parties have become parties to the said Convention. Otherwise, the dispute shall be submitted to the above mentioned ad hoc tribunal.

Mr. Maffezini, an Argentinean national, had not submitted his case to the Spanish courts before presenting his claim to ICSID. In order to justify this procedure he relied on the Chile–Spain BIT where this first step was not provided for, and claimed that the MFN clause in the Argentina–Spain BIT allowed him to invoke Spain's consent in the Chile–Spain BIT. In order to arrive at the conclusion that the prior submission to a national court – which was clearly a condition of the consent to international arbitration given in the Argentina–Spain BIT – could be disregarded, the tribunal entered into the following reasoning. The point of departure was that if it had to interpret the Argentina–Spain BIT alone, 'the Tribunal would have had to conclude that because the Claimant failed to submit the instant case to Spanish courts ... the Centre lacked jurisdiction and the Tribunal lacked competence to hear the case'.[16] But this conclusion was then set aside, using the MFN clause of the Argentina–Spain BIT and the provision of the Spain–Chile BIT, which does not impose a submission to national courts before recourse to arbitration and provides merely that the investor can opt for arbitration after a six-month period allowed for negotiations has expired. In order to conclude that under the Argentina–Spain BIT there was no requirement to submit the dispute first to the Spanish courts, the tribunal followed a reasoning in three steps.

The first step was to consider that the MFN clause applying to 'all matters subject to this Agreement' applied to the dispute settlement procedures: it means that 'matters' has been understood not to refer only to substantive matters or material aspects of the treatment granted to investors, but also to procedural and jurisdictional questions. To arrive at this conclusion, the tribunal relied on the dictum in the *Ambatielos* case, where it was held that:

> it cannot be said that the administration of justice, in so far as it is concerned with the protection of these rights, must necessarily be excluded from the field of application of the most-favored-nation clause, when the latter includes 'all matters relating to commerce and navigation'.[17]

Based on that, the far-reaching rule stated by the ICSID tribunal was quite unambiguous:

> if a third-party treaty contains provisions for the settlement of disputes that are more favorable to the protection of the investor's rights and interests than those in the basic treaty, such provision may be extended to the beneficiary of the most favored nation clause. (paragraph 56)

The second step, then, was to consider that a direct reference to international arbitration is more favourable to the investor than a procedure that first required submission to national courts: as declared by the tribunal, '[t]raders and investors, like their States of nationality, have traditionally felt that their rights and interests are better protected

[16] *Maffezini, supra* n. 14 at paragraph 36. [17] United Nations (1963) RIAA, 107.

by recourse to international arbitration than by submission to domestic courts'.[18] This conclusion was reached in spite of Spain's contention that 'it would have to be proved that the submission of the dispute to Spanish jurisdiction is less advantageous to the investor than its submission to ICSID arbitration'.[19]

The last step was for the tribunal to 'introduce' the consent found in the Chile–Spain BIT, considered as more favourable to the investor, into the Argentina–Spain BIT. This step was probably the most audacious, as far as the interpretation of state consent is concerned, as it disregarded the fact that the Chile–Spain BIT was signed on 2 October 1991 and the Argentina–Spain BIT on 3 October 1991, and that the Argentinian state must have had reasons not to use the same formula as Chile.

It is indeed stated in the award that, if Spain was in favour of direct submission to international arbitration, Argentina was not:

> at the time of the negotiations of the Agreement, Argentina still sought to require some form of prior exhaustion of local remedies, while Spain supported the policy of a direct right of submission to arbitration, which was reflected in the numerous agreements it negotiated with other countries at that time. The eventual role the treaty envisaged for domestic courts, involving the submission of the dispute to these courts for a period of time, not amounting to the traditional exhaustion of local remedies requirement as explained above, coupled with ICSID arbitration, was an obvious compromise reached by the parties.[20]

The outcome of this case could mean that if there is a BIT with absolutely no consent to ICSID and a mere reference to national courts, but a most-favoured nation clause, the absence of consent of the state to ICSID can be disregarded as long as the other contracting state with which the BIT has been entered into, has, among the several BITs it has signed, a single one in which it gives its consent to an ICSID arbitration. Although *Maffezini* does not go this far, one wonders if ultimately the result of the reasoning followed in this case could not be that, if a state Y refuses to consent to ICSID in a BIT with a state X and happens to have entered into another unrelated BIT with another state W where it gives its consent to ICSID arbitration, it can nevertheless be compelled to accept ICSID arbitration with the nationals of state X. As

[18] *Maffezini, supra* n. 14 at paragraph 55. [19] *Ibid*. at paragraph 42.
[20] *Ibid*. at paragraph 57.

stated by the tribunal, 'the application of the most favored nation clause to dispute settlement arrangements in the context of investment treaties might result in the harmonization and enlargement of the scope of such arrangements'.[21] With no doubt, there is an enlargement of the scope of such arrangements, and a harmonization by the systematic spreading of international arbitration – and more precisely of the most favourable access to international arbitration for the foreign investor – but, in my view, to the detriment of the true consent given by the state. The fiction of the state's consent is brought to its ultimate consequence; when the fiction of consent is so far away from reality, as in this context, the question must be raised of its continuing explanatory validity.

It must, however, be mentioned that the tribunal seems to have been conscious of the far-reaching consequences of its decision and has tried to keep things under control, in adding that 'there are some important limits that ought to be kept in mind'.[22] These limits have been summarized in the following manner:

> As a matter of principle, the beneficiary of the clause should not be able to override public policy considerations that the contracting parties might have envisaged as fundamental conditions for their acceptance of the agreement in question, particularly if the beneficiary is a private investor, as is often the case.[23]

Examples of such necessary limits are given: the consent of the state should not be set aside through the MFN clause when the state has conditioned its consent on the exhaustion of local remedies; when it is stated in the BIT that once a choice is made between domestic courts and international arbitration this choice is final and irreversible; when there is a selection of a specific forum like ICSID; or when a reference is made to a highly institutionalized system of arbitration with precise rules of procedures like NAFTA.

The tribunal is aware that 'a distinction has to be made between the legitimate extension of rights and benefits by means of the operation of the clause, on the one hand, and disruptive treaty-shopping that would play havoc with the policy objectives of underlying specific treaty provisions, on the other hand'.[24] The present author, while already not convinced by the general reasoning, does not moreover see where the tribunal draws the line between acceptable and unacceptable extensions

[21] *Ibid.* at paragraph 62. [22] *Ibid.* [23] *Ibid.* [24] *Ibid.* at paragraph 63.

of consent, especially in view of the fact that it went on to declare that 'the requirement for the prior resort to domestic courts spelled out in the Argentina–Spain BIT *does not reflect a fundamental question of public policy*'.[25] One wonders where public policy can be traced if not in such an important provision, quite consistent with the historical position of Latin American countries, and their traditional insistence on the Calvo Clause. The more so, as the ICSID tribunal itself has recognized that there existed a procedure of submission to the national courts 'not amounting to the traditional exhaustion of local remedies',[26] which implies that it is a sort of non-traditional (as it is limited in time) recourse to local remedies; this all the more so as the tribunal, looking at state practice, noted that Spain had signed a BIT with Uruguay similar to the Argentina–Spain BIT, 'probably because of the similarity of *policies* pursued by the two River Plate nations'.[27] Recently, another ICSID arbitral tribunal seems to have given a '*coup d'arrêt*' to the unlimited extension of the use of the MFN clause, the consequence of which would be that it could empty of any meaning the exchange of consent between two states after careful negotiations of the terms of a BIT:

> The Arbitral Tribunal is aware that the Claimant, relying on the decision in the case *Emilio Augustín Mafezzini* v. *Kingdom of Spain* refers in its closing statement to the most favored nation treatment provided for in Article 8(1) of the Agreement in order to enable retroactive application in view of the more favorable treatment in connection with that matter which would be afforded to an Austrian investor under the bilateral treaty on investment protection between the United Mexican States and Austria of June 29, 1998. The Arbitral Tribunal will not examine the provisions of such Treaty in detail in light of such principle, because it deems that matters relating to the application over time of the Agreement, which involve more the time dimension of application of its substantive provisions rather than matters of procedure or jurisdiction, due to their significance and importance, go to the core of matters that must be deemed to be specifically negotiated by the Contracting Parties. These are determining factors for their acceptance of the Agreement, as they are directly linked to the identification of the substantive protection regime applicable to the foreign investor and, particularly, to the general (national or international) legal context within which such regime operates, as well as to the access of the foreign investor to the substantive

[25] *Ibid.* at paragraph 64 (emphasis added). [26] *Ibid.* at paragraph 57.
[27] *Ibid.* at paragraph 59 (emphasis added).

> provisions of such regime. Their application cannot therefore be impaired by the principle contained in the most favored nation clause.[28]

The rule here stated seems very reasonable, and could have been, in the author's view, usefully applied to the *Maffezini* case: it is difficult to consider that the prior reference to the national courts found in the Argentina–Spain BIT was not included in 'the core of matters that must be deemed to be specifically negotiated by the Contracting Parties'. Moreover, there was in this case a problem of determination of the time of the dispute and the relevance of the two BITs to that dispute, which gives rise to another problematic dilution of consent. The Argentina–Spain BIT entered into force on 28 September 1992, while the Chile–Spain BIT entered into force on 29 March 1994. Article II(2) of the Argentina–Spain BIT provides in part: 'However this agreement shall not apply to disputes or claims originating before its entry into force'.

Therefore, it was important to determine when the dispute arose. After a discussion where the tribunal distinguished in the natural sequence of events, first 'the expression of a disagreement and the statement of a difference of views',[29] then 'the dispute in its technical and legal sense',[30] and ultimately 'the claim'[31] arising out of the dispute, the tribunal considered that the critical date was not the date when the claim was presented but the earlier date when the dispute first arose:

> if the dispute arises after the critical date it will qualify for its transformation into a claim, while if the dispute has arisen before such date it will be excluded by the terms of the BIT.[32]

And, without arguing this point extensively, the tribunal declared that 'it is satisfied that in this case the dispute in its technical and legal sense began to take shape in 1994 . . . [t]hat is to say, this dispute came into being after both the Argentina–Spain and the Chile–Spain BITs had entered into force, *although the critical date here is the entry into force of the former*, since this is the basic treaty relevant to this case'.[33] This formulation implies, it seems, that – had the dispute arisen after the coming into force of the Argentina–Spain BIT, but before the coming into force of the Chile–Spain BIT – the tribunal would still have considered that it could 'import' retroactively the consent given by Spain to

[28] *Técnicas Medioambientales Tecmed, SA* v. *United Mexican States*, ICSID Case No. ARB(AF)/00/2, Award, 29 May 2003, paragraph 69.

[29] *Maffezini, supra* n. 14 at paragraph 96.

[30] *Ibid.* at paragraph 98.

[31] *Ibid.* at paragraph 97.

[32] *Ibid.*

[33] *Ibid.* at paragraph 98 (emphasis added).

Chile into the BIT with Argentina. It seems to the author that the acceptable limits of 'deconstruction' of consent are thus crossed.

Concluding remarks

The conclusions reached in this case show the immense possibility of extension of the dispute resolution mechanisms between states and private parties that can rest on the existence of MFN clauses in BITs that include a broad reference to arbitration, as quite clearly explained by Horacio Grigera Naon:

> The presence and operation of the most-favored-nation clause may be construed and interpreted – depending on how it has been worded – as giving access to a private investor in one investment protection treaty to methods of dispute resolution more favorable to it envisaged in another investment protection treaty having the same host State against which the claim is addressed as party but not the country of origin of the private investor.[34]

While the consent of the state fades away – without disappearing completely, it has to be stated – the impression is that slowly but steadily we are walking with giant steps towards a general system of compulsory arbitration involving states for all matters relating to international investments, at the initiative of the private actors of international economic relations. We are engaged in the process of moving from a system of reciprocal consensual commercial arbitration to a completely different system of direct investor-state compulsory international arbitration. It seems that, on the one hand such a system renders states accountable for violations of obligations they have assumed towards investors – which is quite positive – but on the other hand, it opens the door for challenges to perfectly admissible acts of sovereignty, if deemed contrary to the economic interests of international investors, which appears as a more negative aspect. This gives a new dimension to the task of international arbitrators.

Here we must raise a fundamental question once raised by Bruno Oppetit,[35] when he asked: 'L'arbitrage international est-il sous-tendu par une philosophie du droit et si oui laquelle?' As he pointed out, the

[34] H. Grigera Naon, 'The Settlement of Investment Disputes between States and Private Parties' (2000) *Journal of World Investment* 74.

[35] 'Philosophie de l' arbitrage commercial international' (1994) *JDI* 811 at 826.

choice is between two different approaches: either one thinks that 'the arbitrator must only be concerned with the specific relations between the parties to the dispute, without any consideration for the defense of superior interests';[36] or one thinks that 'the arbitrator, as the ordinary judge of the disputes in international economic relations, cannot disregard the general interest'.[37] This second approach, in line with the contemporaneous concern for ethics, pays attention to collective interests that are supposed to be embodied in the state, and not only to individual private economic interests.

This dilemma is exactly the one which the ICSID arbitrator faces today. One should not forget that arbitration is precisely a means to achieve justice by settling conflicting interests – and here the conflicting interests can be private economic interests and general public interests. Bruno Oppetit has stated in a brief but striking formula that 'l'arbitrage est une justice privée, certes, mais c'est une justice'.[38] This should be the ultimate goal of arbitration in investment disputes. And one can be confident that if the arbitrators have the profile and dedication of Florentino Feliciano, this type of justice is not an unreachable goal.

[36] *Ibid.* at 826–27 (author's translation). [37] *Ibid.* at 827 (author's translation).
[38] 'Justice étatique et justice arbitrale' in *Etudes offertes à Pierre Bellet* (Litec, Paris, 1991), p. 420.

19

The Notion of Investment in Recent Practice

RUDOLF DOLZER

Building bridges: a profile of Justice Feliciano

In several respects, Justice Feliciano's personality and career embody at the highest level what it may mean in our contemporary world 'to live greatly in the law'. After the Marrakesh Agreement had successfully strengthened the rule of law in international trade law through the establishment of a formalized dispute settlement mechanism, Justice Feliciano was chosen to be one of the first members of the Appellate Body. This choice was far from self-evident, in as much as Justice Feliciano not only came from the developing world and had the confidence of colleagues and governments from the developing world, but moreover, had no special experience in matters of international trade law. And as the new WTO was a first step towards institution-building for a globalized economy, the experiment of introducing a global rule of law for the trade sector depended, to a large extent, on the success in the initial period of the new dispute settlement system charged with the application and interpretation of new and old rules. Today, ten years after Marrakesh, the WTO dispute settlement system is often considered the most successful effort in the globalizing world to establish the rule of law, all the problems in detail notwithstanding. From 1995 to 2001, Justice Feliciano was a member of the Appellate Body, serving as its Chair from 2000 to 2001.

Remarkably enough, Justice Feliciano's experience in international economic law is not limited to trade law. This is contrary to an understandable, but regrettable, tendency to specialization, not just in international law but within international economic law itself. While the 'trade law community' is, by and large, separate from the 'investment law community', Justice Feliciano was also asked to chair important panels rendering major decisions in ICSID proceedings. As in trade law, these rulings under his chairmanship have left their mark in the development of the rules on foreign investment. As many concepts in investment law and in trade law are identical or functionally equivalent, Justice Feliciano was able to point out the common ground which is mostly ignored in practice and in scholarship.

As if the crossing of lines between investment law and trade law was not enough, Justice Feliciano already had a successful engagement in international financial law behind him before he moved from Manila to Geneva in 1994. In this context, I first had the honour to work with him when we prepared a joint study on the rescheduling of debts after the financial crisis in major countries of the Third World in late 1981. The combination of his soft voice, his firm mind, his insistence on principle, his emphasis on balance, and his natural authority made this task a wonderful experience. What came through in his personality and his approach was, of course, that at that time he already had a successful career in domestic Filipino law behind him, having been a highly respected judge on the Philippines' Constitutional Court, something that had brought him highest recognition in his home country.

In essence, one main characteristic of Justice Feliciano has been his ability and willingness to cross traditional professional lines and to build new professional bridges, from national law to international law, from international to financial law, to trade law and to investment law. Perhaps most importantly, Justice Feliciano has the ability to make us forget, for the moment, on the legal level, the global divide between North and South.

Of course, a career and an intellectual horizon which reaches across so many fields and constituencies is made possible only by his unique personality grounded in personal integrity, in his willingness to work hard, to make a contribution, and, basically, in his belief in law and the legal process to promote justice and the wellbeing of the individual on the basis of personal freedom embedded in a sense of social responsibility.

Ultimately, Justice Feliciano's professional and personal life stands for all the values, in national and international law, which condition and characterize the rule of law and which flow from it. On a personal level, I have seen his strength and his dedication to the rule of law in serving with him on the Board of the International Development Law Organisation in Rome, promoting the training of young lawyers in the developing world. My sense is that this task to strengthen the developing world by strengthening the local legal communities comes as close to his heart as all the other responsibilities which he has assumed in his rich and successful professional life.

The notion of 'investment'

The following observations are meant to take stock briefly of the notion of 'investment' as used in international norms protecting foreign investment and as applied and interpreted in arbitral jurisprudence. Not atypical for many concepts and categories in international economic law, the notion of 'investment' has its origin in economic terminology (as, for example, with 'dumping', 'subsidies', 'capital transfer') and was adopted in legal documents because of its significance and usage, but subsequently turned out to be multifaceted and difficult to define when understood as a legal term.

In economics, it is often assumed that an investment involves the transfer of funds, to a longer-term project, for the purpose of regular income, the participation of the person transferring the funds, at least to some extent, in the management of the project, and a business risk. These elements distinguish foreign direct investment from a portfolio investment (no element of personal management), from an ordinary transaction for purposes of a sale of a good or a service (no management, no continuous flow of income), and from a short-term financial transaction.[1]

On the side of legal state practice in regard to international treaties, Patrick Juillard has rightly pointed out that the term 'investment' has been applied differently in the areas of capital liberalization, and for purposes of the protection of foreign property.[2] But even the narrower comparison of agreements concluded to protect foreign enterprises does not point to a homogeneous usage. Most bilateral agreements define an 'investment' in a very wide sense so as to identify the term with the classical legal notion of any good. A common approach has been to use a broad formula along the following pattern:

> For the purpose of this Treaty:
> the term 'investment' comprises every kind of asset, in particular:
>
> (a) movable and immovable property as well as any other right *in rem*, such as mortgages, liens and pledges;
> (b) shares of companies and other kinds of interest in companies;
> (c) claims to money which has been used to create an economic value or claims to any performance having an economic value;

[1] See also C. Schreuer, *The ICSID Convention* (2001), p. 140.
[2] See D. Carreau and P. Juillard, *Droit international économique* (1998), p. 395.

(d) copyrights, industrial property rights, technical processes, trade-marks, trade-names, know-how, and goodwill;
(e) business concessions under public law, including concessions to search for, extract and exploit natural resources.[3]

Other treaties are phrased more specifically in line with the economic usage of investment and spell out, in one way or another, the elements of the traditional economic term set forth above. Thus, some bilateral treaties spell out that a long-term transfer has to take place: for example, the bilateral investment treaty (BIT) concluded between the Ukraine and Denmark on 23 October 1992[4] states: 'For the purpose of this Agreement, the term "investment" shall mean every kind of asset connected with economic activities acquired for the purpose of establishing lasting economic relations'. The Agreement concluded between the USA and Chile on 6 June 2003 spells out that 'investment means every asset that an investor owns or controls, directly or indirectly, that has the characteristics of an investment, including such characteristics as the commitment of capital or other resources, the expectation of gain or profit, or the assumption of risk'.[5] Similar definitions can be found in recent BITs concluded between Chile and Korea[6] and between the USA and Singapore.[7]

In multilateral treaties as well, no single definition has been adopted. According to Article 17–01 of the Treaty on Free Trade between Colombia, Venezuela, and Mexico,[8] the term investment includes 'any type of asset or right the purpose of which is to produce economic benefits'. However, the same article excludes from this definition claims

[3] Treaty between the Federal Republic of Germany and the Republic of Ghana Concerning the Encouragement and Reciprocal Protection of Investments, (1997) Bundesgesetzblatt 48, p. 2056.

[4] Article 1(1) of the Agreement Concerning the Promotion and Reciprocal Protection of Investments concluded between the Kingdom of Denmark and the Ukraine on 23 October 1992, Lovtidende C, Udenrigsmin. N.4, j.nr. 400.E.9/Ukraine/12.

[5] Article 10.27 of the Free Trade Agreement between the Government of the United States of America and the Government of the Republic of Chile, 6 June 2003, published on the USTR website at www.ustr.gov/new/fta/Chile/final/index.htm

[6] Article 10.1 of the Free Trade Agreement between the Republic of Korea and the Republic of Chile, 15 February 2003, published on the OAS website at www.sice.oas.org/Trade/Chi-SKorea_e/ChiKoreaind_e.asp

[7] Article 15.1, No. 13 of the USA – Singapore Free Trade Agreement, 6 May 2003, published on the USTR website at www.ustr.gov/new/fta/Singapore/final.htm

[8] Treaty on Free Trade between the Republic of Colombia, the Republic of Venezuela, and the United Mexican States, September 1990, published on the OAS website at www. sice.oas.org/Trade/G3_E/G3E_TOC.asp

to money that arise solely from commercial contracts for the sale of goods or services, as does NAFTA Article 1139.[9] The definition of 'investment' in Article 1(6) of the Energy Charter Treaty includes claims to money and claims to performance pursuant to contracts having an economic value 'and associated with an investment'.[10] Other treaties explicitly refer to the more traditional concept of direct investment. For instance, the Free Trade Agreement concluded between the European Free Trade Association (EFTA) and Mexico[11] states:

> For the purpose of this Section, investment made in accordance with the laws and regulations of the Parties means direct investment, which is defined as investment for the purpose of establishing lasting economic relations with an undertaking such as, in particular, investments which give the possibility of exercising an effective influence on the management thereof.

Debates on the definition of the term 'investment' also arose during the negotiations of the Multilateral Agreement on Investment (MAI) within the OECD. The draft consolidated texts[12] provided for a broad definition of the term investment ('Every kind of asset owned or controlled, directly or indirectly, by an investor'), followed by an illustrative list including claims to money, claims to performance, or intellectual property rights. However, it was foreseen that 'an interpretative note will be required to indicate that, in order to qualify as an investment under the MAI, an asset must have the characteristics of an investment, such as the commitment of capital or other resources, the expectation of gain or profit, or the assumption of risk'. The desire to restrict the definition of 'investment' to a more traditional economic sense is also reflected in the commentaries to the consolidated texts, which, for example, tend to exclude from the application of the MAI claims to money arising as a result of the sale of goods and services.[13] The report of 4 May 1998 by the

[9] Article 1139(i) of the North American Free Trade Agreement (NAFTA), (1993) 32 *ILM* 289 at 647.

[10] Energy Charter Treaty Article 1(6) (1995) 34 ILM 360 at 383.

[11] Article 45 of the Free Trade Agreement between the EFTA States and the United Mexican States, 27 November 2000, published on the EFTA website at http://secretariat.efta.int/Web/ExternalRelations/PartnerCountries/Mexico/MX/MX_FTA.pdf

[12] Draft Consolidated Texts of 13 May 1997 (DAFFE/MAI(97)1/REV2), 11 February 1998 (DAFFE/MAI(98)7) and 22 April 1998 (DAFFE/MAI(98)7/REV1), published on the OECD website at www.oecd.org/daf/investment

[13] *Commentary to the Consolidated Text*, DAFFE/MAI(98)8/REV1, 22 April 1998, p. 7, published on the OECD website at www.oecd.org/daf/investment

Chairman to the Negotiating Group[14] proposed to incorporate these elements into the overall definition of the term investment as follows: 'Investment means an asset, owned or controlled, directly or indirectly, by an investor, that has the characteristics of an investment, such as the commitment of capital or other resources, the expectation of gain or profit, or the assumption of risk in the conduct of a business activity'.

Concerning the specific legal setting of ICSID, the issue of defining an investment from a legal perspective necessarily arose, not surprisingly, during the negotiation of the Convention. The delegations and the Secretariat presented several options and preferences. One draft indeed proposed that an investment required a commitment for at least five years.[15] In the end, however, none of these proposals commanded a clear consensus. Under these circumstances, the Secretariat, in the person of Aron Broches, came up with the diplomatic and pragmatic solution to leave the definition up to the parties in each case, pointing out correctly that ICSID jurisdiction always required the consent of both parties.[16] Of course, this approach did not solve all relevant questions inasmuch as Article 25 of the ICSID Convention itself explicitly used the term 'investment' and thus required its interpretation. According to the generally held view,[17] an agreement of both parties to submit the case to ICSID implies a strong presumption that the case involved an 'investment'. The understanding that many, but not all, factual situations could be covered by this construction of Article 25 was expressed subsequently when the rules on ICSID Additional Facility recognized that cases not covered by the ICSID Convention could be submitted under the Additional Rules.[18]

Against this background, the key legal issue remained open – whether or not the term 'investment', if not specifically qualified in accordance with its economic usage, was to be identified with any 'good' or 'asset'. In particular, the question arose for the majority of BITs phrased along the lines of the classical bilateral treaty mentioned above with its illustrative definition on the basis of five designated types. For these treaties,

[14] *Report by the Chairman to the Negotiating Group*, DAFFE/MAI(98)17, 4 May 1998, p. 10, published on the OECD website at www.oecd.org/daf/investment

[15] First Draft (Doc. 43) Article 30 in ICSID, *Documents Concerning the Origin and the Formulation of the Convention* (1968), vol. I, p. 116.

[16] See *Report of the Executive Directors on the Convention on the Settlement of Investment Disputes between States and Nationals of Other States* (1993) 1 ICSID Reports 23 at 28.

[17] See *Ceskoslovenska Obchodni Banka, AS* v. *Slovak Republic*, Decision on Objections to Jurisdiction, 24 May 1999, (2002) 5 ICSID Reports 330 at 351.

[18] See *Fedax NV* v. *Republic of Venezuela*, Decision on Objections to Jurisdiction, 11 July 1997, (2002) 5 ICSID Reports 183 at 193.

ICSID jurisprudence had to decide whether 'investment' in itself must be seen to refer to the traditional economic usage or whether the definition chosen implied that the term was to be understood exclusively in the light of the wording contained in the five illustrative groups, thus including all designated goods without regard to any connection to an investment in the traditional economic sense.

For a long time, ICSID tribunals were only confronted with factual situations which did not require the central issue of interpretation to be addressed. When the tribunals in *Alcoa Minerals of Jamaica Inc.* v. *Jamaica*,[19] *Kaiser Bauxite* v. *Jamaica*,[20] and *Letco* v. *Liberia*[21] were concerned with disputes in the mining business and undertakings in a long-term concession agreement, they were properly satisfied with briefly stating that the case concerned 'an investment' and fell under the jurisdiction of ICSID.

The necessity to take a closer look at the meaning of 'investment' arose for the first time when Fedax NV, a company based in the Netherlands Antilles, being part of the Netherlands, claimed in 1996 that its legal rights under six promissory notes issued by Venezuela fell under the jurisdiction of ICSID.[22] Venezuela raised all the arguments which might have been opposed to this view, but the ICSID tribunal (Vicuña, Heth, Ouren) in 1998 accepted the reasoning submitting by Fedax and decided to hear the case.

In view of this decision by the tribunal, it is widely considered today that the definition of 'investment' has to be a broad one, the definition in the relevant BIT between the Netherlands and Venezuela having been worded along the lines of the classical BIT ('titles to money, to other assets or to any performance having an economic value'). The Fedax tribunal accepted, in paragraph 20, that the interpretation of the BIT had to follow the rules laid down in Article 31 of the Vienna Convention on the Law of Treaties, on which both parties had based their different concepts of 'investment'. The decision emphasizes that the definition chosen by the parties was a very broad one. In its subsequent reasoning, no specific effort is made to highlight the general understanding of

19 *Alcoa Minerals of Jamaica Inc.* v. *Government of Jamaica*, Decision on Jurisdiction and Competence, 6 July 1975 (1979) IV *Yearbook Commercial Arbitration* 206.

20 *Kaiser Bauxite Company* v. *Government of Jamaica*, Decision on Jurisdiction and Competence, 6 July 1975 (1993) 1 ICSID Reports 296.

21 *Liberian Eastern Timber Corporation* v. *Government of the Republic of Liberia*, 31 March 1986 (1994) 2 ICSID Reports 343.

22 *Fedax NV* v. *Republic of Venezuela*, Decision on Objections to Jurisdiction, 11 July 1997 (2002) 5 ICSID Reports 183.

investment and the matter is left open in view of the specific meaning of 'titles to money':

> This definition evidences that the Contracting Parties to the Agreement intended a very broad meaning for the term 'investment'. The Tribunal notes in particular that titles to money in this definition are not in any way restricted to forms of direct foreign investment or portfolio investment, as argued by the Republic of Venezuela. Some such restrictions may perhaps apply to other types of investment listed in such definition, such as rights derived from shares or other similar types of investment, but they do not apply to the credit transactions of different categories that are embodied in the meaning of 'titles to money' as referred to in subparagraph (iii) of the definition set out above. It should be noted, moreover, that titles to money are not necessarily excluded from the concept of foreign direct investment.[23]

In a subsequent passage, however, the same tribunal seems to clarify the matter and emphasizes that promissory notes fall under the concept of 'investment':

> The claimant has rightly argued that promissory notes of this kind have a legal standing of their own, separate and independent from the underlying transaction. It is not disputed in this case that the Government of Venezuela foresaw the possibility that the promissory notes would be transferred and endorsed to subsequent holders, since they explicitly allow for such a possibility. The fact that these notes were denominated in US dollars is further evidence that their eventual international circulation and availability to foreign investors was contemplated from the outset.[24]

The approach of the tribunal reflected in these sentences seems to suggest the view that the various components of the definition of 'investment' are free-standing, without a link to a general notion of investment. Presumably, this result may have been based on the tribunal's emphasis on the ordinary meaning of the terms chosen, consistent with Article 31 of the Vienna Convention. In support of its result, the tribunal also pointed out that Venezuela had not notified ICSID, as possible under section 4 of Article 25 of the Convention, to exclude certain types of investment from the jurisdiction of the Centre. Apparently, the tribunal was inclined to consider that such a declaration would have to be taken into account in the interpretation of the BIT.

[23] *Ibid.* at paragraph 32. [24] *Ibid.* at paragraph 38.

Given this clear-cut focus by the tribunal on the wording of the Treaty, and the independence of the promissory notes from any underlying transaction as the basis for ICSID jurisdiction, it might have been expected that no further analysis of 'investment' was necessary for the decision. However, the tribunal went further than that and did return to the process of interpretation, towards the end of the decision, apparently to analyse the characteristics of the promissory notes in the light of a broader concept of 'investment' (paragraphs 40–3). It remains open as to whether or not this additional line of reasoning indicates that, in the view of the tribunal, the textual analysis of the individual categories of investment listed in the definition of the BIT has to be supplemented by way of placing it in a framework supplied by a general notion of 'investment'.

In this particular case, the tribunal had no reason to elaborate on this point inasmuch as its assessment of the promissory notes led to the result that an 'investment' not only had to be assumed in the light of the wording of the BIT, but also from the perspective of a broader notion of investment along the lines of traditional economic usage. In this part, the tribunal cites academic commentary[25] and notes the element of risk, the public interest involved, the requirement of a 'certain duration', a 'certain regularity of profit and return', the presence of a substantial commitment of the investor, and the significance for the host state's development. The decision turns, in brief sentences, to all of these elements and, without further analysis, affirms their presence in the context of promissory notes intended for international circulation. This is supported by the emphasis on the fact that a claim to implement a right under such notes does not amount to an 'ordinary commercial transaction', that the issuance of the notes involved a 'fundamental public interest', and that the case did not concern 'volatile capital' for quick gains.

Read in its entirety, therefore, the *Fedax* decision is not without ambiguity in its construction of 'investment'. The tribunal addressed the broader issues, but did not have to take a clear position on them in view of the facts of the case.

Subsequent tribunals did not have occasion significantly to advance the discussion. In *Ceskoslovenska Obchodni Banka AS (CSOB)* v. *Slovak Republic*[26] (Buergenthal, Bernardini, Bucher), the tribunal remarked

[25] The tribunal cites Christoph Schreuer, 'Commentary on the ICSID Convention' (1996) 11 *ICSID Review – Foreign Investment Law Journal*, 316.

[26] *Ceskoslovenska Obchodni Banka, AS* v. *Slovak Republic*, Decision on Objections to Jurisdiction, 24 May 1999 (2002) 5 ICSID Reports 330.

(paragraph 64) that investment should be interpreted broadly 'because the drafters of the Convention did not impose any restrictions on its meaning', without specific reference to the discretion left to states in this context.[27] Moreover, the *CSOB* tribunal turned to the Preamble to the relevant BIT, which cites the 'need for international cooperation for international development'; against this background, the tribunal seemed to consider that any international transaction which would promote the objective of the Preamble would qualify as an 'investment'.

In *Salini and others* v. *Morocco,*[28] the tribunal (Briner, Cremades, Fadlallah) explicitly distinguished between the existence of an 'investment' within the meaning of the relevant BIT and the existence of an 'investment' within the meaning of the ICSID Convention. With regard to the second question, the tribunal recalls that no definition of the term 'investment' is given by the Convention. However, the tribunal states that 'ICSID case law and legal authors agree that the investment requirement must be respected as an objective condition of the jurisdiction of the Centre' (paragraph 52). The tribunal then cites academic commentary which requires 'contributions, a certain duration of performance of the contract and a participation in the risks of the transaction' and reads the Convention's Preamble as requiring a 'contribution to the economic development of the host State'. In the view of the tribunal, all conditions were met in the case before it.

Apart from the possible distinction between economic usage and legal terminology, the notion of 'investment' has raised issues in regard to the necessity to clarify the temporal aspect of an 'investment', in particular concerning the initial stages. In *Mihaly International Corporation* v. *Sri Lanka*[29] (Sucharitkul, Rogers, Suratgar), a divided tribunal had to rule on pre-investment expenditures which were incurred by the investor during

[27] 'This statement also indicates that investment as a concept should be interpreted broadly because the drafters of the Convention did not impose any restrictions on its meaning. Support for a liberal interpretation of the question whether a particular transaction constitutes an investment is also found in the first paragraph of the Preamble to the Convention, which declares that 'the Contracting States [are] considering the need for international cooperation for economic development, and the role of private international investment therein'. This language permits an inference that an international transaction which contributes to cooperation designed to promote the economic development of a Contracting State may be deemed to be an investment as that term is understood in the Convention (paragraph 64).

[28] *Salini Costruttori SPA and Italstrade SPA* v. *Kingdom of Morocco*, Decision on Jurisdiction, 23 July 2001 (2003) 42 *ICSID Review – Foreign Investment Law Journal* 609.

[29] *Mihaly International Corporation* v. *Democratic Socialist Republic of Sri Lanka*, 15 March 2002 (2002) 17 *ICSID Review – Foreign Investment Law Journal* 142.

the negotiations with the host state. The claimant argued that it was necessary to interpret 'investment' broadly, so as to cover the costs in view of the encouragement to the flow of capital into developing countries. The tribunal analysed the negotiations and concluded that all three documents on which the parties had agreed were to be characterized as letters of intent or other types of agreement which were non-binding in nature. In view of the wording of the relevant USA–Sri Lanka BIT concerned, the tribunal concluded that the term 'investment' could not be extended to cover pre-investment expenses where the negotiations failed to lead to a binding commitment of the host state. Remarkably, the tribunal added 'that *de lege ferenda* the sources of international law on the extended meaning or definition of investment law will have to be found in conventional law or in customary law' (paragraph 60). In an obiter dictum, the tribunal went so far as to argue that even in a case in which the circumstances had led to a duty to negotiate in good faith between the host state and the investor, such a duty would not be arbitrable under the Convention (paragraph 51). Perhaps, a matter of such complexity would have deserved a broader discussion or could have been omitted from the reasoning in this particular case.

It would not be surprising if other case scenarios arise in the future, which would require tribunals to elaborate on the temporal aspect of 'investment'. For instance, an 'agreement to agree' would raise new questions in this context, as would a unilateral but binding statement (in whatever legal form) on the part of the host state to admit an investment or a class of investments.

Another side of the notion of 'investment', which may only be alluded to here, concerns those types of complex investment which comprise a number of segments or even companies operating to some extent independent of each other. In such a setting, the legal status of a segment or company not in itself qualifying as an 'investment' may have to be discussed. In *Holiday Inns* v. *Morocco*,[30] *Klöckner* v. *Cameroon*,[31] *Amco* v. *Indonesia*,[32] and *AGIP* v. *Congo*,[33] the tribunals were inclined to

30 See P. Lalive, 'The First "World Bank Arbitration" (Holiday Inns v. Morocco)' (1993) 1 ICSID Reports 645.

31 *Klöckner Industrie-Anlagen GmbH and others* v. *Republic of Cameroon*, 21 October 1983 (1994) 2 ICSID Reports 9.

32 *Amco Asia Corporation and others* v. *Republic of Indonesia*, Decision on Jurisdiction, 25 September 1983 (1993) 1 ICSID Reports 389.

33 *Agip Spa* v. *Government of the People's Republic of Congo*, 30 November 1979, (1993) 1 ICSID Reports 306.

consider that the direct relationship to the broader investment operation sufficed to bring the individual component under the protection of an 'investment'.[34] Here, as well, the specific circumstances of each case will have to be considered in detail. It would appear, though, that the general approach in the above cases will find broad approval.

A third area of uncertainty worth mentioning relates to the territorial dimension of foreign investments. In a number of settings, the issue may arise whether or not any movement of assets will be required to satisfy the requirement of an investment. Both the *Fedax* decision (paragraph 41) and the *CSOB* ruling (paragraph 78) assumed that the absence of a physical transfer of funds will not stand in the way of the existence of an 'investment'. Without explaining the rationale for this view in any detail, the *Fedax* tribunal considered apparently that it is sufficient that the funds made available by the investor are utilized by the host country as the beneficiary of the transaction, so as to finance its various governmental needs.

These short remarks may suffice to show that while considerable progress has been made by ICSID jurisprudence in determining the definition of an 'investment', significant issues remain to be clarified. Apart from the absence of a centralized system leading to uniformity of jurisprudence, the open issues point to the methodology of interpretation of BITs. Of course, there is general agreement that the rules of interpretation laid down in Article 31 of the Vienna Convention on the Law of Treaties will be applicable.[35] As in other areas of international law, the various principles contained in Article 31 do not automatically lead to hard and fast results. In the particular context of investment treaties, three lines of reasoning within the framework of Article 31 are conceivable.

One approach may emphasize the object and purpose of the treaty, highlighted in Article 31, and in this context focus on the Preamble which typically will refer to the desire of both parties to increase the flow of investments.[36] In principle, such a teleological perspective may lead to an interpretation which, in the case of doubt, favours the investor rather than the host state. For example, in *Metalclad* v. *Mexico*,[37] the tribunal (Lauterpacht, Civiletti, Siqueiros) explicitly referred to the NAFTA

[34] See also C. Schreuer, *The ICSID Convention* (2001), p. 173 *et seq.*

[35] According to Article 31 of the Vienna Convention on the Law of Treaties, 'A treaty shall be interpreted in good faith in accordance with the ordinary meaning to be given to the terms of the treaty in their context and in the light of its object and purpose'.

[36] See R. Dolzer and M. Stevens, *Bilateral Investment Treaties* (1995), pp. 17, 20.

[37] *Metalclad Corporation* v. *United Mexican States*, 30 August 2000 (2002) 5 ICSID Reports 209 at 225.

Preamble, which declares the host country's resolution to ensure 'a predictable commercial framework for business planning and investment', before concluding that Mexico had failed to comply with its contractual commitments. A similar approach was adopted by the tribunal in *Tradex* v. *Albania*[38] (Böckstiegel, Fielding, Giardina), which cautiously took the position that a relevant Albanian law should, in case of doubt, be interpreted in favour of investor protection. In a broader context, a comparable teleological approach can be found in the 1982 *Aminoil* arbitration (Reuter, Sultan, Fitzmaurice) with regard to the determination of the amount of compensation: 'as regards States which welcome foreign investment, and which even engage in it themselves, it could be expected that their attitude towards compensation should not be such as to render foreign investment useless, economically'.[39] In 2004, the two ICSID decisions in *SGS* v. *Philippines*[40] and *Tokios Tokelés* v. *Ukraine*[41] have, in principle, adopted the same approach.

A second approach may place an emphasis on the wording of the text without special regard to the object and purpose of the treaty. Thus, with regard to the interpretation of the NAFTA rules, the tribunal in *ADF* v. *United States*[42] (Feliciano, de Mestral, Lamm) found:

[38] *Tradex Hellas SA* v. *Republic of Albania*, Decision on Jurisdiction, 24 December 1996 (1999) 14 *ICSID Review – Foreign Investment Law Journal*, 161 at 194.

[39] Award in the Matter of an Arbitration between Kuwait and the American Independent Oil Company (Aminoil), 24 March 1982 (1982) 21 *ILM* 976 at 1033.

[40] *SGS Société Générale de Surveillance* v. *Republic of Philippines*, Decision on Objections to Jurisdiction, 29 January 2004 (available at www.worldbank.org/icsid/cases/awards.htm), paragraph 116: 'The object and purpose of the BIT supports an effective interpretation of Article X(2). The BIT is a treaty for the promotion and reciprocal protection of investments. According to the preamble it is intended "to create and maintain favourable conditions for investments by investors of one Contracting Party in the territory of the other". It is legitimate to resolve uncertainties in its interpretation so as to favour the protection of covered investments.'

[41] *Tokios Tokelés* v. *Ukraine*, Decision on Jurisdiction, 29 April 2004 (available at www.worldbank.org/icsid/cases/awards.htm), paragraph 31: 'The object and purpose of the Treaty likewise confirm that the control-test should not be used to restrict the scope of "investors" in Article 1(2)(b). The preamble expresses the Contracting Parties' intent to "intensify economic cooperation to the mutual benefit of both States" and "create and maintain favourable conditions for investment of investors of one State in the territory of the other State".' The Tribunal in *SGS* v. *Philippines* interpreted nearly identical preambular language in the Philippines–Switzerland BIT as indicative of the treaty's broad scope of investment protection (footnote omitted). We concur in that interpretation and find that the object and purpose of the Ukraine–Lithuania BIT is to provide broad protection of investors and their investments.

[42] *ADF Group Inc.* v. *United States*, 9 January 2003, paragraph 147, available online at www.state.gov/documents/organization/16586.pdf

> We understand the rules of interpretation found in customary international law to enjoin us to focus first on the actual language of the provision being construed. The object and purpose of the parties to a treaty in agreeing upon any particular paragraph of that treaty are to be found, in the first instance, in the words in fact used by the parties in that paragraph.[43]

With regard to jurisdictional clauses, the tribunal in *Amco Asia*[44] (Higgins, Lalonde, Magid) emphasized that ICSID was 'not to be construed restrictively, nor, as a matter of fact, broadly or liberally', but 'in good faith, that is to say by taking into account the consequences of their commitments the parties may be considered as having reasonably and legitimately envisaged'. The same position was essentially expressed by the tribunal in *SOABI* v. *Senegal*[45] (Broches, Mbaye, Schultsz). In *SPP* v. *Egypt*,[46] the Tribunal (Aréchaga, El Mahdi, Pietrowski) used similar language and added that jurisdiction will be found to exist 'if – but only if – the force of arguments militating in favor of it is preponderant'.

A third approach, emphasizing the classical principle of interpretation of '*in dubio mitius*', narrowing the scope of limitations on the part of the states concerned, is found in *Société Générale de Surveillance* v.

[43] The tribunal continues: 'We do not suggest that the general objectives of NAFTA are not useful or not relevant. Far from it. Those general objectives may be conceived of as partaking of the nature of *lex generalis* while a particular detailed provision set in a particular context in the rest of a Chapter or Part of NAFTA functions as *lex specialis*. The former may frequently cast light on a specific interpretative issue; but it is not to be regarded as overriding and superseding the latter. Clearly, NAFTA is a complex document . . . Thus, the specific provisions of a particular Chapter need to be read, not just in relation to each other, but also in the context of the entire structure of NAFTA if a treaty interpreter is to ascertain and understand the real shape and content of the bargain actually struck by the three sovereign Parties.'

[44] *Amco Asia Corporation and others* v. *Republic of Indonesia*, Decision on Jurisdiction, 25 September 1983 (1993) 1 ICSID Reports 376 at 393.

[45] *Société Ouest Africaine des Bétons Industriels* v. *Senegal*, 25 February 1988 (1994) 2 ICSID Reports 190, at 205: 'In the Tribunal's opinion, an arbitration agreement must be given, just as with any other agreement, an interpretation consistent with the principle of good faith. In other words, the interpretation must take into account the consequences which the parties must reasonably and legitimately be considered to have envisaged as flowing from their undertakings. It is this principle of interpretation, rather than one of *a priori* strict, or, for that matter, broad and liberal construction, that the Tribunal has chosen to apply.'

[46] *Southern Pacific Properties (Middle East) Ltd* v. *Arab Republic of Egypt*, Decision on Jurisdiction, 27 November 1985 (1995) 3 ICSID Reports 101 at 143.

Pakistan in August 2003[47] (Feliciano, Faurès, Thomas). The decision refers to this principle in interpreting the rule in a BIT that a state must observe its undertakings with a foreign investor. Perhaps not surprisingly, this tribunal chaired by Justice Feliciano has supported its reasoning by way of reference to recent jurisprudence of the Appellate Body of the WTO.

In the future, the weight and the acceptance of these three approaches will presumably be assessed not just in the context of the term 'investment'. The interpretation of such general clauses as 'fair and equitable' or 'full protection and security' will also depend on which of the three modes of interpretation will gain acceptance. At this moment, the diversity of reasoning of the tribunals makes it difficult to predict the direction of future jurisprudence.[48]

[47] *SGS Société Générale de Surveillance SA* v. *Islamic Republic of Pakistan*, Decision on Objections to Jurisdiction, 6 August 2003, (2003) 18 *ICSID Review – Foreign Investment Law Journal*, 307 at 366.

[48] The tribunal cites *European Communities – Measures Concerning Meat and Meat Products (Hormones)*, WT/DS48/AB/R, 16 January 1998, paragraphs 163–5; see also the citations to the same case in the *ADF* decision at paragraph 147, note 152.

20

Arbitration of Investment Disputes under UNCITRAL Rules and the Choice of Applicable Law

GIORGIO SACERDOTI

Arbitrating bilateral investment treaties disputes under UNCITRAL Rules: *CME and Lauder* v. *Czech Republic* arbitrations (1999–2001)

A recent international investment dispute, the *CME and Lauder* v. *Czech Republic* arbitrations, has attracted widespread attention beyond specialized circles, for a number of peculiarities.

This is possibly the first publicly known dispute under a bilateral investment treaty (BIT) decided through international commercial arbitration proceedings (in accordance with the UNCITRAL Rules) instead of within ICSID. The national courts of the country where the award was rendered, *in casu* Sweden, have had to decide the challenge to set aside the award brought by the losing state in accordance with the local arbitration statute. Under the ICSID Convention, by contrast, no such control by national courts would be admissible. The same acts by the Czech Republic were subject to two separate arbitrations at the same time: this has highlighted the conflict of procedures, of governing treaty provisions and of awards that the intricate, non-coordinated network of bilateral investment treaties may entail, when international commercial arbitration is resorted to, thus potentially bringing a backlash to the legal security surrounding international investments.[1] On the other hand, the speedy completion of all litigation (including full payment by the state concerned), notwithstanding these complexities, indicates that

The author appeared as an expert witness in international law on behalf of CME before the Court of Appeal of Stockholm in the annulment proceedings of the CME – Czech Republic award in 2003.

[1] See Charles Brower, Charles H. Brower, and Jeremy Sharpe, 'The Coming Crisis in the Global Adjudication System' (2003) 19 *Arbitration International* 413 at 424.

international commercial arbitration, when available under relevant BITs, may be an alternative practicable avenue for aggrieved investors.

The dispute arose from the interference in 1996–9 by Media Council, an agency of the Czech government, with the contractual scheme under which CME Czech Republic BV, a Dutch company controlled by Mr Ronald Lauder, was operating in partnership with a local investor TV Nova, the most successful commercial television in Czechoslovakia, bringing about the exclusion of CME and the destruction of its valuable investment.

CME started arbitration against the Czech Republic in 2000 in accordance with the provisions of Article 8 of the BIT of 1991 between the Netherlands and the Czech and Slovak Federal Republic, claiming unfair treatment and expropriation without compensation. This article provides that disputes between a contracting state and an investor of the other contracting state concerning an investment of the latter shall be submitted to an ad hoc arbitral tribunal, which shall determine its own procedure 'applying the arbitration rules of the UN Commission for International Trade Law (UNCITRAL)'. The article also includes a clause on applicable law and a reference to the Stockholm Chamber of Commerce; based on this link, arbitration took place in Stockholm.

The proceedings and the award between Mr Lauder (an American citizen) and the Czech Republic, were likewise the result of an UNCITRAL arbitration, initiated in 1999 and carried out in London in conformity with similar provisions found in Article VI of the BIT of 1991 between the USA and the Czech and Slovak Federal Republic, based on the fact that CME's investment was 'controlled directly or indirectly by Mr Lauder (Art.I.1 (a) of the BIT)'. Differing from the Dutch BIT, the treaty with the USA gave the investor the alternative option to resort to ICSID but Mr Lauder chose UNCITRAL arbitration.

In its award of 3 September 2001, the London tribunal found no injury although it concluded that the government had acted unfairly in some respects. The Stockholm tribunal, however, in a partial award of 13 September 2001, found that the Czech Republic had violated several articles of the BIT causing therefore *de facto* expropriation of CME's investment.

The Czech government challenged this award before the competent Court of Appeal of Stockholm according to the Swedish Arbitration Act of 1999,[2] claiming *inter alia* major procedural errors and lack of

[2] An English translation of the Act is reprinted in (2001) 17 *Arbitration International* 425; see especially Articles 33 and 34 on invalidity and setting aside of awards.

jurisdiction, in that the arbitrators had disregarded the principles of *lis pendens* and *res iudicata* in the light of the London proceedings and award. The award of the Stockholm tribunal was further challenged for 'excess of mandate' in having failed to apply Czech law in accordance with Article 8.6 of the BIT, having relied instead on public international law, and for being *ex aequo et bono*. The Court of Appeal rejected all challenges against the Stockholm award. Shortly thereafter the tribunal concluded the *quantum* phase of the arbitration, awarding about US$250 million in damages to CME.[3]

Direct arbitration in BIT

This litigation offers several interesting aspects for reflection. I will focus here only on some peculiarities involved in submitting to international commercial arbitration claims under a BIT, namely (a) the identification and interpretation of the arbitration agreement when represented by the BIT itself, (b) the choice of the applicable law (especially as to international law), highlighting the differences with respect to ICSID dispute settlement.

I find it appropriate to dedicate this essay to Florentino Feliciano, in view of his manifold contribution to international justice and arbitration, including his services as an international arbitrator both in commercial and in investment disputes.

The starting point is undoubtedly the massive expansion of BITs since the 1970s, now numbering more that 2000. As stated in a UN publication:

> Given the controversy surrounding customary international law relating to foreign investment, international agreements could provide a source of clear and certain rules ... At the multilateral level, the adoption of agreements on investment has proved to be far more difficult ... Thus, over the years, for many countries BITs have provided the second best solution in the absence of a universal investment agreement ... BITs constitute at present a principal source of substantive and, especially, procedural rules for international protection of [foreign direct investment].[4]

[3] For the text of the *Lauder* award of 3 September 2001 see (2002) 14 *World Trade and Arbitration Materials* 35; for the *CME* partial award of 13 September 2001 see (2002) 14 *World Trade and Arbitration Materials* 109; for the final award of 14 March 2003 see (2003) 15 *World Trade and Arbitration Materials* 83. For the Svea Court of Appeals of Stockholm decision of 15 May 2003 see (2003) 42 ILM 919. All the decisions are available at www.cetv-net.com

[4] UNCTAD, *Bilateral Investment Treaties in the Mid 1990s* (1998), p. 4.

They lay down both standards for the substantive treatment of foreign investments by nationals and companies of any of the signatories in the territory of the other, as well as direct arbitration procedures for the settlement of possible disputes.

In BITs, the availability of direct arbitration against the host state by an aggrieved foreign investor of the other contracting state relies upon the advanced consent of the contracting states. Arbitration with the foreign investor is by now a standard feature and indeed a basic element of the 'protection' of foreign investment that is among the basic purposes of these treaties. On the other hand, the exact regulation of arbitration is one of the areas where individual BITs differ most. This is a fact first as to the kind of disputes that can be brought to arbitration,[5] especially whether they are limited to claims of BIT breach or include those alleging claims of contract and domestic legislation violation; procedural requirements as to settlement negotiations or local remedies exhaustion as condition precedent, and finally the type of arbitration procedures that are made available.

Direct arbitration between foreign investors and host governments has become the preferred method of resolving disputes ever since the entry into force of the Washington Convention establishing ICSID in 1965. Indeed, the main purpose of the Convention was that of 'depoliticizing' the underlying conflicts by ensuring an impartial, efficient arbitral mechanism, administered by an international organization, whereby disputes would be resolved by application of legal rules and with due respect for international legal principles.[6] Before and apart from ICSID, ad hoc arbitration based on relevant clauses of 'state contracts' or 'investment agreements' between major foreign investors and host states had been frequent.[7] Arbitral tribunals and authors have been striving to decide whether these relations, the law applicable to them and the awards pertain to international or transnational law, rather than to the private law of contract and arbitration. Whatever the solution, private parties have often been prevented from pursuing effectively arbitral

[5] Compare the Netherlands–Czech Republic BIT (Article 8.1) covering 'all disputes concerning an investment' with the USA-Czech Republic BIT, limited to claims alleging breach of the BIT itself or of an investment authorization (Article VI.1).

[6] See generally *Report of the Executive Directors of the IBRD on the Convention*, reprinted in *ICSID Convention, Regulations and Rules* (ICSID, 2003), paragraphs 37, 40; Aron Broches, 'The Convention on the Settlement of Investment Disputes between States and Nationals of Other States' (1972–11) 136 *Rec. des cours* 3.

[7] See especially the *Aramco* case, *Arabian-American Oil Co.* v. *Saudi Arabia* (1958) 27 ILR 117, the award in *Aminoil* v. *Kuwait* (1982) 21 ILM 976, and the 'Libyan oil cases', *Texaco* v. *Libya* (1978) 17 ILM 1, *Llamco* v. *Libya* (1981) 20 ILM 78.

proceedings and from enforcing favourable awards due to state sovereign interference and immunity in respect to execution.[8]

Arbitration without privity under BITs

Direct investor-state arbitration provided for in BITs and in other treaties dealing with investments (such as NAFTA) has been encapsulated in the expression 'arbitration without privity'.[9] The relevant treaty provision makes it unnecessary that the investor and the state consent explicitly in writing in a contract clause or otherwise to submit an existing or eventual dispute to a given arbitration procedure, as is normal practice under domestic law and international conventions. The treaty provision constitutes the 'advance consent' of the state, as some treaty clauses specify (such as Article 8(2) of the Netherlands–Czech Republic BIT); the consent of the private investor results instead from it starting an arbitration proceeding, thus 'accepting' the 'standing offer' made by the state in the treaty.[10] Thus, the investor may start arbitration 'unilaterally', without having ever consented specifically beforehand to arbitration with the country concerned. Consent of both parties is expressed by the convergence of these separate declarations made at different times. This kind of 'arbitration without privity',[11] which eliminates the need for a consensual (contractual) arbitration undertaking (*compromis* in respect of an existing dispute or *clause compromissoire* in respect of future disputes), has

[8] See Karl-Heinz Bockstiegel, *Der Staat als Vertragsparner Auslandischer Unternehmungen* (1971); Giorgio Sacerdoti, *I Contratti tra Stati e Stranieri nel Diritto Internazionale* (1972); Charles Leben, 'Quelques reflexions théoriques à propos des contrats d'Etat' in *Souverainété étatique et Marches Internationaux à la Fin du XX Siècle* (2000), p. 119; M. Sornaraj, *The Settlement of Foreign Investment Disputes* (2000), p. 25.

[9] See Jan Paulsson, '*Arbitration Without Privity*' (1995) 10 *ICSID Review – Foreign Investment Law Journal* 232.

[10] Antonio R. Parra, 'Applicable Substantive Law in ICSID Arbitrations Initiated under Investment Treaties' (2001) 16 *ICSID Review – Foreign Investment Law Journal* 20 at 21–4 (mentioning twenty-eight ICSID cases brought by investors under BITs and eight under NAFTA and examining the five awards rendered on the merits). Other relevant cases include: *LANCO International Inc.* v. *Argentine Republic*, Preliminary Decision on Jurisdiction of the Tribunal, 8 December 1998, (2001) 40 ILM 457; *Salini Costruttori SpA and Italstrade SpA* v. *Morocco* (2002) J Droit Int'l 196; *Antoine Goetz and others* v. *Republic of Burundi*, Case No. ARB/95/3 (2000) 15 *ICSID Review – Foreign Investment Law Journal* 457.

[11] Some BITs do require a separate consent to arbitration in writing by the investor. See, e.g., USA–Czech Republic BIT Article VI(3). This formality does not affect the qualification of the arbitration as 'without privity'.

become so relevant currently, that most arbitrations pending at ICSID are based on such a BIT clause rather than on contract.[12]

The widespread participation of states in ICSID (about 140 ratifications presently) and the guarantees of efficient and impartial proceedings surrounding ICSID would justify its arbitration as being exclusively referred to in BITs. This, however does not appear to be the case for a number of reasons: if one or both states are not (yet) party to the ICSID Convention at the time of the signature of the BIT, providing for an alternative is inevitable. Even in case of participation of both states to the ICSID Convention the tendency is to list other mechanisms to which the parties to a dispute, in practice a foreign investor as claimant, can resort.

As stated by a leading UN publication:

> The earliest investor-to-State dispute provisions contained each contracting party's consent only to ICSID arbitration. The recent trend is to give investors a choice of mechanisms. One choice authorized by some BITs is arbitration through some institutions other than ICSID or the affiliated Additional Facility. Other institutions include the International Chamber of Commerce or the Stockholm Chamber of Commerce. Another choice is ad hoc arbitration, that is arbitration before a single individual appointed, or a tribunal specially constituted, for a particular dispute ... The decision to provide alternatives to ICSID arbitration is the result of a number of considerations. First, there was concern at one point that ICSID awards might be particularly vulnerable to annulment. Second, the successful use of UNCITRAL rules by the Iran-United States Claims Tribunals seemed to suggest that these rules were especially adaptable to investor-to-State dispute-settlement.[13]

The Netherlands–Czech Republic BIT appears peculiar in this respect, as it does not allow ICSID arbitration, but provides only for international commercial arbitration in accordance with the UNCITRAL Rules.[14]

Relevant clauses not referring to ICSID list ad hoc arbitration based on the UNCITRAL Rules (with or without indication of an appointment authority in case of need) and/or institutionalized arbitration such as

[12] *News from ICSID* (Summer 2003), p. 2, indicates that the latest fifteen cases registered since January 2003 had all been based on BIT clauses.

[13] UNCTAD, *Bilateral Investment Treaties*, p. 95.

[14] It is true that the Czech Republic was not yet party to the ICSID Convention when it entered into the BIT with the Netherlands in 1991 (which entered into force in 1992). However, this fact did not prevent the Czech Republic from agreeing to the application of the ICSID Convention in the BIT with the USA in the same year, in light of its future adhesion to ICSID, which occurred in 1993 and is a prerequisite for having recourse to it.

under the ICC Rules or those of the Stockholm Chamber of Commerce. All these models share the common feature of pertaining to the category of international commercial arbitration; arbitration is governed in last resort by municipal law (often following the UNCITRAL Model Law of 1985); awards are subject to challenge and control according to local arbitration statutes in the country where they are rendered, while recognition and enforcement abroad is subject to the New York Convention of 1958. Awards rendered pursuant to the rules of the ICSID Additional Facility, which is also provided for in some BITs and in NAFTA Chapter 11 (Article 1130), are also subject to the New York Convention.

Notwithstanding this variety of options usually made available, most, if not all, generally known investment arbitration under BITs has been conducted within ICSID, so that any question of application of the model of international commercial arbitration to BITs investment disputes has been subject to limited attention, if any at all. The *CME and Lauder* case seems the first instance of a major investment dispute arising under BITs where UNCITRAL arbitration (a term that is used here as synonymous with international commercial arbitration) has been resorted to, evidencing a number of specific questions, if not problems, that may arise from the combination of BIT clauses on arbitration with recourse to standard international commercial arbitration.

International commercial arbitration for investment disputes under BITs

By adopting or admitting recourse to the UNCITRAL Rules, BITs refer investor-state disputes to 'international commercial/trade/economic arbitration', the preferred method by which most international disputes having an economic content between subjects of different countries are resolved today. In providing for the direct settlement of investment disputes between states and foreign investors through this type of arbitration, BITs add some peculiar features to the otherwise applicable scheme of international commercial arbitration that must be taken into account.[15]

The instruments of international commercial arbitration to which BITs refer directly or indirectly include:

- New York Convention of 1958 on the Recognition and Enforcement of Foreign Arbitral Awards ('the New York Convention'), dealing

[15] This is the case also for several articles of NAFTA Chapter 11.

with the recognition by State courts of arbitration agreements and awards made in other countries or under foreign law;

- European Convention of 1961 on International Commercial Arbitration ('the Geneva Convention') on the same subject;
- UNCITRAL Arbitration Rules, unanimously approved and commended by the UN General Assembly in 1974 for the conduct of ad hoc arbitration;
- UNCITRAL Model Law on International Commercial Arbitration of 1985, also recommended by the UN General Assembly 'in view of the desirability of uniformity of the law of arbitral procedures and the specific needs of international arbitration practice'.

The specificity (autonomy) of international commercial arbitration is recognized both in domestic laws and in the relevant international instruments, distinguishing it from purely domestic arbitration both at the seat and as to recognition in other countries, especially for the purpose of limiting interference by local courts.[16] The UNCITRAL Model Law was drafted, and has been used extensively, as a basis for national legislation addressing the regulation, recognition, and enforcement of international arbitration taking place in the forum or abroad without distinction.[17] States have now come to accept and view the existence of this widespread practice favourably; they tend to facilitate and support the effectiveness of this type of arbitration within their territories and cross-border through appropriate special domestic legislation and the above-mentioned international instruments.

Thus, the UNCITRAL Model Law defines arbitration as international if, in the first instance, 'the parties to an arbitration agreement have, at the time of the conclusion of that agreement, their place of business in different States' (Article 1(3)). The New York Convention does not rely on a definition of the 'international' character of arbitration. In fact, in conformity with its title, it focuses on the 'recognition and enforcement of foreign arbitral awards', i.e. those 'made in the territory of a State other than the State where the recognition and enforcement of such

[16] Giorgio Bernini, 'The Enforcement of Foreign Arbitral Awards by National Judiciaries: A Trial of the New York Convention's Ambit and Workability', in Jan C. Schultsz and Albert Van der Berg (eds.), *The Art of Arbitration: Essays on International Arbitration, Liber Amicorum Pieter Sanders* (1982), pp. 51, 59.

[17] The Swedish Arbitration Act of 1999 has taken the UNCITRAL Model Law into account, though not followed it in all respects, as is the case, e.g., with the German Arbitration Act of 1998. See Kaj Hobér, 'Arbitration Reform in Sweden' (2001) 17 *Arbitration International* 351 at 352.

awards are sought, and arising out of differences between persons whether physical or legal' (Article I(1)). The Convention does not regulate the proceedings either directly or indirectly; it does not deal, therefore, with the prerequisites, if any, that make the choice of arbitration to settle a given dispute admissible, nor with the constitution of an arbitral tribunal, nor with the conduct of the proceedings. These matters, which are within the responsibility of the parties and of the arbitrators, are covered by other instruments (Arbitral Rules, UNCITRAL Model Law), mostly on an optional basis.

It is unanimously recognized that disputes between government or state entities on the one hand and private businessmen or enterprises of another country on the other, can also properly be subject to the dispute resolution procedures of international commercial arbitration. This practice is indeed current and has been an important feature of international economic intercourse for decades:[18]

> In principle, there can be little doubt, if any, that international arbitration arising from a dispute between States and foreign subjects, under a contractual relationship between the parties, should be put on the same level as arbitrations between two private parties, and not as arbitrations between States, which are governed as such by public international law ... [T]here is no reason to believe that the general legal principles applying to international commercial arbitration ... do not apply when one of the parties is a State or another public entity, only in view of this particular circumstance. As far as the applicable international conventions are concerned, this does not seem to be open to doubt, especially in view of the broad wording, and even more the broad policy of the New York Convention. The practice of courts and arbitral tribunals confirms this assumption.[19]

Even if the dispute is not contractual (as in the case of investment disputes based on BITs):

> Arbitration of a dispute arising in the course of an international economic transaction involving one or more public entities will be

[18] The Annual Report of the International Chamber of Commerce for 2001 reported that almost 10 per cent of the new arbitral proceedings under the ICC Rules of Arbitration in that year involved at least one state or state entity.

[19] Riccardo Luzzatto, 'International Commercial Arbitration and the Municipal Law of States' (1977) 157 *Hague Rec. des Cours* 87.

> considered as commercial, particularly where the arbitration takes place between a state, a state-owned entity, and a foreign private undertaking.[20]

The fact that the dispute at issue cannot be properly defined as 'commercial' as the term is used in civil law is immaterial, since it is generally agreed that the term 'commercial' found in most international instruments on arbitration is intended to have a purely economic meaning, not a restrictive meaning, so that it does not prevent recourse to arbitration in respect of relationships that would not be defined as commercial under the commercial law or statutes of a given country.[21] This understanding explains why the terms 'trade' or 'economic' arbitration are preferred by many authors, when such a qualification is intended to distinguish these procedures from those applied in inter-state arbitration.[22]

As to the UNCITRAL Model Law, a note to the official edition by the United Nations regarding Article 1, which states 'this law applies to international commercial arbitration', specifies that '[t]he term "commercial" should be given a wide interpretation so as to cover matters arising from all relationships of a commercial nature, whether contractual or not'. New York Convention Article I(3) follows the same approach in that it requires contracting states to make a specific declaration (which very few have

[20] Emmanuel Gaillard and John Savage (eds.), Fouchard, Gaillard, *Goldman on International Commercial Arbitration* (1999), p. 40, paragraph 69.

[21] *Ibid.* at p. 41, paragraph 70.

[22] Also under the NAFTA Treaty of 1994 establishing the North American Free Trade Area, arbitration of investment disputes between one of the members (USA, Canada, Mexico) and investors of another member can be settled, based on the contracting states advanced consent expressed in the treaty, by international commercial arbitration with application of the UNCITRAL Rules (NAFTA Chapter 11 Article 1130(b)). The arbitral tribunal 'shall hold an arbitration in the territory of a Party that is a party to the New York Convention' and all claims submitted to arbitration 'shall be considered to arise out of a commercial relationship or transaction for the purposes of Article I of the New York Convention' (Article 1136(7)).

Following the same principles, the awards rendered between aggrieved American investors and Iran by the Iran-United States Claims Tribunal in the Hague, established by the Algiers Agreement of 1981 between these two countries, are generally held to pertain to international commercial arbitration, both because private claimants are parties and in view of the application of the UNCITRAL Rules to the procedure. A French court, before which an American investor sought recognition of an award, has held that the French provisions on recognition of international/foreign (economic) awards were applicable: *Golshani* v. *Iran*, 28 June 2001, Cour d'appel de Paris, (2002/1) *Revue de l' Arbitrage* 163; see also (2002) 2 *Cahiers de l'Arbitrage* 13 (summarizing the decision and noting the particular features of the Iran-United States Claims Tribunal and the effect those features have on the applicability of provisions of French law dealing with foreign arbitral awards).

made) if they want to restrict it to arbitration of disputes 'arising out of legal relationships, whether contractual or not, which are considered as commercial' under their national law.

Modifications by BITs of applicable arbitration rules

The lack of contractual privity in the arbitration clauses of BITs highlights that BIT protection may be invoked even in the absence of any contractual or other relationship between the investor and the state. Not being based on private law, arbitration based on treaty clauses has some additional peculiarities, altering 'the private nature of the dispute by introducing certain aspects of inter-State disputes'.[23] The treaty may include provisions that complement or modify, enlarge or restrict, access to arbitration and/or other features of arbitration in respect to the otherwise applicable rules, be they found in the ICSID Convention, the New York Convention, the UNCITRAL Rules, or in other texts.

Many BITs prescribe a compulsory preliminary attempt to negotiate an amicable settlement and that the arbitration may not be initiated before a definite period of time for that purpose, such as six months from a formal notice of dispute by the investor to the host government. NAFTA Article 1135 provides for the possibility of consolidating connected arbitration, a unique innovative feature. The coordination between the multilateral instrument and the bilateral may create difficulties. There is no doubt that bilaterally, the ensuing modifications are valid in accordance with Article 41 of the Vienna Convention of 1969 on the Law of Treaties concerning 'Agreements to modify multilateral treaties between certain of the parties only'. This development might be viewed alternatively as a selective application of some provisions of the multilateral instrument to a different context by a separate treaty.

Another kind of modification is represented by treaty clauses indicating the applicable law. This clause is present in some BITs, such as in Article 8(6) of the Netherlands–Czech Republic BIT.[24] This modification affects

[23] Phillipe Pinsolle, 'The Annulment of ICSID Arbitral Awards' (2000) 1 *J World Investment* 243 at 257. See also, Bernardo M. Cremades and David J. A. Cairnes, 'The Brave New World of Global Arbitration' (2002) 3 *J World Investment* 173 at 183–4 (describing a 'new field of arbitral activity – a hybrid between private arbitration and inter-state arbitration' arising from investor-state arbitrations).

[24] Only a few of the Netherlands BITs include such a provision, which is not typical in BITs. For example, choice of law provisions have only been used 'occasionally' by Switzerland. See Jean-Christophe Liebeskind, 'State-Investor Dispute Settlement

the procedural and substantive rules that would otherwise be applicable; on the one hand, the applicable law provisions 'pre-empt' any choice of law that the parties to the dispute could have otherwise made (a choice that would be difficult to make since there is as a rule no separate arbitration agreement); on the other hand, they indicate to the arbitrators the applicable law(s) in the absence of choice by the parties, instead of having them follow the otherwise applicable arbitration rules in this respect.

Thus, despite the commercial arbitration procedures invoked, this investor-state arbitration has a 'quasi-public character, or at least an inescapably public element'[25] which is relevant from various points of view. The jurisdiction of the tribunal is not based on a private agreement by the parties to the dispute, but is predetermined by the two states. Possibly it cannot be restricted by the will of the parties to the dispute; nor can the rights stemming from the treaty, including obtaining a decision once the procedure has been set in motion, be reduced by the operation of other normative texts, including other BITs. The right of action to start arbitration is given directly to the foreign investor by the BIT, and he can make use of it in the event a dispute arises, thus displacing the jurisdiction of domestic courts that might be otherwise competent on the same subject matter. The arbitral jurisdiction provided for by the treaty is exclusive as to claims based on the treaty, as was held in various precedents on the point.[26]

Application of public international law v. domestic law in UNCITRAL investment disputes arbitration

In international commercial arbitration on the basis of the generally accepted notion of 'party autonomy',[27] parties may, as to substantive law, not only choose among different national laws, be they objectively connected in some way to their contract or not. They may choose even rules not part of a definite legal system, such as trade usages, or 'merchant law' *(lex mercatoria)*, i.e., the principles of commercial law commonly used

Clauses in Swiss Bilateral Investment Treaties' (2002) 20 *ASA Bulletin* 27 at 51. The practice of the USA is not to include choice of law provisions in BITs.

25 Cremades and Cairnes, 'Brave New World', 184–5.

26 See, e.g., *Lamco* v. *Argentina* and *Salini* v. *Morocco, supra* n. 10 (so holding notwithstanding contractual clanses providing for the competence of domestic courts). For a partially different solution see *SGS* v. *Philippines*, 29 January 2004, available at www.worldbank.org/icsid/cases

27 Gaillard and Savage, *International Commercial Arbitration*, pp. 579–81.

and recognized in international trade.[28] Further, the choice of public international law, alone or in combination with other sources, is admitted – especially when a state is party to the arbitration.[29]

The purpose and features of BITs explain the prominent role of international law as the law to be applied in cases of investor-state arbitration of disputes under the treaty.[30] Complaints by private investors against the host state invoking the treaty protections have normally as their object the claim that rights established under the treaty have been breached by the host state. The breach of treaty provisions is obviously a matter of international law and the existence of any such breach has to be determined by application of its rules and principles.

In fact, one of the basic features of BITs is that the standard of treatment and protection agreed by the two contracting states for the benefit of their respective investors can be directly invoked by any such aggrieved investor of a contracting state against the other (host) state through the agreed direct investor-state arbitral dispute settlement mechanism. In the absence of such a procedural right, typically granted to private investors under the BITs, it would be for the home country of the investor to raise the question with the other country making use of the right of diplomatic protection. Thus, BITs do not only grant procedural remedies to investors, but also allow them to invoke directly in arbitration the relevant norms and standards of public international law.

[28] Ole Lando, 'The Law Applicable to the Merits of the Dispute' in Julian D. M. Lew (ed.), *Contemporary Problems in International Arbitration* (1986), pp. 101, 104–5; René David, *Arbitration in International Trade* (1985), pp. 344–7 (describing the flexible application of national laws).

[29] See Prosper Weil, 'Principes généraux du droit et contrats d'Etat' in *Le Droit des Relations Économiques Internationals: Etudes Offertes à Berthold Goldman* (1982), p. 387; Ibrahim F. I. Shihata and Antonio R. Parra, 'Applicable Substantive Law in Disputes between States and Private Foreign Parties: The Case of Arbitration under the ICSID Convention', in *Planning Efficient Arbitration Proceedings: The Law Applicable in International Arbitration* (International Council for Commercial Arbitration, Congress Series No. 7, 1996), p. 294, 298; Stephen M. Schwebel, 'The Law Applicable in International Arbitration: Application of Public International Law' in *ibid.* at p. 562; David, *Arbitration in International Trade*, pp. 347–9. Professor Schreuer also considers the choice of public international law admissible for contracts submitted to ICSID arbitration: internationalization of the state-foreign investor agreement is recommended as '[i]n most situations, a more realistic way to protect the investors' interests against the vagaries of the host State's law'. Christoph H. Schreuer, *The ICSID Convention: A Commentary* (2001), p. 562.

[30] Cremades and Cairns, 'Brave New World', 183.

How does this feature interact with UNCITRAL arbitration? Article 33(1) of the Rules provides that: 'the arbitral tribunal shall apply the law designated by the parties as applicable to the substance of the dispute. Failing such designation by the parties, the arbitral tribunal shall apply the law determined by the conflict of law rules which it considers applicable.' The approach is thus typical of private law. This would not, however, prevent a tribunal set up under a BIT to apply, in the absence of any indication as to the applicable law, public international law to an alleged treaty breach as the law properly applicable to such state conduct under the BIT which represents the 'terms of reference' of the tribunal.[31]

The *CME* case was different because the relevant BIT includes a clause on applicable law. Article 8(6) of the BIT provides as follows:

> The arbitral tribunal shall decide on the basis of the law, taking into account in particular though not exclusively:
>
> 1. the law in force of the Contracting Party concerned;
> 2. the provisions of this Agreement, and other relevant Agreements between the Contracting Parties;
> 3. the provisions of special agreements relating to the investment;
> 4. the general principles of international law.

This clause, which was agreed in the BIT by the contracting parties, is equivalent to a choice of law clause agreed upon by the parties to a contract or to a dispute. Since Article 8(5) subjects the procedure to the UNCITRAL Rules, Article 8(6) would fit into the first sentence of Article 33(1) of the Rules ('The arbitral tribunal shall apply the law designated by the parties as applicable to the substance of the dispute.'). The above clause is binding upon the tribunal. However, the basis of its application is not a choice of law by the parties to and for the dispute. This results from the initiation of an arbitration under the BIT, which in turn implies acceptance of the relevant provisions of the treaty, including Article 8(6).

In an arbitration without privity, such as in the case of BITs, an indication of the applicable law made directly in the treaty by the

[31] As stated in 1989 by the Institut de Droit International in its Resolution on Arbitration between States, State Enterprises or State Entities, and Foreign Enterprises: 'The parties have full autonomy to determine the procedural and substantive rules that are to apply in the arbitration. In particular, (1) a different source may be chosen for the rules and principles applicable to each issue that arises and (2) these rules and principles may be derived from different national legal systems as well as from non-national sources such as principles of international law, general principles of law and the usage of international commerce.' (1990–11) *Annuaire de l'Institut de Droit International* 330.

contracting parties displaces and renders inapplicable altogether the choice of law provisions of the applicable arbitration rules, in our case Article 33(1) of the UNCITRAL Rules, including those which apply where the parties have made no choice. Article 8(6) thus replaces the second sentence of Article 33(1): 'Failing such designation by the parties, the arbitration tribunal shall apply the law determined by the conflict of laws rules which it considers applicable.'

The same approach was taken in what appears to be the only precedent for an arbitration of an investment dispute based on a BIT containing a (similar) choice of law clause, namely the ICSID award in the *Goetz* v. *Burundi* case.[32] In that case the arbitral tribunal considered that the clause on applicable law in the Belgium-Burundi BIT was an indirect choice of law by the parties, and that the criteria to be applied under Article 42(1) of the ICSID Convention in case of absence of parties' choice ('the law of the Contracting State party to the dispute and such rules of international law as may be applicable') were therefore irrelevant.[33]

Article V of the Algiers Agreement establishing the Iran-United States Claims Tribunal, which was also to apply the UNCITRAL Rules, is another interesting precedent in that it indicated directly the applicable law(s) derogating from Article 33 of the UNCITRAL Rules. The Iran-United States Claims Tribunal adopted the content of Article V in its Rules for the selection in each case of the applicable law.[34] A commentator has noted that '[i]n some respects the Tribunal's modified rule places limits on the extensive party autonomy so insistently pursued by the UNCITRAL drafters'.[35]

A further peculiarity of provisions such as Article 8(6) is that they must of course be interpreted as a treaty clause in accordance with the principles of interpretation of treaties under public international law, and not as contract clauses. The main difference in this respect is that an objective interpretation of the treaty provision is required rather than one seeking to determine the intent of the parties to a contract. It is also worth observing that Article 8(6) is peculiar in respect of the flexibility

[32] *Goetz* v. *Burundi*, *supra* n. 10 at 454. [33] *Ibid.* paragraphs 94–9.

[34] See Article 33(1) of the Rules of Procedure of the Iran-United States. Claims Tribunal: 'The arbitral tribunal shall decide all cases *on the basis of respect for law*, *applying* such choice of law rules and principles of commercial and international law as the arbitral tribunal determines to be applicable, *taking into account* relevant usages of the trade contract provisions and changed circumstances' (emphasis added).

[35] Stewart Abercrombie Baker and Mark David Davis, *The UNCITRAL Arbitration Rules in Practice: The Experience of the Iran-US Claims Tribunal* (1992), p. 177.

(discretion) it grants to the tribunal in selecting the legal rules to be applied: the arbitration tribunal is directed to 'decide on the basis of the law, taking into account in particular though not exclusively . . . '. Thus, the fundamental requirement of the treaty is that any award must be based on legal rules and principles. However, the provision grants to the tribunal a remarkable discretion as to which law to apply. It must 'take into account' but not 'exclusively' the set of rules listed thereafter.[36]

It is worth noting that the list includes both items, which are 'law' in the sense of a definite legal system (such as 'the law in force of the Contracting Party concerned '), and specific legal provisions or 'rules of law', such as the BIT itself ('this Agreement') and 'other relevant Agreements between the Contracting Parties'. The list refers also to contractual provisions, which are not by themselves 'law' ('the provisions of special agreements relating to the investment').[37] In accordance with the explicit discretion in the clause, there is neither order nor priority between the various categories of law listed in Article 8(6) that the tribunal has to take into account 'particularly though not exclusively' to decide 'on the basis of the law'. As recognized by the Court of Appeal of Stockholm, no indication is given as to the respective roles of 'the law in force of the Contracting Party concerned' (Czech law) on the one hand, and the provisions of the BIT and 'the general principles of international law', on the other hand.[38]

36 There is a difference between an obligation to 'take into account' and an obligation to 'apply'. A basic example of this distinction is in the Iran-United States Claims Tribunal Rules, cited *supra* n. 34, which direct the tribunal to *apply* certain rules and to take into account others.

37 Professor Schreuer, in his Commentary to the ICSID Convention in relation to Article 42(1), which spells out the freedom of the parties to select 'rules of law' of their choice, states that the sentence 'refers to "rules of law" rather than to systems of law. Therefore, it is generally accepted that the parties are not restricted to accepting an entire system of law *tel quel* but are free to combine, to select and to exclude rules or sets of rules of different origin'. Schrever, *ICSID Commentary*, p. 565.

38 Based on a textual interpretation, the last expression is equivalent to 'international law' or 'customary/general international law', which is of course relevant for the interpretation of the BIT provisions including Article 8(6). As a Dutch author has observed based on a comparison of many BITs, expressions such as 'general principles of international law', 'general rules and principles', 'generally accepted/recognised rules and principles' of international law are common in these BIT clauses: 'Most of these presumably mean the same thing: all rules and principles of general international law and customary international law which the tribunal considers applicable'. Paul Peters, 'Dispute Settlement Arrangements in Investment Treaties', (1991) 22 *Netherlands Yearbook of International Law* 91 at 113.

In a case where claims are for treaty violations, international law alone is relevant because international obligations of states are governed exclusively by international law. If the 'cause of action' at issue arises under international law, then international law applies to evaluate the lawfulness of the state's conduct even if the legal relationship (or a contract where applicable) is governed, as is normally the case, by domestic law.[39]

In its challenge of the Stockholm award before the Court of Appeals of Stockholm, the Czech Republic complained that the arbitrators had breached Article 8(6) in not having applied Czech law. In rejecting this challenge the court stated that:

> The wording that the arbitral tribunal shall 'take into account in particular though not exclusively' must be interpreted such that the arbitrators may also use sources of law other than those listed ... The unnumbered list almost gives the impression that the contracting States have left to the arbitrators the determination, on a case by case basis, as to which source of law shall be applied. If the case concerns an alleged violation of the Investment Treaty, it might be relevant first of all to apply international law, in light of the Investment Treaty's purpose of affording protection to foreign investors by prescribing norms in accordance with international law ... The interpretation which can be given to the words of the clause is thus hereby confirmed, namely that the clause leaves to the arbitral tribunal to take into account Czech law and other sources of law insofar as such are relevant to the dispute.[40]

The court observed further that 'if the case concerns an alleged violation of the Investment Treaty, it might be relevant first of all to apply international law, in light of the Investment Treaty's purpose of affording protection to foreign investors by prescribing norms in accordance with international law'.

The irrelevance of internal law in such a situation is reinforced by two basic principles of international law, namely that: '[a] party may not invoke the provisions of its internal law as justification for its failure to perform a treaty';[41] and, more generally, that in case of international responsibility for a wrongful act (namely for an act 'which is attributable to the state under international law', and which 'constitutes a breach of an international obligation of the state') '[t]he characterization of an act

[39] See *Case of Certain Norwegian Loans* (*France* v. *Norway*), 6 July 1957, (1957) ICJ Rep. 9 at 37 (Separate Opinion Lauterpacht).

[40] See *supra* n. 3 at 93. [41] Vienna Convention of the Law of Treaties Article 27.

as internationally wrongful is governed by international law'. Additionally, '[s]uch characterization is not affected by the characterization of the same act as lawful by internal law'.[42]

The same principle is spelled out by the ILC Articles in Part II of its text, regarding the consequence of wrongfulness, namely the obligation to make 'full reparation' for the injury caused, which 'includes any damage, whether material or moral, caused by the internationally wrongful act of the State'.[43] As stated in Article 32: 'The responsible State may not rely on the provisions of its internal law as justification for failure to comply with its obligations under this part'. All the above provisions by the ILC reflect basic principles of customary international law.[44]

What is then the relevance of the reference to the domestic law of the party concerned in Article 8(6) of the BIT? The answer lies in the text of Article 8(4) which, as mentioned before, and differently from some other BITs (notably those of the USA), submits to direct arbitration not just the disputes stemming from a claim of breach of the BIT's obligations but any dispute between a contracting state and an investor of the other state 'concerning an investment of the latter'.[45]

Disputes having as their object contractual or legal rights of the foreign investor under domestic law, as was in part the case in the *Goetz* v. *Burundi* dispute, are thus also amenable to arbitration under the BIT and would have to be decided applying the law of the state involved, should the investor also bring such a claim against the host state. The breach of domestic law may not necessarily entail breach of international law, as held by the International

[42] International Law Commission Articles on Responsibility of States for Internationally Wrongful Acts, Articles 2 and 3. These articles have been included as Annex by the UN General Assembly to its Resolution 56/83 of 12 December 2001 and commended to the attention of the UN member governments. As the Commentary by the ILC to Article 3 makes clear, the principle that domestic law cannot prevent wrongfulness under international law is a basic customary principle. James Crawford, *The International Law Commission's Articles on State Responsibility: Introduction, Text and Commentary* (2002), p. 86.

[43] ILC Articles on State Responsibility Article 31.

[44] Ian Brownlie, *Principles of Public International Law* (5th edn., 1998), p. 34.

[45] See Giorgio Sacerdoti, 'Bilateral Treaties and Multilateral Instruments on Investment Protection' (1997) 269 *Hague Rec. des Cours* 261 at 445 ('BITs' clauses that direct the tribunal to apply both domestic and international law indicate . . . that the arbitral dispute settlement procedure is not only applicable to disputes concerning an alleged breach of international law (including the BITs' provisions). Depending upon the language of the text as to the types of disputes covered, arbitration may be available for other disputes between the investor and the host State arising under its domestic law with respect to a covered investment.').

Court of Justice in the *ELSI* case.[46] On the other hand, by violating some provision of its domestic law in respect of the foreign investor, the host state may also have committed, at the same time, a breach of the treaty (or of customary international law) and therefore be liable under international law. In such a case the arbitral tribunal may have to interpret and apply domestic law as a preliminary step in order to pinpoint the exact conduct of the state. This step may be required even if the BIT provision does not mention domestic law as a law to be taken into account. However, domestic law in either case is considered as a fact from the point of view of international law, when the latter has to be applied in order to evaluate the lawfulness or unlawfulness of state conduct under international law.[47]

Applicable law: a comparison with ICSID arbitration

Even when Article 42(1) of ICSID is applicable and the parties have made no choice of law,[48] the reference to the host state's law and 'such rules of international law as may be applicable'[49] has consistently been interpreted and applied as requiring that ICSID tribunals, being international in that they are constituted and operate pursuant to an international convention, apply rules of international law in lieu of any domestic law provision that would be contrary to international law.[50] Decisions based on Article 42(1), second sentence, have given precedence to international law whenever some otherwise applicable provision of domestic law was found contrary to rules of international law on the treatment of foreigners. Conflicting domestic law was not applied, neither concurrently nor otherwise.[51] Thus,

46 *Case Concerning Elettronica Sicula SpA (ELSI)* (*United States* v. *Italy*), 20 July 1989, (1989) ICJ Rep. 4, paragraph 124.

47 Brownlie, *supra* note 45, at 39.

48 ICSID Article 42(1): 'The Tribunal shall decide a dispute in accordance with such rules of law as may be agreed by the parties. In the absence of such agreement, the Tribunal shall apply the law of the Contracting State party to the dispute (including its rules on the conflict of laws) and such rules of international law as may be applicable.'

49 For the contentious *travaux préparatoires* of this text, see Aron Broches, 'The Convention on the Settlement of Investment Disputes between States and Nationals of Other States' (1972–11) 136 *Rec. des Cours* 345 at 390. Aron Broches was at the time the General Counsel of the World Bank and became the first Secretary-General of ICSID.

50 Shihata and Parra, 'Applicable Substantive Law', 312–13.

51 In our opinion the contrary view of Prof. Michael Reisman who would limit the precedence of international law in case of conflicts to peremptory norms (*ius cogens*) is not supported by practice nor by systemic considerations. See Michael Reisman, 'The Regime for "Lacunae" in the ICSID Choice of Law Provisions and the Question of its Threshold' (2000) 15 *ICSID Review – Foreign Investment Law Journal* 362.

in *Amco* v. *Indonesia* (in which the parties did not agree upon the applicable law), the Ad hoc Committee found that Article 42(1) empowers the tribunal to apply the rules of international law in order to fill a lacuna in the municipal law and also to ensure the prevalence of the norms of international law when there is a contradiction with municipal law.[52] The Ad hoc Committee in *Klockner* v. *Cameroon* (the first and controversial annulment under the ICSID Convention), where the parties had again not selected the applicable law, similarly decided that Article 42(1) grants precedence to the rules of international law in cases in which the municipal law cannot be reconciled with the principles of international law.[53] The tribunal in the case of *Letco* v. *Liberia* made statements of a similar nature.[54]

This is also the conclusion of Professor Schreuer in his ICSID Commentary, based on an impressive list of ICSID awards: 'ICSID tribunals have frequently applied rules of customary international law either under the first or second sentence of Article 42(1)'.[55] Other commentators have taken the same position in all instances where there was a conflict between domestic law and international law, sharing the view that international law rules are preferentially and solely applicable in case of breach of international law by domestic law. Thus, Broches lists among the cases of application of international law by an ICSID tribunal the case 'where the law of the contracting State party to the dispute, or action taken under that law, violates international law. In this instance international law operates as a corrective to national law.'[56] As stated by Hirsch, '[t]he arbitral awards of the Centre and the works of prominent scholars have determined that when there is a contradiction between the municipal law of the host State and international law, the latter prevails.'[57]

More generally, in case of arbitration on the basis of a BIT, international law, *in primis* the very BIT provisions and the standards of treatment and protection they refer to, have to be applied, including when the BIT does not contain any indications as to the applicable law. As Broches points out 'an ICSID tribunal will have occasion to apply

[52] *Amco* v. *Indonesia* (1986) 25 ILM 1439 at 1445, paragraph 20.

[53] *Klöckner Industrie-Anlagen GmbH and others* v. *United Republic of Cameroon and Société Camerounaise des Engrais*, Case No. ARB/81/2, Ad hoc Committee Decision, 3 May 1985 (1994) 2 ICSID Rep. 95 at paragraph 69.

[54] *Liberian Eastern Timber Corp.* v. *Republic of Liberia*, Case No. ARB/83/2 (1987) 26 ILM 647 at 658.

[55] Schreuer, *ICSID Commentary*, p. 612. [56] Broches, 'The Convention', 392.

[57] Moshe Hirsch, *The Arbitration Mechanism of the International Centre for the Settlement of Investment Disputes* (1993), p. 140.

international law . . . (iii) where the subject matter or issue is directly regulated by international law, for instance by a treaty between the State party to the dispute and the State whose national is the other party to the dispute'.[58] Antonio Parra (currently the deputy Secretary-General of ICSID) has drawn the following conclusion from an analysis of the twenty-eight ICSID cases submitted on the basis of a BIT, which had led then to five published awards:

> The cases that have come to ICSID under these treaties have had a number of important dimensions. Not least among these concerns the rules of law applicable to the substance of the dispute. These mainly have been the rules set out in the substantive provisions of the treaty themselves. In most instances, this follows simply from the investor's invocation of those rules in bringing the claim, such reliance on the rules being explicitly or implicitly authorised by the investor-to-State dispute-settlement provisions of the treaty. The treaty being an instrument of international law, it is I think also implicit in such cases that the arbitrators should have recourse to the rules of general international law to supplement those of the treaty. The NAFTA and some BITs leave none of this to inference. They specifically require the investor-to-State disputes to be settled by the arbitrators in accordance with the treaty and the applicable rules of international law – the BITs often also referring in this context to the law of the State party to the dispute.[59]

A number of ICSID awards confirm this. As Parra has stressed, in *AAPL* v. *Sri Lanka*, for instance, which was based on the United Kingdom–Sri Lanka BIT and did not include a clause on the applicable law, the tribunal applied the international standard of 'full protection and security'.[60] In *AMT* v. *Zaire*, the tribunal applied the standard referred to in the relevant BIT of 'protection and security . . . not less than that recognised in international law'.[61]

In *Fedax* v. *Venezuela*, the issue was whether Venezuela was liable to pay certain promissory notes that the Dutch claimant had acquired through endorsement from the original holder. Here, too, the tribunal directly applied the BIT for the purpose of determining that Venezuela had 'to honor the specific payments established in the promissory notes'

58 Broches, 'The Convention', 392.
59 Parra, 'Applicable Substantive Law', 21.
60 See *Asian Agricultural Products Ltd* v. *Democratic Socialist Republic of Sri Lanka*, Case No. ARB/87/3, Award and Dissenting Opinion, 27 June 1990, (1991) 6 *ICSID Review – Foreign Investment Law Journal* 526 at 533, paragraph 21.
61 *American Manufacturing and Trading, Inc.* v. *Democratic Republic of the Congo*, Case No. ARB/93/1, Award, 21 February 1997, (1997) 36 ILM 1534, paragraphs 6.05–6.14.

concerned.[62] It was only for the purpose of ascertaining preliminarily the rights of a holder and whether the notes were endorsable and how, that the tribunal had to turn to Venezuelan law in order to ascertain the legal regime of these private law instruments governed by Venezuelan law. Having done that, as required by the particularities of that case, the tribunal applied the BIT and international law in order to decide the merits of the case.

This is consistent with the principle of international law that, except when and insofar as international tribunals may be called upon to decide a case (a claim) on the basis of domestic law (which may and does happen, as mentioned, in direct arbitration of investment disputes on the basis of BIT clauses or ICSID Article 42(1)), municipal laws are merely 'facts' to be ascertained.[63] *Maffezzini* v. *Spain* is another example of a treaty claim where, even though brought under ICSID, the tribunal distinguished the types of claims made and their legal basis in order to ascertain whether or not 'the claim seeks the vindication of rights guaranteed in a treaty, for example, which empowers the tribunal to interpret and to apply the treaty'. The tribunal decided the case on the basis of the treaty, having found that 'here the parties have a treaty right to obtain a final determination from the international tribunal on the scope of their rights under the treaty'.[64]

The *Goetz* v. *Burundi* case is an example of BIT arbitration based on a choice of law provision in the treaty. In that case, the Belgian claimants requested the tribunal to order that a ministerial decision revoking certain tax and customs privileges originally granted to the investor be annulled; that the taxes and duties paid as a result of the withdrawn privileges be reimbursed; and that the damages suffered because of consequential interruption of activity be indemnified. In accordance with the terms of the BIT, the tribunal was required to examine the claims under both Burundi law and international law, and in case of conflict, the parties agreed that the law most favourable to the investor would apply.[65] Having concluded that the revocation and other connected actions by the state authorities were not in violation of Burundi law,[66] the tribunal examined

62 See Parra, 'Applicable Substantive Law', 23 (referring to the 1998 decision of *Fedax NV* v. *Republic of Venezuela*).

63 *Certain German Interests in Upper Silesia*, 25 May 1926, PCIJ, Ser. A, No. 7, 4 at 19; Brownlie, *Principles*, pp. 39–41.

64 *Emilio Augustín Maffezini* v. *Kingdom of Spain*, Case No. ARB/97/7, Decision on Jurisdiction, 25 January 2000, (2001) 16 *ICSID Review – Foreign Investment Law Journal* 223, paragraph 30 (emphasis added).

65 *Goetz* v. *Burundi*, *supra* n.10 at 502.

66 *Ibid.* at paragraphs 117 and 119.

the actions at issue under international law and the BIT. The tribunal took the view that national law and international law each have their own sphere of application,[67] rather than relying on any hierarchy or applying international law only to fill gaps or if in contradiction to local law. It concluded that the actions of the government were tantamount to an expropriation but Burundi would not be liable if it withdrew the measure or paid compensation as stipulated in the BIT.

In conclusion, while Article 42 of the ICSID Convention has no bearing on the selection of the applicable law in non-ICSID arbitration, whether a choice of law provision is or is not included in the relevant BIT, the results tend to be the same: international law must be applied where relevant to decide the claim and it prevails over conflicting domestic provisions.

The main differences of ICSID arbitration lie, thus, in the procedural framework (within an international organization such as ICSID), the nature of the awards, the admissible challenges (only ad hoc annulment as regulated by the Washington Convention with no interference by state courts). The *CME and Lauder* dispute shows, however, that the limited control exercised by domestic courts, mainly at the place of the seat of the arbitration (which do not include reviewing the choice of law by the arbitrators nor their interpretation nor application of the selected law), when properly exercised, neither obstructs recourse to UNCITRAL arbitration as a means for the impartial, competent and speedy settlement of the dispute, nor the implementation of the award.

[67] *Ibid.* at paragraph 97.

PART IV

New challenges in international adjudication

21

From Preston to Prescott: Globalizing Legitimate Expectation

FRANCISCO ORREGO VICUÑA

Discretionary acts and legitimate expectation: concepts central to a new approach

Two principal concepts have come to dominate the legal approach to the review of administrative acts by the judiciary. A long-standing tradition has established the discretionary nature of acts of the administration, which generally meant that such acts were not subject to judicial review.[1] However, this very concept was qualified in a number of ways, particularly when some form of abuse of power or procedural irregularity tainted the act.[2] The second and more recent concept has been that of legitimate expectation, dealing in part with procedural matters but also with substantive expectations. Both concepts, while originating in domestic decisions, have come to an important degree of global application, mainly by means of the work of international administrative tribunals and in some specialized matters by tribunals established under the ICSID Convention. This contribution will examine the main evolution of these jurisprudential developments and how they offer new perspectives on the approaches taken by domestic and international tribunals in handling the issue of individual rights in the context of the administrative acts of the state.

Regulatory power and its limits

In order to better understand the issues underlying this evolution, it is necessary first to identify which are the main legal interests that need to be taken into account and protected to the extent appropriate by the law.

[1] See, e.g., the decision adopted by the French Conseil d'Etat in *Abbé Bouteyre*, 10 May 1912, cited in M. Long *et al.*, *Les Grands Arrêts de la Jurisprudence Administrative* (2001), p. 150.

[2] Conseil d'Etat, *Daudignac*, 22 June 1951, cited in Long, *Les Grands Arrêts*, p. 447.

The first such interest is the right of the state to adopt regulatory measures in implementation of legislation and other expressions of sovereignty. This right, generally brought under the vague concept of administrative or police powers, has not been questioned, nor could it be unless one is aiming at the total dissolution of state functions. Even in the context of a globalized legal structure, this dissolution is not quite evident nor is it likely to be so in the future. The second legal interest at stake is that regulatory authority cannot be validly exercised if it violates the framework of legal rights and obligations in which it operates. It is quite clear today, for example, that regulatory measures cannot be validly adopted contrary to constitutional standards, legislative mandate, or human rights. This will be subject to scrutiny both by constitutional bodies, judicial entities, or even international mechanisms. As noted above, the concept of discretionary powers has been progressively qualified so as to prevent the abuse of discretion that ultimately results in abuse of power. Courts have been generally open to consider the review of irregularities that could have such a result, first in the context of procedural irregularities and next in substantive terms, dealing with issues such as improper motive and discrimination. Beyond the tradition of domestic courts, it is of interest to note that some key decisions adopted by international administrative tribunals incorporated this very approach into international law.

The contribution of international administrative tribunals

As was explained by Judge Gentot at a recent Conference convened by the World Bank Administrative Tribunal on the comparative experience of these entities:

> All tribunals appear to allow for the possibility of limited reviews of cases involving the exercise of discretionary power, although the language used to describe such reviews is not always identical (even within the same tribunal). It is a widely held belief that while discretionary power is not synonymous with arbitrary action (and that it therefore must be subject to review), judges should not substitute their own assessments for those of organizations (meaning their reviews must therefore be limited). Whatever the terminology used, it would seem that judges have the right – and the duty – to censure decisions (even if the decisions resulted from the exercise of discretionary power) which were issued by an authority that was not competent to act in the situation, which were taken in violation of procedural rules, which were based on errors of

fact or of law, or which indicate the existence of abuse or misuse of authority.[3]

This approach has been constantly affirmed since the *Desgranges* case, decided in 1953 by the Administrative Tribunal of the International Labor Organization.[4] As explained by Judge Valticos in the same Conference referred to above, 'the *Desgranges* opinion had, as early as 1953, begun to sound the death knell of an absolutist concept of discretionary power'.[5] Recent decisions of the Administrative Tribunals of the International Labor Organization,[6] the International Monetary Fund,[7] the World Bank,[8] and the Council of Europe[9] have all confirmed this understanding of the limits of discretionary power and the existence of a limited power of judicial review. As with the decisions of domestic courts, the gradual refinement of the limits of discretionary powers has been noticeable in the jurisprudence of international tribunals. The grounds for review have generally been related to the concept of *détournement de pouvoir*, substantive irregularities, or procedural irregularities. In this connection, for example, the most common phrase appearing in the decisions of the World Bank Administrative Tribunal is that the Tribunal will not interfere with the exercise of discretion unless the decision contested 'constitutes an abuse of discretion, being arbitrary, discriminatory, improperly motivated or carried out in violation of a fair and reasonable procedure'.[10]

[3] Michel Gentot, 'Review of Discretionary Power by International Administrative Tribunals', paper presented at Conference convened by the World Bank Administrative Tribunal on the occasion of its twentieth anniversary, April 2001, Paris, p. 2.

[4] *Desgranges*, International Labor Organization Administrative Tribunal, Judgment No. 11, 1953.

[5] Nicolas Valticos, 'Checks Exerted by Administrative Tribunals over the Discretionary Powers of International Organizations', paper presented at Conference, *supra* n. 3, p. 2.

[6] See, e.g., *Beaucent* v. *UPU*, 3 February 2000, ILO Administrative Tribunal.

[7] See, e.g., *Mrs. C*, Administrative Tribunal of the International Monetary Fund, No. 1997–1, 22 July 1997.

[8] See, e.g., *Ezatkhah*, World Bank Administrative Tribunal, Decision No. 185, 15 May 1998.

[9] See, e.g., *Sixto*, Administrative Tribunal of the Council of Europe, Appeal No. 210, 26 April 1996.

[10] See, e.g., *Montasser*, World Bank Administrative Tribunal, Decision No. 156, 1997, paragraph 10.

Extending the protection of individual rights

Various developments, however, have taken this broad definition further so as to take care of changing concerns in respect of individual rights. Some particularly noteworthy developments are the following:

(i) Processes: in many cases a tribunal will be concerned not so much with a single decision that might affect an individual but with a decisional process as a whole. While a decision in itself might not be seriously objectionable, the aggregate of decisions taken might eventually amount to an abuse of discretion. Such adverse process can reveal 'errors of judgment which taken together amount to unreasonableness and arbitrariness'.[11]

(ii) Commitments: tribunals generally, and the World Bank Administrative Tribunal in particular, have emphasized the need for the administration to honour the commitments made to individuals. It has thus been held, for example, that the 'possibility exists also that there may be something in the surrounding circumstances which creates a right to the conversion of a fixed-term appointment to a permanent one'.[12] In a recent case it was found that a promise of conversion had been validly made and that the applicant had met the required conditions; a decision not to convert was therefore held to be an abuse of discretion.[13]

(iii) Quasi-judicial powers: some discretionary powers amount in fact to the exercise of a quasi-judicial function by the administration, as is typically the case of the adoption of disciplinary measures. The standard of review generally becomes stricter in this connection and might lead the tribunal to examine the decision *de novo*, as if the tribunal itself had been requested to take the decision originally.[14]

(iv) Appellate jurisdiction: in some matters administrative tribunals are given a special appellate jurisdiction. This jurisdiction is both

[11] See, e.g., *Chhabra*, World Bank Administrative Tribunal, Decision No. 139, 1994, paragraph 57.

[12] See, e.g., *Mr. X*, World Bank Administrative Tribunal, Decision No. 16, 1984, paragraph 38.

[13] See *Bigman*, World Bank Administrative Tribunal, Decision No. 209, 1999.

[14] See generally C. F. Amerasinghe, *The Law of the International Civil Service* (1994), vol. 1, p. 267.

exceptional and broader than the mere review of managerial discretion.[15]

(v) Legislative functions: in the leading case of *de Merode*, the World Bank Administrative Tribunal gave a first step in reviewing administration policies that might affect fundamental and essential elements of the rights and duties of staff members.[16] In that case it introduced a meaningful limitation to the exercise of discretion in this context, holding that such elements, unlike those which are less fundamental, cannot be changed without the consent of the individual concerned. A second step in this direction relates to the regular review by tribunals of legislation that entails discrimination or other anomalies.[17]

Judicial review of legislative authority

Recently, however, the need arose to take this review a step further on account of the legislation enacted by the World Bank on pension reform. In *Crevier* and other cases that followed, the applicant and the Staff Association raised, in addition to discrimination and other alleged deficiencies, an objection to the very objective pursued by the reform and its inspiring philosophy, independently from the manner in which this could affect the individual claimant.[18] The World Bank Administrative Tribunal examined each aspect of the applicant's contentions in order to establish the reasonableness and fairness of the Bank's legislation, which it upheld. It follows, therefore, that in certain circumstances the enactment of legislation by administrative bodies can be reviewed as a discretionary power subject to limitations.

Evolving scope of legitimate expectation

The marked evolution characterizing judicial review of discretionary powers gradually led to the emergence of the second concept of interest,

[15] See, e.g., *Shenouda*, World Bank Administrative Tribunal, Decision No. 177, 1997, paragraph 12.

[16] See *de Merode*, World Bank Administrative Tribunal, Decision No. 1, 1981, paragraphs 41, 42.

[17] Francisco Orrego Vicuña, 'The Review of Managerial Discretion by International Administrative Tribunals: Comments in the Light of the Practice of the World Bank Administrative Tribunal', paper presented at Conference, *supra* n. 3, p. 4.

[18] See *Crevier*, World Bank Administrative Tribunal, Decision No. 205, 1999.

that of legitimate expectation. English courts in particular have refined the application of this concept, also following a gradual progression. As with many other contemporary legal developments, it was Lord Denning who emphasized the role of legitimate expectation in protecting the rights of the citizen before the state.[19] It has been rightly explained that at first the main ground for the intervention of the courts in the light of this concept was to enforce procedural rights, and hence emphasis was placed on how decisions were adopted rather than on their content.[20] This soon led, however, to the *Wednesbury* principle allowing for judicial intervention when the content of a decision is manifestly unreasonable.[21] Although at first the standard of review was not entirely clear or defined, in 1985 the House of Lords gave an important step forward in the *Preston* case.[22] A decision may be *ultra vires* and amount to an abuse of power through unfairness, arbitrariness, or other situations. As expressed by Lord Templeman: 'Judicial review is available where a decision-making authority exceeds its powers, commits an error of law, commits a breach of natural justice, reaches a decision which no reasonable tribunal could have reached or abuses its powers.'[23] Similarly, Lord Scarman stated that 'the principle of fairness has an important place in the law of judicial review'.[24] A century earlier, Lord Russell had also underlined that the limits of the court's benevolence is related to those regulations that are 'manifestly unjust, partial, made in bad faith or so gratuitous and oppressive that no reasonable person could think them justified'.[25] Or in the words of Judge Bingham, 'the doctrine of legitimate expectation is rooted in fairness'.[26] As cases determined a progression in the reasoning underlying the concept of legitimate expectation, many views were expressed either in support or criticism of new approaches.[27] The fact is, however, that the progression continued. This is perhaps well evidenced in the recent case *R* v. *North and East Devon Health Authority, ex parte Coughlan*,[28] where the Court

[19] Mark Elliott, 'Case and Comment. House of Lords Decisions: "Legitimate Expectation: The Substantive Dimension"' (2000) 59 *Cambridge Law Journal* 421 at 423.
[20] *Ibid.* at 422.
[21] *Associated Provincial Picture Houses Ltd* v. *Wednesbury Corp.* [1947] 2 All ER 680, [1948] 1 KB 223, CA.
[22] Preston v. IRC [1985] 2 All ER 327, [1985] AC 835. [23] [1985] 2 All ER 327 at 337.
[24] *Ibid.* at 329. [25] *Kruse* v. *Johnson* [1898] 2 QB 91, [1895–9] All ER Rep. 105.
[26] *R* v. *IRC, ex parte MFK Underwriting Agents Ltd* [1990] 1 WLR 1545 at 1569–70.
[27] Elliott, 'Case and Comment', 423–4.
[28] *R* v. *North and East Devon Health Authority, ex parte Coughlan* [2000] 3 All ER 850.

of Appeal in England sought to redress the inequality of power between the citizen and the state.[29] In this case it was held that:

> Where the Court considers that a lawful promise or practice has induced a legitimate expectation of a *benefit which is substantive*, not simply procedural, authority now establishes that here too the court will in a proper case decide whether to frustrate the expectation is so unfair that to take a new and different course will amount to an abuse of power. Here, once the legitimacy of the expectation is established, the court will have the task of weighing the requirements of fairness against any overriding interest relied upon for the change of policy.[30]

The Court, having examined prior cases, then added:

> The court's task in all these cases is not to impede executive activity but to reconcile its continuing need to initiate or respond to change with the legitimate interests or expectations of citizens or strangers who have relied, and have been justified in relying, on a current policy or extant promise.[31]

Reasonableness and fairness thus became the central tenets of the conceptual evolution linking the control of discretionary power with legitimate expectation and not just with the traditional standards guiding the role and availability of judicial review.

Legitimate expectation before international tribunals

Just as the evolution of the review of discretionary powers before national courts led to a subsequent development in the same direction before international tribunals, so too the emergence of legitimate expectation attending rather to the substance of the claim has had similar repercussions before such international tribunals. The various directions indicated above in respect of processes, commitments, appellate jurisdiction, quasi-judicial powers, and legislative functions were largely related to the issues of fairness and reasonableness, in addition to elements connected with due process. Procedure and substance thus came together, albeit many times inadvertently. The questions of fairness and reasonableness became paramount in a series of recent cases decided by the World Bank Administrative Tribunal in respect of the

[29] Elliott, 'Case and Comment', 421. [30] *Coughlan* [2000] 3 All ER 850, paragraph 57.
[31] *Ibid.* at paragraph 65.

pension reform enacted by the Bank and its implications for non-regular staff members, who were not included in the reform. Unjustifiable differentiation was one of the arguments raised in the claims concerning this situation, thus pointing again in the direction of the substantive content of the decisions questioned. In *Caryk* and *Madhusudan*, after considering various initiatives directed to correct adverse consequences of the pension reform, the Tribunal held:

> These examples of policy initiatives or studies . . . show that the Respondent, far from being involved in a *détournement de pouvoir* and *détournement de procedure*, was sensitive to a wide range of different, and occasionally conflicting, factors. The task of the Tribunal cannot possibly be to judge whether the Respondent could have been wiser.[32]

Procedural and substantive aspects thus became intertwined in the reasoning of the Tribunal, but the observance of the privileges of managerial discretion still prevailed. This reasoning was taken a step further in the *Prescott* case where considerations of fairness came to prevail over managerial discretion. The Tribunal thus held:

> As a general principle, the Bank did not have an obligation to regularize the Applicant. This was a discretionary decision, which was final unless the decision constituted an abuse of discretion, being arbitrary, discriminatory, improperly motivated or carried out in violation of a fair and reasonable procedure. But under the applicable policy and rules, and in the context of contemporaneous communications to staff and managers, the Bank had an obligation to consider his regularization after four years in the light of the unique circumstances of the case. The Bank undertook no such consideration and thus failed to comply with this obligation. Moreover, the Bank at the time offered no valid reason for this failure.[33]

The Tribunal concluded that the managers concerned had abused their discretion because the decision was tainted by some form of arbitrariness.[34] While not explicitly mentioning legitimate expectation, in fact the whole case dealt with the legitimate expectation of Mr Prescott to be regularized in the light of the policies and the statements of the Bank's managers. This legitimate expectation was violated and hence the

[32] *Caryk*, World Bank Administrative Tribunal, Decision No. 214, 1999, paragraph 40; *Madhusudan*, World Bank Administrative Tribunal, Decision No. 215, 1999, paragraph 49.
[33] *Prescott*, World Bank Administrative Tribunal, Decision No. 253, 2001, paragraph 25.
[34] *Ibid.* at paragraphs 27–8.

Tribunal upheld the claim, not quite on the consideration of procedural aspects, but rather, on the importance attached to fairness and substantive rights of the individual. On the basis of this decision the Bank's management and the staff later came to an agreement about extending the pension reform and related benefits to some classes of non-regular staff. Although the conceptual evolution examined has been mostly related to the field of administrative law, whether domestic or international, its implications for the broader spectrum of international law are becoming increasingly evident. There is also a growing connection of this matter with the international law of human rights.[35]

Influencing the law on foreign investments

It is first important to note that this concept has not only permeated the work of international administrative tribunals but also that of a number of other tribunals dealing in particular with foreign investment. The case law of ICSID and NAFTA shows an increasing concern for the right interpretation of the 'fair and equitable' treatment and other standards of substance embodied in bilateral investment treaties (BITs) and similar instruments.[36] Although there are wide variations in the reasoning of tribunals on this question, the basic underlying premise seems to be that what is reasonable and fair on the part of states and investors alike ought to prevail, but what is abusive ought to be controlled. Next, it is also evident that the process of protecting foreign investment is becoming global through numerous BITs.[37] To this extent the standards of treatment become global in their application. This phenomenon is enhanced by other concurrent developments, most notably the enactment of

35 For a discussion of the decisions of English courts and the related views of the European Court of Human Rights, see, e.g., Jane Wright, 'The Retreat from Osman: Z v United Kingdom in the European Court of Human Rights and Beyond' in D. Fairgrieve *et al.* (eds.), *Tort Liability of Public Authorities in Comparative Perspective* (2002), pp. 55–80.

36 Asan Sedigh, 'What Level of Host State Interference Amounts to a Taking under Contemporary International Law?' (2001) 2 *Journal of World Investment* 631; Thomas Wälde and Abba Kolo, 'Environmental Regulation, Investment Protection and "Regulatory Taking" in International Law' (2001) 50 *International and Comparative Law Quarterly* 811.

37 See generally UNCTAD, *World Investment Report 2002*; and Eloise Obadia, 'ICSID, Investment Treaties and Arbitration: Current and Emerging Issues' in Gabrielle Kaufmann-Kohler *et al.* (eds.), *Investment Treaties and Arbitration* (Swiss Arbitration Association, 2002), pp. 67–76, both reporting over 2,000 BITs in force.

broad multilateral conventions such as the Energy Charter Treaty,[38] or the application of the most-favoured nation clause to both procedural arrangements and substantive treatment accorded to foreign investors.[39] Since a good number of claims deal with administrative decisions by governments and local authorities, the reasoning that international tribunals might wish to apply is not altogether different from the reasoning that domestic tribunals have followed. In many instances, legitimate expectation arising from contracts or other forms of agreement and from legal principles of general application will be at the heart of the dispute, thus allowing the tribunal to examine with grater ease the substantive treatment embodied in the treaties or applicable legislation and principles. The process as a whole relates then to a broader question of legal interpretation.

Influencing the development of international law

It is in this process also that the role of general international law becomes important. The 'fair and equitable treatment' or other standards of protection might change from case to case, be broader or narrower in the light of BITs, the NAFTA, the Energy Charter Treaty, or, to the extent applicable, customary law,[40] but what finally matters is that such standards and their judicial implementation cannot fail to protect individual rights from arbitrariness and excess on the part of regulatory bodies.[41] The philosophy underlying these developments is then the same. There is still one other development that must be borne in mind, for it might have important implications for international law. Thus far, the immunities of states before foreign courts have included

[38] Antonio R. Parra, 'Provisions on the Settlement of Investment Disputes in Modern Investment Laws, Bilateral Investment Treaties and Multilateral Instruments on Investment' (1997) 12 *ICSID Review – Foreign Investment Law Journal* 287.

[39] Francisco Orrego Vicuña, 'Bilateral Investment Treaties and the Most-Favored-Nation Clause: Implications for Arbitration in the Light of a Recent ICSID Case' in Kaufmann-Kohler, *Investment Treaties*, pp. 133–44.

[40] See, e.g., the discussion of fair and equitable treatment by a NAFTA tribunal in the light of customary law and domestic legislation in *Mondev* v. *United States* (2003) 42 *ILM* 85, paragraphs 94–127.

[41] An interesting example of application by British courts of the legitimate expectation doctrine to the judicial review of the traditional privilege of foreign policy decisions in the context of diplomatic protection of citizens abroad is found in *R (Abbasi and another)* v. *Secretary of State for Foreign and Commonwealth Affairs and another* Case No. C/2002/0617A; 0617B, 6 November 2002, Court of Appeal, Civil Division, [2002] EWCA Civ. 159.

without hesitation administrative law matters, as they are associated with the concept of sovereign power and the exercise of discretionary power by states. However, as noted by Lady Fox, '[t]he exclusive powers of regulation of its civil service and internal administration for which States have reciprocally granted each other immunity dates from a period before the development of judicial review of governmental activities'.[42] Because in later periods both domestic and international courts have increasingly resorted to judicial review of discretionary acts, the inevitable question is then: 'Should the law of State immunity accommodate this increased supervision of government by including within the commercial exception matters which have given rise to a legitimate expectation on the part of an individual?'[43] This proposition has been met with both favourable and unfavourable opinions. The latter are, of course, associated with the view that no court can sit in judgment on the sovereign acts of foreign states.[44] However, Professor Ian Brownlie has already cautioned against a distinction that would allow private law claims to be decided by foreign courts and not allow the same right in respect of other relationships which, although not being of a private law character, are equally based on good faith and legal security.[45] Often the acts of the administration fall under this last category when they affect the rights of individuals. Lady Fox has also examined this potential development: 'Another approach is to treat the legitimate expectation raised by an administrative decision or act as an approximation to a private law right, and hence not immune because the restrictive rule allows such private law rights to be pursued against a foreign State by way of exception to State immunity.'[46]

Democratization, globalization and individual rights

In the end, the essential element both in domestic and international legal developments is that '[t]he democratization of the internal government of States and their subjection to the rule of law has led to increased accountability before their own domestic courts of the executive branch

[42] Hazel Fox, *The Law of State Immunity* (2002), p. 298. [43] *Ibid.* at p. 299.
[44] *Ibid.*
[45] Institut de Droit International, Resolution on Contemporary Aspects concerning Jurisdictional Immunities of States, Article 2(d), (1991-II) *Annuaire de l'Institut de Droit International* (Basle Session) 64 at 266, as discussed by Fox, *Law of State Immunity*, p. 299.
[46] *Ibid.* at pp. 299–300.

of government . . . [and] national courts increasingly take it upon themselves to determine the appropriate balance between executive effectiveness and protection of the citizen'.[47] In a globalized international society, international courts and tribunals are gradually moving in the same direction, just as eventually foreign courts will do.

[47] *Ibid.* at p. 298.

22

The Independence of the International Judiciary: Some Introductory Thoughts

PHILIPPE SANDS

Florentino Feliciano has contributed greatly to the development of international law as scholar, practitioner, judge, and arbitrator. He has a deserved reputation for excellence, independence, and integrity. Amongst his many contributions, I feel especially privileged to have benefited from his counsel and advice as a founding member of the Steering Committee of the Project on International Courts and Tribunals. He was amongst those who actively encouraged the Project to focus on the independence of the international judiciary. This is a subject that has attracted greater attention as international courts and tribunals increase in number and in influence.

The first efforts to establish a standing international court occurred in the 1890s; they foundered for the simple reason that the states involved in the diplomatic negotiation of the Hague Peace Conference of 1899 could not agree on the method of appointing the judges, in particular how to balance the competing interests of, on the one hand, the desire of every participating state to have a judge on the court with, on the other hand, the need for a tribunal of manageable proportions (imagine a national Supreme or Constitutional Court of fifty or more judges . . .).

The first international court – the Central American Court of Justice – was established in 1907, between a small enough number of states to dispose of the obstacle on which the Hague discussions foundered. At this court each participating state had a judge on the bench. The intimate connection between the states parties to the instrument establishing an international court and the provenance, number, and identity of the judges – with all that these factors imply for independence – remains a live issue today.

The Central American Court had a short life. The next international court to be established was the Permanent Court of International Justice (PCIJ) in 1922, based in The Hague. The PCIJ was succeeded by the

International Court of Justice (ICJ) in 1946, with the creation of the United Nations, of which it is the principal judicial organ. Until 1960, the ICJ and its fifteen judges had a monopoly on the judicial resolution of international disputes. Since then there has been a marked increase in the number of international courts, and the situation today is much changed.[1] And, of course, almost all of these international courts and tribunals are organs of, or are otherwise connected to, international organizations, giving rise to issues of independence. Beyond the ICJ there is now an International Tribunal for the Law of the Sea (ITLOS) (Hamburg, twenty-three judges); a regional European Court of Human Rights (ECtHR) connected to the Council of Europe (Strasbourg, forty-one judges) and equivalent bodies for the Americas and Africa; the Court of Justice of the European Communities and the European Court of First Instance (ECJ), forming the judicial organs of the European Union (Luxembourg, fifty judges) and equivalent economic courts in parts of Africa and Latin America. There is the World Trade Organization's Dispute Settlement Understanding (DSU), which provides for the resolution of international trade disputes by dispute settlement panels with appeals on points of law to a seven-member Appellate Body (in Geneva), arguably the single most economically powerful court anywhere in the world. There is an International Criminal Tribunal for Rwanda (ICTR) (Arusha, with fourteen judges) and an International Criminal Tribunal for the former Yugoslavia (ICTY) (The Hague, with fourteen judges), both established by and in continuing relationship with the UN Security Council and the International Criminal Court (ICCt). The Statute of the ICCt (also in The Hague, with eighteen judges), was adopted in Rome in 1998 and came into force on 1 July 2002 (with a Prosecutor whose independence from the permanent members of the Security Council provides much of the reason why the USA will not ratify). There are also standing arbitration institutions, such as the World Bank's International Centre for the Settlement of Investment Disputes (ICSID), providing (amongst other matters) for compulsory arbitration of disputes between foreign investors and the three NAFTA states (and, in effect, reviewing decisions of

[1] See generally P. Sands, R. Mackenzie, and Y. Shany, *Manual of International Courts and Tribunals* (Butterworths, 1999). See also the website of the Project on International Courts and Tribunals (www.pict-pcti.org) and the Centre on International Courts and Tribunals (www.ucl.ac.uk/laws/cict/index.html).

US federal courts, including the US Supreme Court). There are inspection panels at various multilateral development banks, providing for administrative review of lending decisions, and there are international administrative tribunals resolving disputes between employees and the various multilateral development banks for which they work. For each of these bodies, issues of independence arise in relation to the institution which established finances or governs them.

Amongst the standing, permanent bodies there are now more than 200 international judges. Compared to most national legal systems this is a small number, although it is supplemented by the appointment of ad hoc judges (at some international courts, a state involved in a case may appoint a judge where it has no national on the bench) and of ad hoc arbitrators where disputes are taken to arbitral tribunals established to deal with a particular case. Notwithstanding their modest numbers, these judges exercise an avowedly judicial function (in England, the UK judge at the ECJ, the ECtHR, the ICCt, and the ICJ is treated as an equivalent to a High Court judge), and they do so on a wide range of politically and economically sensitive topics, including areas which touch on the functioning of international organizations. The international judiciary is therefore a permanent feature of the legal landscape, and one which is now the subject of institutional study.

What has received rather less attention, however, is the subject of the 'independence' of these international judges. It is a feature of each and every international court and tribunal that the judges are to be 'independent' and 'impartial' (we do not here address the distinction between these two separate but related concepts). Article 2 of the Statute of the ICJ, for example, provides that:

> The Court shall be composed of a body of independent judges, elected regardless of their nationality from among persons of high moral character, who possess the qualifications required in their respective countries for appointment to the highest judicial offices, or are jurisconsults of recognized competence in international law.

The seven members of the WTO Appellate Body are to be:

> persons of recognized authority, with demonstrated expertise in law, international trade and the subject matter of the covered agreements generally. They shall be unaffiliated with any government. The Appellate Body membership shall be broadly representative of membership in the WTO. (DSU Article 17).

During their term of office, the judges of the European Court of Human Rights 'shall not engage in any activity which is incompatible with their independence, impartiality or with the demands of a full-time office' (European Convention on Human Rights Article 21.3). Arbitrators appointed under the ICSID arbitration rules are persons 'who may be relied upon to exercise independent judgment', and may be disqualified if they do not meet this standard (ISCID Convention Articles 14 and 57). The judges of the International Criminal Court are to be 'chosen from among persons of high moral character, impartiality and integrity who possess the qualifications required in their respective States for appointment to the highest judicial offices' (ICC Statute Article 36.3(a)).

In many cases these general formulations are supplemented by more detailed rules, determining what international judges can and cannot do, the cases upon which they ought to recuse themselves, etc. In some cases, the international courts have very clear and strict rules or practices prohibiting, for example, all forms of 'outside activity' as a means of promoting independence. In other cases, the practices (or rules/guidelines) are more flexible. Although the formulations and practices vary, the stated and general commitment to 'independence' and 'impartiality' is apparent. *Prima facie*, the requirement that there should be an 'independent judiciary' applies equally in respect of the international judges (although there have been only very few instances in which the issue of independence has been formally raised and then reported, as it was, for example, in a recent case before the ICTY concerning the impartiality of a judge, see below). As with the national level, the legitimacy and authority of the courts is perceived to be related to their independence. What is less apparent is what independence and impartiality mean in the context of these international bodies.

Does 'independence' fall to be assessed by reference to the standards or approach applying to judges at the domestic level (it is apparent that the idea of 'independence' is culturally specific). Is the 'independence' of a national judge at the ICJ or the WTO Appellate Body measured by reference to national standards, or to the standard of the ICJ, or to such common international (minimum) standard as might exist? If international norms exist or emerge, might they begin to inform the content and application of national standards? Could they even weaken those standards? And, more broadly, should national courts give effect to international judicial decisions and rules which have been developed by judges who might not be considered to be independent according to certain domestic standards? (This last question assumes considerable relevance given that the standards governing judicial independence in common law countries differ markedly from the Roman or civil law or Islamic traditions, and that the common law approach will often find itself in a minority on the international bench.) And, as an umbrella question, one might ask whether it is appropriate at all to treat the independence of the international judiciary as one would consider the independence of national judges, or whether there is something qualitatively different about international law and courts (i.e., the popular refrain that international justice is merely international politics writ large), with the result that we should apply different – i.e., lesser – standards?

These and other questions are part of a research agenda waiting to be carried out. There is very little written on the subject of the independence of the international judiciary, whether in the context of their relations with international organizations or other aspects. There are many other questions which could be asked, and it is curious that they are not yet being asked more often in relation to the international judiciary.

To put these questions in an international context, I set out four examples of recent practice before some of the international courts. The developments assume a broad view of the idea of 'independence', touching upon independence by reference to the judge's relationship with his or her state of origin, with the political organs of the institution with which his or her court is connected, and with the parties to a dispute.

Identity and background of judges

Candidates for international judicial office are put forward by individual states. When a state nominates or appoints an individual to international judicial office it does so in the knowledge that the judge may be involved in deciding a contentious case involving the interests of the state of his or her nationality, or an advisory opinion on which his or her state has a clear view. It would be unreasonable to expect that a nominating or appointing state would not seek to put forward as a candidate to international judicial office a person who generally shares the value systems of the nominating state and who might be considered by the nominator to be a 'safe pair of hands'. But how far is a state entitled to go in ensuring 'safety', and at what point should one conclude that any prior relationship between the judge and the state precludes international judicial appointment? The question arises because it is an unremarkable feature (for public international lawyers) of many international courts that a nominated candidate might have been a former legal adviser of the nominating state, or a former member of the diplomatic corps of that state involved in the activities of associated international organizations,[2] or even a former parliamentarian. This everyday feature elicits little or no comment in the international legal literature. Should it be considered to be an issue worthy of attention?

Let me provide an illustration, which touches upon independence, but also the right to a fair hearing (which is related to, but distinct from, our interest in 'independence'). In one ICJ case, the following was observed: whilst counsel for a state party to a case made comments criticizing a political decision of another state, the judge who was a national of the state being criticized (and formerly the legal adviser of its Ministry of Foreign Affairs) was seen to remove his headphones (through which simultaneous interpretation was being provided) and place them on the table in front of him, not putting them back on until the counsel had moved on to his next (non-political) point. He appeared to be expressing a view on counsel's performance, indeed on the arguments of the state concerned, and this raised an issue of judicial propriety, and of independence, since independence assumes that the international judge will listen to all arguments put to him.

Appointment

A second issue concerns the appointment of international judges. There has been considerable attention given to the relationship between the independence of the judge and the manner of his or her appointment or election, and appointment and re-election. Although the appointment process of the international judges varies from body to body, the general approach is similar. The states involved in the appointment process are entitled to nominate a single candidate (an exception is the ECtHR, where the forty-one states involved put forward three candidates, who

[2] See, e.g., the Appeals Chamber of the ICTY in *Prosecutor* v. *Furundzija*, judgment, 21 July 2000, where the Chamber rejected as a ground of appeal the issue of refusal of Judge Mumba, the Presiding Judge in the appellant's trial, on the grounds that she was not impartial or gave the appearance of bias (on the issue of rape as genocide) and should have been disqualified pursuant to Rule 15 of the ICTY Rules because of her former involvement with the United Nations Commission on the Status of Women (UNCSW). See www.un.org/icty/furundzija/appeal/judgement/index.htm at paragraphs 164–214.

are then assessed and voted upon by the Parliamentary Assembly of the Council of Europe, and one is elected by the Parliamentary Assembly). That candidate is then subject to an election process. In the case of the ICJ, the fifteen judges are elected by the UN General Assembly and Security Council for a renewable term of nine years. No two judges can have the nationality of the same state and the entire bench is to represent the main forms of 'civilization' (as Article 9 of the Statute of the ICJ puts it) and the principal legal systems. In practice, the five permanent members of the UN Security Council always have a judge (United Kingdom, USA, France, Russia, China). This is an unwritten custom which may, in the eyes of some observers, raise issues about independence, although others take the view that it is nothing more than an appropriate mechanism to guarantee that the principal judicial organ of the United Nations remains broadly representative of political realities. The other ten judges comprise two from each of the five regional groupings in the UN system (Latin America and the Caribbean; Western European and others; Eastern Europe; Africa; Asia).

Elections to many international courts are highly politicized affairs. In the context of the ICJ, ITLOS, and the WTO Appellate Body, without the support of some of the more powerful states the electoral prospects for any candidate will be slim. The electoral process often involves meetings between the candidates and diplomatic representatives of members of the United Nations or other electing organization. The state proposing a candidate will use its clout to push the candidate (if it does not the candidate will be perceived not to have the support of the state and the candidacy will be in difficulty, as the recent re-election of one judge to the ICTY demonstrated). It is not unheard of for a President (of a permanent member) to lobby in support. I have received invitations from sitting international judges (on the bench of a tribunal before which I have appeared and was currently acting) asking whether I would be willing to make an 'introduction' to some of the states with which I had worked, in the context of a re-election process (I declined). Other international judges have told me how 'unseemly' they find the whole process, particularly since there is no independent assessment of the candidates' background or abilities. For judges who are standing for re-election it would be astonishing if the election process did not concentrate the mind on cases which are to be decided in the run-up to an election. This is the political context in which many international judges are elected and re-elected. It raises eyebrows. But is there any evidence that it leads to a more or less independent judge than, say, the electoral process for state judges in the USA, or that we should be unduly concerned about the consequences of the process?

Outside activities

A third aspect related to the independence of the international judiciary concerns the permissibility of 'outside activities'. At the national level – certainly in the USA and the United Kingdom – it is established that any person holding judicial office is barred from performing a range of outside activities, e.g., sitting on boards, holding university appointments, acting as arbitrator or judge elsewhere – and certainly from being remunerated for these kinds of activities.

Some international courts (ICTY, ICTR, ECJ, ECtHR) prohibit such activities almost entirely. But others are more flexible. In the case of the ITLOS, where judges are part-time, it is perhaps not inappropriate that some of the judges should continue to hold teaching positions, or might even consult in matters entirely unrelated to the law of the sea. ICJ judges are full-time, but the court appears to take a flexible attitude with regard to certain 'outside' activities. Some of the judges have accepted appointments to act as arbitrators, for example. The practice apparently began in the 1970s when the court was not very busy. Now that the court has a relatively full docket, the practice may still not raise concerns where the arbitral dispute is between two states, neither of which is involved in proceedings before the ICJ. But should – as has happened – an international judge be able to accept appointment as a party-appointed arbitrator (as opposed to appointment as the independent president of a tribunal) by a foreign investor involved in a commercial dispute with a state which may be involved in proceedings before that judge's court?

Relations between judicial organs and political organs

A fourth, and more classical, issue concerns the relationship between the judiciary, on the one hand, and the legislature and executive, on the other. This issue is not limited to the national context, and there exists a considerable literature concerning the proper relationship between the ICJ and the UN Security Council (in particular whether the ICJ may judicially review one or more decisions of the Security Council in the context of sanctions imposed against Libya following the Lockerbie incident). The issue is not limited to the ICJ.

Recently the WTO Appellate Body found itself in the following situation. The WTO rules are silent on the question of whether the Appellate Body may accept *amicus curiae* briefs from interested parties (e.g., NGOs, corporations). In a May 2000 decision, the WTO Appellate Body interpreted the silence of the rules as an indication that states had not intended to prohibit *amicus* briefs, and, in fact, held that it had the right to accept and consider *amicus* briefs.[3] In November 2000, to avoid the floodgates opening in a particular case, the Appellate Body adopted an Additional Procedure governing the conditions under which *amicus* briefs could be filed, and setting a deadline of 27 November 2000 for such briefs to be filed. The Additional Procedure was communicated to the Chairman of the WTO Dispute Settlement Body on 8 November 2000, described as a case-specific measure taken in the interests of fairness and an orderly procedure in the conduct of an appeal in the dispute concerning a ban on the importation into France of asbestos from Canada.[4] On 22 November 2000 an extraordinary meeting of the WTO General Council was held, during the course of which strong hostility was expressed towards the approach taken by the Appellate Body in its Additional Procedure.[5] The Appellate Body received applications from seventeen interested parties to file such briefs, of which only six came within the stated timetable. All seventeen applications were refused. The only reason given by the Appellate Body was that none of the applications had met the conditions set forth in the guidelines. One is bound to wonder whether the decision of the Appellate Body might have been influenced by the view of the General Council, the political organ of the WTO and, if so, what that implies for the independence of the judicial organ vis-à-vis the political organ. That said, it must be recognized that WTO rules remain in their early stages of development, and there may be something to be said for the Appellate Body moving cautiously in its interpretation and application of those rules, taking account of signals from the political organs.

[3] Appellate Body Report, *United States – Imposition of Countervailing Duties on Certain Hot-Rolled Lead and Bismuth Carbon Steel Products Originating in the United Kingdom*, WT/DS138/AB/R, 7 June 2000, paragraph 42.

[4] WT/DS135/9, 8 November 2000 (available at www.wto.org/english/news_e/news00_e/ds135_9.doc, visited on 3 May 2002).

[5] See minutes of the meeting, WT/GC/M/60, 23 January 2001, referred to in P. Mavroidis, 'Amicus Curiae Briefs before the WTO: Much Ado about Nothing' in A. von Bogdandy, P. Mavroidis, and G. Meny, *Festschrift für Claus-Dieter Ehlermann* (Kluwer, 2002) at n. 6 (also available at www.jeanmonnetprogram.org/papers/01/010201–02.html#P26_2553).

Conclusions

The issues raised in this contribution reflect some of the broader themes that international lawyers are faced with as they address the independence of their judiciary. There are other issues which will have to be addressed, including the very real problem of the impact on the independence of the international judiciary of the severe financial resource constraints which face many international organizations. For present purposes, it is sufficient to recall that the issue of the relationship between international judicial bodies and the international organizations, of which they form a part, is an important one, and that in the eyes of many, enhanced independence is ultimately closely connected with legitimacy and effectiveness.

23

'Straddling and Highly Migratory Flags' before the International Tribunal for the Law of the Sea

TULLIO TREVES

Flagging and reflagging in the cases before ITLOS

Reflagged vessels and vessels flying flags of convenience (two phenomena that most often coexist) are a frequent feature in cases brought before the International Tribunal for the Law of the Sea (ITLOS). Of all the cases decided by the ITLOS,[1] only two had nothing to do with this phenomenon: the *Southern Bluefin Tuna* cases and the *MOX Plant* case.[2] Only the former involves ships in some way, as it concerns fishing. The *Saiga* cases,[3] the *Camouco*, the *Monte Confurco*, the *Grand Prince*, and the *Volga* cases[4] all concern ships which had been reflagged one or more times; and all concern ships flying a flag belonging to a state that has modest connections with the ship. If we take the substantive criteria for ship registration used in the ill-fated United Nations Convention on the Registration of Ships of 7 February 1986,[5] namely that the flag state

'Straddling and Highly Migratory Flags' is an expression borrowed from the title of a Panel of a Law of the Sea Institute Symposium held at the University of California at Berkeley in 2003. Participation in that panel made the author start reflecting on the subject.

1 All judgments and orders, and the records of oral proceedings, as well as most of the written proceedings, are available at the ITLOS website: www.itlos.org. Judgments and Orders are published in ITLOS, Reports of Judgments, Advisory Opinions and Orders (ITLOS Reports) and most of them also in *International Legal Materials*.

2 Orders for provisional measures under Article 290, paragraph 5 of the United Nations Convention for the Law of the Sea (UNCLOS) respectively of 17 August 1999 and 3 December 2001.

3 Judgment, 4 December 1997 (*Saiga (No. 1)*, prompt release case) and judgment of 1 July 1999 (*Saiga (No. 2)*, merits case).

4 Judgments respectively of 7 February 2000, 18 December 2000, and of 23 December 2002.

5 (1987) 26 ILM 1229. UNCLOS has not reached the forty ratifications or accessions corresponding to 25 per cent of world tonnage needed under Article 19 for its entry into force. It has been ratified or acceded to only by eleven states, fourteen others have

or its nationals participate as owners or in the ownership of the ship, and that 'a satisfactory part of the complement consisting of officers and crew' be 'nationals or domiciled or lawfully in permanent residence' in the flag state,[6] we see that neither of them is satisfied in each of the above-mentioned five cases. Of course, the reference to these criteria is broad and general. It does not mean that under the Convention, which indicates the two criteria as alternative and not as cumulative and provides for exceptions and loopholes, the ships involved would not qualify for registration. It seems, nonetheless, interesting to consider the situation in the five cases in light of the broad criteria of national ownership and national manning:

(a) The *Saiga*: the flag state was (allegedly) Saint Vincent and the Grenadines. The owner was a company of Cyprus and was managed by a company in Scotland. The beneficial owners were not known. The complement of officers, including the master, and crew was mostly Ukrainian.[7] The ship had previously flown the flag of Malta.
(b) The *Camouco*: the flag state was Panama. The owner was a company of Panama, with Spanish companies as beneficial owners. The master and most of the crew were of Spanish nationality. The ship after its release was reflagged twice before its final forfeiture by the French authorities.[8]
(c) The *Monte Confurco*: the flag state was the Seychelles. Its owner was a company registered in the Seychelles. The beneficial owners were presumably Spanish. The master was Spanish and the crew of various countries.[9]

signed it: http://untreaty.un.org/bible/englishinternetbible/Part I/ChapterXII/treaty 16-asp, visited on 23 September 2003.

6 Articles 7 to 9 of the 1986 Convention.

7 Counsel for Saint Vincent and the Grenadines, Mr Howe, indicated that the vessel 'is registered under the flag of Saint Vincent and the Grenadines. The owner of the M/V *Saiga* is Tabona Shipping Co. Ltd and she is managed by Messrs Seascott Shipping Ltd who are based in Glasgow in Scotland. The vessel has a Ukrainian Master and the crew totalling 24 of Ukrainian and Senegalese nationality'. ITLOS PV/98/1, p. 25.

8 See the Affidavit by Geoffrey Rohan, Australian Statement of Response in the *Volga* case, pp. 71–2; and the pleadings of Mr Campbell and of Prof. Crawford, ITLOS PV/02/02, pp. 6 and 19.

9 Counsel for the Seychelles, Mr Gallardo, gave this description: 'We have a Seychelles vessel, we have an international crew, Spanish, Peruvians, Chileans, Mauritians and Namibians, belonging to a mixed, Spanish company established in the Republic of the Seychelles'. ITLOS PV/00/5/rev.1.

(d) The *Grand Prince*: the flag State was (allegedly) Belize. The owner was a company with its seat in Belize.[10] The beneficial owners were apparently Spanish.[11] The master had Spanish nationality. The crew was composed of Spaniards and Chileans.[12]
(e) The *Volga*: the flag state was the Russian Federation. The owner was a Russian company.[13] There were no satisfactory indications at to the nationality of the beneficial owners.[14] The master had Russian nationality. The chief mate, the fishing master, and the fishing pilot were of Spanish nationality, while the rest of the crew was composed mostly of Chinese and Indonesian nationals.

In the judgments concerning two of these cases (the *Saiga* and the *Grand Prince*) the question of the nationality of the ship was discussed thoroughly as its solution was decisive for the disposal of the case. Also, in the remaining three cases, the fact that the master and crew, as well as the beneficial owners, were not nationals of the flag state had some relevant impact. It is further to be noted that all these cases, with the exception of the *Saiga*, were 'prompt release' cases concerning fishing for toothfish in the Southern Ocean. It seems therefore useful to consider separately these four 'toothfish prompt release cases' and the two 'nationality of ship cases' (although, admittedly, the *Grand Prince* case belongs to both categories).

The 'toothfish prompt release' cases

The 'toothfish prompt release' cases follow a common pattern. Fishing vessels flying various flags and involving most often Spanish interest (as beneficial owners, as masters, as crew-members) engage in long-term fishing cruises in the waters of the Southern Ocean. Their base-port is in the southern hemisphere very far from the fishing grounds (Port Louis, Mauritius; Walwis Bay, Namibia, or Durban, South Africa, for instance).

10 See the Memorial of Belize, p. 4.
11 Judgment, paragraph 32. In particular, as to the beneficial owner of the vessel, it is indicated that: 'the Agent of the Applicant stated that the owners of the vessel were Paik Commercial Corporation [with its seat in Belize City] and the Agent of the Respondent stated that France was unaware of the actual owners of the vessel'.
12 Judgment, paragraph 34.
13 The Agent of the Russian Federation, Mr Dzubenko, stated that 'the ship is owned by Albers Company Limited, is registered in the Russian ship register and is entitled to fly the Russian flag'. ITLOS PV/02/01, p. 7.
14 Australia insisted on having particulars on the subject, but to no avail. See judgment, paragraph 75.

The wealth of fish – especially Patagonian toothfish – in the waste expanses of the Southern Ocean, combined with the relatively small chance of being caught while fishing in the economic zones of France (Kerguelen and Crozet islands) and Australia (Heard and McDonald Islands), are the main attractions for such expeditions. The financial stakes appear in a clear light if one considers that the value of a full cargo of Patagonian toothfish can equal or exceed the very value of the fishing vessel involved. This emerged clearly in the *Monte Confurco* case (value of the vessel accepted by the ITLOS, US$345,000, amount for which the cargo was sold, FF 9 million, approximately US$1.5 million)[15] and in the *Volga* case (uncontested value of the vessel, AUS$1.8 million, amount for which the catch was sold, approximately AUS$1.9 million).[16]

These fishing cruises are considered by concerned coastal states as prime examples of illegal, uncontrolled, undeclared fishing (IUUF), facilitated by frequent reflagging. France underlined this aspect in its pleadings in the *Monte Confurco* case. Its Agent observed:

> These facts are very serious but, beyond that, we have a more serious and broader problem of organised, illegal fishing that endangers the future of these fish resources ... Illegal fishing has indeed been structured in a perfectly well organised manner. There are powerful economic and financial interests involved, attracted by considerable profits from these activities. The vessels that carry out illegal fishing are supported by specialist lawyers, which one always finds in this kind of business, and very often they are the first to know about such incidents ...
>
> These vessels often change their names. They very often change their flags and are very often the property of so-called 'one ship companies'. This is a very useful formula by which to hide the identity of the true interests of the people for whom they are working and also to prevent proper action being taken against the people responsible. It is also a useful means by which to avoid the high fines that are being imposed on such small companies. These vessels are organised in a network. They communicate with each other, thanks to codes such as the one that we found on the *Monte Confurco*. It is true that they try to escape the surveillance of coastal states, but they are also ready to help each other and are extremely efficient at doing so.[17]

15 *Monte Confurco*, judgment, paragraphs 84 and 85.
16 *Volga*, judgment, paragraph 71.
17 *Trinquier*, ITLOS/PV 00/6/Rev.1, 7 December 2000, pm, pp. 5–6.

Similar remarks were made by the Agent of Australia in the *Volga* case:

> A fundamental fact of the present case is Australia's justified concern that, upon release, the *Volga* will resume its role, perhaps under a different flag, perhaps under a different name, in the plunder of the resources of the Southern Ocean ...
>
> One can see a cycle developing that is inimical to the proper management and conservation of the marine living resources of the Southern Ocean ...
>
> Australia's concerns are shared by other sovereign States with a stake in the conservation and management of the resources of the Southern Ocean.[18]

Fishing in the Southern Ocean (including the Australian EEZ of Heard and McDonald Islands, but excluding the French EEZ of Kerguelen and Crozet islands) is regulated by the Convention on the Conservation of Antarctic Marine Living Resources (CCAMLR).[19] An aspect adding to the concerns of the coastal states is that the states whose flags have been flown by the ships involved in the cases have not been parties to it. The exception is Russia, which, nonetheless, according to Australia, was not diligent in applying to the *Volga* the Convention's provisions.[20]

The coastal states parties to the cases here examined urged the ITLOS to take these aspects of the factual background of the cases into consideration in order to support the conclusion that the severe penalties imposable and the high bonds imposed were reasonable. This was put in a particularly clear manner by the New Zealand Diplomatic Note of 6 December 2002, to be found in the Annexes to the Australian Statement in Response in the *Volga* case:[21]

> In New Zealand's view, the Tribunal ought to be cognisant of the serious and growing problem of IUU fishing in these waters, a result of enforcement difficulties and the very high value of the fishery. These factors mean that the incentive for vessel owners and operators to engage in IUU fishing is significant. Similarly, high rewards are available to vessels released from detention upon the posting of a financial security following detention for suspected earlier IUU fishing. Coastal States, and States Parties to UNCLOS and regional fisheries management organizations, including CCAMLR, must take steps to compel and encourage better observance with the provision of these instruments. *It is clear that the Tribunal also has a role to play.*

18 *Campbell*, ITLOS/PV 02/ 02 12, 12 December 2002, pm, pp. 6–7.

19 Concluded at Canberra, 20 May 1980, (1980) 19 ILM 841.

20 See the observations by P. Weckel, 'Chronique de jurisprudence internationale' (2003). *Revue Générale de Droit International Public* 187.

21 At pp. 50–6 (emphasis added).

In the same vein, Professor Crawford, counsel for Australia in the same case, argued as follows:

> the Tribunal should at all times seek to act in aid of regional fisheries arrangements which are the only way, now and in the long term, of preserving the world's fish stocks ... The relevant regional fisheries organization here is that established by CCAMLR.[22]

The ITLOS was not insensitive to these appeals. Its response was, nevertheless, rather restrained. In the *Camouco* judgment the point was mentioned only in dissenting opinions.[23] In the *Monte Confurco* judgment, the ITLOS summarized the arguments concerning the 'general context of unlawful fishing in the region' and stated 'The Tribunal takes note of this argument'.[24]

In the *Volga* judgment, the ITLOS having, again, taken note of this argument, made a step forward in adding:

> The Tribunal understands the international concerns about illegal, unregulated and unreported fishing and appreciates the objectives behind the measures taken by States, including the States Parties to CCAMLR, to deal with the problem.[25]

The ITLOS did not consider it possible, however, to go beyond such 'taking note', 'understanding', and 'appreciating', even when challenged not to become 'an unwitting accomplice to criminal activity'.[26]

The reasons were made explicit in the *Volga* judgment. Immediately after taking note of the issue and expressing its understanding and appreciation of it, the ITLOS stated that:

> The Tribunal must, however, emphasize that, in the present proceedings, it is called upon to assess whether the bond set by the Respondent is reasonable in terms of article 292 of the Convention. The purpose of the procedure provided for in article 292 of the Convention is to secure the prompt release of the vessel and crew upon the posting of a reasonable bond, pending the completion of the judicial procedure before the courts of the detaining State.[27]

[22] ITLOS/PV 02/ 02, 12 December 2002, pm, p. 21.
[23] Judges Anderson and Wolfrum.
[24] *Monte Confurco*, judgment, paragraph 79. Judge Anderson in his dissenting opinion states that '[t]his "factual background" is relevant in balancing the respective interests of France and the applicant'.
[25] *Volga*, judgment, paragraph 68.
[26] Crawford, pleading for Australia in the *Volga* case, ITLOS/PV 02/02, p. 18.
[27] *Volga*, judgment, paragraph 69.

The constraints of the prompt release proceedings are at the basis of this explanation. They are that the specific purpose of Article 292 is to obtain release of vessels and crews detained in violation of a narrow group of rules of UNCLOS, and the consequential requirement not to prejudice the merits.

Reflagging and the use of flags of convenience would seem to be, among the elements of the factual background of the toothfish prompt release cases, those concerning which some limits to the use of prompt release proceedings might emerge. As is well known, in the *Grand Prince* case a request for prompt release of a vessel arrested in circumstances similar to those of the *Camouco* and the *Monte Confurco* was dismissed by the ITLOS for lack of jurisdiction. The Tribunal found that the nationality of Belize, on behalf of which the request of prompt release had been submitted, was not established satisfactorily, as the documentation gave inconsistent indications. This was possibly connected to the fact that, when apprehended, the *Grand Prince* was on its way to Brazil where it had already begun to seek reflagging. Whatever the merits of the conclusions of the ITLOS, and whatever other reasons might have been in the mind of the Tribunal, the attention paid *proprio motu* to the question of nationality, in order to ascertain its jurisdiction, seems to be a clear indication of an intention to consider, whenever legally possible, the 'background' of prompt release cases.

With the exception of the *Volga* case, all the toothfish prompt release cases were submitted to the ITLOS, as permitted by Article 292, paragraph 2, 'on behalf' of the flag state, and not directly by it. This possibility was introduced in UNCLOS Article 292 as a compromise between those who considered it preferable to give the private persons interested in the vessel *locus standi* in prompt release proceedings, and those who wished not to make an exception to the principle that disputes under UNCLOS (apart from those concerning the International Seabed Area) should be state-to-state disputes. In practice, Article 292 has resulted as an expedient tool for states that wish to avoid the responsibilities of actively protecting ships flying their flag through prompt release proceedings in Hamburg, while, at the same time, obtaining an equivalent result, and consequently enhancing their attractiveness as flag states, through the action of the private interested persons.

This has made crucial the authorization which private persons wishing to submit to the ITLOS an application for prompt release on behalf of a state are required to obtain from that state.

The Tribunal, in its dealings with prospective applicants, has made it clear that the authorization must come from members of the government entitled to represent the state in foreign relations, such as the Minister of Foreign Affairs or the Attorney-General. The ITLOS wishes to minimize the risk of proceeding on the basis of an application signed by an official who is later disowned by higher authorities, or whose authority is challenged in the proceedings.[28]

Flag states may assess the relative pros and cons of authorizing prompt release proceedings on their behalf, acting directly, or of taking neither course of action. Policy and bilateral relations considerations will be relevant. Also, diplomatic pressure from the state that has arrested the vessel and possibly pressure of public opinion and non-governmental organizations (NGOs) may play a part in the decision of the flag state. While diplomatic notes of France to the Seychelles aiming at discouraging it from bringing the *Monte Confurco* case to the ITLOS are on record, only rumours exist as regards NGO pressure or diplomatic considerations explaining why certain prompt release cases did not reach Hamburg. The desire to avoid such pressures might be part of the explanation of the decision of a big power, not generally known as a 'flag of convenience state', the Russian Federation, to submit directly to the Tribunal the *Volga* case, even though in fact its defence in the case was mostly conducted by the lawyers of the private company interested.

A further consequence of cases submitted 'on behalf' of a flag (of convenience) state is that the function of Agent is taken by the private lawyer representing the private interest in the ship. While the situation of a private lawyer acting as Agent of a state is not unprecedented before the International Court of Justice, the roles of Agent and counsel remain separate, even though raising some concerns.[29] In the 'on behalf' prompt release cases, Agent and counsel become one. This situation may raise doubts as to whether the Agent can always be considered as the representative of the state party and may create difficulties when questions requiring answers on matters of domestic law of the flag state arise. Ad hoc Judge Cot gave expression to the uneasiness raised by this situation in the ITLOS. He stated in his declaration to the *Grand Prince* judgment:

[28] Unfortunately, there is no published evidence of the indications given as to the policy of the ITLOS, which are based on the author's insider knowledge. The author believes that he does not betray anything confidential in giving expression to this policy which is already known to some parties to disputes before the Tribunal.

[29] Judge Oda, Declaration to the ICJ Order on Provisional Measures in the Case concerning Armed Activities on the Territory of the Congo (*Congo* v. *Uganda*) 1 July 2000, paragraph 8, (2000) 39 ILM 1100 at 1114.

The delegation of sovereignty by the flag State in appointing a lawyer as agent raises a different kind of problem. The dispute before the Tribunal remains an inter-State dispute. However, the lawyer-agent is not necessarily in close contact with the authorities of the flag State. The credibility and reliability of the information he provides as to the legal position of the flag State may be questionable. In the present case, the Tribunal had to be satisfied with incomplete and contradictory information concerning the registration of the vessel and the position of Belize as to the nationality of the *Grand Prince*.[30]

The 'nationality of ships' cases

The *Saiga (No. 2)* judgment of 1999 (the only judgment on the merits of a contentious case so far handed out by the ITLOS), and the already mentioned *Grand Prince* judgment of 2001, are the two instances in prompt release cases in which the Tribunal considered directly questions concerning the nationality of ships.

The *Saiga (No. 2)* case is particularly rich on this matter. I will briefly review three aspects which seem particularly significant.

First, the judgment of the ITLOS decided that the *Saiga* had retained Vincentian nationality, even though the validity of its certificate of registration had lapsed, by invoking in particular the practice of both parties to the dispute as well as the needs of justice in the case.[31] This seems to show that the ITLOS had in mind a distinction, that has been supported in scholarly works,[32] between nationality and proof of nationality, which makes it possible to substitute factual elements indicating nationality for the missing registration.

Secondly, the judgment states that:

> The purpose of the provisions of the Convention on the need for a genuine link between the ship and the flag State is to secure more effective implementation of the duties of the flag State, and not to establish criteria

[30] Declaration of Ad hoc Judge Cot, paragraph 14. See also J. P. Cot, 'Appearing "For" or "on Behalf of" a State: The Role of Private Counsel Before International Tribunals' in N. Ando, E. McWhinney, and R. Wolfrum (eds.), *Liber Amicorum Shigeru Oda* (The Hague, 2002), pp. 835–47.

[31] *Saiga (No. 2)*, judgment, paragraph 73.

[32] Recently, with references, Schiano di Pepe, 'La questione della nazionalità delle navi dinanzi al Tribunale per il diritto del mare' (2002) 85 *Rivista di diritto internazionale* 329 at 336, 341–4.

by reference to which the validity of the registration of ships in a flag State may be challenged by other States.[33]

This statement, while far from being 'politically correct',[34] is supported, in the view of the Tribunal, by the evolution of the 'genuine link' provision from its formulation in the Geneva High Seas Convention to that set out in the 1982 UN Convention on Conditions for Registration of Ships, and by subsequent practice. Such practice includes the inability of the 1986 UN Convention to enter into force and the weakness of its contents, and, especially, the fact that the recent Straddling Stocks Agreement of 1995[35] and the FAO Agreement to Promote Compliance with International Conservation and Management Measures by Fishing Vessels on the High Seas (Compliance Agreement) of 1993,[36] 'set out . . . detailed obligations to be discharged by the flag States of fishing vessels but do not deal with the conditions to be satisfied for the registration of fishing vessels'.[37]

It seems significant to add that negotiations leading to the above-mentioned 1993 FAO Compliance Agreement had started as concerning 'the flagging of vessels fishing on the high seas to promote compliance with internationally agreed conservation and management measures'. This shift of the focus of the states negotiating the agreement from 'flagging' to the consequences of flagging had been the main cause of a dispute which the European Court of Justice had decided in 1996.[38] Its significance for the concept and function of the 'genuine link' did not escape the attention of the ITLOS, even though it chose to refer to it with the rather elliptic sentence just quoted.

[33] *Saiga (No. 2)*, judgment, paragraph 83.

[34] See M. Kamto, 'La nationalité des navires en droit international' in *La Mer et son Droit, Mélanges offertes à Laurent Lucchini et Jean-Pierre Quéneudec*, (Paris, 2003), pp. 343–73 at p. 353. The view set out in the judgment of the ITLOS is approved by A. Oude Elferink, 'The Genuine Link Concept: Time for a Post Mortem?' in Ige F. Dekker and H. G. Post, *On the Foundations and Sources of International Law* (The Hague, 2003), pp. 41–63, esp. 56–7, 61–3; and by A. Soons, 'Comment' in *ibid.* at pp. 65–71.

[35] Agreement for the Implementation of the Provisions of the United Nations Convention on the Law of the Sea of 10 December 1982 relating to the Conservation and Management of Straddling Fish Stocks and Highly Migratory Fish Stocks, New York, 4 December 1995, (1995) 34 ILM 1542.

[36] Rome, 24 November 1993, in United Nations Food and Agriculture Organization, *International Fisheries, Instruments with Index* (New York, 1998), p. 41.

[37] *Saiga (No.2)* judgment, paragraph 85.

[38] Judgment of 19 March 1996, C-25/95 *Commission of the EC* v. *Council of the EU* [1996 ECR 329]. See T. Treves, 'The European Community and the Law of the Sea Convention: New Developments' in E. Cannizzaro (ed.), *The European Union as an Actor in International Relations* (The Hague, 2002), pp. 279–96 at p. 287.

Thirdly, the judgment provides an interesting clarification as to the scope of the nationality of ships from the perspective of nationality of claims for the purposes of diplomatic protection. In discussing whether the flag state could make claims for violations allegedly committed by Guinea to the detriment of persons connected to the *Saiga* (crew members, ship owners, owners of the cargo) which were not of Vincentian nationality, the ITLOS referred to various articles of the Convention (namely, Articles 94, 106, 110, 217, and 292) to support its conclusion that:

> the Convention considers a ship as a unit, as regards the obligations of the flag State with respect to the ship and the right of a flag State to seek reparation for loss or damage caused to the ship by acts of other States and to institute proceedings under article 292 of the Convention. Thus the ship, every thing on it, and every person involved or interested in its operations are treated as an entity linked to the flag State. The nationalities of these persons are not relevant.[39]

This conclusion was strengthened by referring to

> two basic characteristics of modern maritime transport: the transient and multinational composition of ships' crews and the multiplicity of interests that may be involved in the cargo on board a single ship. A container vessel carries a large number of containers, and the persons with interests in them may be of many different nationalities. This may also be true in relation to cargo on board a break-bulk carrier. Any of these ships could have a crew comprising persons of several nationalities. If each person sustaining damage were obliged to look for protection from the State of which such person is a national, undue hardship would ensue.[40]

As regards the *Grand Prince* judgment, commentators (and dissenting judges)[41] have identified some inconsistency between the approach that led the ITLOS in that case to conclude that the ship had lost the nationality of Belize, and the approach followed in the 1999 judgment, which led the Tribunal to conclude that the *Saiga* had maintained Vincentian nationality. I do not wish to state a view as to whether this inconsistency is real or apparent.[42] Considerations of justice in the specific case (explicitly mentioned in the *Saiga (No. 2)* judgment) may have been relevant, also in light of the above-mentioned 'background' of

[39] *Saiga (No. 2)*, judgment, paragraph 106. [40] *Saiga (No. 2)*, judgment, paragraph 107.

[41] Dissenting opinion of Judges Caminos, Marotta Rangel, Yankov, Yamamoto, Akl, Vukas, Marsit, Eiriksson, and Jesus, paragraph 11.

[42] See the balanced observations by di Pepe, 'La questione della nazionalità', 349.

frequent reflagging which the ITLOS has learned to recognize, as mentioned above, as a constant feature of the toothfish prompt release cases.

A further relevant aspect of the *Grand Prince* judgment is that the ITLOS had to deal with the possibility, afforded by the law of Belize to its authorities, to cancel registration of a ship as a punitive measure for violations of the conditions set out in the fishing licence. While this was a background element to the alleged loss of nationality of the vessel, its wisdom is not discussed in the judgment. It did not, however, escape the attention of judges. Judge Wolfrum on one side, and the seven dissenting judges, on the other, stated directly opposing views. Judge Wolfrum stated:

> I would like to highlight the newly introduced provision in the legislation of Belize that permits the Belizean authorities to de-register a vessel for violations of international conventions and agreements. I consider this to be a commendable approach which in an innovative manner strengthens the role of the flag State with the view to a more effective protection of national and international fishery resources or of the marine environment. It is for Belize to ensure that the respective decisions are not taken in an arbitrary manner and that the ship owners may have recourse to a procedure in which they can defend their rights.[43]

According to the seven dissenting judges:

> The decision of the Tribunal has the effect, perhaps unintended, when depriving Belize of its rights as a flag State, albeit for the limited purposes of actions under article 292 of the Convention, also of condoning a system under which a flag State can in certain circumstances absolve itself of its duties as a flag State, including those laid down in article 94 of the Convention. It will be recalled that, under article 94, paragraph 1, every State must effectively exercise its jurisdiction and control in administrative, technical and social matters over ships flying its flag. It certainly cannot suffice for a flag State to seek to comply with this obligation merely by revoking, without more, the registration of ships flying its flag.[44]

Conclusions

Nationality of ships remains an axis of the law of the sea. Interstate relations concerning activities at sea depend on it. It remains a well-defended

[43] Judge Wolfrum's Declaration, paragraph 5.

[44] Dissenting opinion of Judges Caminos, Marotta Rangel, Yankov, Yamamoto, Akl, Vukas, Marsit, Eiriksson, and Jesus, paragraph 16.

preserve of the sovereignty of states. Attempts at conditioning the sovereign right to fix the conditions for the granting of nationality to ships have not been very successful. The needs underlying these attempts have, however, obtained the effect of extending, in geographical and substantive terms, the powers of coastal states to the detriment of the flag states, and of making the consequences of granting nationality to a ship more precise in terms of duties and responsibilities of the flag state. The cases brought before the ITLOS seem to reflect this situation rather accurately.

24

Collective Security and the Personalization of Peace

CHARLOTTE KU

Contemporary international political and legal environment

Although I have long admired the work of Justice Florentino Feliciano, I have met him only once. The meeting was, however, memorable because it provided a rare occasion where my professional and family lives crossed. As Justice Feliciano and I walked together after dinner in Annecy, in France on a beautiful summer evening in 1990, we discovered a common admiration, affection, and respect for Anita Magsaysay Ho, the distinguished Filipina painter who is also my aunt. We recalled my aunt's deep love for the Philippines and her strong portrayals of Filipina women at work. Therefore, by honouring Justice Feliciano, I hope to honour, in a small way, the beautiful land that he served and that I came to know through my aunt's eyes.

Flashed across the front pages of newspapers and magazines across the world, the image of a man dressed in a white shirt and black trousers facing down a tank on one of the main avenues of Beijing during the Chinese government's crackdown of the pro-democracy movement in June 1989 is one of the more memorable photos of that dramatic event. However, the photo also represents the convergence of several world-wide 'patterns of conduct'[1] that emerged from the twentieth century with important implications for the international system of the twenty-first century. These include the personalization and internationalization of activities previously thought to be exclusively within the purview of states. Louis Henkin described the convergence of these phenomena:

> State autonomy remains a powerful value, but the distinction between state and human values continues to converge. The right of a state 'to be

[1] Hendrik Spruyt, *The Sovereign State and its Competitor: An Analysis of Systems Change* (Princeton University Press, 1994), p. 189.

> let alone' subsumes the rights of its inhabitants to be let alone, to maintain their traditions and culture, as well as their ways of life.[2]

What this particular quotation does not include is that the 'rights of its inhabitants to be let alone', has now become a matter of international concern and interest.

The result is that in contemporary international political and legal relations, individuals have now moved to the centre stage long occupied by states alone. It matters little that states themselves took the steps that produced this transformation. It is, however, significant that this change is here to stay, and that to influence the course of international relations today means to take into account multiple layers of authority, politics (interests), and law. These layers include those at the state, outside-the-state, and substate levels. Outside the state, we find regional and international organizations created by states to fulfil certain functions. At the substate level, we find the elements of civil society – non-governmental organizations, private enterprise, and the individual.

As an indicator of state behaviour, a survey of the nearly 6,000 multilateral treaties concluded since 1648 illustrates this development. Of eighty-six treaties concluded by states between 1648 and 1750, eighty-five dealt with political and military issues. The one non-political/military treaty addressed commerce and navigation rights in France and was concluded in 1691. The next multilateral treaty to address a non-political/military subject did not appear until 1815 and dealt with navigation of the Rhine River. From 1850 to 1995, both the number of treaties and the number of subject areas covered by treaties mushroomed. It is worth noting, however, that despite the growth in subject areas covered by multilateral treaties after 1850, the number covering political and military areas continued to grow, and accounted for 20 to 50 per cent of all multilateral treaty activity from 1850 to 1995.[3]

The economic area is the next most prominent category of multilateral treaty activity, accounting for nearly 40 per cent of such activity between 1850 and 1995. What is perhaps noteworthy is the 10 per cent or less number of multilateral treaties under the heading of human welfare, a figure that includes the human rights conventions. Given the important role these treaties have played in changing the nature and character

[2] Louis Henkin, 'Politics, Values and Functions at the Turn of the Century' in *International Law: Politics and Values* (Martinus Nijhoff Publishers, Dordrecht, 1995), p. 284.

[3] See Charlotte Ku, *Global Governance and the Changing Face of International Law* (ACUNS Reports and Papers, 2001), pp. 2–5.

of international relations, it shows that quantity of treaties and their relative impact are not necessarily related.

International trade was the area where the simultaneous importance of multiple private, national, and international layers was first developed, and most prominently recognized. Since the mercantilist aspirations of the great European state trading companies like the Dutch and British East India Companies gave way to free enterprise, states have promoted the private interests of their entrepreneurs in international competition. The inability of the interwar trading environment to support productive enterprise due to high national tariff barriers and ruinous exchange rates caused post-Second World War planners to focus during the war on creating the conditions that would provide for a stable trading environment, but not stifle free enterprise. The institutions that emerged from these plans adopted at Bretton Woods, New Hampshire, were the International Monetary Fund and the World Bank. The International Trade Organization foundered, but gave way to the General Agreement on Tariffs and Trade that developed into the World Trade Organization in 1995.

The issues faced by these financial institutions and the methods they adopted to deal with them created an intergovernmental institutional structure within which private actors could act. This can be found in the dispute settlement mechanisms developed by these institutions – the WTO Dispute Settlement Understanding and the International Centre for the Settlement of Investment Disputes. Ronald Brand observed that:

> The twentieth century has seen new recognition of the direct application of international law to relationships between individuals and states. The law of economic relations is one area in which international law (traditionally considered only applicable between and among 'sovereign' states) has grown to encompass rules that provide rights for individuals in their relationships with states.[4]

And these dispute settlement mechanisms have not only provided a means to address the treatment of private party interests by states, but have also over time allowed for the direct participation of private parties in the negotiation and representation of their own interests. Brand continued:

[4] Ronald A. Brand, 'Sovereignty: The State, the Individual, and the International Legal System in the Twenty First Century' (2002) 25 *Hastings International and Comparative Law Review* 290.

> The twentieth century witnessed the return of the merchant to a significant role in determining the rules applicable to commercial conduct. National codes have been accompanied by rules established directly by merchant groups, and ultimately by the movement to treaties through which the rules once again become truly international in nature and context. In the process, 'international law' rules are developed specifically for the purpose of measuring the conduct of private parties . . . Thus, private parties participate in the creation and become the subjects of international legal rules.[5]

Significant as this development would be by itself, the effect has been even more profound, considering other factors also present. These include the emergence of the norms and institutional structures of human rights, intensified transborder activities described generally as globalization, the power which communications technology has placed in the hands of individuals, and the increasing prominence of individuals and groups of individuals in international activities.

But where does this leave the state in today's international system? In his study of structural change, Hendrik Spruyt examined the 'long historical process' that led to the system of sovereign states. His study concluded with some scenarios for contemporary change. One such scenario is described as self-help, where 'there will be relatively little change in the nature of formal political institutions but considerable change in how social actors order international transactions themselves'.[6] As Spruyt reminds us, the important question when examining systems change is to understand 'that the *character* of the units in the system creates patterns of conduct'.[7] The patterns of conduct that we can observe in the security arena and their implications are the focus of this chapter.

Individuals and non-states as factors in international security

Although the issues of terrorism have been on the world's agenda since 1963 with the conclusion of the Tokyo Convention on Offences and Certain Other Acts Committed on Board Aircraft, the scope and

[5] Brand, 'Sovereignty: The State, the Individual', 293. Contrast this with the observation made by Donald McRae in Thomas J. Schoenbaum, Junji Nakagawa, and Linda C. Reif (eds.), *Trilateral Perspectives on International Legal Issues: From Theory into Practice* (Transnational Publishers, Ardsley, 1998) as reviewed by Charlotte Ku, (2000) 94(2) *American Journal of International Law* 443.

[6] Spruyt, *The Sovereign State*, p. 189. [7] *Ibid.* at p. 193.

potential of terrorism as a threat to the international system after 11 September 2001 have heightened international concern. President George W. Bush described this new security environment in his commencement address to the 200th graduating class of the US Military Academy at West Point:

> The gravest danger to freedom lies at the crossroads of radicalism and technology. When the spread of chemical and biological and nuclear weapons along with ballistic missile technology – when that occurs, even weak states and small groups could attain a catastrophic power to strike great nations.[8]

What the President was describing were the security needs of a globalized world. As Joseph Nye put it, '[g]lobalization . . . has proved itself to be more than just an economic phenomenon'.[9] The globalized world is one that encourages the free movement of goods and people, with unprecedented numbers of people directly linked to each other through technology. It is also a world with shifting political arrangements among individual states, states that pool their sovereignty (as do members of the European Union), regional arrangements, and international organizations. These political entities are further supported and complemented by a growing private sector of non-governmental organizations, including private foundations, think tanks, and aid organizations. Individuals within these groups further interact across borders in transnational networks that exert influence through their ability to coordinate actions in a particular area.[10]

What terrorism and the attacks on the USA of 11 September 2001 highlight is the extent to which globalization can also serve the causes of violence and destruction. President Bush recognized that the security requirements of the future had changed now, to include dealing with 'shadowy terrorist networks with no nations or citizens to defend'.[11] But, as with so many presidents before him, President Bush did not stop

[8] As quoted in *The National Security Strategy of the United States of America* (September 2002), p. 13.

[9] Joseph S. Nye, Jr., 'U.S. Power and Strategy After Iraq' (2003) *Foreign Affairs* (July/August) 62.

[10] See Anne-Marie Slaughter, 'Governing Through Government Networks' in Michael Byers (ed.), *The Role of Law in International Politics* (Oxford University Press, 2000), pp. 177–205.

[11] George W. Bush, Commencement Address at the US Military Academy at West Point, 1 June 2002.

at identifying the threat, he went on to outline a vision of the world after the present conflict:

> And finally, America stands for more than the absence of war. We have a great opportunity to extend a just peace by replacing poverty, repression and resentment around the world with hope of a better day ... The 20th century ended with a single surviving model of human progress based on nonnegotiable demands of human dignity, the rule of law, limits on the power of the state, respect for women and private property, and free speech, and equal justice and religious tolerance.[12]

Although globalization emphasizes the transnational activities of individuals, post-conflict international attention to the status and wellbeing of individuals is not altogether new. More than eighty years ago, when Woodrow Wilson outlined American war aims on entering the First World War, he proposed a concert of peace in his Fourteen Points Speech in January 1918. Point XIV provided that: 'A general association of nations must be formed under specific covenants for the purposes of affording mutual guarantees of political independence and territorial integrity to great and small states alike'.[13] At the same time, Point V introduced the notion that the 'interests of the populations concerned must have equal weight with the equitable claims of the government'. However, true to the times, these interests remained those of states to be advanced by and through governments.[14]

Concerned that Article 10 of the League of Nations Covenant, which called on League members 'to respect and preserve as against external aggression the territorial integrity and existing political independence of all Members of the League' would tie the USA to commitments that would not be in its national interest, the USA did not join the League. Whether American absence doomed the League security system to failure or not, the League's inability to respond to the security challenges that faced it throughout the 1930s failed to provide the security that states sought from it. This failure made retaining the League impossible, and early in the post-Second World War planning process, it was decided that a new international organization would be created.[15]

[12] *Ibid.*
[13] Woodrow Wilson, Fourteen Points Speech, 8 January 1918, see http://isinfo.state.gov/usa/infousa/democrac/51.htm at p. 3.
[14] *Ibid.*
[15] See Townsend Hoopes and Douglas Brinkley, *FDR and the Creation of the UN* (Yale University Press, 1997).

The USA considered what the world would look like after the war even before it became a belligerent in the Second World War. On 6 January 1941, President Franklin D. Roosevelt offered an alternative to the Fascist objectives of the Axis powers, and closed his address to Congress by saying that: 'We look forward to a world founded upon four essential human freedoms':[16]

- freedom of speech and expression;
- freedom of every person to worship God in his own way;
- freedom from want; and
- freedom from fear.

The post-Second World War system of international organizations embraced these four freedoms both in rhetoric and in institutional structure. The Preamble to the United Nations Charter states:

> We the peoples of the United Nations, determined to save succeeding generations from the scourge of war, which twice in our life-time has brought untold sorrow to mankind, and to reaffirm faith in fundamental human rights, in the dignity and worth of the human person, in equal rights of men and women and of nations large and small, and to establish conditions under which justice and respect for the obligations arising from treaties and other sources of international law can be maintained, and to promote social progress and better standards of life in larger freedom, and for these ends, to practice tolerance and live together in peace with one another as good neighbors, and to unite our strength to maintain peace and security, and to ensure, by the acceptance of principles and the institution of methods, that armed force shall not be used, save in the common interest, and to employ international machinery for the promotion of the economic and social advancement of all peoples, have resolved to combine our efforts to accomplish these aims.

To achieve these ends, the United Nations was organized into six principal organs: the General Assembly, Security Council, Economic and Social Council, Trusteeship Council, International Court of Justice, and Secretariat. The UN Charter also recognized the importance of individual wellbeing to the security system it was establishing when, in Article 55, it stated that:

[16] F. D. Roosevelt, 'Four Freedoms Speech', 6 January 1941, see http://wiretap.area.com/gopher/gov/US-history at p. 4.

> With a view to the creation of conditions of stability and well-being which are necessary for peaceful and friendly relations among nations based on respect for the principle of equal rights and self-determination of peoples, the United Nations shall promote:
>
> a) higher standards of living, full employment, and conditions of economic and social progress and development;
> b) solutions of international economic, social, health, and related problems; and international cultural and educational co-operation; and
> c) universal respect for, and observance of, human rights and fundamental freedoms for all without distinction as to race, sex, language, or religion.

The UN specialized agencies were established and directed to develop and work towards the 'purposes of Article 55'.

But notable in this structure was also the clear separation between the organs charged with security (the UN Security Council) and those charged with the stability and wellbeing of individuals (the Economic and Social Council, the Trusteeship Council, and the specialized agencies). Under the provisions of Article 10, the General Assembly 'may discuss any questions or any matters within the scope of the present Charter', except for issues dealt with by the Security Council. The General Assembly was to refrain from acting on matters before the Security Council unless the Security Council requested it to do so, or the procedures of the Uniting for Peace Resolution were activated once the Security Council became deadlocked because of the threat of a veto by one of its Permanent Members.[17] So, although the importance of the wellbeing of individuals was recognized in the UN structure, human welfare was regarded as an issue separate from issues of state security.

The UN security system reflected a certain hierarchy that started with ensuring the security of member states. States, in turn, would be relied on to ensure the safety and wellbeing of the people in their territories. Taken collectively, these actions would provide for global stability. It was a state-centred vision of world order. It is difficult to know whether this would have worked or not, since the UN security system was blocked from functioning fully by the rivalry of the Cold War. Labouring under the threat of a veto, the UN Security Council avoided areas of specific interest to either of the superpowers. What we do know is that, although many expected the UN security system to operate as its founders had envisaged once the Cold War ended, by the time the Soviet

[17] UN General Assembly Resolution 377 (1950).

Union collapsed in 1991, the world had changed to an extent that this became impossible.

In fact, the end of the Cold War marked another turning point in the world's understanding of security, with conflicts erupting over intrastate issues and in response to deliberate government policies of extermination and displacement of portions of their populations. These conscience-shocking events forced a re-examination of the obligations of non-interference in the domestic affairs of states and the formulation of standards to address instances where international action needs to be taken against an unfolding atrocity. But even before the end of the Cold War, the United Nations, through UN Secretary-General Javier Perez de Cuellar, had already recognized the need for a broad and multidimensional strategy for conflict prevention, and described it in 1982 as one to include 'peace and security, development, human rights and humanitarian affairs'.[18]

This move towards including human rights and humanitarian concerns in the security agenda was further developed after the end of the Cold War, following the historic 1992 Security Council summit where then UN Secretary-General Boutros-Boutros Ghali was asked to prepare a report on the prevention of conflicts. His 1992 Agenda for Peace explicitly made the connection between human rights and conflict prevention:

> The sources of conflict and war are pervasive and deep. To reach them will require our utmost effort to enhance respect for human rights and fundamental freedoms, to promote sustainable economic and social development for wider prosperity, to alleviate distress and to curtail the existence and use of massively destructive weapons.[19]

In and of itself, this was an unexpected conclusion for a UN Charter system that in 1945 had defined breach and threat to the peace as the violation of the territorial integrity and political independence of a member state.[20] If we consider the nature of the conflicts the United Nations and NATO have addressed between 1946 and 2003, this conclusion seems less surprising. Of the seventy-seven operations authorized by the United Nations and NATO between 1946 and 2003,

[18] Bertrand G. Ramcharan, *The Security Council and the Protection of Human Rights* (Martinus Nijhoff Publishers, The Hague, 2002), p. 63.
[19] A/47/277-S/24111, paragraph 5 as quoted in Ramcharan, *The Security Council*, p. 65.
[20] UN Charter, Article 1, paragraph 4.

sixty-two, or 80 per cent, were intrastate.[21] Not only were intrastate conflicts prevalent, they were often accompanied by massive violations of human rights and genocide. The difficulty of dealing with conflicts stemming from a gross violation of human rights was brought to a head in 1994, when the international community failed to respond to the massacre occurring in Rwanda. This prompted UN Secretary-General Kofi Annan to ask:

> if humanitarian intervention is, indeed, an unacceptable assault on sovereignty, how should we respond to a Rwanda, to a Srebrenica – to gross and systematic violations of human rights that affect every precept of our common humanity?[22]

One answer came from the International Commission on Intervention and State Sovereignty (ICISS) through its concept of 'the Responsibility to Protect'. The ICISS defined the Responsibility to Protect as 'the idea that sovereign states have a responsibility to protect their own citizens from avoidable catastrophe – from mass murder and rape, from starvation – but that when they are unwilling or unable to do so, that responsibility must be borne by the broader community of states'.[23]

On 12 September 2001, the UN Security Council took another step in expanding the scope of security when it adopted Resolution 1368, recognizing the inherent right of individual or collective self-defence against the terrorist acts that took place in New York and Washington, DC. By doing so, the UN Security Council expanded its understanding of security and self-defence to include acts committed against member states and their citizens by non-state actors – the first time in its history against an act of terrorism. The Security Council moved again to expand its definition of security when it passed Resolution 1373 on 28 September 2001. Resolution 1373 called on member states, under Chapter VII of the UN Charter, to take specific measures to 'refrain from organizing, instigating, assisting or participating in terrorist acts in another State or acquiescing in organized activities within its territory directed towards the commission of such acts'.[24] Recalling Hendrik Spruyt's conclusion that changes to the international system are the product of historic

[21] See Charlotte Ku and Harold K. Jacobson, *Democratic Accountability and the Use of Force in International Law* (Cambridge University Press, 2003).
[22] Report of the International Commission on Intervention and State Sovereignty, *The Responsibility to Protect* (December 2001), p. vii.
[23] *Ibid.* at p. viii. [24] UN Security Council Resolution 1373 (28 September 2001).

processes and patterns of conduct, a review of Security Council practice shows that this move towards acknowledging an expanded concept of security to include human rights had been in the works since sanctions were voted by the UN Security Council in the 1960s and 1970s against Southern Rhodesia and South Africa for their violations of human rights through the practice of apartheid.[25]

The new security environment and the personalized dimension of peace

Since the end of the Cold War, the international community has struggled to act in the face of menace and brutality by governments against their own populations. As the international community has faced these crises, it has come to realize that it is not enough to recognize that gross violations of human rights are threats to international peace and security, and to express outrage. Such gross violations compel collective action. Again responding to a plea by the UN Secretary-General to 'put people at the centre of everything we do',[26] the Commission on Human Security, spearheaded by the government of Japan and headed by former UN High Commissioner for Refugees, Sadako Ogata, and Nobel Laureate Amartya Sen, described this changed environment:

> The international community urgently needs a new paradigm of security. Why? Because the security debate has changed dramatically since the inception of state security advocated in the 17th century. According to that traditional idea, the state would monopolize the rights and means to protect its citizens. State power and state security would be established and expanded to sustain order and peace. But in the 21st century, both the challenges to security and its protectors have become more complex. The state remains the fundamental purveyor of security. Yet it often fails to fulfill its security obligations – and at times has become a source of threat to its own people. That is why attention must now shift from the security of the state to the security of the people – to human security.[27]

[25] See UNSC 2332 (1966) and UNSC 418 (1977).

[26] Kofi A. Annan, *We the Peoples: The Role of the United Nations in the 21st Century* (United Nations, New York, 2000), p. 7.

[27] Commission on Human Security, *Human Security Now* (New York, 2003), p. 6 (available at www.humansecurity-chs.org/).

This appeal for a new paradigm echoes President George W. Bush's assessment that: 'With the collapse of the Soviet Union and the end of the Cold War, our security environment has undergone profound transformation'.[28] And most recently, Javier Solana, the European Union's High Representative for the Common Foreign and Security Policy, noted that:

> Bad governance is often at the heart of these problems. Corruption, abuse of power, weak institutions and lack of accountability corrode states from within and contribute to regional insecurity. Security is a precondition of development. Conflict not only destroys infrastructure, including social infrastructure; it also encourages criminality, deters investment and makes normal economic activity impossible. A number of countries and regions risk becoming caught in a downward spiral of conflict, insecurity and poverty.[29]

This expanded view of the foundations of security is also present in the US National Security Strategy:

> A strong world economy enhances our national security by advancing prosperity and freedom in the rest of the world. Economic growth supported by free trade and free markets creates new jobs and higher incomes. It allows people to lift their lives out of poverty, spurs economic and legal reform, and the fight against corruption, and it reinforces the habits of liberty.[30]

Prior to the late twentieth century, the nexus between individuals and the international system was the state. The system acknowledged that governments had a monopoly of coercive power internally, with the understanding that they would provide security for individuals and that this monopoly of power would not be abused. When states concluded that the use of force was to be subjected to international scrutiny and authorization through the United Nations, there was an explicit assumption that Chapter VII would not be used abusively against any individual state. This assumption seemed immutable until states, working through the institutions they had created – the United Nations, the North Atlantic Treaty Organization, and other regional organizations – concluded that they would respond to gross violations of human rights

[28] *National Security Strategy of the United States of America* (September 2002), p. 13.

[29] Javier Solana, EU High Representative for the Common Foreign and Security Policy, *A Secure Europe in a Better World* (20 June 2003), p. 3.

[30] *National Security Strategy of the United States of America* (September 2002), p. 17.

even where it would intrude on the internal actions of a state. When this occurred, the globalized security realm pierced the veil of the sovereign state, and joined the economic and human rights areas that had pioneered a role and status for individuals and non-state actors in their respective international frameworks. As the Commission on Human Security noted, this focus on individuals now includes the post-conflict and state-building phases of peace-making.

Since wars are fought to stop gross violations of human rights, international concern has extended to the forging of long-term peace. But as the work in Cambodia, Kosovo, East Timor, and Afghanistan demonstrates, to do so requires the personalization of the peace to address the needs of individuals within states. The wars of the late twentieth and the early twenty-first centuries have revealed the continuing importance of one of the purposes of international law – to provide for the 'peace and harmony of nations'.[31] This is attained today, not only by regulating war and peace, but also through trade, human rights, and protection of the environment. Indeed, it is becoming clear that because the peace and harmony of nations remain central to world order, maintenance of this peace and harmony must reach beyond the security of states to the security and wellbeing of individuals. Where a state is unable to provide this for its own citizens, or intentionally declines to do so, the international community has discovered the cost of the violence that can result. The citizens of other states frequently also pay a price in losing a measure of their own security in the wake of such violence, as occurred in France following the independence of Algeria, in the refugee flows that came from the break-up of the former Yugoslavia, and in the USA following 11 September 2001.

This new realm of international security joins the established practice of states to defend and protect their own people in the face of danger or threat. However, as the debate leading up to the 2003 American-led war in Iraq demonstrated,[32] the internationalization of war has made it difficult even for the world's militarily most powerful state to provide such protection on its own. If the international community is unable (or unwilling) to take the necessary steps to stabilize the situation in a particular trouble spot, it might consider what its role and responsibility

[31] Philippe Sands, 'Turtles and Torturers: The Transformation of International Law' (2001) 33 *New York University Journal of International Law and Politics* 559.

[32] See, e.g., the range of views expressed in 'Agora: Future Implications of the Iraq Conflict' (2003) 97 *American Journal of International Law* 553.

needs to be following a conflict. Given the common interest to prevent a recurrence of violence, the international community may now need to understand and to develop the collective means to provide for the long-term wellbeing of individuals as a foundation for durable peace. As the twentieth century worked to develop a collective interest in stemming war, the twenty-first century will have to work beyond avoiding war to developing a collective interest in maintaining peace.

25

Some Thoughts on 'Asian' Approaches to International Dispute Resolution

M. C. W. PINTO

Toy Feliciano and I met for the first time nearly forty years ago, when he came to Washington as legal counsel to a Philippine delegation negotiating with the World Bank. A brilliant academic and professional career saw him rise to the highest level of his country's judiciary, and eventually grace the international judicial system in the field of trade law. He moves with ease between the often separate worlds of domestic and public international law, bringing to bear in each of them the same rigorous standards of legal scholarship and integrity, uniquely benefiting both.

Introduction

A recent work on dispute resolution in Asia opens with the question: 'Is there an "Asian" style of dispute resolution?', recalling in this context references to 'Asian values' and to 'the Asian way' of doing business. After a careful review of their material, the authors incline to a response in the negative:

> It is very difficult to identify any common cultural and legal norms or sources or positive law that are shared from the former Soviet Far East to Sulawesi. We cannot point to unifying systemic characteristics of law in Asia today because there is no organic relationship linking the cultural and legal histories of all the countries loosely identified as 'Asia'.[1]

They later conclude:

> Local legal, commercial and political culture and economic endowments cannot be reduced to core components that will remain static and polarized. Understanding the profile of individual Asian legal systems at a

[1] V. Taylor and M. Pryles, 'The Cultures of Dispute Resolution in Asia' in M. Pryles (ed.), *Dispute Resolution in Asia* (2nd edn., 2002), p. 1.

> given point in time is essential, but essentializing a region-wide 'Asian' approach to dispute resolution and law when 'Asia' itself is an artificial construct is probably a futile exercise.[2]

The authors suggest that the tendency in the 1970s and 1980s to recognize a 'unique, non-legal character of Asian commercial dispute resolution', and to contrast an 'Asian' mindset with 'Western' approaches to business relationships and law, might be to fall into the trap of Orientalism identified by Edward Said, and described by them as the manufacture and dissection of a Western representation of Asia, in preference to seeking accurate data about it.[3] While one could agree that the structures and processes of dispute resolution vary over the vast expanse of the continent, from Islamic 'west' Asia, across the Indian Ocean hinterland to that of the Pacific, certain commonalities do exist, particularly in expectations as to the outcomes of those processes.

That, at least, would appear to be the conclusion of scholars from the region. In what follows, some roots of a possible common Asian cultural bias as to dispute resolution outcomes are discussed. Such a bias ought not, however, to be thought of as immutable in an age of rapid if not instantaneous communication, and in which countries compete to obtain capital and technology from those outside the region who insist on strict adherence to core elements of their own legal cultures that have served them well. The reception of such core elements may well take place over time, but may also coexist for even longer with different expectations as to outcomes.

An 'Asian' dispute resolution culture?

The *ICC International Court of Arbitration Bulletin* once recalled that, early in the decade of the 1980s, when an Asian company was invited to send a speaker to a conference on international arbitration, the company's response had been to the effect that 'while the invitation was very much appreciated, Asia had a very old civilization which had over the centuries come to learn that negotiation and conciliation were the preferred means of resolving disputes, much better than the confrontation which would inevitably be entailed in arbitration', and accordingly declined to participate in

[2] *Ibid.*

[3] *Ibid.* For a somewhat different view, see M. Wiley, 'The Practicalities of Cross-Cultural Arbitration' in S. N. Frommel and B. A. K. Rider (ed.), *Conflicting Legal Cultures in Commercial Arbitration* (1999), pp. 79, 94–5.

the conference.[4] Having surveyed the extent to which international commercial arbitration has been received in some countries in East Asia, one distinguished jurist from the region contrasts the Western concept of arbitration, described as 'legalistic and adversarial in nature', with an Eastern approach which he finds 'more flexible'. He observes that, in countries of the region, the arbitrator:

> cannot divorce himself from his primary role as conciliator and as an active promoter of dispute solving. In Japan, for example, the arbitrator is free to advise parties to settle; he participates actively in forming the terms of settlement. This, of course, may not be acceptable to those who have been brought up on arbitration as understood by the West. There is thus a fundamental difference of approach between East and West in dispute resolution.[5]

As one writer describes the dispute settlement aspect of the Confucian tradition as it prevails in China:

> there is a concept known as li, which concerns the social norms of behaviour within the five natural status relationships: emperor and subject, father and son, husband and wife, brother and brother, or friend and friend. Li is intended to be persuasive, not compulsive and legalistic, a concept that governs good conduct and is above legal concepts in societal importance. The governing legal concept fa, is compulsive and punitive. While having the advantage of legal enforceability, fa is below li in importance. The Chinese have always considered the resort to litigation as the last step, signifying that the relationship between the disputing parties can no longer be harmonized. Resort to litigation results in loss of face, and discussion and compromise are always to be preferred. Over time, the concepts of fa and li have become fused, and the concept of maintaining the relationship, and, therefore, face, has become part of the Chinese legal system.[6]

[4] Cited by M. J. Moser, 'Arbitration in Asia: An Overview' in *ICC International Court of Arbitration Bulletin, International Commercial Arbitration in Asia* (Special Supplement, 1998), Proceedings of the 'Asian Update' Conference, 6 November 1997, Hong Kong.

[5] M. Kusuma-Atmadja, presentation at a Seminar on Legal Aspects of Regional Co-operation, 29 April 1996, organized by the Asian Development Bank, *Proceedings*, p. 15. See also as to the preference for conciliation over 'adjudicatory' methods, L. Marasinghe, 'Third World Jurisprudence for the Twenty-first Century' in A. Anghie and G. Sturgess (eds.), *Legal Visions of the Twenty-first Century: Essays in Honour of Judge Christopher Weeramantry* (Kluwer Law International, 1998), pp. 49–71, at pp. 68–9.

[6] M. S. Donahey, 'The Asian Concept of the Conciliator/Arbitrator: Is it Translatable to the Western World?' (1995) 10 *ICSID Review – Foreign Investment Law Journal* 120 at 121, citing Nafziger and Jiafang, 'Chinese Methods of Resolving International Trade, Investment and Maritime Disputes' (1987) 23 *Willamette Law Review* 619.

An expert on international arbitration seems to distinguish three types of 'arbitration culture'. He observes: (1) that lawyers educated in the common law system (e.g. USA, United Kingdom) have left their imprint on the system of arbitration by seeking to conduct arbitration proceedings in the same manner as procedures before their domestic courts; (2) while types in 'continental Europe' are placed in one group, he finds that approaches to conflict resolution differ as between areas with Germanic cultural roots and those within what he calls 'the Latin zone of cultural influence'; and finally, (3) that 'East Asian, Arabic and Islamic societies are known for their emphasis on conciliation'.[7]

Another commentator suggests a parallel differentiation of 'dispute resolution cultures', primarily into a 'litigation' culture and a 'conciliation' (including negotiation and mediation) culture. According to him:

> The western world is traditionally characterized, to varying degrees, by the litigation culture, perhaps with the United States and Germany at the extreme end of the scale. Asia, especially East Asia, is known for its emphasis on conciliation. For centuries, a conciliation culture comprising a variety of forms has flourished there. A typical example is Japan. Under a stable feudal regime which lasted for more than 250 years until 1868 (Tokugawa period), the practice of law was not allowed. There was a strong communal system to promote amicable settlement of disputes and to suppress litigation. Litigation was condemned as a moral wrongdoing to the society and to the other party. A good judge was not supposed to give a judgment but to try to bring about a good conciliation. This tradition was deeply embedded in the people's mind and formed the dispute resolution culture of Japan.[8]

[7] B. Cremades, 'Overcoming the Clash of Legal Cultures: The Role of Interactive Arbitration' (1998) 14 *Arbitration International* 158. As to what might be considered 'key aspects of an arbitral culture', see H. Holtzmann, 'The Permanent Court of Arbitration and the Evolution of a Worldwide Arbitration Culture' in *Proceedings of the Centenary Conference of the Members of the PCA* (17 May 1999).

[8] Y. Taniguchi, 'Is There a Growing International Arbitration Culture? An Observation from Asia', *Proceedings of the 1996 Seoul Conference of the International Council for Commercial Arbitration (ICCA)*, pp. 31–40 at p. 31. The Max Planck Institute's Encyclopedia of Public International Law deals with 'Conciliation and Mediation' under a single heading, and opens with the statement (vol. 1, p. 47): 'No clear distinction can be drawn between the terms conciliation and mediation. Both describe the intervention of a third party in disputes between States with the aim of settling them or contributing to their settlement'. For the purpose of that particular presentation, the author declares that he will use the term 'mediation' to describe such intervention by a state, and the term 'conciliation' for intervention by a private person. Some distinctions between the two processes may be implied, e.g., (1) the entry in the Encyclopedia itself

Another authority confirms that:

> Arab and Islamic societies [were] characterized by the existence of a strong communal system to promote amicable settlement of disputes through 'negotiation/mediation' as a first step that could lead ultimately at a later stage to 'conciliation/arbitration'. According to results obtained through serious anthropological research studies, the region had been culturally pro-conciliation even before the appearance of Judeo-Christian and Islamic ideals of moral harmony and peaceful settlement of disputes within the community without confrontation through litigation. This characteristic survived until the mid-twentieth century where 80% of all disputes used to be amicably settled outside of State courts by recourse to an elder respected and popular person chosen for his wisdom and known integrity, either in the village rural community, among the heads of the nomadic tribes or among city merchant circles. Such a person ... played the role of a semi-arbitrator keen to conciliate the conflicting interests in a no victory–no defeat manner, in other words, rendering a morally binding decision mainly based on fairness and justice without abiding by a specific rule of law or being obliged to conform with a system of judicial procedures.[9]

A reader may well wonder whether frequent references to 'culture' in discussions of such concrete legal problems might not be based on evidence that is essentially anecdotal, and is yet to be supported by the results of empirical study. However, the frequency with which a range of commentators make reference to 'cultural' differences of the kind described, and the existence of 'serious anthropological research studies'

notes that a state or international organization can either mediate on its own initiative or in response to a request from one or both parties, while in the case of conciliation, no third party can become active unless a request is addressed to it by the parties to the dispute or, under a compulsory system, by one of them; (2) although both mediation and conciliation are characterized by their informality, it would appear that recent initiatives have tended to push conciliation in the direction of increased formality. UNCITRAL, the International Chamber of Commerce and the Permanent Court of Arbitration have all prepared sets of 'Conciliation Rules'. For an account of various instances of settlement through processes described as mediation, see J. Bercovitch and J. Z. Rubin (eds.), *Mediation in International Relations* (1992).

[9] A. S. El-Kosheri, 'Is There a Growing International Arbitration Culture in the Arab-Islamic Juridical Culture?', *Proceedings of the 1996 Conference of ICCA*, p. 47. See also by the same author, 'The Inter-relation Between Worldwide Arbitral Culture and the Islamic Traditions' in *Proceedings of the Centenary Conference of the Members of the PCA* (17 May 1999). Citing passages from the Koran, another writer confirms: 'alternative dispute settlement mechanisms to court litigation are deeply rooted in Islam – a fact evidenced by many historical events': Hamid G. Gharavi, 'The 1997 Iranian International Commercial Arbitration Law' (1999) 15 *Arbitration International* 85.

attested to by the authority just cited, do indicate the influence of a 'cultural' factor, and are reason enough to speculate on the origin of such differences, their current impact, and prospects for evolution. It should also be noted that a recent study of the role of law and legal institutions in six Asian countries (China, India, Japan, Korea, Malaysia, and Taipei China) prepared for the Asian Development Bank, does confirm that 'Asia shows a preference for the mechanisms of mediation and conciliation available through traditional dispute settlement institutions'.[10]

Possible origins of differences among 'dispute resolution cultures'

Civilizations (in which different/various 'cultures' may be subsumed) may diverge in their approaches to political organization, and ultimately to law and dispute resolution,[11] under the influence of different religious beliefs acted upon by different histories. One writer[12] draws attention to such a divergence, which he attributes to different ways in which populations have perceived their relationships to their environments. What he describes as 'purely' Asian ways of thought introduced by Aryan settlers and transmitted through Hindu, Buddhist, Confucian, and, more recently, Gandhian philosophy, derived knowledge inductively, through direct observation. Thus, political organization found its moral basis in 'an intuitively felt continuum of immediacy or in the patriarchal family relationship or ethnological species given inductively by natural history science'. Rules were derived from 'warm-hearted intuition or the family, caste and tribal relations observed inductively'. The associated religious goal is thought of as 'non-dualistic', or 'immediate immersion of oneself in the all-embracing formlessness which is the non-Aryan Brahman, Nirvana or the Confucian vastness'.

By contrast, the Western approach to political organization, he suggests, was influenced by Greek science, through which nature ceased to be described merely in terms of the way we feel it 'when, through naïve observation, we become aware of ourselves as immersed in its

[10] K. Pistor and P. A. Wellens, 'Executive Summary', *The Role of Law and Legal Institutions in Asian Economic Development, 1960–1995*, p. 13.

[11] This is recognized implicitly in the requirements for election of judges of the International Court of Justice (Statute of the ICJ Article 9), and of members of the UN International Law Commission (Statute of the Commission Article 8).

[12] F. S. C. Northrop, *The Taming of the Nations: A Study of the Cultural Bases of International Policy* (1952), pp. 186–204.

continuum of impressionistic aesthetic immediacy'. Instead, nature is conceived as something inferred from this naively felt and observed nature, but not immediately seen in it. The relationship of humans to nature is not known through being directly sensed: it is the 'thesis of Greek science that any truly known thing or event is an instance of a theoretically conceived determinate law'. If good conduct is conduct which proceeds from true knowledge about man and his fellow men in nature, and if knowledge of man and nature reveals man and other entities in nature to be instances of determinate laws not derived inductively from family, village, or tribal relations, then the moral basis of political organization becomes free from such limitations.

According to the author, Greek science was responsible for the creation of the Roman 'technically conceptualized science of law', which transformed Hebrew culture and religion into the form of Christianity that became the foundation of Western civilization. The new way of thinking was centred on free individuals who were nevertheless subject to a body of law, and, where this culture prevailed, brought about a transformation in living law habits, beliefs, and emotions of persons necessary to sustain new positive legal and political forms. It laid the foundation for the Western concept of 'the just State as a theoretically constructed constitutionalism valid for all men because of its universalism which gave to the diversity and pluralism which moral freedom generates ... effective political unity, order and peace'.[13]

The contrast between the author's 'purely Asian' and Western (Christian) approaches is well expressed in the following passage:

> With the locus of the model of justice in theoretically conceived nature rather than in the intuitively felt continuum of immediacy or in the patriarchal family relationship and the ethnological species given inductively by natural history science, fathers were, as Jesus said, put against son, mother against daughter and daughter-in-law against mother-in-law. Forthwith belief in a determinately expressed doctrine rather than loyalty to one's parents, ancestors, caste or technological group determined the morally good and just men. And with respect to a particular determinate, theoretically expressed doctrine which is believed, father and son, daughter-in-law and mother-in-law, nation and nation, and even man-to-manness can differ without any moral sense of failure of loyalty to family or tribe or God.[14]

[13] *Ibid.* at p. 209. [14] *Ibid.* at pp. 195–6.

From this observation we may be led to conclude that if the decision of a third party seized of a dispute were to go against a party with a 'Western' (i.e., concept- and rule-accustomed) approach to dispute settlement, the decision is likely to be accepted with good grace and complied with in due course; while if the decision were to go against the party with the postulated 'purely Asian' mindset, it may not be taken in good part. It may even be rejected, and in any event may generate resentment born of a 'moral sense of failure', thought of as reflecting adversely on the 'loser's' dignity or reputation. It is doubtful if such a proposition can be sustained. No disputant, whether 'Asian' or 'Western', is likely to be enthusiastic about a decision that is perceived as adversely affecting its interests. As to acceptance and implementation of a decision, a variety of factors would affect the 'loser's' attitude, including the quality of the decision and the reasons on which it purports to be based, the 'importance' of the dispute, the symmetry or otherwise of the political influences of the parties, and the relations prevailing between them. Resentment at 'loss of face' and a lingering sense of grievance are not attributes solely of 'Asian' losing parties. Of course, the reasons for such sentiments and their intensity and outcome may be expected to vary as between categories of parties. It is not necessary, however, to accept the writer's thesis in its entirety to recognize that the existence of perceptions of differences potentially so fundamental, present a formidable challenge to those who would seek commonalities and attempt to forge a synthesis of dispute resolution cultures as contemplated below.

In the sixteenth century, Western civilization entered a new phase, changing in significant ways under pressure from the new spirit of enterprise, which released long-suppressed human energies and sanctioned their use in the pursuit of material gain. Greed and the desire for power were recognized as important aspects of human nature,[15] and were thus not to be thwarted, but rather tempered or moderated by the

[15] In the film 'Wall Street', the central character, Gordon Gekko, makes an impassioned speech to shareholders of a company he hopes to acquire, on the quality and function of greed: 'The point is, that "greed" – for want of a better word – is good. Greed is right. Greed works. Greed clarifies and cuts through and captures the essence of the evolutionary spirit. Greed in all its forms – greed for life, for money, for love, knowledge – has marked the upward surge of mankind. And greed – you mark my words – will not only save Teldar Paper, but also that other malfunctioning corporation called the United States of America'.

gentle teachings of Christ.[16] Correspondingly, primitive Christian beliefs were re-interpreted to accommodate the upward spiral of material progress based on buying cheap and selling dear, not to mention the gold, slaves, textiles, and spices taken from 'the Indies'.

This vision of the real world had far-reaching consequences for European law. Seventeenth-century Europe saw the growth of a natural law based no longer solely on theology, not on the will of God, but on reason. Under the influence of Grotius and Leibniz it was thought to be good sense not to do injury to your neighbour, and that any such injury should give rise to a right of redress. Justice was seen as the charity of the wise. It was not bad morals to demand excessive interest for the use of money: it was merely bad business to do so.[17] This worldview would lead in Europe to the division between the realms of church and state, and between religion and law. Following the dissolution of the Holy Roman Empire and the Peace of Westphalia, the new wave produced, through the work of Pufendorf, Wolff, and Vattel, an international law which saw nation states as separate individuals, sovereign and independent of one another, with equal rights, but compelled by reason (the law of nature) to allow each other their equal exercise. A bias in the direction of the individual showed that, in case of conflict between the duty of a nation to itself, and its distributive duties to other nations, the duty towards itself – the *raison d'état* – would prevail.

Most importantly, it placed the individual at the centre of social effort, and allowed the virtually unrestrained pursuit of profit.[18] This

[16] As one distinguished writer encapsulates the implications of Calvin's teachings: 'capital and credit are indispensable; the financier is not a pariah, but a useful member of society; and lending at interest, provided that the rate is reasonable and that loans are made freely to the poor, is not per se more extortionate than any other of the economic transactions without which human affairs cannot be carried on. That acceptance of the realities of Calvinism and its offshoots took their stand on the side of the activities which were to be most characteristic of the future, and insisted that it was not by renouncing them, but by untiring concentration on the task of using for the glory of God the opportunities they offered, that Christian life could and must be lived': R. H. Tawney, *Religion and the Rise of Capitalism* (1926, Peregrine Books reprint 1987), pp. 116–17.

[17] See C. F. Murphy, *The Search for World Order: A Study of Thought and Action* (1985), p. 29 *et seq.*

[18] 'That creed was that the individual is absolute master of his own, and, within the limits set by positive law, may exploit it with a single eye to his pecuniary advantage, unrestrained by any obligation to postpone his own profit to the well-being of his neighbours, or to give account of his actions to higher authority. It was in short, the theory of property, which was later to be accepted by all civilized communities': Tawney, *Religion and the Rise of Capitalism*, p. 151 (emphasis added).

liberty was circumscribed only by limits set by positive law, which would at the same time provide protection from the excessive demands or tyranny of the Prince. These notions regarding the individual were also consistent with a fundamental belief in each human being's possession of a unique soul, which retained its special distinctive character even in the transition to an after-life, and would, still in that form, be redeemed or condemned for its conduct on earth.

After the first wave of European adventures in search of souls to be won for Christ (not averse however, to the acquisition of gold for an expectant patron), the imperial powers propagated among the colonies their worldview founded on the spirit of enterprise and individualism. That view was reflected not only in their religious beliefs, but also in their laws, languages, and literature, all of which were transplanted to the lands under their control. The consequences of such efforts on communities in which an indigenous religion, government, and law lay, yet, inextricably mingled, and whose social history had not been affected by currents of thought such as those that had sparked Europe's economic progress,[19] were complex in the extreme, and continue so until today, after more than three centuries. Where imperial conquest did not extinguish entire populations, Euro-Christianity (and the spirit of enterprise and individualism that travelled with it) encountered societies in which the prevailing religion, culture, and moral code demanded subordination of the welfare of the individual to that of the community,[20] or reinforced customs and an ethic with that goal. Moreover, Euro-Christianity and its ways were not introduced by the dominant power for acceptance or rejection by the colony at its option. They represented an imposed doctrine, one that was perceived as

[19] 'The Western belief that progress should result in ever greater scope for individual autonomy is not taken as self-evident by most Asians, who are more inclined to believe that greater happiness comes from suppressing self-interest in favour of group solidarity. The success of the Japanese, and now of the Koreans, Taiwanese and Singaporeans, in building modern institutions through strong group loyalties suggests that individualism does not have to be either a prerequisite or a consequence of economic development': Lucian W. Pye, *Asian Power and Politics: The Cultural Dimensions of Authority* (1985), p. 26.

[20] '[A] reverence for individualism can blind Westerners to the fact that Asians can find satisfaction and security in knowing that their social fabric is firm and that they have the blessings of belonging to some larger and coherent community. The pluralism which seems so desirable to Westerners was rejected in those Asian cultures in which there were only two alternatives of consensus: loyalty and conformity, or selfishness and opportunistic scheming': *ibid.* at pp. 26–7.

inconsistent with the mores that had prevailed in the country since time immemorial, and threatened to disrupt and overturn hallowed and familiar social concepts and structures. It was a doctrine imposed, moreover, by a foreigner, who sought dominance through a strategy of trade; and imposition was often accomplished by force of arms. In contrast to an indigenous religion, which might see the notion of 'self' as an impediment to spiritual development, as perpetuating a cycle of death and rebirth that needed to be broken to enable the false notion of self to dissolve and merge finally with the infinite,[21] Euro-Christianity did not merely acknowledge the existence of 'self', but gave it a permanent and central place.[22] Its introduction through promise of material advancement, or by forms of compulsion, together with the deprivation of land that accompanied colonial penetration, left the wounds which today appear to some to portend a 'clash of civilizations' in the future.

Impact of imperialism

As the power of certain Western nations climbed toward its zenith in the nineteenth century, leading to their expansion into countries in Asia and Africa, it was inevitable that free enterprise and individualism should form the basis of the legal and administrative systems they established in those countries. While those systems served the overall purposes of the

[21] '[T]he idea of an abiding, immortal substance in man or outside, whether it is called Atman, "I", Soul, Self, or Ego, is considered only a false belief, a mental projection. This is the Buddhist doctrine of Anatta, No-Soul or No-Self': Revd. Walpola Rahula, *What the Buddha Taught* (rev. edn. 1967, reprint 1982), p. 55; also: 'From passions liberate, quit of self, Of arrogance, impatience, anger, pride; ... Such a one grows to oneness with the Brahm; Such a one, growing one with Brahm, serene, Sorrows no more, desires no more': *The Bhagavadgita* (trans. Sir Edwin Arnold, 1899; Dover Publications, 1993), ch. 18.

[22] Adda Bozeman suggested that 'Asian and African traditions had been at one for millennia in stressing the primacy of the group, assigning essentially role-playing functions to the individual, and keeping thought subordinate to custom and authority. Impressive conceptual systems ... were recorded in the Orient, but, as administered by elites claiming a monopoly of knowledge, they proved to be impediments rather than stimuli to secular, innovative thinking. This was so firstly because they instructed men to aim at the elimination rather than the development of the personality; and secondly, because ... they did not allow for the evolution either of distinct categories of thought or of politically significant ways of perfecting society. No possibility thus existed either in [the Orient] or in Africa of disengaging "law" as a separate system of norms, of fathoming "contract" as a structuring principle for human relationships, and of rendering rights and obligations in the language of legal abstractions': A. B. Bozeman, *The Future of Law in a Multicultural World* (1971), pp. 162–3.

foreign administering powers within which they had evolved, and whose agents were well acquainted with their use and potential, they were little understood by native populations in which social norms had evolved differently. The essence of the impact of Western legal concepts and systems on indigenous dispute settlement processes may be found in the imposition of rules which treated each disputant as individual and separate: separate from the associations with ancestors, clan, caste, or guild that had characterized earlier informal settlement methods. Henceforth, the social context of a dispute would not necessarily be relevant to its resolution. Only the facts of the case would be examined. This 'isolation', which had taken centuries to evolve in Europe, and had there become one of the parameters of an impersonal and impartial 'justice', had now to be accepted by disputants in the colony, depriving them of important support from traditional loyalties.

For generations the new processes were treated with reserve, either because disputants preferred the application of familiar indigenous religious and ethical norms with which the new systems seemed inconsistent; because the language of administration was foreign (e.g., English, French), and frustrated efforts to understand the systems' meaning and implications; because of disputants' failure to appreciate the benefits those processes might bring in the long term; or because of mere prejudice. Thus, old informal methods of dispute settlement continued to exist side by side with the courts and other formal means introduced through colonial legislation.

The objective of colonial administrators familiar with either common law or civil law systems (both being influenced considerably by Roman law) was to bring their own order and method, and a predictable uniformity, to the informal dispute settlement arrangements established by tradition so that they themselves could comprehend and control them. In India, for example, which had a well-developed informal system for resolving local disputes,[23] extension of the British system of the administration of justice to cover the subcontinent meant the

[23] In addition to the *panchayats* or village tribunals, disputes might be referred to the *Kula* (a group bound by family ties), the *sreni* (an assembly of tradesmen and artisans), and the *puga* (a group of local dignitaries belonging to various social divisions). While these appear to represent a kind of hierarchy, their relationship to one another and the source of their authority are not fully understood. Appeal always lay to the King. See, for recent summary, V. Raghavan, 'New Horizons for Alternative Dispute Resolution in India' (1996) 13 *Journal of International Arbitration* 5 at 6–7; see also, R. Lingat, *The Classical Law of India* (1973), pp. 246–7.

establishment of a hierarchy of courts, the introduction of rules of evidence and procedure, and a system of legal education. Regulations concerning arbitration were introduced in various parts of India as early as in the eighteenth century; but it was in 1859, with the enactment of the first Code of Civil Procedure, that a law to govern arbitration became applicable throughout India. The first legislation dealing entirely with arbitration was enacted in 1899, based on the British Arbitration Act 1889, but was applied only in major metropolitan areas. The Arbitration Act 1940 was intended to consolidate arbitration law in India, but it appears to have met resistance from the courts of the time. In part for that reason, and in part because of intrinsic complexities, the Act failed to form an adequate basis for a satisfactory arbitration regime.

India's laws relating to international commercial arbitration were consolidated by the Arbitration (Protocol and Convention) Act 1937, which enabled India to give effect to its undertakings as party to the 1923 Geneva Protocol on Arbitration Clauses and to the 1927 Geneva Convention on Foreign Arbitral Awards. After independence, India became a party to the New York Convention on the Recognition and Enforcement of Foreign Arbitral Awards 1958, the Foreign Awards (Recognition and Enforcement) Act 1961 being enacted as the basis for its implementation.

The Arbitration and Conciliation Act, No. 8 of 1996, which is based on UNCITRAL's Model Law on International Commercial Arbitration (and grants statutory recognition to conciliation applying UNCITRAL's conciliation rules), seems to be welcomed by prospective arbitrating parties and practitioners alike. As one commentator puts it 'Alternative Dispute Resolution in India has finally come of age'.[24] Covering, as it does, international commercial arbitration and conciliation, in addition to local arbitration, the Act is likely to increase investor confidence and to fit well with India's 'reform'-oriented policies concerning trade and foreign investment.

The systematic introduction of British dispute resolution processes, commencing very early in the colonial association, and inevitably accompanied by the infusion of British, and generally European, legal doctrine through legislature, courts, and institutions for legal education, may have resulted in a more complete reception of such processes in India than appears to have occurred in some other jurisdictions in Asia.

[24] Raghavan, 'New Horizons', 42. The foregoing summary of the legislative history of arbitration in India is based on its presentation in V. Raghavan's fine essay.

Today, India possesses a range of dispute settlement mechanisms from a system of courts, and a judiciary of exemplary competence, courage, and independence, to arbitration, conciliation, and other forms of 'alternative' dispute resolution. However, the extent of the 'reception' of Western legal concepts and systems in colonized territories varied widely depending on many factors too diverse and complex to be considered here; but it would seem that these Western concepts and systems are more firmly entrenched today in the Indian subcontinent and its immediate neighbours than in territories further east.

Resistance to some Western legal imports remains. The manner in which international arbitration has been developed in Asia under pressure from the capital-exporting countries has been the subject of sharp criticism. One author,[25] focusing on the concept of the internationalization of state contracts with foreign investors, and undertakings to submit any related disputes to international arbitration, rather than to the law and the courts of the host state, rejects both concept and outcome. Host state distrust of international arbitration of such disputes is justified, he suggests, for at least three reasons. First, 'internationalization' of state contracts with foreign firms is tantamount to elevation of the contract to the status of a treaty between sovereign states and its objective is to place it beyond the reach of the national legal and judicial system of the host state. This transmutation he finds unwarranted, without precedent, and contrary to the principles of international law

[25] M. Sornarajah, *International Commercial Arbitration: The Problem of State Contracts* (1990). Compare also the conclusion reached by another commentator: 'To say, therefore, that the obligations arising out of arbitration between a state and a foreign private party are international could at best be only a half truth. The state party could potentially be bound under international law, but the private party could never be bound. This fundamental inequality of obligation is the strongest indication that these arbitrations are not creatures of international law . . . the process of mixed arbitration itself is not a manifestation of international law': S. J. Toope, *Mixed International Tribunals: Studies in Arbitration between States and Private Persons* (1990), pp. 388–9. It may be noted that the Iran–United States Claims Tribunal, established by an international agreement between Iran and the USA, and empowered to decide intergovernmental claims, as well as claims by the nationals of one state party against the government of the other state party, has held: 'Under contemporary international law, the fact that an individual or a private entity is party to proceedings before a forum created by an international agreement does not deprive that forum and its proceedings of their international nature. The Tribunal is clearly an international tribunal . . . By definition, international arbitral awards, if final, are binding. Recourse to this Tribunal implies the undertaking to respect its awards'. *Islamic Republic of Iran* v. *United States* Award No. 586-A27-FT (1998), paragraph 58.

recognized by the Permanent Court of International Justice (PCIJ), according to which it is precisely that national system that should properly be applied in resolving such disputes.[26] The host state having thus agreed to refer the dispute for resolution to an international tribunal by the application of international norms, the process of internationalization demands that the host state take a further step in consequence, i.e. (the second reason) to agree to inclusion of a 'stabilization clause', whereby it would undertake not to change its policy (and its laws), thereby divesting itself of the sovereign right to enact legislation that would return the contract and any related disputes to the domain of its national law and judicial institutions. Finally, as another consequential step in the process of internationalization, the host state is required to recognize that the 'arbitration clause', the undertaking to submit disputes to binding international arbitration, would survive the parent contract if the latter were to be found to be inoperative for any reason.[27]

Having considered the doctrines advanced in support of the theory of internationalization of state contracts (*pacta sunt servanda*, the sanctity of property rights, and the principle of acquired rights), he finds that theory unsound, and its application by arbitral tribunals since the award in the Sapphire Petroleum Arbitration[28] to be a departure from 'standards of neutrality which are central to the evolution of an acceptable system of international arbitration'.[29] In his view, for international arbitration to recover the confidence of the capital-importing states, tribunals should accord greater weight to what he calls 'competing norms', such as those comprehended in an evolving 'law of development', whose theoretical foundations, though they might be weak, are actually no less reliable than those advanced in support of 'internationalization' of state contracts.[30]

[26] He cites in support the PCIJ's dictum in the 'Serbian Loans' case that 'any contract which is not a contract between states in their capacity as subjects of international law is based on the municipal law of some country': (1929) PCIJ Rep. Ser. A. No. 20, at 41, and see the *Panevezys-Saldutiskis Railway Co.* case (1939) PCIJ Rep. Ser. A/B No. 76, at 18, 'in principle, the property rights and the contractual rights of individuals depend in every State on municipal law and fall therefore more particularly within the jurisdiction of municipal tribunals'.

[27] *Ibid.* at 6–22.

[28] (1963) 35 ILR 136. The tribunal held that the law applicable to a contract between Sapphire Petroleum and Iran could not have been Iranian law, as the latter would have been subject to change at will by the government, but was, in fact, 'the general principles of law recognized by civilized nations'.

[29] Sornarajah, *International Commercial Arbitration*, p. 29.

[30] *Ibid.* at pp. 29–48.

Selective application or synthesis of approaches to dispute resolution?

If there are at least two cultural approaches to law, to justice, and thus to dispute resolution, and if, indeed, they differ fundamentally in that, in the one ('Asian', 'African', 'Islamic') the communal element is absolutely dominant, while in the other (European, Atlantic) the dominant feature is the principle of individuation, is there any prospect of forging from them a synthesis and, in relation to our topic, establishing an international dispute resolution culture? A formidable number of experts in legal philosophy would seem to suggest a negative answer to the question. For example:

> When two countries governed by dialectically related (i.e. logically incompatible) ideals . . . face an international dispute, the dispute is completely misunderstood and falsely conceived if it is described as a difference merely of ways to a common goal. A goal is meaningless except as it is specified by a given ideology or the factors of knowledge which that ideology designates. Hence, when the ideologies are incompatible, the goals are also. Being in its essence dialectical, justice with respect to such a dispute simply cannot consist in the mediational, pacifistic Gandhian purely Asian technique of softening down or covering up the determinately expressed doctrinal differences as if they were of secondary importance and merely verbal.
>
> To ask a people or nation with a theoretically formulated morality to compromise the basic principles of that morality is, from the standpoint of the spiritual foundations of Western civilization here outlined, to ask them to stop being moral men.[31]

Adda Bozeman, in her profound reflections on cultural differences in approaches to law, draws attention to those differences as they relate to time perspectives. Attributing to African and Asian perspectives the tendency to remain concentrated on the past, seen by them as the trusted abode of truth and authority, and therefore able to instruct or dominate the present, she contrasts the Western perspective, a by-product of the curiosity, the urge to free inquiry, inherited from the Greeks, which demands looking to the future, and planning ahead, so that 'the uncertain future may be partially divested of its unpredictability by human effort'. Consciously distinguishing among past, present, and future, the

[31] Northrop, *The Taming of the Nations*, p. 197.

Western mind thus strives on the one hand for 'development' and on the other, simultaneously, for 'stability'. In her view, the institution that best illustrates the 'complementarity' of the two contrasting dispositions towards time, is the:

> contract – the core of all associational life in this civilization and . . . the source of constitutional government. What makes contract a unique expression of the European time sense, is the theory of confidence that it encloses: confidence not only in the ability of men to pre-empt and order time that lies ahead of them by means of promises to do or refrain from doing something, but confidence also in the binding nature of obligations assumed in the past. All Western constitutions, bills of rights and acts of legislation that are normative . . . are in the final analysis emanations of this mode of thinking. That is to say, they cannot be transplanted effectively into other civilizations, ruled by totally different political traditions and philosophies of time.[32]

Northrop's work was published in 1952, just after some of the independence movements in Asia had triumphed, and while others were gathering momentum. While Western initiatives at the United Nations had hitherto been assured of a sympathetic hearing (outside the sphere of Soviet influence), the situation seemed likely to change with the admission of new members with hubris born of sovereignty regained, anxious to emphasize policy differences with the former imperial powers, and to validate them by reference to the ancient glory of their cultural heritages. It was necessary for the West to study those cultural heritages in order to determine whether there was anything in the phenomenon which could threaten the stability of the modern world order, which they saw as being essentially of their creation. Adda Bozeman's book first appeared in 1971, by which time the Soviet Union and its allies formed a countervailing influence to the West, the Non-aligned Movement was gathering strength, and at the United Nations the 'Group of 77' could insist on being addressed as a caucus in every negotiation of consequence. Communism, as well as Asian and African ideas concerning law and political organization, were seen as threatening to destabilize a world order created by an Atlantic society that had developed, *inter alia*, by faithful adherence to the principle of individuation and the institution of contract, and was now based upon and protected by international law. Her work was a call to Atlantic

[32] Bozeman, *The Future of Law*, p. xvi.

society and to the USA in particular, to beware the multiple threats to the foundations of their world and especially to its protective fabric of international law, from alien cultures and ideologies.

Brilliant as are analyses such as those of Northrop and Bozeman, their relevance may well have diminished through one of the elements on which they themselves laid stress: time. The time sense of the European may well differ today from that of neighbours in Asia and Africa; but it is equally certain that time passes, and with its passage comes change. Changes in a culture may, indeed, be slow, held back by human agencies which thrive on stagnation and are themselves protected by complex and ancient taboos. However, other human agencies are at work in all countries, oriental and occidental, which will inevitably, if gradually, and perhaps painfully, alter habits of thought that seemed immutable. From the time of Socrates (469–399 BC), who, as Cicero said, brought philosophy down from heaven to earth, to the emergence of an 'Atlantic society', inspired, it has been argued, by the currents of reason generated in his time, we may count more than twenty centuries. Its realization in Europe was hindered and delayed at various times by war, famine, the Dark Ages, and a variety of disasters, many wrought by human agencies.

Given the rapid development of communications and transportation systems, and the now generalized facilities for countries to engage in trade, the global interaction that results will, perhaps in less than a century, see the convergence of the basic concepts of the West and of Asia in relation to law and political organization, notwithstanding what today appear to be 'cultural' obstacles. This does not seem likely to occur, neither through the triumph of the 'communal element' (said to be emphasized in Asian thought) nor of the 'principle of individuation' (said to be the foundation of Western political and economic achievement), but rather by recognition that both have their roots in 'reason', and through their interaction with one another. In the field of international commercial dispute settlement, that process may have already begun, and the outcome will not be 'Western' or 'Asian' or 'African', but international.

One European authority on international commercial arbitration, recalling the doctrine that an arbitrator's duty should not be mixed with any mediating activity or intent to reconcile, lest he be exposed to the risk of challenge, concedes that the participation in international commercial arbitration of jurists from different legal cultures, including those of the Far East for whom 'conciliation is something closer to the mentality . . . than litigation or arbitration', has caused that doctrine to be questioned. He finds, moreover, that it is 'excessive 'judicialization' of international commercial arbitration . . . [that] has, in fact, led to the search for alternative dispute resolution techniques distinct from both litigation and arbitration'.[33] As a means of avoiding a conflict of legal cultures, he proposes that arbitrators adopt an 'increased interactive approach' to the parties, leading to open discussion and eventual harmonization of such 'cultural' differences.[34]

An Asian authority on international commercial arbitration similarly suggests that, in the West, pursuit of 'the ideal of procedural due process' has:

> pushed arbitration towards the litigation culture [and] . . . brought about an excessive legalization of arbitration . . . [making] the arbitration culture almost indistinguishable from the litigation culture.[35]

Observing that it may be difficult for 'the arbitration culture' and 'the conciliation culture' to coexist, he suggests that we conceive the arbitration culture as comprehending a range of processes, from those resembling litigation to others which admit 'amiable composition', and thus resemble conciliation. However, he sees this as a phase in a process of evolution towards an attainable 'single international commercial arbitration culture', which might combine elements of both conciliation and arbitration.[36]

A survey of a range of jurisdictions in relation to the extent to which, and the manner in which, conciliation and arbitration may be combined in the course of a dispute settlement process, places at one end the virtually inextricable combination of roles of arbitrator and conciliator inherent in the Chinese model, whereby 'the arbitrator may become a conciliator, then become an arbitrator again at any stage of the proceedings'.[37] At the opposite end of the range, the author would place the Western view that 'the role of an arbiter is that of an unbiased "truth" seeker, who then strictly applies the law to the truth that has been discovered

[33] B. M. Cremades, 'Overcoming the Clash of Legal Cultures: The Role of Interactive Arbitration' (1998) 14 *Arbitration International* 157 at 162–3.

[34] *Ibid.* at 160. [35] Taniguchi, 'An Observation from Asia', pp. 31–40 at 37.

[36] *Ibid.* at p. 160.

[37] M. S. Donahey, 'The Asian Concept of the Conciliator/Arbitrator: Is it Translatable to the Western World?' (1995) 10 *ICSID Review – Foreign Investment Law Journal* 120 at 125. However, under the 1994 Rules adopted by the China International Economic and Trade Arbitration Centre (CIETAC), this may occur only with the consent of the parties; and the Rules provide restrictions on the use of information gained during the conciliation effort.

and renders a decision based solely on such application, without regard to the effect on the parties' relationship'. The epitome of this approach is the UNCITRAL Rules of Conciliation, which do not permit a conciliator to act as an arbitrator in the same dispute. The basis of the Western view is that offers to compromise and disclosures of confidential information made during, and essential to, the conciliation process, might affect the ability of the conciliator to act as an unbiased arbitrator in the same dispute. Recalling the critical importance of maintaining harmonious personal (and business) relationships in East Asian cultures such as those of Korea and Japan, the author concludes – in the view of this writer, correctly – that:

> if there is one principle which can be said to lead to the combining of the role of arbitrator with that of conciliator it is that of preserving the harmonious relationship between the parties to the dispute. This principle is one that is frequently cited by western arbitral institutions in promoting the use of commercial arbitration over litigation.[38]

He notes that within Asia there exists a spectrum of ways of combining conciliation with arbitration, citing Indonesia and Korea as instances where an arbitrator will be permitted to conciliate a dispute at the outset, prior to the commencement of the arbitration; or, if the parties were to agree to conciliation during the course of arbitration, an arbitrator would suspend arbitration during the period that conciliation is to be attempted. In Japan, where efforts at conciliation fail, the conciliator may, with the advance written consent of the parties, issue a binding decision that is then converted in a judgment by a court. In Hong Kong, a conciliator may act as arbitrator, and vice versa, provided that information received in confidence by persons who act as both arbitrators and conciliators is disclosed, upon termination of the conciliation attempt, to the extent that the arbitrators/conciliators deem such information to be material.[39] In India and neighbouring Asian countries in which more than a century of British legislation governing

[38] *Ibid.* at 123.

[39] *Ibid.* at 124, 126. As to the practice of combining different settlement methods (mediation, conciliation, arbitration) in relation to the same dispute, see the contributions of M. E. Schneider, Tang Houzhi, M. Hoellering, T. Oyekunle, and C. N. Netto, in 'Legal Aspects of Regional Co-operation', *Proceedings*, pp. 55–135. See also as to legislation providing for both conciliation and arbitration, and rules governing their consecutive application in the same dispute, H. M. Holtzmann and D. F. Donovan, 'Recent Legislation that Combines Conciliation and Arbitration' in *Proceedings of ICCA/CIETAC 1994 International Commercial Arbitration Conference* (Beijing, 1994).

litigation and arbitration gave the pre-existing legal cultures an overtly 'Western' orientation, the separation of arbitration from conciliation would appear to be complete.[40]

These developments seem to represent a gradual absorption by the 'conciliation culture' of elements of the 'litigation culture'. They are occurring, however, as a result of the desire of governments in 'conciliation culture' countries to meet the demand by potential foreign private investors (or investment insurers) from 'litigation culture' countries, for a system of international arbitration acceptable to them, before investment funds actually begin to flow.[41] They do not necessarily signal – even in the case of India, which now has arbitration and conciliation laws on the Western pattern – that a country has embraced a litigation-type arbitration

[40] Raghavan, 'New Horizons'.

[41] Many Asian countries have adopted modern statutes on the Western pattern governing international commercial arbitration, often using UNCITRAL's Model Law and Arbitration Rules as guides, and arrange for disputing parties to receive institutional support: in Singapore, the International Arbitration Act 1995 was amended in 2001, 2002 to harmonize domestic and international arbitration and see the Singapore International Arbitration Centre (SIAC) Rules; in Malaysia, an amendment to the Arbitration Act 1952 allows international disputes to be referred by the parties to the Kuala Lumpur Regional Arbitration Centre, and to be governed by the KLRAC Arbitration Rules, 1978; in Thailand, the Arbitration Act 1987 allows international disputes to be dealt with at the Ministry of Justice's Arbitration Institute, by application of the Institute's Arbitration Rules and Conciliation Rules, 1990; in Indonesia, parties to an international commercial dispute may, by agreement, refer it to a tribunal constituted in accordance with the procedures of the Indonesian Board of Arbitration established in 1997 by the Indonesian Chamber of Commerce with government support; in Vietnam, international commercial arbitrations are dealt with by the Vietnam International Arbitration Centre (VIAC) established in 1993 on the pattern of SIAC, and by application of VIAC Rules similar to those of SIAC; in China, international commercial disputes are governed by the Arbitration Law 1995, and may be resolved by application of the 1994 Revised CIETAC Arbitration Rules, which are based on the ICC Arbitration Rules; in Japan, international commercial arbitration may be resolved by application of the Japan Commercial Arbitration Association's Arbitration Rules, revised 1992: see Kusuma-Atmadja, 'Legal Aspects of Regional Co-operation', *Proceedings*, pp. 17–23. In India, international commercial disputes are governed by the Arbitration and Conciliation Ordinance 1996 and may be referred for settlement under the auspices of either the Indian Council of Arbitration (1965) or the International Centre for Alternative Dispute Resolution (1995); in Sri Lanka, arbitration proceedings and the enforcement of arbitral awards, including foreign awards, are governed by the Arbitration Act 1995. All of the foregoing are parties to the New York Convention on the Recognition and Enforcement of Arbitral Awards 1958. However, the efficiency of the functioning of the international arbitral process across this range of countries is reported to be highly variable, particularly in the matter of enforcement. As to Iran's 1997 Law on International Commercial Arbitration, see Gharavi, 'The 1997 Iranian Law'.

culture through conviction as to its general efficacy, although it may be a step in that direction. There is little indication, moreover, that 'litigation culture' is absorbing, through arbitration, elements of 'conciliation culture', such as might foreshadow a true synthesis of the two philosophies; nevertheless, it has been suggested that the express provision in the British Columbia International Commercial Arbitration Act for an arbitrator to act as conciliator at any stage of the proceedings, with the agreement of the arbitrating parties, might have been introduced through interaction between Canadian populations of Asian origin with their Asian trading partners on the Pacific rim.[42]

The search for a genuinely international dispute resolution culture continues. As one writer wisely observes:

> the American ADR movement and underlying Japanese cultural norms for dispute resolution are compatible; if lawyers and businessmen concentrate on the commonalities of these processes (rather than their different roots), they can evolve a system of international dispute resolution which avoids or more efficiently resolves disputes and, therefore, leads to increased productivity and efficiencies for industry in both countries.[43]

Prospects for evolution of a single international arbitration culture

A study of the role of law and legal institutions in Asian economic development, prepared at the request of the Asian Development Bank, acknowledges that the imperial powers found in Asia (1) informal dispute settlement institutions relying primarily on voluntary compliance, as well as (2) formal institutions empowered to enforce primarily criminal and administrative law. The key question the study attempts to answer is whether the essentially formal institutions (systems of courts, binding arbitration) that were transplanted from the West into Asian communities, which had previously shown a preference for the processes of mediation and conciliation available through traditional dispute settlement institutions, had eventually come to play an important

[42] Donahey, 'The Asian Concept', 126. He observes further: 'it should not be surprising that the concept of the arbitrator/conciliator has been accepted most completely by western dispute resolution centers on the Pacific Rim' (at 121).

[43] C. R. Ragan, 'Emerging Dispute Resolution Techniques in the Pacific Basin' (1993) 9 *Arbitration International* 131 at 145.

role in settling commercial disputes. The study found that, although those institutions had remained unused or under-utilized for a long period, they had become more active during the recent increase in the level and complexity of entrepreneurial activity, and resulting economic growth. The authors' conclusion, 'a qualified "yes"', confirms a theory that, as markets expand, informal dispute settlement mechanisms become less reliable, and formal institutions with powers of enforcement become more important.[44]

Thus, the study suggests that, as the level of economic development of countries in Asia (and elsewhere) converges with those in the West, and as the former become more rule-conscious, so will their preference shift from informal to formal procedures. Although the forecast of such a shift may be justified on the basis of studies of disputes between non-state entities, it may not be made with quite the same confidence in relation to disputes where one party is a state, or to interstate disputes.

It seems both feasible and desirable that any evolving international dispute resolution culture should remain, as far as possible, neutral in relation to national cultural predispositions (i.e., oriented neither towards the pro-conciliation mindset, nor towards the pro-litigation mindset). This may indicate that the current range of separate dispute resolution mechanisms should remain, and even be made more diverse, so as to be able to be appropriately responsive to the needs of parties in the exercise of their autonomy, while awaiting the merger of dispute resolution cultures to take place, as forecast, when the disparity among levels of economic development of states has become less acute.

Another approach worthy of study is that referred to above, proposed by Professor Taniguchi, i.e., to conceive the 'arbitration culture' as in fact comprehending a range of arbitral processes, from those resembling litigation (favoured by those from a 'litigation culture'), to others which invariably admit 'amicable composition', and are favoured by those from a 'conciliation culture'.[45] The present writer, when attempting some years ago to discover the 'essence' of international arbitration, suggested that the current 'judicial' mode of that process had evolved among the states on either side of the Atlantic, which had engaged in interstate arbitrations most frequently in the course of the twentieth century; and that this particular concept of arbitration, which made the process virtually indistinguishable from judicial settlement, may prevail

44 Pistor and Wellons, 'Executive Summary', pp. 12–13.
45 Taniguchi, 'An Observation from Asia'.

only among those states, and might not be shared by others who believed that the element of 'conciliation' or 'amiable composition' was inherent in the process, and was, in fact, the very feature that led them to prefer arbitration to the submission of the dispute to a court.[46]

To the latter group of states, the litigation culture's engagement in elaborating ever more comprehensive sets of rules of arbitral procedure seemed to be gradually altering the pristine 'flexible' (if vulnerable) character of arbitration.[47] The very act of establishing sets of 'watertight' rules, notwithstanding their merely being available for voluntary acceptance, had the effect of upsetting the desirable level nature of the parties' playing field: for even if described as 'models' or 'optional', the embodiment of the 'judicial' (litigation culture) mode in these comprehensive rules: (1) made it appear that that mode was being endorsed and being established in the corpus of international law even though this might be occurring largely as the result of the superior bargaining position and the vigilance, enterprise, and resources of some Western states; and (2) made elimination of any of the 'optional' rules that might be unacceptable to one party a matter for prior negotiation, in which the party seeking to apply the rules in their entirety would be in a favoured position. In order to preserve the neutrality of the rules and prevent their being tilted either towards the 'litigation' or the 'conciliation' mode of arbitration, it seems desirable that only those rules which could be agreed at a diplomatic conference by consensus should be included in the main body of the 'optional' rules, while others, among them some which might be designed to protect the integrity and uninterrupted working of the process, could be presented in the form of model clauses annexed to the main body, and available for inclusion therein if both parties to the dispute were to agree to do so.

As to the outcome of the arbitral process, the difference between that expected by adherents of the litigation culture, and that looked for by those of the conciliation culture, can best be demonstrated

[46] M. C. W. Pinto, 'Structure, Process, Outcome: Thoughts on the "Essence" of International Arbitration' in S. Muller and W. Mijs (eds.), *The Flame Rekindled: New Hopes for International Arbitration* (1994), pp. 43–66.

[47] 'The features of arbitration law which offer so many avenues of escape and which serve in the [International Law] Commission's eyes as excuses for shirking international undertakings, may be the very features which attract states to enter into social undertakings': J. Stone, *Legal Controls of International Conflicts* (1954), p. 736. Similar observations were made by the Netherlands government concerning the ILC's Model Rules on Arbitral Procedure, see (1953–11) 5 *Yearbook of the International Law Commission* 235.

by contrasting the reference to decisions *ex aequo et bono* in the 'applicable law' provision included in the UNCITRAL Arbitration Rules 1976, with the corresponding reference in a statement of principle by F. L. Oppenheim, then Whewell Professor of International Law at Cambridge.

Article 33 (Applicable Law) of the UNCITRAL Arbitration Rules reads in relevant part:

> 1. The arbitral tribunal shall apply the law designated by the parties as applicable to the substance of the dispute . . .
> 2. The arbitral tribunal shall decide as amiable compositeur or ex aequo et bono only if the parties have expressly authorized the arbitral tribunal to do so and if the law applicable to the arbitral procedure permits such arbitration.[48]

Oppenheim, on the other hand, declared that:

> an arbitral tribunal is not a court in the real sense of the word, for its decisions are not necessarily based on rules of law, and it does not necessarily deal with legal matters. An arbiter, *unless the terms of reference otherwise provide* [emphasis added] decides ex aequo et bono, whilst a judge founds his decision on rules of law and is only applied to on legal issues . . .
>
> The experience which we have so far had of arbitral tribunals shows that they make praiseworthy efforts to arrive at a finding which shall as far as possible satisfy both parties, and that they have in view a compromise rather than a genuine declaration of law.[49]

Oppenheim was writing in 1921. In just over half a century, the Atlantic states, which had been the principal users of international arbitration in the period, had inducted the arbitral process into the litigation culture, and given it its present character. Those states which might have had a different 'conciliation culture' concept of arbitration were, for most of that period, either colonies, or under the cultural, economic, and political influence of the Atlantic states, and could not be heard in their own right. When the latter did regain their independence, any attempt to effect a radical change in the (by then entrenched) 'litigation' mode of arbitration, would have involved a form of confrontation with the Atlantic states that seemed, at best,

48 Compare Article 38, paragraph 2 of the Statute of the International Court of Justice.
49 F. L. Oppenheim, *The Future of International Law* (1921), pp. 46–7 (emphasis added).

impolitic, since 'conciliation culture' states had begun to court private investment from Atlantic states, and were doing so in competition among themselves.

It may be, however, that Professor Taniguchi's 'litigation culture' and 'conciliation culture' are not as distinct and wide apart as may sometimes appear. Instead of inspiring different forms of the arbitral process, it may be that every arbitration, whether taking place between states, or between parties only one of which is a state, is influenced by both cultures, and that this subsisting influence-amalgam represents an actual, if unexpressed (even covert) international arbitration culture. It is perhaps because 'litigation' and 'conciliation' perspectives remain, that the adherents of each, upon subjecting the outcomes of particular arbitrations to critical appraisal, sometimes find that an award leans towards one culture or the other, and conclude that the apparently determining culture was the only one that had influenced the proceeding. The existence of such an unexpressed international dispute resolution, discernible in relation to both process and outcome, has been suggested by several scholars. Thus, Professor Simon Roberts observes:

> Because the arbitrator depends for his authority to make a decision upon the disputants' agreement that he should do so, he must be sensitive towards their opinions as to what an acceptable decision might be; otherwise, the chances of his decision being complied with, and his being approached to deal with subsequent quarrels, will be small. Such considerations are not present in the case of the adjudicator who hears and decides a dispute by virtue of his office in the community. Not only is he entitled to hear the dispute but he is also likely to have force at his disposal to ensure compliance with his decision if the parties do not like it. Only in the much longer term can unpopular decisions affect his legitimacy.[50]

A scholarly review of the work of 'mixed arbitral tribunals' seems to reach very similar conclusions. Having noted that arbitration is a means of dispute resolution rooted in party autonomy and therefore dependent for its smooth operation upon the continuing consent of the parties, the author emphasizes the value of compromise:

[50] S. Roberts, *Order and Dispute: An Introduction to Legal Anthropology* (1979), p. 78. For a criticism of the 'anthropological approach', see J. Frank, *Courts on Trial: Myth and Reality in American Justice* (1973), pp. 378–9.

> throughout the process, arbitrators attempt to employ the rules so as to encourage the continuing participating of the parties and voluntary compliance with the resulting award.[51]

He cites another authority to the effect that the award, too, should be such as not to alienate one party completely:

> [m]ediate solutions acceptable to both parties are the goal, and, as a practical matter, few arbitrators would find much employment if they did not develop a record of providing such solutions.[52]

To determine the existence of an international dispute resolution culture, or the potential for its evolution, taking into account inputs of the 'litigation' culture as well as those of the 'conciliation' culture, would require a global study of surviving arbitration concepts. While being as comprehensive as feasible in the collection of available data, and unbiased in analysis of that data, the study should be given direction: to isolate and define the commonalities universally recognized as elements of an international arbitration culture. Left exclusively to legal experts, understandably impatient on behalf of their clients to provide a basis for expedient, practical solutions, the study may fail to take adequate account of an existing legal pluralism. The study should thus be interdisciplinary, an experiment in collaborative research, with lawyers working together with experts in such fields as political science, some branches of psychology and sociology, and legal anthropology.[53]

Although dispute resolution cultures may be converging in the wake of increased and more complex entrepreneurial activity in countries where social structures had previously hindered it, that process could take generations to mature, even at an accelerated pace, when compared to similar developments in the West. Until then, designing or refining aspects of international arbitration might be assisted if, through a study

[51] Toope, *Mixed International Tribunals*, p. 392.

[52] M. Shapiro, *Courts: A Comparative and Political Analysis* (1981), p. 4. See also M. S. Donahey, who observes: 'A common criticism of commercial arbitration in the United States arises from the perception that an arbitrator has a tendency to "split the baby", or reach a compromise result. Arbitration associations go to great lengths to dispel this perception, citing statistics which show that arbitrators tend to decide cases largely in favour of one party or the other': 'The Asian Concept', 126 n. 23.

[53] See in this connection prescriptions for future research on Asian law in C. Antons, 'Analysing Asian Law: The Need for a General Analytical Concept' in (1994) 5 *Finnish Yearbook of International Law* 429.

of the type suggested, a broader awareness and knowledge of the existing cultural pluralism could be promoted. Through it may also be gained a better understanding of 'the process whereby disputing mechanisms maintain and legitimize the distribution of power, and the means by which the powerful control disputing mechanisms'.[54]

[54] L. Nader and H. F. Todd (eds.), *The Disputing Process: Law in Ten Societies* (1978), p. 20. 'When individuals are no longer dependent on each other for their welfare, the tendency is for the powerful to manipulate legal means for their exclusive advantage': *ibid.* at p. 21.

26

The Cameroon v. Nigeria; Equatorial Guinea Intervening (Land and Maritime Boundary) Judgment

BARBARA KWIATKOWSKA

Introduction

It is a great honour to dedicate this chapter to Justice Florentino P. Feliciano, whose friendship for the past decade has been of valuable support in my searching for fairness and justice in international law. While his involvement in international commercial arbitrations has always been of general interest to me,[1] Feliciano's promotion when Justice of the Philippine Supreme Court of the principle of the protection of the environment for present and future generations three years prior to its endorsement by the landmark 1997 *Hungary/Slovakia Gabcikovo-Nagymaros Project* judgment,[2] and as the then President of the WTO Appellate Body, his promotion of this and other principles of the modern environmental law codified and progressively developed by this judgment, have been of illuminating impact upon the area of my specialization, the international law of the sea.[3] Justice Feliciano was a member of the inaugural Annex VII *Southern Bluefin Tuna* Arbitral

1 For the *SGS Société Generale de Surveillance SA* v. *Pakistan* (Jurisdiction) Award rendered in 2003 under Florentino P. Feliciano's presidency, see ICSID, www.worldbank.org/icsid and ASIL, www.asil.org/ilib/ilib0616.htm For an excellent appraisal of his WTO experience, see F. P. Feliciano and P. L. H. van den Bossche, 'The Dispute Settlement of the WTO' (2000) 75 *Philippine Law Journal* 1. See also Stephen Schwebel, Chapter 17, at pp. 241–5.

2 See *Minors Oposa* v. *Secretary of the Department of Environment*, judgment of the Supreme Court, including Separate Opinion of Justice Florentino Feliciano (1994) 33 ILM 173 and A. Oposa, *A Legal Arsenal for the Philippine Environment* (2002), pp. 102–11; *Hungary* v. *Slovakia (Gabcikovo-Nagymaros Project)*, judgment, President Stephen M. Schwebel, [1997] ICJ Rep. 41, paragraph 53, at 68, paragraph 112 and at 78, paragraph 140, www.icj-cij.org

3 1997 *Gabcikovo* judgment, *supra* n. 2 at 18, 31–7, 41, 44, 62, 64–8, 73–4, 77–80, Separate Opinion of Vice-President Weeramantry, 88–119; as reaffirmed by Appellate Body Report, *United States – Import Prohibition of Certain Shrimp and Shrimp Products*, WT/DS58/AB/R, 12 October 1998 and Appellate Body Report, *European*

Tribunal,[4] presided over by the then ICJ President Stephen M. Schwebel and also comprising Judge Per Tresselt, Ambassador Chusei Yamada, and Sir Kenneth Keith, which has remarkably enriched, through its 2000 Award, the procedural principles of peaceful settlement of the oceans and environmental disputes laid down in the UN Convention on the Law of the Sea (UNCLOS)[5] in accordance with the United Nations Charter.[6] However, as the *Southern Bluefin Tuna* Award involved highly

Communities – Measures Concerning Meat and Meat Products (Hormones), WT/DS26/AB/R, 13 February 1998, and other decisions surveyed in B. Kwiatkowska, *Decisions of the World Court Relevant to the UN Convention on the Law of the Sea* (2002). For analysis of the outstanding contributions of the *Gabcikovo* judgment to the development of modern environmental law, the law of international watercourses, the law of treaties and other issues, see, e.g., Rosalyn Higgins, 'Natural Resources in the Case Law of the International Court' in D. Freestone (ed.), *International Law and Sustainable Development: Past Achievements and Future Challenges* (1999), pp. 87–111; Stephen M. Schwebel, 'The Inter-Active Influence of the ICJ and the ILC' in C. AA. Barea (ed.), *Liber Amicorum for Judge Jose Maria Ruda* (2000), pp. 479–505; Stephen C. McCaffrey, 'International Watercourses in the Jurisprudence of the World Court' in N. Ando (ed.), *Liber Amicorum Judge Shigeru Oda* (2002), pp. 1055–68; Statement of ICJ President Gilbert Guillaume to the sixth (Legal) Committee of the fifty-seventh UN General Assembly, 30 October 2002, www.icj-cij.org; B. Kwiatkowska, 'The Law of the Sea Related Cases in the International Court of Justice During the Presidency of Judge Stephen M. Schwebel (1997–2000) and Beyond', updated as of 27 March 2003 at NILOS, www.law.uu.nl/nilos – Publications, Online Papers.

4 The inaugural *Southern Bluefin Tuna* arbitration was followed by two other UNCLOS Annex VII arbitrations, *Ireland* v. *United Kingdom (Mox Plant)* and *Malaysia* v. *Singapore (Land Reclamation)*, which are both pending, see www.pca-cpa.org

5 For the current status of the 1982 UNCLOS and the 1994 Part XI Agreement, see (2005) 55 *UN Law of the Sea Bulletin* and the excellent website of the UN Division for Ocean Affairs and the Law of the Sea (UNDOALOS) at www.un.org/Depts/los/

6 *Southern Bluefin Tuna (Jurisdiction and Admissibility)*, Award, 4 August 2000 ('the 2000 SBT Award'), President Stephen M. Schwebel, reprinted in 119 ILR 508; (2000) 39 ILM 1359; available with pleadings and the related ICSID news releases at the website of the International Centre for Settlement of Investment Disputes (ICSID), www.worldbank.org/icsid/bluefintuna/main.htm and (2001) 17(1) *ICSID News*, www.worldbank.org/icsid/news/n-17–1–3.htm; as reported in the Report of the Secretary-General, *Oceans and the Law of the Sea*, UN Doc. A/56/58, 80–81 (2001), www.un.org/Depts/los/; and B. Kwiatkowska in (2001) 95 *American Journal of International Law* 162.

See also contributions in Ando, *Liber Amicorum Oda*, by Stephen M. Schwebel, 'The Southern Bluefin Tuna Case', at pp. 743–8, B. Kwiatkowska, 'The Southern Bluefin Tuna Award (Jurisdiction and Admissibility)', at pp. 697–730, Y. Otani, 'Quelques réflexions sur la juridiction et la recevabilité vis-à-vis de l'Affaire du thon à nageoire bleu', at pp. 731–42, Chusei Yamada, 'Priority Application of Successive Treaties Relating to the Same Subject Matter: The Southern Bluefin Tuna Case', at pp. 763–71; see also B. Kwiatkowska, 'The Australia and New Zealand v. Japan Southern Bluefin Tuna (Jurisdiction and Admissibility) Award of the First Law of the Sea Convention Annex VII Arbitral Tribunal' (2001) 16 *International Journal of Marine and Coastal Law* 239, www.kluwerlawonline.com/document.php?id = 357926 and W. R. Mansfield, 'Letter to

developed states (Australia, New Zealand, and Japan) and the editors of this *Liber Amicorum* chose to focus it on developing states, my chapter will instead survey the 2002 *Cameroon* v. *Nigeria; Equatorial Guinea Intervening (Land and Maritime Boundary) (Merits)* judgment.

The 2002 judgment, along with the 2001 *Qatar* v. *Bahrain (Maritime Delimitation and Territorial Questions) (Merits)* judgment,[7] as well as the preceding 1998 *Eritrea* v. *Yemen (Territorial Sovereignty and Scope of the Dispute) (Phase I)* and the 1999 *Eritrea* v. *Yemen (Maritime Delimitation) (Phase II)* Awards,[8] provide landmark instances of application of the modern law of equitable maritime boundary delimitation in combination with the law

the Editor in Chief: The Southern Bluefin Tuna Arbitration: Comments on Professor Kwiatkowska's Article' (2001) 16 *IJMCL* 361, www.kluwerlawonline.com/document.php?id = 357934, and www.mft.govt.nz/support/legal/disputes/seapol.html, with that article as updated at www.law.uu.nl/nilos, announced in (2003) 1(3) *Global Oceans Forum Newsletter*, www.globaloceans.org/newsletters.html; T. L. McDorman, 'The Southern Bluefin Tuna Award' (2000) 11 *Yearbook of International Environmental Law* 582; Shabtai Rosenne, 'The Perplexities of Modern International Law: General Course' (2002) 291 Collected Courses of The Hague Academy 111 at 130–1, 305; S. Rosenne, 'Reflections on Fishery Management Disputes' at the 57th UN General Assembly Commemorating the 20th Anniversary of the Convention on the Law of the Sea, 9 December 2002, www.un.org/Depts/los; B. Kwiatkowska, 'The Southern Bluefin Tuna Arbitral Tribunal Did Get It Right: A Commentary and Reply to the Article by David A. Colson and Dr. Peggy Hoyle' (2003) 34 *Ocean Development and International Law* 369.

7 *Qatar* v. *Bahrain (Merits)*, judgment, President Gilbert Guillaume, [2001] ICJ Rep. 40, reprinted in (2001) 40 ILM 847; summarized in ICJ Press Releases 2001/9 and 2001/9 *bis*, 16 March 2001; www.gna.gov.bh/bahrain-qatar/news/title-e1.html; (2001) 46 *UN Law of the Sea Bulletin* 87. See G. Guillaume, *La Cour Internationale de Justice à l'aube du XXIème siècle* (2003), pp. 287–318; Ph. Weckel, 'CIJ: Arret du 16 mars 2001 (fond)' (2001) 105 *Revue Générale de Droit International Public (RGDIP)* 443; T. Yoshifumi, 'Reflections on the Concept of Proportionality' 16 *IJMCL* 433 at 452–3; G. Plant, 'The *Qatar* v. *Bahrain (Merits)* judgment' (2002) 96 *AJIL* 198; J. R. Crook, 'The 2001 Judicial Activity of the ICJ' (2002) 96 *AJIL* 397; M. G. Kohen, 'Les questions territoriales dans l'Arrêt de la C. I. J. du 16 mars 2001 en l'affaire Qatar c. Bahrein' (2002) 106 *RGDIP* 295; A. P. Palomar, 'La qualification juridique des formations maritimes dans l'Arrêt du 16 mars 2001' (2002) 106 *RGDIP* 329; P. Weil, 'Les hauts-fonds découvrants dans la délimitation maritime' in Ando, *Liber Amicorum Oda*, pp. 307–21; B. Kwiatkowska, 'The Qatar v. Bahrain Maritime Delimitation and Territorial Questions Case,' (2003) 3(6) *IBRU Maritime Briefing*, www-ibru.dur.ac.uk/pubs/mb.html

8 1998 *Eritrea* v. *Yemen (Territorial Sovereignty and Scope of the Dispute) (Phase I)*, Award, and the 1999 *Eritrea* v. *Yemen (Maritime Delimitation) (Phase II)*, Award, President Sir Robert Jennings, (2001) 40 ILM 900 at 983; 114 ILR 1 and 119 ILR 417; UNRIAA XXII, 211, 335; PCA at www.pca-cpa.org; Yemen Gateway at www.al-bab.com/yemen/pol/int.htm. See also Statement of Eritrea's Foreign Ministry of 20 December 1999, UN Doc. S/1999/1265; (2001) 44 *UN Law of the Sea Bulletin* 77.

See P. Hamilton *et al.* (eds.), *The Permanent Court of Arbitration: International Arbitration and Dispute Resolution* (1999), pp. 3, 26–7 (J. G. Merrills), p. 196 (Summary); W. M. Reisman, Case Reports on the *Eritrea* v. *Yemen* Awards (*Phase I*) at

of territorial acquisition, as developed in the notably successful and mutually reinforcing jurisprudence of the International Court of Justice, arbitral tribunals, and other third party fora.[9] The maritime delimitation settlements, which as Judge Stephen M. Schwebel put it, remain 'more plastic than formed'[10] and 'as variable as the weather of The Hague',[11] have also significantly contributed to the development of rules governing the legal regimes of all maritime spaces and other issues dealt with in this context, and the same often applies to territorial settlements, such as the 1998 *Eritrea/Yemen (Phase I)* Award, the 2002 UN *Eritrea/Ethiopia Boundary (Merits)* decision[12]

(1999) 93 *AJIL* 668, and (*Phase II*) at (2000) 94 *AJIL* 721; A. S. Millet, 'Erythree/ Yemen – CPA: Sentence du 9 octobre 1998' (1999) 103 *RGDIP* 189; G. Distefano, 'La Sentence Arbitrale du octobre 1998 dans l'affaire du differend insulaire entre le Yemen et l'Erythree' (1999) 103 *RGDIP* 851; J.-F. Dobelle and J.-M. Favre, 'La Sentence Arbitrale du 9 octobre 1998' (1998) 44 *Annuaire Français de Droit International* 337; Ph. Weckel, 'CPA: Sentence du 17 décembre 1999' (2000) 104 *RGDIP* 511; G. Distefano, 'La sentence arbitrale du 17 décembre 1999' (2000) 46 *AFDI* 255; M. D. Evans, 'The Maritime Delimitation Between Eritrea and Yemen' (2001) 14 *LJIL* 141; B. Kwiatkowska, 'The Eritrea/Yemen Arbitration: Landmark Progress in the Acquisition of Territorial Sovereignty and Equitable Maritime Boundary Delimitation' (2000) 8(1) *IBRU Boundary and Security Bulletin* 66 and (2001) 32 *ODIL* 1, available in revised and updated version at www.law.uu.nl/nilos, Publications – Online Papers.

9 See Annual Statements of Presidents Stephen M. Schwebel and Gilbert Guillaume to the 52nd to 57th UN General Assembly in 1997–2002, stressing that the Court has played and will continue to play a notably prominent role in contributing to the maintenance of international peace and security by resolution of territorial and maritime disputes: see www.icj-cij.org, as reaffirmed by the 2002 ICJ Message on the Occasion of the 20th UNCLOS Anniversary, ICJ Press Release 2002/38, 10 December 2002, and UN General Assembly Resolution 57/141 on Oceans and the Law of the Sea, 12 December 2002, paragraph 11; Kwiatkowska, *Decisions of the World Court*, pp. 57–111 and elsewhere (via Index of Cases); *Judge Schwebel's Reflections on International Adjudication and Arbitration* (Yale Reading Materials, 8 October 2004), www.law.yale.edu/outside/html/alumni_affairs/alum-wkndreadings.htm

10 *Gulf of Maine*, Separate Opinion of Judge Schwebel, [1984] ICJ Rep. 357, as reaffirmed in *Libya* v. *Malta (Continental Shelf) (Merits)*, Dissenting Opinion of Judge Schwebel, [1985] ICJ Rep. 187.

11 *Denmark* v. *Norway (Jan Mayen)*, Separate Opinion of Judge Schwebel, [1993] ICJ Rep. 120.

12 For exposition of the concept of 'the perpetuation of the traditional fishing regime in the region', see the 1998 and 1999 *Eritrea* v. *Yemen* Awards, *supra* n. 8. For the authoritative interpretation of 'disclaimers' placed on the United Nations maps, see the 2002 UN *Eritrea* v. *Ethiopia (Boundary) (Merits)* decision, President Sir Elihu Lauterpacht, paragraphs 3.26–3.28 and Appendix A, paragraphs A26-A32; as relied upon in the *Indonesia* v. *Malaysia (Merits)* hearings, CR2002/29, 42–3 (Counsel Malintoppi, 4 June 2002).

For the texts of the 2002 UN *Eritrea* v. *Ethiopia (Boundary Delimitation) (Merits)* decision, 13 April 2002, which delimited boundary lines involving rivers within the

or the 2002 *Indonesia/Malaysia Sovereignty over Pulau Ligitan and Pulau Sipadan (Merits)* judgment.[13]

The course of the proceedings and delivery of the judgment

The *Land and Maritime Boundary between Cameroon and Nigeria* proceedings were procedurally the most complex in the ICJ's history and consisted of the phases of provisional measures, preliminary objections, interpretation of the judgment on preliminary objections, as well as the phase of merits, including counterclaims and intervention, and the pending phase of implementation involving a third party (United Nations). This, as well as the *Libya/Chad*, *Botswana/Namibia*, *Eritrea/Yemen*, *Eritrea/Ethiopia*, and *Benin/Niger* cases illustrate the view of then President Stephen M. Schwebel that: 'Stability and certainty of boundaries, and the need for clear principles, fairly applied have been matters of particular importance to African States emerging from the colonial era'.[14]

Along with many other cases, they also illustrate that, as the UN General Assembly Statements of both Presidents Schwebel and Gilbert Guillaume

central and western sectors (Chapters II, IV, V, VII, VIII) (S/2002/423; (2002) 41 ILM 1057), and which was followed by *ibid.* (Interpretation) decision, 24 June 2002, as well as *ibid.* (Interim Measures) and (Demarcation) Orders, 17 July 2002 (S/2002/853), Determinations, 7 November 2002, Observations, 21 March 2003 (S/2003/257/Add.1; (2003) 42 ILM 1010) and Article 15B Decision, 7 July 2003 (S/2003/752) concerning the phase of demarcation, see PCA at www.pca-cpa.org and United Nations at www.un.org/NewLinks/eebc arbitration/ websites. See Judge Bruno Simma and D. E. Khan, in Ando, *Liber Amicorum Oda*, pp. 1179–96; Ph. Weckel, 'Decisions du 13 avril et 24 juin 2002' (2002) 106 *RGDIP* 695 at 705; J. Donaldson and M. Pratt, 'International Boundary Developments' (2004) 9 *Geopolitics* 501 at 502, 506–7.

13 For clarification of Indonesia's archipelagic regime and baselines under Act No. 4, 18 February 1960 (*The Law of the Sea: Practice of Archipelagic States* (United Nations, 1992), pp. 45–53), see 2002 *Indonesia* v. *Malaysia (Merits)*, judgment, [2002] ICJ Rep. 625, President Gilbert Guillaume, paragraphs 84, 130–1, 137; Hearings, CR 2002/27, 15 (Agent Wirajuda, 3 June 2002), CR 2002/29, 51, 53–6 (Counsel Pellet, 4 June 2002), CR 2002/30, 13 (Agent Mohamad, 6 June 2002), 22 (Co-Agent Ariffin), CR 2002/32, 27–9 (Counsel Crawford, 7 June 2002), CR 2002/34, 33 (Pellet, 10 June 2002), www.icj-cij.org See D. A. Colson, 'The Malaysia/Indonesia (Merits) Judgment' (2003) 97 *AJIL* 355 at 356, 398–406 and on this dispute generally, see R. Haller-Trost, *The Contested Maritime and Territorial Boundaries of Malaysia* (1998); D. M. Ong, 'Case Between Indonesia and Malaysia Concerning Sovereignty over Pulau Ligitan and Pulau Sipadan' (1999) 14 *IJMCL* 399; Ko Swan Sik, 'The Attitude of Asian States Towards the International Court of Justice Revisited' in Ando, *Liber Amicorum Oda*, pp. 165, 172–4.

14 S. M. Schwebel, 'The Impact of the International Court of Justice' in *Boutros Boutros-Ghali Amicorum Discipulorumque Liber: Paix, Développement, Démocratie* (1998), pp. 663, 668–9. See also the 2001 Harvard Interview with Judge Schwebel on 'International Law and the World Court,' www.npwj.org/pressmon/20010110_HIR.shtml

appreciated, the African states have been in the forefront of acquiring the 'judicial habit', contributing to the continuously busiest docket in the ICJ's history.[15] As in *Guinea-Bissau* v. *Senegal*, the parties to *Cameroon* v. *Nigeria* did not qualify for obtaining assistance from the UN Secretary-General's Trust Fund, which is currently being extended from cases brought by means of a *compromis* to all types of cases.[16]

The 1996 *Cameroon* v. *Nigeria (Provisional Measures)* Order exemplified, in the view of President Schwebel, political and judicial resolution of disputes by the Security Council and the ICJ respectively, working in parallel, and it provided an important instance of what he perceives as the 'considerable and constructive' influence of the ICJ on the progressive development of the international law of human rights.[17] In the 1998 *Cameroon* v. *Nigeria (Preliminary Objections)* judgment, which importantly consolidated the consent-based system of the Optional Clause under Article 36.2(4) of the ICJ Statute, the Court, presided over by Judge Schwebel, rejected seven preliminary objections of Nigeria to its jurisdiction and declared that the eighth objection (supplementary to the seventh one) did not have, in the circumstances of the case, an exclusively preliminary character.[18]

[15] See UN General Assembly Statements of Presidents Schwebel and Guillaume, *supra* n. 9. On the first 'decolonization' case relating to the African Continent, which was brought by Cameroon and led to *Cameroon* v. *United Kingdom (Northern Cameroons) (Preliminary Objections)*, judgment, [1963] ICJ Rep. 15, see D. H. N. Johnson, 'The Northern Cameroons Case' (1964) 13 *ICLQ* 1143.

[16] See (1989) 28 ILM 1589; UN Doc. A/57/373 (2002) and A/59/372 (2004).

[17] *Cameroon* v. *Nigeria (Provisional Measures)*, Order, [1996] ICJ Rep. 13, and Statement of President Stephen M. Schwebel to the 53rd UN General Assembly, UN Doc. A/53/PV.44, 27 October 1998, pp. 1, 5, in (1998–9) 53 *ICJ Yearbook* 316; S. M. Schwebel, *Justice in International Law: Collected Writings of Judge Stephen M. Schwebel* (1994), pp. 146–68; S. M. Schwebel, 'Clean Hands Doctrine' in *The World Bank, International Financial Institutions and the Development of International Law* (ASIL, 1999), pp. 74–8. See J. Sztucki, 'The 1996 Cameroon v. Nigeria (Provisional Measures) Order' (1997) 10 *Leiden JIL* 341.

[18] *Cameroon* v. *Nigeria (Land and Maritime Boundary) (Preliminary Objections)*, judgment, President Stephen M. Schwebel, [1998] ICJ Rep. 275; www.crtv.cm/actualite_det.php?code = 563. For Optional Clause Declarations, see (1999–2000) 54 *ICJ Yearbook* 106 (Cameroon), 129 (Nigeria). In connection with the first preliminary objection, the 1998 judgment consolidated the regime laid down in Article 36(2)–(4) of the ICJ Statute for depositing and transmitting Optional Clause Declarations and the condition of reciprocity. See C.-A. Fleischhauer, 'The Constitutional Relationship Between the Secretary-General of the United Nations and the International Court of Justice' in *Boutros-Ghali Liber*, pp. 462–3; G. Ziccardi Capaldo, 'The 1998 Cameroon v. Nigeria (Preliminary Objections) Judgment' (2001) 1 *Yearbook of International Law and Jurisprudence* 181.

Subsequently, Nigeria's Request for Interpretation of the 1998 judgment, in pursuance of Article 60 of the ICJ Statute, was found by the 1999 *Nigeria* v. *Cameroon (Interpretation)* judgment to be inadmissible.[19] Similarly, the 2002 UN *Ethiopia* v. *Eritrea Boundary (Interpretation)* decision and the 2003 *Yugoslavia* v. *Bosnia and Herzegovina (Revision)* judgment dismissed Ethiopia's request for interpretation and Yugoslavia's for revision, as inadmissible.[20]

In the course of the phase of merits pending during Judge Schwebel's Presidency, the 1999 *Cameroon* v. *Nigeria (Counter-Claims)* Order admitted counterclaims of Nigeria under Article 80 of the Rules of Court,[21] while the 1999 *Cameroon* v. *Nigeria (Application by Equatorial Guinea for Permission to Intervene)* Order authorized Equatorial Guinea to intervene in the *Cameroon* v. *Nigeria* case as a non-party pursuant to Article 62 of the ICJ Statute.[22] After authorization by the ICJ of the production by Cameroon of certain new documents concerning events subsequent to its Reply (documents which Cameroon found necessary, in view of Nigeria's Rejoinder), the oral hearings were held on 18 February–21 March 2002.[23]

[19] *Nigeria* v. *Cameroon (Land and Maritime Boundary) (Interpretation of the 1998 Judgment)*, judgment, President Stephen M. Schwebel, [1999] ICJ Rep. 31 (entered under General List No. 101, separate from No. 94 of the principal case). See H. Barati, 'Frontière Terrestre et Maritime (Cameroun c. Nigéria) Exceptions Préliminaires, Interprétation, Intervention' (1999) 45 *AFDI* 371; G. Ziccardi Capaldo, 'The 1999 Nigeria v. Cameroon Judgment' (2001) 1 *YILJ* 205. On procedural issues of the proceedings on interpretation, see S. Rosenne, 'Controlling Interlocutory Aspects of Proceedings in the International Court of Justice' (2000) 94 *AJIL* 307 at 308.

[20] See the 2002 UN *Ethiopia* v. *Eritrea (Interpretation)* decision, *supra* n. 12; and *Yugoslavia* v. *Bosnia and Herzegovina (Revision)*, judgment, President Gilbert Guillaume, ICJ Press Release 2003/8, 3 February 2003 and [2003] ICJ Rep. 7.

[21] *Cameroon* v. *Nigeria (Counter-Claims)* and *Cameroon* v. *Nigeria, Equatorial Guinea Intervening (Counter-Claims)*, Orders, [1999] ICJ Rep. 983 and [2001] ICJ Rep. 9. See Rosenne, 'Controlling Interlocutory Aspects', 309.

[22] *Cameroon* v. *Nigeria (Intervention)*, Order [1999] ICJ Rep. 1029, reprinted in (2000) 38 ILM 112, unanimously adopted by President Schwebel, Vice-President Weeramantry, Judges Oda, Bedjaoui, Guillaume, Ranjeva, Herczegh, Shi, Fleischhauer, Koroma, Vereshchetin, Higgins, Parra-Aranguren, Kooijmans, Rezek, Judges ad hoc Mbaye (designated by Cameroon) and Ajibola (designated by Nigeria). See Barati, 'Frontière Terrestre' J. G. Merrills, 'The International Court of Justice and the Adjudication of Territorial and Boundary Disputes' (2000) 13 *Leiden JIL* 873 at 880–1; Ph.Weckel, 'Ordonnance du 21 octobre 1999,' (2000) 104 *RGDIP* 248; E. Doussis, 'Interet juridique et intervention devant la CIJ' (2001) 105 *RGDIP* 55.

[23] ICJ Press Releases 2002/1 and 11, 28 January and 22 March 2002; CR 2002/1–26; 2002 *Cameroon* v. *Nigeria; Equatorial Guinea Intervening (Merits)*, judgment, paragraphs 22–4.

A notable significance of these multiphase proceedings for the global system of peace and security was reflected by an appeal of the UN Standing Advisory Committee on Security Questions in Central Africa of 30 August 2002 that the two parties 'refrain from taking any action that could create difficulties for the application of the final judgment of the Court'.[24] It was followed by an unusual prior commitment expressed by the Presidents of Cameroon and Nigeria at their meeting held with UN Secretary-General Kofi A. Annan in Paris on 5 September 2002 that they would respect and implement the ICJ's judgment and restore their fraternal and neighbourly relations.[25] In his Statement summarizing the *Cameroon* v. *Nigeria; Equatorial Guinea Intervening (Land and Maritime Boundary) (Merits)* judgment upon its delivery on 10 October 2002,[26] President Gilbert Guillaume welcomed on behalf of the ICJ the result of the Paris meeting and hoped that the judgment '[would] contribute to friendly relations between the two brother countries'.[27] In his parallel Statement of the same day, Secretary-General Kofi Annan reiterated his 'call on both parties to respect and implement the Court's decision', commended Nigeria and Cameroon for resorting to the ICJ for a peaceful settlement of their territorial dispute, and reaffirmed the United Nations' readiness to assist both countries in the judgment's implementation.[28] In his Statement to the fifty-seventh UN General Assembly on 29 October 2002, having reported upon the importance of the Court's decisions, President Guillaume concluded that: 'This Judgment is final.

24 UN Doc. A/57/380-S/2002/988, 6 September 2002, at pp. 4–5.

25 'Meeting with Annan, Cameroon and Nigeria Agree to Follow ICJ Border Decision and Statement of UN Secretary-General Kofi Annan', Press Release SG/SM/8368-AFR/476, 5 September 2002, www.un.org/News/Press/docs/2002/sgsm8368.doc.htm

26 *Cameroon* v. *Nigeria; Equatorial Guinea Intervening (Merits)*, judgment, [2002] ICJ Rep. 303, ICJ Press Release 2002/26, 10 October 2002. Present: President Guillaume, Vice-President Shi, Judges Oda, Ranjeva, Herczegh, Fleischhauer, Koroma, Higgins, Parra-Aranguren, Kooijmans, Rezek, Al-Khasawneh, Buergenthal, Elaraby, and Judges ad hoc Mbaye (Cameroon) and Ajibola (Nigeria), www.icj-cij.org. See P. H. F. Bekker in (2003) 97 *AJIL* 387; Ph. Weckel in (2003) 107 *RGDIP* 168.

27 Statement of President Guillaume, 10 October 2002, paragraph 9, www.icj-cij.org. See also *Cameroon* v. *Nigeria; Equatorial Guinea Intervening (Merits)*, judgment, paragraph 313, referring to *Libya* v. *Chad (Territorial Dispute)*, judgment, [1994] ICJ Rep. 6; (1994) 33 ILM 571 at 619, and 2002 Separate Opinion of Judge Ranjeva, paragraph 1. On the *Libya* v. *Chad* judgment, see Guillaume, *La Cour*, pp. 319–31; Schwebel, 'The Impact', 669.

28 Statement of UN Secretary-General Kofi A. Annan, 10 October 2002, www.un.org/apps/sg/sgstats.asp?nid=104

It is binding on the Parties. It thus brings legal closure to the frontier dispute between the two countries'.[29]

Less than one-third of the 285 paragraph legal reasoning of the ICJ (paragraphs 39–324) deals with the equitable maritime boundary delimitation (paragraphs 226–307, 318), with respect to which the Court took four decisions (operative paragraph 325.IV.(A)-(B)). The remaining part of this landmark decision concerns the disputed territorial sovereignty, determines the lengthy land boundary of 1,800 km, including the rivers,[30] and deals with state responsibility and counterclaims of Nigeria. The issues concerned include:

- the boundary line in Lake Chad (paragraphs 40–70, 312, 318 and operative paragraph 325.I.(A)-(B));
- the seventeen-sector boundary line from Lake Chad to the Bakassi Peninsula (paragraphs 71–192, 318 and operative paragraph 325.II.(A)-(B));
- sovereignty over the oil-rich Bakassi Peninsula, which was attributed to Cameroon, and the boundary line (paragraphs 193–225, 312, 318 and operative paragraph 325.III.(A)-(C));[31]
- Cameroon's submissions concerning Nigeria's state responsibility and Nigeria's counterclaims concerning Cameroon's state responsibility, which were both unanimously rejected (paragraphs 308–324 and operative paragraph 325.V.(D)-(E));[32]

[29] Statement of President Guillaume (to the 57th UN General Assembly), *supra* n. 9, 3–4. For the ensuing UNSG summits and UN Cameroon/Nigeria Commission's meetings see UNOWA, www.un.org/Depts/dpa/prev_dip/africa/office_for_srsg/cnme/preleas/sgstmts.htm; C. Paulson, 'Compliance with Final Judgments of the ICJ' (2004) 98 *AJIL* 434 at 449–52.

[30] On boundaries in international rivers and lakes, see also, *inter alia*, *El Salvador* v. *Honduras*; Nicaragua Intervening (Land, Island and Maritime Frontier Dispute) (Merits), judgment, [1992] ICJ Rep. 351, Chamber's President Jose Sette-Camara; 1994/1995 *Chile* v. *Argentina* (Laguna del Desierto), Awards, 113 ILR 1 at 17, 194; UNRIAA XXII, 3, 153; *Botswana* v. *Namibia* (Kasikili/Sedudu Island), judgment, President Stephen M. Schwebel, [1999] ICJ Rep. 1045; (2000) 39 ILM 310; 2002 UN *Eritrea* v. *Ethiopia* decisions, *supra* n. 12, and the pending *Benin* v. *Niger (Frontier Dispute)* case and *El Salvador* v. *Honduras (Gulf of Fonseca) (Revision)*, judgment, [2003] ICJ Rep. 392, www.icj-cij.org

[31] 2002 *Cameroon* v. *Nigeria; Equatorial Guinea Intervening (Merits)*, judgment, operative paragraph 325.III, with all three decisions having been taken by a 13:3 vote. In favour: President Guillaume, Vice-President Shi, Judges Oda, Ranjeva, Herczegh, Fleischhauer, Higgins, Parra-Aranguren, Kooijmans, Al-Khasawneh, Buergenthal, Elaraby, and Judge ad hoc Mbaye (designated by Cameroon); against: Judges Koroma, Rezek, and Judge ad hoc Ajibola (designated by Nigeria).

[32] See *supra* n. 21.

- withdrawal by each of the parties of their administration and military and police forces from sectors now determined as falling within the sovereignty of another party and affording by Cameroon protection to Nigerians living in the Bakassi Peninsula and in the Lake Chad area (paragraphs 312–18 and operative paragraph 325.V.(A)-(C)).[33]

The ICJ decided that the respective sectors of land boundary referred to above were determined by a number of colonial treaties,[34] including an Anglo-German Agreement of 11 March 1913, pursuant to which sovereignty over the Bakassi Peninsula was found to lie with Cameroon. With respect to the Lake Chad area and Bakassi, the Court rejected, moreover, the theory of historical consolidation and the *effectivités* relied upon by Nigeria which could not displace the established treaty titles.[35] In the 2002 *Indonesia* v. *Malaysia (Merits)* judgment, the treaty title and title by succession were rejected and the disputed Ligitan and Sipadan were attributed on the basis of *effectivités* to Malaysia.[36] The 2002 *Eritrea* v. *Ethiopia (Boundary) (Merits)* decision, basing itself on the 1999 *Botswana* v. *Namibia* approach, combined reliance on colonial treaties (of 1900, 1902, and 1908 applicable to the central, western, and eastern sectors respectively) with that on rules of international law relating to the effects of conduct of the parties, including maps, *effectivités* and a range of diplomatic and other similar exchanges.[37]

In its description of the geographical setting of the dispute, the 2002 *Cameroon* v. *Nigeria; Equatorial Guinea Intervening (Merits)* judgment noted that the coastal region where the southern part of the land boundary ends is the area of the Bakassi Peninsula, which is bounded by the River Akwayafe to the west and by the Rio del Rey to the east.[38] It is an amphibious

[33] See also *infra* n. 113.

[34] In the Lake Chad area, the treaty boundary was affirmed by the work of the Lake Chad Basin Commission (LCBC) carried out on the demarcation in 1983–91. The LCBC was established under Fort Lamy (N'Djamena) Convention and Statute on the Development of the Lake Chad Basin of 22 May 1964, as amended on 22 October 1972. See 2002 *Cameroon* v. *Nigeria; Equatorial Guinea Intervening (Merits)*, judgment, paragraphs 53–5.

[35] But see 2002 *Cameroon* v. *Nigeria; Equatorial Guinea Intervening (Merits)*, Separate Opinion of Judge Al-Khasawneh and Dissenting Opinions of Judge Koroma and Judge ad hoc Ajibola.

[36] 2002 *Indonesia* v. *Malaysia (Merits)*, judgment, *supra* n. 13.

[37] 2002 *Eritrea* v. *Ethiopia (Boundary) (Merits)*, decision, *supra* n. 12, paragraphs 3.14, 3.30, quoting 1999 *Botswana* v. *Namibia*, judgment, *supra* n. 30, at 1101–2, paragraphs 91–3.

[38] 2002 *Cameroon* v. *Nigeria; Equatorial Guinea Intervening (Merits)*, judgment, paragraph 30. On the region's high (land and coastal) oil potential, see J. Servant, 'The USA and the

environment, characterized by an abundance of water, fish stocks, and mangrove vegetation. The Gulf of Guinea, which is concave in character at the level of the Cameroonian and Nigerian coastlines, is bounded by other states, in particular by Sao Tome and Principe and by Equatorial Guinea, whose Bioko Island lies opposite the parties' coastlines.[39]

In contrast to the *Eritrea* v. *Yemen* and *Qatar* v. *Bahrain* cases, where only one of the parties (Yemen and Bahrain) ratified the UNCLOS, both Cameroon and Nigeria ratified it on 19 November 1985 and 14 August 1986 respectively. By virtue of Law No. 16 of 5 December 1974, and Decree of 1967, as amended by Decree No. 1 of 1 January 1998, Cameroon and Nigeria each proclaimed a twelve-mile territorial sea (TS), while by virtue of Decree No. 28 of 5 October 1978, Nigeria also established a 200-mile Exclusive Economic Zone (EEZ).[40] Equatorial Guinea, which, by virtue of Act No. 15 of 12 November 1984, proclaimed a twelve-mile territorial sea and 200-mile EEZ, ratified the UNCLOS some two years prior to filing its Application for Permission to Intervene in the *Cameroon* v. *Nigeria* proceedings, i.e., on 21 July 1997, and shortly prior to that Application it designated by Act No.1 of 6 March 1999 the equidistant line as its maritime boundary with Nigeria and Cameroon.[41] Subsequently, Equatorial Guinea and Sao Tome and

Gulf Oil States', *Le Monde Diplomatique*, January 2003, http://mondediplo.com/2003/01/08oil; 'New Oil Finds in West Africa', *International Herald Tribune*, 4 November 2003, www.iht.com/articles/116160.html and 8 June 2004, www.rigzone.com/news/article.asp?a_id = 13731

39 2002 *Cameroon* v. *Nigeria; Equatorial Guinea Intervening (Merits)*, judgment, paragraph 30 and Sketch-Map No. 11. See also Libreville Convention on the Regional Development of Fisheries Gulf of Guinea (COREP), 21 June 1984, (1987) 91 *RGDIP* 1115; Dakar Regional Convention on Fisheries Cooperation Among African States Bordering the Atlantic Ocean, 5 July 1999, (1912) UNTS 54; the UNEP Abidjan Convention for Cooperation in the Protection and Development of the Marine and Coastal Environment of the West and Central African Region and Protocol on Cooperation in Combating Pollution in Cases of Emergency, 23 March 1981 (in force 5 August 1984, (1981) 20 ILM 729; www.unep.ch/seas/rshome.html); (2003–4) *Yearbook of International Cooperation on Environment and Development* 173.

40 Cameroon's TS Law No. 16, *The Law of the Sea: National Legislation on the Territorial Sea*, (United Nations, 1995), p. 78; Nigeria's TS Decree No. 1, (1998) 38 *UN Law of the Sea Bulletin* 53; Nigeria's EEZ Decree No. 28, *The Law of the Sea: National Legislation on the Exclusive Economic Zone* (United Nations, 1993), p. 250; (1999) 39 *UN Law of the Sea Bulletin* 41 at 45.

41 Act No. 15, (1985) 6 *UN Law of the Sea Bulletin* 19; Act No. 1, (1999) 40 *UN Law of the Sea Bulletin* 31. For Equatorial Guinea's Declaration of 20 February 2002 under UNCLOS Article 298(1)(a), see (2002) 49 *UN Law of the Sea Bulletin* 14. On the Bioko Biodiversity Programme established to protect the wildlife of Bioko Island, see www.bioko.org/

Principe concluded the Maritime Boundary Delimitation Treaty of 26 June 1999,[42] followed by the Nigeria–Equatorial Guinea Maritime Boundary Treaty of 23 September 2000[43] and the Nigeria–Sao Tome and Principe Joint Development Zone Treaty of 21 February 2001.[44]

Equitable maritime boundary delimitation

The process of equitable maritime boundary delimitation in the phase of merits had been enriched by intervention of Equatorial Guinea, coupled with reconsideration and reaffirmation by the ICJ of its holdings concerning the seventh and eighth preliminary objections raised by Nigeria in the jurisdictional phase.

As in the *Eritrea* v. *Yemen* and the *Qatar* v. *Bahrain* cases, the single all-purpose boundary was drawn between both the twelve-mile territorial seas and the 200-mile exclusive economic zones and the continental shelf (CS) of Cameroon and Nigeria. It reinforced the governing role of equidistance as the equitable boundary not only between the opposite, but now also between the adjacent states under both Article 15 (TS) and Articles 74 and 83 (EEZ/CS) of the UNCLOS,[45] subject to interests of third states. While none of the other relevant circumstances were ultimately found to be of relevance on the actual course of the boundary line, the 2002 *Cameroon* v. *Nigeria; Equatorial Guinea Intervening (Merits)* judgment appraised the role of an island of a non-party state (Equatorial Guinea) and that of the oil practice (concessions and wells), even though without giving attention to mineral resources straddling the boundary.[46]

Third state intervention

After the 1990 *El Salvador* v. *Honduras (Gulf of Fonseca) (Intervention)* judgment of the Chamber for the first time granted Nicaragua permission

42 (2001) 47 *UN Law of the Sea Bulletin* 39.
43 (2001) 45 *UN Law of the Sea Bulletin* 68. See 2002 *Cameroon* v. *Nigeria; Equatorial Guinea Intervening (Merits)*, judgment, paragraphs 243, 284, Separate Opinion of Judge ad hoc Mbaye, paragraph 136; *infra* n. 79.
44 (2003) 50 *UN Law of the Sea Bulletin* 42. See 21 May and 18 June 2003, www.gulf-news.com/Articles/news.asp?ArticleID = 88242 and www.rigzone.com/news/article.asp?a_id = 7049; 28 October 2003, http://news.bbc.co.uk/2/hi/africa/3219409.stm
45 On the lack of geodetic datum, see *infra* nn. 85 and 111.
46 See *infra* nn. 89 and 106–9.

to intervene as a non-party under Article 62 of the ICJ Statute,[47] the 1999 *Cameroon* v. *Nigeria (Intervention)* Order, now rendered unanimously by the full Court, presided over by Judge Stephen M. Schwebel, marked the second instance of such an intervention by Equatorial Guinea.[48] Significantly, while President Schwebel was not a Member of the *Gulf of Fonseca* Chamber, he importantly contributed to such a more liberal approach to third state intervention through Opinions filed by him – along with that Chamber's Members, Judges José Sette-Camara, Shigeru Oda, and Sir Robert Jennings – in the preceding negative *Tunisia* v. *Libya* and *Libya* v. *Malta* decisions.[49] Although in both Libyan cases the requests for permission to intervene (opposed by each of the respective principal parties) were not granted, the 1981 *Tunisia* v. *Libya (Application by Malta for Permission to Intervene)* and the 1984 *Libya* v. *Malta (Application by Italy for Permission to Intervene)* judgments, including their Opinions, might be regarded as having opened up a new perspective for international litigation.[50] In particular, the requests of the two would-be interveners, Malta and Italy, had the effect of reducing considerably the areas of the congested and politically sensitive central Mediterranean Sea, which the

[47] *El Salvador* v. *Honduras (Gulf of Fonseca) (Intervention)*, judgment, [1990] ICJ Rep. 92 and the 1992 Gulf of Fonseca (Merits) judgment, *supra* n. 30, rendered by the Chamber consisting of President Sette-Camara, Judges Oda and Sir Robert Jennings, Judges ad hoc Valticos (designated by El Salvador) and Torres Bernardez (designated by Honduras). On the Chamber's composition, see also *El Salvador* v. *Honduras (Revision)*, Declaration of Judge Oda, [2002] ICJ Rep., www.icj-cij.org; Rosenne, 'Controlling Interlocutory Aspects, 310–11.

[48] 1999 *Cameroon* v. *Nigeria (Intervention)* Order, *supra* n. 22.

[49] For reliance on Judge Schwebel's *Tunisia* v. *Libya (Intervention)* Separate Opinion, [1981] ICJ Rep. 35, and *Libya* v. *Malta (Intervention)* Dissenting Opinion, [1984] ICJ Rep. 131, see 1984 *Libya* v. *Malta (Intervention)*, Separate Opinion of Judge ad hoc Jimenez de Arechaga, paragraph 28; *Gulf of Fonseca (Intervention)* Hearings, C4/CR90/1, 28 (Agent Argüello, 5 June 1990), 34 (Counsel Brownlie), C4/CR90/5, 12 (Argüello, 8 June 1990); *Indonesia* v. *Malaysia* (Intervention), Dissenting Opinion of Judge Oda, paragraph 7 and Separate Opinion of Judge ad hoc Weeramantry, paragraphs 19 and 27; 2002 *Cameroon* v. *Nigeria; Equatorial Guinea Intervening (Merits)*, Declaration of Judge Herczegh, www.icj-cij.org.

[50] *Tunisia* v. *Libya (Intervention)*, judgment, [1981] ICJ Rep., President Sir Humphrey Waldock, Separate Opinions of Judges Morozov at 22, Oda at 23 and Schwebel at 35; *Libya* v. *Malta (Intervention)*, judgment, [1984] ICJ Rep., President Elias, Separate Opinions of Judges Morozov at 30, Nagendra Singh at 31, Mbaye at 35, Judge ad hoc Jimenez de Arechaga (designated by Libya) at 55, Dissenting Opinions of Vice-President Sette-Camara at 71, Judes Oda at 90, Ago at 115, Schwebel at 131, and Sir Robert Jennings at 148, quoting (at 133, 156) *Colombia* v. *Peru Haya de la Torre (Intervention)*, judgment, [1951] ICJ Rep. 76.

ICJ found came within its jurisdiction in these cases. It might, therefore, be argued that, in spite of the Court's decision dismissing the applications to intervene, the would-be interveners, to an important extent, had achieved their objectives.[51]

In his Separate Opinion, which was the only one appended to the 1990 *Gulf of Fonseca (Intervention)* judgment, Judge Shigeru Oda concurred with the Chamber's judgment permitting Nicaragua to intervene, but criticized the scope of this intervention, which was limited (in accordance with Honduras' contention) to the legal regime of the waters within the Gulf of Fonseca, as determined by the 1917 *El Salvador* v. *Nicaragua (Gulf of Fonseca)* judgment.[52] Judge Oda regretted that this limitation excluded from the intervention the questions of delimitation within the Gulf and of the legal situation of the maritime spaces (including their prospective delimitation) outside the Gulf. However, the Chamber's position would appear to be justifiable in view of the aim of Honduras to confine the relevant area for the purposes of a hypothetical delimitation with El Salvador to the western sectors within and outside the Gulf of Fonseca. A clear confinement to these sectors, limited by perpendicular lines drawn from the midpoint on the closing line of the Gulf back inside the Gulf to reach the Honduran coast on the one hand, and out to the 200-mile limit on the other hand, would not prejudice any future delimitation which Nicaragua might seek either within or outside the Gulf.[53]

From a jurisdictional perspective, the 1990 *Gulf of Fonseca (Intervention)* judgment was in entire conformity with the previous decisions of the ICJ and could be regarded as but a gloss on their effect. In particular, in accordance with the principle of judicial consistency, the Chamber fully accepted that the lack of a jurisdictional link between

[51] See 1985 *Libya* v. *Malta (Merits)*, Dissenting Opinion of Judge Schwebel, *supra* n. 10 at 172–4, 177–8; Shabtai Rosenne, *Intervention in the International Court of Justice* (1993), pp. 136, 139–42.

[52] 1990 *Gulf of Fonseca (Intervention)*, judgment, *supra* n. 47 at 102–206, 120–2 and 137, operative paragraph 105, and Separate Opinion of Judge Oda, at 138–44; Hearings, C4/CR90/4, 27–53 (Counsel Bowett, 7 June 1990), C4/CR90/5, 53–59 (8 June 1990). For 1917 *El Salvador* v. *Nicaragua (Gulf of Fonseca)*, judgment of the Central American Court of Justice, see (1917) 11 *AJIL* 674; (1923) 17 *AJIL* 309; Kwiatkowska, *Decisions of the World Court* (via Index of Cases).

[53] 1990 *Gulf of Fonseca (Intervention)* judgment, *supra* n. 47 at 123; *Memorial of Honduras*, vol.2 (1 June 1988), Map C.5 (within the Gulf) at 704, and Map C.6 (outside the Gulf) at 720; Bowett (in C4/CR90/4), *supra* n. 52) and C4/CR91/44, 11–14 (Counsel Bowett, 10 June 1991).

the state seeking to intervene and the parties to the case is a fundamental stumbling block to a would-be intervener.[54] But since Nicaragua obviously had an effective legal interest in the case as required by Article 62 of the ICJ Statute, the Chamber allowed intervention without the intervening state having the status of a party to the dispute, thus holding that where there is no jurisdictional link a third state cannot be a party, even though it might intervene. Not being a party makes a material difference and precludes the application of Article 59 of the ICJ Statute and the respective provisions of the Rules of Court.[55] A significant element of the Chamber's decision thus lies in the distinction between an intervening party and a mere intervener, which does permit some kind of useful intervention while allowing full logical effect to the lack of any jurisdictional link.[56]

During the complex *Cameroon* v. *Nigeria* proceedings, the issue of third state intervention first revealed itself in the phase of jurisdiction and admissibility, in connection with the interrelated seventh and eighth preliminary objections of Nigeria, which concerned the whole Cameroon–Nigeria maritime boundary up to Point G and beyond (TS-CS/EEZ) and that boundary's sector beyond Point G (CS/EEZ), respectively. After Equatorial Guinea was granted permission to intervene in 1999, both these objections were again considered in the 2002 *Cameroon* v. *Nigeria; Equatorial Guinea Intervening (Merits)* judgment prior to the determination by the ICJ of a single, two-sector boundary (up to Point G and beyond).

The seventh preliminary objection of Nigeria that there was no legal dispute between the two parties over maritime boundary delimitation was rejected in the 1998 *Cameroon* v. *Nigeria (Preliminary Objections)* judgment

[54] 1990 *Gulf of Fonseca (Intervention)* judgment, *supra* n. 47 at 130–6; as reaffirmed by the 1999 *Cameroon* v. *Nigeria (Intervention)* Order, *infra* nn. 67–71.

[55] When Nicaragua declared its intention to be bound by the Chamber's 1990 judgment, *supra* n. 47 at 109, paragraph 38 in fine, it probably did not contemplate the possibility of being allowed to intervene as a non-party. If Nicaragua meant only that Article 59 would presumably apply, its declaration had no meaning or effect, which would be against the rules of interpretation. See also 1992 *Gulf of Fonseca (Merits)* judgment, *supra* n. 30 at 609–10, paragraphs 422 and 424; Rosenne, *Intervention*, p. 155; *Libya* v. *Malta (Intervention)*, Dissenting Opinions of Judges Sette-Camara, Schwebel, and Jennings, [1984] ICJ Rep. 87 at 134, 157–60; *Pakistan* v. *India (Jurisdiction)*, judgment, [2000] ICJ Rep. 24, paragraph 26.

[56] See 1981 *Tunisia* v. *Libya* (Intervention), Separate Opinion of Judge Schwebel, *supra* n. 50 at 40; 1984 *Libya* v. *Malta (Intervention)*, Dissenting Opinions of Judges Sette-Camara, *supra* n. 50 at 71–8, 84–8, Oda at 90–4, Schwebel at 139–47, and Sir Robert Jennings at 155–60; Rosenne, *Intervention*, pp. 188–90, 200; *infra* nn. 73–4.

by a twelve to five majority vote.[57] In the first place, the ICJ dismissed Nigeria's argument that no determination of a maritime boundary was possible prior to the determination of title over the Bakassi Peninsula on the ground that this matter could not be the basis of a preliminary objection, but lay within the Court's discretion of arranging the order of addressing the issues concerned.[58] As to Nigeria's second argument that Cameroon's Application was inadmissible because a precondition of prior negotiations was not fulfilled under UNCLOS Articles 74/83, the ICJ considered that it had not been seized on the basis of Article 36(1) of the ICJ Statute and UNCLOS Part XV, but on the basis of the Optional Clause Declarations which were made under Article 36(2) of the Statute and did not contain any condition relating to prior negotiations to be conducted within a reasonable time period.[59] In addition, the ICJ observed that not only had neither of the parties raised the question whether, beyond Point G, the dispute was defined with sufficient precision for the Court to be validly seized of it, but Cameroon and Nigeria had 'entered into negotiations with a view to determining the whole of the maritime boundary' and drew up the 1975 Maroua Declaration (up to Point G). As this Declaration was subsequently held to be binding by Cameroon, but not by Nigeria, and as the parties had not been able to agree on the continuation of the negotiations beyond Point G, the dispute between them was precise enough to be brought before the ICJ.[60]

With respect to Nigeria's eighth preliminary objection that maritime delimitation beyond Point G 'necessarily involves the rights and interests of third States and is to that extent inadmissible', the 1998 *Cameroon* v. *Nigeria (Preliminary Objections)* judgment found, by a twelve to five majority vote, that it did 'not possess, in the circumstances of the case, an exclusively preliminary character'.[61] The judgment pointed out that:

> the geographical location of the territories of the other States bordering the Gulf of Guinea, and in particular Equatorial Guinea and Sao Tome

[57] 1998 *Cameroon* v. *Nigeria (Preliminary Objections)* judgment, *supra* n. 18 at 322–5, paragraphs 103–11, and at 326, operative paragraph 118(1)(g). In favour: President Schwebel, Vice-President Weeramantry, Judges Bedjaoui, Guillaume, Ranjeva, Herczegh, Shi, Fleischhauer, Vereshchetin, Parra-Aranguren, Rezek, Judge ad hoc Mbaye (designated by Cameroon); against: Judges Oda, Koroma, Higgins, Kooijmans, Judge ad hoc Ajibola (designated by Nigeria).

[58] *Ibid.* at 320–1, paragraph 106. [59] *Ibid.* at 321–32, paragraph 109.

[60] *Ibid.* at 321, paragraph 107 and at 322, paragraph 110.

[61] *Ibid.* at 322–5, paragraphs 112–17, and at 326, operative paragraph 118(2). The twelve to five vote was the same as in the case of the seventh objection, *supra* n. 57.

> and Principe, demonstrates that it is evident that the prolongation of the maritime boundary between the Parties seawards beyond point G will eventually run into maritime zones where the rights and interests of Cameroon and Nigeria will overlap those of third States. It thus appears that rights and interests of third States will become involved if the Court accedes to Cameroon's request.[62]

Having noted that the ICJ could not therefore give a decision on the eighth objection as a preliminary matter, the Court remarked that:

> In order to determine where a prolonged maritime boundary beyond point G would run, where and to what extent it would meet possible claims of other States, and how its judgment would affect the rights and interests of these States, the Court would of necessity have to deal with the merits of Cameroon's request. At the same time, the Court cannot rule out the possibility that the impact of the judgment required by Cameroon on the rights and interests of the third States could be such that the Court would be prevented from rendering it in the absence of these States, and that consequently Nigeria's eighth preliminary objection would have to be upheld at least in part. Whether such third States would choose to exercise their rights to intervene in these proceedings pursuant to the Statute remains to be seen.[63]

As the 1999 *Cameroon* v. *Nigeria (Intervention)* Order recalled, the 1998 holdings quoted above were relied upon in the Application of Equatorial Guinea of 27 June 1999, which specified that it did 'not seek to become a party to the case'.[64] Instead, the purpose of its intervention was to inform the ICJ of Equatorial Guinea's legal rights and interests so that these may remain unaffected as the Court proceeds to address the question of the maritime boundary between Cameroon and Nigeria. Referring to Article 81(2)(a) of the Rules of Court, Equatorial Guinea set out its 'interest of a legal nature which [it] considers may be

[62] 1998 *Cameroon* v. *Nigeria (Preliminary Objections)*, judgment, *supra* n. 18 at 324, paragraph 116, reaffirming the third state-related holdings of the *Portugal* v. *Australia (East Timor)*, judgment, [1995] ICJ Rep. 101, paragraph 26 and at 104, paragraph 34, and *Nauru* v. *Australia (Preliminary Objections)*, judgment, [1992] ICJ Rep. 261, paragraph 55, Dissenting Opinions of President Sir Robert Jennings and Judge Schwebel at 301–2, 329–43.

[63] 1998 *Cameroon* v. *Nigeria (Preliminary Objections)* judgment, *supra* n. 18 at 324, paragraph 116; as relied upon in *Indonesia* v. *Malaysia (Intervention)*, Hearings, CR2001/1, 11 (Counsel Reisman, 25 June 2001) www.icj-cij.org

[64] 1999 *Cameroon* v. *Nigeria (Intervention)* Order, *supra* n. 22, paragraph 2, quoting 1998 *Cameroon* v. *Nigeria (Preliminary Objections)* judgment, *supra* nn. 62–3.

affected by the decision in that case', not as involving the ICJ's determination of its boundaries with Cameroon or Nigeria, but as confined to its wish that 'any Cameroon–Nigeria maritime boundary that may be determined by the Court should not cross over the median line with Equatorial Guinea'.[65] In pursuance of Article 81(2)(b) of the ICJ Rules of Court, 'the precise object of Equatorial Guinea's intervention' was thus:

first, to protect its legal rights in the Gulf of Guinea by all legal means available, and in this regard, to make use of the procedure established by Article 62 of the Statute;
secondly, to inform the Court of the nature of the legal rights and interests of Equatorial Guinea that could be affected by the Court's decision in the light of maritime boundary claims advanced by the parties to the case.[66]

As to the critical issue of a jurisdictional link between the intervening state and the parties to the case under Article 81.2(c) of the Rules of Court, Equatorial Guinea restated that it did not seek to be a party to the *Cameroon* v. *Nigeria* case. It had neither adhered to the Optional Clause under Article 36(2) of the Statute, nor was there any agreement in force between the three states conferring jurisdiction on the Court under Article 36(1).[67] Although it would be open to the three states to seek such an agreement, Equatorial Guinea preferred to continue to seek determination of its maritime boundaries with its neighbours through negotiations.

While none of the principal parties objected to such a non-party intervention, the ICJ, on its part, was of the opinion that Equatorial

[65] 1999 *Cameroon* v. *Nigeria (Intervention)* Order, *supra* n. 22, paragraph 3; and *supra* nn. 41–3. See also 2002 *Cameroon* v. *Nigeria, Equatorial Guinea Intervening (Merits)* judgment, paragraph 29, quoting contention of Equatorial Guinea that '[s]afeguarding the interests of the third State in these proceedings means that the delimitation between Nigeria and Cameroon decided by the Court must necessarily remain to the north of the median line between Equatorial Guinea's Bioko Island and the mainland'; and see paragraph 284.

In *Indonesia* v. *Malaysia (Sovereignty over Pulau Ligitan and Pulau Sipadan) (Intervention)*, judgment, President Gilbert Guillaume, paragraphs 59, 67, 82, [2001] ICJ Rep. 575, www.icj-cij.org, the ECJ dismissed the request of the Philippines to intervene as a non-party with a view to protecting its claim of sovereignty over North Borneo, because the Philippines had not discharged its burden of showing that it had a legal interest that could be affected within the terms of Article 62 of the ICJ Statute.

[66] 1999 *Cameroon* v. *Nigeria (Intervention)* Order, *supra* n. 22 at paragraph 4; also paragraph 6; as reaffirmed by 2001 *Indonesia* v. *Malaysia (Intervention)* judgment, *supra* n. 65 at paragraphs 49 and 87.

[67] 1999 *Cameroon* v. *Nigeria (Intervention)* Order, *supra* n. 22 at paragraph 5.

Guinea sufficiently established that it had 'an interest of a legal nature which could be affected' by 'any' judgment determining the Cameroon–Nigeria maritime boundary.[68] In this context, the Court reaffirmed the 1990 *Gulf of Fonseca (Intervention)* holding that '[s]o far as the object of [a state's] intervention is "to inform the Court of the nature of the legal rights [of that state] which are in issue in the dispute", it cannot be said that this object is not a proper one: it seems indeed to accord with the function of intervention'.[69] In view of the absence of jurisdictional link, the 1999 *Cameroon* v. *Nigeria (Intervention)* Order also reaffirmed the landmark *Gulf of Fonseca* holdings, which crowned a more liberal approach to third state intervention as now consolidated, under Article 62 of the ICJ Statute, by asserting that:

> It follows . . . from the juridical nature and from the purposes of intervention that the existence of a valid link of jurisdiction between the would-be intervener and the parties is not a requirement for the success of the application. On the contrary, the procedure of intervention is not to ensure that a State with possibly affected interests may be permitted to intervene even though there is no jurisdictional link and it therefore cannot become a party.[70]

Accordingly there was nothing to prevent the Application by Equatorial Guinea from being granted, as such, the ICJ unanimously permitted it to intervene, pursuant to Article 62, to the extent, in the manner, and for the purposes set out in that Application.[71]

[68] 1999 *Cameroon* v. *Nigeria (Intervention)* Order, *supra* n. 22 at paragraph 13; as relied upon in *Indonesia* v. *Malaysia (Intervention)*, Hearings, CR2001/2, 27 (Counsel Cot, 26 June 2001).

[69] 1999 *Cameroon* v. *Nigeria (Intervention)* Order, *supra* n. 22 at paragraph 14, quoting 1990 *Gulf of Fonseca (Intervention)* judgment, *supra* n. 47 at 130, paragraph 90; as both reaffirmed by 2001 *Indonesia* v. *Malaysia (Intervention)* judgment, *supra* n. 65 at paragraph 88. See also 2001 judgment at paragraph 35, quoting 1990 *Gulf of Fonseca (Intervention)* judgment, *supra* n. 47 at 133–4, paragraphs 97–8; and *supra* nn. 47–56.

[70] 1999 *Cameroon* v. *Nigeria (Intervention)* Order, *supra* n. 22 at paragraph 15, quoting 1990 *Gulf of Fonseca (Intervention)* judgment, *supra* n. 47 at 135, paragraph 100; as both reaffirmed by 2001 *Indonesia* v. *Malaysia (Intervention)* judgment, *supra* n. 65 at paragraph 35, also adding that according to the 1990 judgment, paragraph 99, such a jurisdictional link is required only if the state seeking to intervene is desirous of 'itself becoming a party to the case'; 2001 Dissenting Opinion of Judge Oda, paragraph 7, Separate Opinion of Judge Weeramantry, paragraphs 19 and 27; Hearings, CR2001/2, 24 (Counsel Cot, 26 June 2001) www.icj-cij.org

[71] 1999 *Cameroon* v. *Nigeria (Intervention)* Order, *supra* n. 22 at paragraph 16 and operative paragraph 18(1).

The eighty-one paragraph legal reasoning of the 2002 *Cameroon* v. *Nigeria, Equatorial Guinea Intervening (Merits)* judgment related to equitable maritime boundary delimitation (paragraphs 226–307) commenced, in accordance with Article 79(7) of the Rules of Court, with consideration of Nigeria's eighth objection, which the 1998 *Cameroon* v. *Nigeria (Preliminary Objections)* judgment found not to 'possess, in the circumstances of the case, an exclusively preliminary character' and which was now dismissed by a thirteen to three majority vote.[72] Having examined the positions of the parties, the Court considered that Article 59 of the ICJ Statute might not sufficiently protect Equatorial Guinea as a non-party intervener or Sao Tome and Principe from the effects – even if only indirect – of a judgment affecting their legal rights, and that, therefore, the ICJ had to ensure that it did not adopt any position which could affect the rights of these states.[73] In connection with this Court's holding concerning Article 59, Judge Geza Herczegh recalled, in his concurring Declaration, the view of Judge Stephen M. Schwebel that 'Article 59 cannot, by any cannon of interpretation, be read so as to read Article 62 out of the Statute'.[74] At the same time, as both parties agreed, the ICJ was not entitled to fix the Cameroon–Nigeria–Equatorial Guinea tripoint in

[72] 2002 *Cameroon* v. *Nigeria; Equatorial Guinea Intervening (Merits)* judgment, *supra* n. 26 at paragraphs 226–38 and operative paragraph 325.IV.(A), quoting (at paragraphs 227, 237, and 325.IV.(A)) the 1998 *Cameroon* v. *Nigeria (Preliminary Objections)* judgment, *supra* nn. 61–4. In favour: President Guillaume, Vice-President Shi, Judges Ranjeva, Herczegh, Fleischhauer, Higgins, Parra-Aranguren, Kooijmans, Rezek, Al-Khasawneh, Buergenthal, Elaraby, and Judge ad hoc Mbaye (designated by Cameroon); against: Judges Oda, Koroma, and Judge ad hoc Ajibola (designated by Nigeria). Dame Rosalyn Higgins and Judge Kooijmans, who voted against operative paragraph 118(2) of the 1998 judgment, *supra* n. 61, were now in the majority.

[73] 2002 *Cameroon* v. *Nigeria; Equatorial Guinea Intervening (Merits)* judgment, paragraphs 227–36 (positions of the parties) and paragraph 238, quoting *Tunisia* v. *Libya (Merits)*, judgment, [1982] ICJ Rep. 91, paragraph 130. Although Sao Tome and Principe did not request permission to intervene, the 2002 judgment followed the 1998 *Cameroon* v. *Nigeria (Preliminary Objections)* judgment, *supra* nn. 62–3, in considering its rights along with those of Equatorial Guinea. See 1981 *Tunisia* v. *Libya (Intervention)*, Separate Opinion of Judge Schwebel, *supra* n. 50 at 37, doubting with respect to the 1981 judgment paragraph 33 whether there were interests of the same kind of other states than Malta (intervener) and Italy (non-intervener) – other than Tunisia and Libya – within the central Mediterranean region.

[74] 2002 *Cameroon* v. *Nigeria; Equatorial Guinea Intervening (Merits)*, Declaration of Judge Herczegh, quoting 1984 *Libya* v. *Malta (Intervention)*, Dissenting Opinion of Judge Schwebel, *supra* n. 50 at 134, paragraph 9. On the positions of the parties on Article 59 of the ICJ Statute, see 1998 *Cameroon* v. *Nigeria (Preliminary Objections)* judgment, *supra* n. 18 at paragraphs 113–14. See also *supra* nn. 55–6.

determining the boundary line beyond Point G. The Court concluded that the mere presence of the two third states, whose rights could be affected by its decision, did not in itself preclude the Court from having jurisdiction over a maritime delimitation between the parties, Cameroon and Nigeria, although it had to remain mindful of the limitations on its jurisdiction that such presence imposed.[75] The ICJ then turned to giving a renewed consideration in the 2002 *Cameroon* v. *Nigeria, Equatorial Guinea Intervening (Merits)* judgment to the inter-related seventh objection of Nigeria that the requirement of prior negotiations has not been satisfied, and to reaffirming the findings of the 1998 *Cameroon* v. *Nigeria (Preliminary Objections)* judgment which dismissed that objection.[76] While Nigeria accepted the 1998 judgment's holding that the ICJ had not been seized on the basis of Article 36(1) of the ICJ Statute and UNCLOS Part XV, but on that of Article 36(2) of the Statute, it argued that this judgment only concerned the Court's jurisdiction and not the substantive law laid down in UNCLOS Articles 74 and 83.[77] Moreover, while Nigeria accepted the 1998 finding that 'Cameroon and Nigeria entered into negotiations with a view to determining the whole of the maritime boundary', it insisted that those negotiations were not even remotely concerned with the line now claimed by Cameroon, but solely related to areas around Point G and the location of the Cameroon–Nigeria–Equatorial Guinea tripoint.[78] In the view of Cameroon, intense negotiations between the two parties focused, from the outset, on, as the ICJ stated, 'the whole of the maritime boundary'. Since it was the bad faith conduct of Nigeria that led to an impasse in achieving a negotiated agreement, Nigeria could not now take advantage of its own wrongful behaviour to prevent Cameroon from achieving full settlement of the dispute by the Court. Were the ICJ to refrain from delimiting the maritime areas beyond

[75] 2002 *Cameroon* v. *Nigeria; Equatorial Guinea Intervening (Merits)* judgment, paragraph 238.

[76] 2002 *Cameroon* v. *Nigeria; Equatorial Guinea Intervening (Merits)* judgment, paragraphs 226, 239–45, quoting (at paragraphs 239–44) the 1998 *Cameroon* v. *Nigeria (Preliminary Objections)* judgment, *supra* nn. 57–60.

[77] 2002 *Cameroon* v. *Nigeria; Equatorial Guinea Intervening (Merits)* judgment, paragraphs 239–40 (Nigeria) and 242 (Cameroon), quoting the 1998 *Cameroon* v. *Nigeria (Preliminary Objections)* judgment, *supra* n. 59.

[78] 2002 *Cameroon* v. *Nigeria; Equatorial Guinea Intervening (Merits)* judgment, paragraphs 241 (Nigeria) and 243 (Cameroon), quoting the 1998 *Cameroon* v. *Nigeria (Preliminary Objections)* judgment, *supra* n. 60.

Point G, it would, according to Cameroon, leave a major source of conflict between the two parties.[79]

The Court reaffirmed its 1998 findings that negotiations under UNCLOS Articles 74 and 83 concerning the entire Cameroon–Nigeria boundary up to Point G and beyond have indeed been conducted in good faith.[80] It added that if, following unsuccessful negotiations, judicial proceedings are instituted and one of the parties then alters its claim, Articles 74 and 83 would not require that the proceedings be suspended while new negotiations were conducted, even though the new claim would have to be dealt with exclusively by judicial means. In the view of the ICJ, it did not follow from Articles 74 and 83 that the drawing of the boundary between Cameroon and Nigeria presupposed that simultaneous negotiations between them and third states had taken place. The Court was, therefore, in a position to proceed to the delimitation of that boundary insofar as the rights of Equatorial Guinea and Sao Tome and Principe were not affected.[81]

A single all-purpose equidistant (median) line

The single Cameroon–Nigeria equidistant (median) boundary was constructed by the ICJ in two sectors, which were relied upon by Cameroon and which comprised of:

the southern sector of partially overlapping TSs up to Point G, and
the northern sector of partially overlapping CS/EEZs beyond Point G.

As the course of the boundary up to Point G was found by the ICJ to be determined by valid international agreements between the parties, it

79 2002 *Cameroon* v. *Nigeria; Equatorial Guinea Intervening (Merits)* judgment, paragraph 243, quoting the 1998 *Cameroon* v. *Nigeria (Preliminary Objections)* judgment, *supra* n. 60, and adding that the ECJ's abstention would implicitly uphold the 2000 Nigeria–Equatorial Guinea Agreement (*supra* n. 43) which was concluded in utter disregard of Cameroon's own rights. For Equatorial Guinea's view that Cameroon cannot seek to benefit from that Treaty, see 2002 judgment, paragraph 284.

80 2002 *Cameroon* v. *Nigeria; Equatorial Guinea Intervening (Merits)* judgment, paragraph 244, quoting the 1998 *Cameroon* v. *Nigeria (Preliminary Objections)* judgment, *supra* n. 60, and noting that under UNCLOS Articles 74 and 83 and international law generally, the good faith negotiations do not need to be successful. See also 1997 *Gabcikovo-Nagymaros Project* judgment, *supra* n. 2 at 78, paragraph 141, reaffirming the *North Sea Continental Shelf* judgment [1969] ICJ Rep. 47, paragraph 85.

81 2002 *Cameroon* v. *Nigeria; Equatorial Guinea Intervening (Merits)* judgment, paragraph 245.

was only with respect to the sector beyond Point G that the Court referred to the concept of a single all-purpose boundary, which was agreed to by both parties and which, as the 2001 *Qatar* v. *Bahrain (Merits)* judgment held:

> [d]oes not stem from multilateral treaty law but from State practice and . . . finds its explanation in the wish of States to establish one uninterrupted boundary line delimiting the various – partially coincident – zones of maritime jurisdiction appertaining to them.[82]

The 2002 *Cameroon* v. *Nigeria; Equatorial Guinea Intervening (Merits)* judgment also reaffirmed holdings of the *Gulf of Maine* Chamber, which for the first time applied a single boundary line and whose views were already relied upon by the *Qatar* v. *Bahrain (Merits)* judgment.[83]

Boundary line up to Point G

The sector of Cameroon–Nigeria boundary delimiting their partially overlapping territorial seas was determined by a thirteen to three majority vote (the same as in the case of awarding sovereignty over the Bakassi Peninsula to Cameroon) to extend from the mouth of the Akpakorum (Akwayafe) River to Point 12 and from the latter up to Point G.[84] The boundary was defined by a series of geodetic lines joining Points 1 to 12 and A to G, which were specified in degrees, minutes, and seconds of the geographic latitude and longitude (without indication of the geodetic datum) and were indicated, for illustrative purposes only, in a sketch-map attached to the 2002 *Cameroon* v. *Nigeria; Equatorial Guinea Intervening (Merits)* judgment.[85] Since Point 1 of the maritime boundary corresponds with the ending point

[82] 2002 *Cameroon* v. *Nigeria; Equatorial Guinea Intervening (Merits)* judgment, paragraphs 25–7, 226, 272 (Cameroon), 26–7, 276 (Nigeria) and paragraph 286, quoting 2001 *Qatar* v. *Bahrain (Merits)* judgment, *supra* n. 7 at paragraph 173.

[83] 2002 *Cameroon* v. *Nigeria; Equatorial Guinea Intervening (Merits)* judgment, paragraph 287, quoting *Gulf of Maine* judgment, [1984] ICJ Rep. 327, paragraph 194 and *supra* n. 10; as reaffirmed by 2001 *Qatar* v. *Bahrain (Merits)* judgment, *supra* n. 7 at paragraph 173.

[84] 2002 *Cameroon* v. *Nigeria; Equatorial Guinea Intervening (Merits)* judgment, paragraphs 32, 38, 211–15, 223, 246–68 and operative paragraph 325.IV.(B), adopted by thirteen to three majority vote, the same as in the case of operative paragraph 325.III, *supra* n. 31.

[85] 2002 *Cameroon* v. *Nigeria; Equatorial Guinea Intervening (Merits)* judgment, operative paragraph 325.IV.(B) and Sketch-Map No. 12. See also the *Cameroon* v. *Nigeria* Relevant Lines map of Sovereign Geographic, Inc., www.sovereigngeographic.com, 'Portfolio'. On the lack in the 2002 judgment – by contrast to the 1999 *Eritrea* v.

of the land boundary determined by the ICJ in the Bakassi Peninsula, the maritime boundary starts from the point of intersection of the centre of Akwayafe's navigable channel with the straight line joining Bakassi Point and King Point, as determined by the Anglo-German Agreement of 11 March 1913 Articles XVIII and XXI.[86] Accepting Cameroon's contentions, the ICJ upheld the validity of instruments, pursuant to which the Heads of State of Nigeria and Cameroon agreed upon their boundary and determined:

- that Points 1 to 12 of the boundary follow 'the compromise line' drawn in the Yaounde II Declaration of 4 April 1971 and British Admiralty Chart No. 3433 annexed to that Declaration, with precise coordinates of those twelve points having been determined by the Joint Commission at its meeting in Lagos in June 1971, and
- that from Point 12, the boundary line connecting Points A to G follows the line adopted in the Maroua Declaration of 1 June 1975, as corrected by the Exchange of Letters of 12 June and 17 July 1975, and as accordingly marked up at British Admiralty Chart No. 3433 (not specifying the geodetic datum).

The ICJ rejected Nigeria's argument that the Maroua Declaration was a nullity due to its non-ratification by the Nigerian Supreme Military Council and held that this Declaration's wording testified to its having entered into force immediately upon its signature. If the 1975 Maroua Declaration, which expressly confirmed the line contained in the 1971 Yaounde II Declaration, was an international agreement binding on both parties, it necessarily followed that the Yaounde Declaration was binding on them as well.[87] As the ICJ also dismissed Nigeria's arguments that its constitutional rules regarding the conclusion of treaties were not complied with and that Cameroon knew, or ought to have known, that the Head of State of Nigeria had no power legally to bind Nigeria without consulting the Nigerian government, it concluded that the 1971 Yaounde II and the 1975 Maroua Declarations had to be considered as binding and as establishing a legal obligation on

Yemen (Phase II) Award and the 2001 *Qatar* v. *Bahrain (Merits)* judgment – of the geodetic datum required by UNCLOS, see B. Ravanas, 'Datums et Projections' in *Colloque International sur le Processus de Délimitation, Monaco, 27–29 March 2003* (Bruylant, 2004) www.indemer.org

86 2002 *Cameroon* v. *Nigeria; Equatorial Guinea Intervening (Merits)* judgment, paragraphs 30 (*supra* n. 38), 213–14, 250, 261, 268, 292 (*infra* n. 100) and operative paragraphs 325.III.(C) and 325.IV.(B).

87 *Ibid.* at paragraphs 263–4.

Nigeria.[88] Consequently, it was unnecessary for the ICJ to address Nigeria's contentions concerning the oil practice in the present sector of the boundary line up to Point G.[89]

Boundary line beyond Point G

In the decision-making process which led to its unanimous determination of a single maritime boundary delimiting partially overlapping CS/EEZ areas of Cameroon and Nigeria beyond Point G,[90] the ICJ first carefully considered contentions and submissions of both parties and the non-party intervener Equatorial Guinea.[91] In connection with the application of a single all-purpose boundary, the Court reaffirmed the 1985 *Libya* v. *Malta (Merits)* holding that as the UNCLOS demonstrates, 'the two institutions – continental shelf and exclusive economic zone – are linked together in modern law'.[92] Although without invoking the 1993 *Denmark* v. *Norway (Jan Mayen)* pronouncements to this effect, the 2002 *Cameroon* v. *Nigeria; Equatorial Guinea Intervening (Merits)* judgment also reaffirmed, as did the 1999 *Eritrea* v. *Yemen (Phase II)* Award, the 2001 *Qatar* v. *Bahrain (Merits)* judgment and other decisions, that the 'equidistance/special circumstances' and the 'equitable principles/relevant circumstances' rules (or methods) applicable to delimitation of the TS and the CS/EEZ, respectively, are 'very similar' and it expressly invoked UNCLOS Articles 74 and 83 in that latter

[88] *Ibid.* at paragraphs 265–8. On the location of Point G to the east of the equidistance, and on the course of the boundary from Points G to X where it meets the equidistance, see *ibid.* paragraph 307, *infra* n. 111.

[89] 2002 *Cameroon* v. *Nigeria; Equatorial Guinea Intervening (Merits)* judgment, paragraphs 256 and 268. See also *ibid.* at paragraph 211, referring to Nigeria's arguments that 'the area in dispute was the subject of competing exploration activities' and that 'the incidence of oil-related activities was not ... regarded [by the parties] as conclusive of the issue of sovereignty'; paragraphs 214–15, noting that, in the view of the ECJ, the geographic pattern of the oil concessions granted by the two parties up to 1991 was consistent with their understanding evidenced elsewhere, as to pre-existing Cameroon title in Bakassi; paragraph 223; *supra* nn. 38, 46; and *infra* nn. 106–9.

[90] 2002 *Cameroon* v. *Nigeria; Equatorial Guinea Intervening (Merits)* judgment, paragraphs 246–8, 269–307 and operative paragraph 325.IV(C)–(D), *infra* nn. 111–12.

[91] 2002 *Cameroon* v. *Nigeria; Equatorial Guinea Intervening (Merits)* judgment, paragraphs 25–7, 270–5 (Cameroon), 26–7, 276–83 (Nigeria), 29, 284 (Equatorial Guinea) (*supra* n. 65); and *supra* n. 78.

[92] See *supra* nn. 82–3; and 2002 *Cameroon* v. *Nigeria; Equatorial Guinea Intervening (Merits)* judgment, paragraph 287, quoting *Libya* v. *Malta Continental Shelf (Merits)* judgment, [1985] ICJ Rep. 33, paragraph 33; as reaffirmed by 2001 *Qatar* v. *Bahrain (Merits)* judgment, *supra* n. 7 at paragraph 226.

context.[93] It followed, as the previous equitable jurisprudence of the ICJ and arbitral tribunals held, that the maritime boundary delimitation was to be effected through a two-stage decision-making process of (1) first drawing provisionally an equidistant line,[94] and then (2) considering whether there are circumstances which must lead to an adjustment of that line.[95]

At the first stage of constructing a provisional equidistance, the ICJ rejected Cameroon's contentions, on the one hand, that account should be taken of the coastline of the Gulf of Guinea from Akasso (Nigeria) to Cap Lopez (Gabon) in order to delimit Cameroon's maritime boundary with Nigeria, and, on the other, that no account should be taken of the greater part of the coastline of Bioko Island.[96] In the view of the Court, the Cameroon–Nigeria maritime boundary could only be determined by reference to points on the coastlines of these states and not of third states, while the presence of Bioko belonging to Equatorial Guinea made itself felt from Debundsha, at the point where the Cameroon coast turns south-south-east. North and east of Bioko Island the maritime rights of Cameroon and Equatorial Guinea have not yet been determined. As the part of the Cameroon coastline beyond Debundsha Point faces Bioko, it could not be treated as facing Nigeria, so as to be relevant to maritime delimitation between the two parties.[97]

[93] 2002 *Cameroon* v. *Nigeria; Equatorial Guinea Intervening (Merits)* judgment, paragraph 288. Reference to UNCLOS Articles 74 and 83, *ibid.* at paragraph 285, by contrast to its absence in the 2001 *Qatar* v. *Bahrain* judgment, paragraph 231, now resulted from forming part by these provisions of Nigeria's seventh preliminary objection referred to in the 2002 judgment paragraphs 26–7, 239–45, 270 and 278, *supra* nn. 76–81. See also *Denmark* v. *Norway (Maritime Delimitation) (Jan Mayen)*, judgment, [1993] ICJ Rep. 58, Separate Opinions of Judge Oda at 106–9 and Judge Schwebel at 127–8; 1999 *Eritrea* v. *Yemen (Phase II)* Award, *supra* n. 8 at paragraphs 13, 23–4, 116, 131–3; 2002 *Newfoundland and Labrador* v. *Nova Scotia (Phase II)* Award, paragraphs 2.27, 5.2, www.boundary-dispute.ca

[94] For definition of equidistance, see 2002 *Cameroon* v. *Nigeria; Equatorial Guinea Intervening (Merits)* judgment, paragraphs 290 and 292, quoting 2001 *Qatar* v. *Bahrain (Merits)* judgment, *supra* n. 7 at paragraph 177.

[95] 2002 *Cameroon* v. *Nigeria; Equatorial Guinea Intervening (Merits)* judgment, paragraphs 288–90, quoting 1993 *Denmark* v. *Norway (Jan Mayen)* judgment, *supra* n. 93 at 61–2, paragraphs 51, 55, as previously reaffirmed by 2001 *Qatar* v. *Bahrain (Merits)* judgment, *supra* n. 7 at paragraphs 227–34.

[96] 2002 *Cameroon* v. *Nigeria; Equatorial Guinea Intervening (Merits)* judgment, paragraphs 272–5, referring to Cameroon's contentions relying on the 1985 *Guinea* v. *Guinea-Bissau (Maritime Boundary)* Award ((1986) 25 ILM 251) and other decisions of the ICJ and arbitral tribunals, and 2002 judgment paragraph 291.

[97] 2002 *Cameroon* v. *Nigeria; Equatorial Guinea Intervening (Merits)* judgment, paragraph 291 and Sketch-Map No. 11 (*supra* n. 39).

The ICJ did not refer to baselines proclaimed by the parties, but just observed that the establishment of the base points in accordance with the *Qatar* v. *Bahrain (Merits)* holdings was to enable it to determine the equidistant line between their relevant coastlines.[98] Moreover, whatever the base points used, the limitation on the length of the equidistant line was necessitated by the fact that this line could not be extended beyond a point where it could affect rights of Equatorial Guinea.[99] Given the configuration of the coastlines and the limited area within which the Court had jurisdiction to effect the delimitation, it considered that for the purpose of constructing its provisional equidistance, no base points were necessary other than the land-based anchorage West Point (at 8° 16′ 38″ longitude east and 4° 31′ 59″ latitude north) and East Point (at 8° 30′ 14″ longitude east and 4° 30′ 06″ latitude north), corresponding to the most southerly points on the low-water line for Nigeria and Cameroon to either side of the bay formed by the estuaries of the Akwayafe and Cross Rivers, as determined on the 1994 edition of British Admiralty Chart No. 3433.[100]

At the second stage, during its consideration of whether the provisional single equidistant line had to be adjusted to take into account relevant circumstances, the ICJ examined but rejected Cameroon's contentions concerning the concavity of the coastline, the presence closer to Cameroonian coast of Bioko Island being part of Equatorial Guinea, and the disparity between the length of the respective coastlines, as well as Nigeria's arguments concerning the oil practice (concessions and wells). By means of a general approach, the Court reaffirmed its classic *North Sea* holdings that 'equity does not necessarily imply equality' and that it is not required to take all geographical particularities into account in order to adjust or shift the provisional delimitation line, because:

[98] *Ibid.* at paragraph 292, reaffirming 2001 Qatar v. Bahrain (Merits) judgment, *supra* n. 7 at paragraph 177. For the respective legislation and treaties, see *supra* nn. 40–4. On implementation of UNCLOS Articles 16, 47(8)–(9), 76(9), 75 and 84, and 134(3), see Report 5 of the Secretary-General, *Oceans and the Law of the Sea* UN Docs A/56/58 (2001) at 20–1, A/57/57 at 18–19 (2002) and A/58/65 at 12 (2003), www.un.org/Depts/los

[99] 2002 *Cameroon* v. *Nigeria; Equatorial Guinea Intervening (Merits)* judgment, paragraph 292. See also *supra* nn. 41–3, 65, 68, 75, 78–9, 81, 96–7 and *infra* nn. 102–3, 112.

[100] 2002 *Cameroon* v. *Nigeria; Equatorial Guinea Intervening (Merits)* judgment, paragraph 292. See also *supra* n. 86. See also holdings on the low-water line (normal baselines) under UNCLOS Article 5, in 1999 *Eritrea* v. *Yemen (Phase II)* Award, *supra* n. 8 at paragraphs 133–5, 146 and 2001 *Qatar* v. *Bahrain (Merits)* judgment, *supra* n. 7 at paragraph 184.

> [i]t is not a question of totally refashioning geography whatever the facts of the situation, but given a geographical situation of quasi-equality as between a number of States, of abating the effects of an incidental special feature from which an unjustifiable difference of treatment could result.[101]

The Court noted that while the 1985 *Guinea* v. *Guinea-Bissau* Award took account of the concavity of the coastline between the two parties, such concavity did not occur in the sectors of coastline of Cameroon and Nigeria relevant to the present delimitation, but only in the sector of Cameroon's coastline facing Bioko Island.[102] Consequently, this concavity was not a circumstance that would justify any shift of the equidistance. The same applied, as Judge ad hoc Keba Mbaye (designated by Cameroon) in both instances regretted, to the presence of Bioko, whose reducing effect on the seaward projection of the Cameroonian coastline was regarded by the Court to be an issue between Cameroon and Equatorial Guinea and not between Cameroon and Nigeria.[103]

In a notable departure from the previous equitable jurisprudence of the ICJ as well as the *Eritrea* v. *Yemen* and other arbitral tribunals,[104] neither the 2001 *Qatar* v. *Bahrain (Merits)* nor the 2002 *Cameroon* v. *Nigeria; Equatorial Guinea Intervening (Merits)* judgments specified what were the exact ratios of the coastal length of the parties and their

[101] 2002 *Cameroon* v. *Nigeria; Equatorial Guinea Intervening (Merits)* judgment, paragraph 295, quoting 1969 *North Sea* judgment, *supra* n. 80 at 49–50, paragraph 91.

[102] 2002 *Cameroon* v. *Nigeria; Equatorial Guinea Intervening (Merits)* judgment, paragraphs 296–7, quoting 1985 *Guinea* v. *Guinea-Bissau* Award, *supra* n. 96 at paragraph 104.

[103] 2002 *Cameroon* v. *Nigeria; Equatorial Guinea Intervening (Merits)* judgment, paragraphs 298–9, noting (at paragraph 299) that islands were sometimes relevant circumstances 'when such islands lay within the zone to be delimited and fell under the sovereignty of one of the parties', and Separate Opinion of Judge ad hoc Mbaye, paragraphs 132–7; *supra* nn. 96–7. See holdings on Saint Pierre et Miquelon made in the 2002 *Newfoundland and Labrador* v. *Nova Scotia (Phase II)* Award, *supra* n. 93, paragraphs 3.16, 4.26–4.29.

[104] See, e.g., 1984 *Gulf of Maine* judgment, *supra* n. 83 at 334–7, paragraphs 218–22, specifying (at paragraph 222) that the ratio between the coastal fronts of the USA and Canada on the Gulf of Maine to be applied for the purposes of determining the location of the corrected equidistance would be 1.32:1 in place of 1.38:1, and Separate Opinion of Judge Schwebel at 353–8 (*supra* n. 10); 1999 *Eritrea* v. *Yemen (Phase II)* Award, *supra* n. 8 at paragraphs 20, 39–43, 117 and 165–8, quoting (at paragraphs 39, 165) the 1969 *North Sea* judgment, *supra* n. 80 at 52, paragraph 98, at 54, operative paragraph 101(D)(2), and specifying (at paragraph 168) that the *Yemen* v. *Eritrea* ratio of coastal length was 387026 to 507110 metres (or 1:1.31), while the ratio of their water areas (including TS) was 25535 to 27944 square kilometres (or 1:1.09); 2002 *Newfoundland and Labrador* v. *Nova Scotia (Phase II)* Award, *supra* n. 93 at paragraphs 1.28, 2.34, 4.11/24 and 5.14/19.

water areas. At the same time, by contrast to the 1969 *North Sea* and 1984 *Gulf of Maine* judgments and the 1999 *Eritrea* v. *Yemen (Phase II)* Award, which applied proportionality as an *a posteriori* test of the equitableness of a result arrived at by other means, both the *Qatar* v. *Bahrain* and *Cameroon* v. *Nigeria; Equatorial Guinea Intervening* judgments followed the pattern of the 1993 *Denmark* v. *Norway (Jan Mayen)* judgment of applying proportionality *ex ante* as an independent principle of delimitation. Since whichever coastline of Nigeria was regarded as relevant, the relevant coastline of Cameroon was not longer than that of Nigeria, there was no reason to shift the equidistance line, as Cameroon submitted, in its favour.[105]

With respect to the oil practice (concessions and wells), the ICJ followed its own jurisprudence and that of arbitral tribunals, testifying that this practice is not in itself considered as a relevant circumstance impacting upon the course of a boundary unless it is based on express or tacit agreement between the parties, which was lacking in the instant case.[106] In his Statement of 10 October 2002, President Gilbert Guillaume stressed, however, that the 'delimitation thus effected for the most part respects existing oil installations'.[107] Given that 'oil dominates the land and the sea' ('le pétrole domine la terre et la mer'),[108] the ICJ should have – both in the present and the *Qatar* v. *Bahrain (Merits)* judgment – reaffirmed the important obligations expounded in the 1999 *Eritrea* v. *Yemen (Phase II)* Award with respect to the basic duties of the parties to inform and consult one another and to give every consideration to the shared or joint or unitized exploitation of mineral resources which may be discovered that straddle the maritime boundary or that lie in its vicinity.[109]

[105] 2002 *Cameroon* v. *Nigeria; Equatorial Guinea Intervening (Merits)* judgment, paragraph 291 (*supra* n. 97) and paragraphs 300–1, quoting 1984 *Gulf of Maine* judgment, *supra* n. 83 at 336, paragraphs 221–2, and 1993 *Denmark* v. *Norway (Jan Mayen)* judgment, *supra* n. 93 at 34, paragraph 68. See also 2001 *Qatar* v. *Bahrain (Merits)* judgment, *supra* n. 7 at paragraphs 241–3.

[106] 2002 *Cameroon* v. *Nigeria; Equatorial Guinea Intervening (Merits)* judgment, paragraphs 302–4; *supra* n. 89.

[107] Statement of President Guillaume, *supra* n. 27 at paragraph 4. This respect seems to be confirmed by the concurring vote of Judge ad hoc Ajibola (designated by Nigeria) with regard to the course of the boundary beyond Point G, *infra* n. 111.

[108] 2001 *Qatar* v. *Bahrain (Merits)*, Joint Dissenting Opinion of Judges Bedjaoui, Ranjeva, and Koroma, paragraph 215, paraphrasing the classic 'land dominates the sea' ('la terre domine la mer') maxim, reaffirmed by the 2001 judgment, *supra* n. 7 at paragraph 185.

[109] 1999 *Eritrea* v. *Yemen (Phase II)* Award, *supra* n. 8 at paragraphs 75–86, 132, citing, *inter alia*, the 1969 *North Sea* judgment, *supra* n. 80 at 54, operative paragraph 101(D)(2), as reaffirmed by the 1985 *Libya* v. *Malta (Merits)* judgment, *supra* n. 92

As there were no other reasons necessitating an adjustment of the equidistant line, the 2002 *Cameroon* v. *Nigeria; Equatorial Guinea Intervening (Merits)* judgment concluded that this line represented an equitable result for the delimitation of the area in respect of which the ICJ had jurisdiction to give a ruling.[110] In the process of determining the course of the Cameroon–Nigeria boundary line, the ICJ considered that since according to the 1975 Maroua Declaration, Point G lay to the east of the equidistance, Cameroon was entitled to request that from that point the boundary should return to the equidistant line. Consequently, the single maritime boundary in the present sector of partially overlapping CS/EEZ beyond Point G was determined by two unanimous decisions of the ICJ, which essentially endorsed Nigeria's contentions and which held:

- that from Point G, the boundary line between the maritime areas appertaining respectively to Cameroon and Nigeria followed a loxodrome having an azimuth of 270° as far as the equidistant line passing through the midpoint of the line joining West Point and East Point; the boundary met this equidistance at a Point X, with coordinates (slightly different from those put forward by Cameroon) 8° 21′ 20″ longitude east and 4° 17′ 00″ latitude north; and
- that from Point X, the boundary turned and continued southwards along the equidistance, following a loxodrome having an azimuth of 187° 52′ 27″.[111]

at 41, paragraph 50; the 1969 *North Sea* judgment, Separate Opinion of Judge Philip C. Jessup, [1969] ICJ Rep. 81; and M. Miyoshi, 'The Joint Development of Offshore Oil and Gas in Relation to Maritime Boundary Delimitation' (1999) 2(5) *IBRU Maritime Briefing*. See also D. M. Ong, 'Joint Development of Common Offshore Oil and Gas Deposits' (1999) 93 *AJIL* 771; B. Kwiatkowska, 'The Peaceful Settlement of Maritime Disputes by the ICJ', Guest Lectures at Centre René-Jean Dupuy, Senghor University, Alexandria and Egyptian Society of International Law, Cairo, 9–10 November 1999, www.cdupuy-usenghor.org/word/confe.pdf For analysis of these 1999 *Eritrea* v. *Yemen (Phase II)* holdings, see D. M. Ong, 'The New Timor Sea Arrangement 2001' (2002) 17 *IJMCL* 79 at 90. For reliance on these *Eritrea* v. *Yemen* holdings, see 2002 *Newfoundland and Labrador* v. *Nova Scotia (Phase II)* Award, *supra* n. 93 at paragraphs 3.4/23 and 5.11; 2002 OAS *Belize* v. *Guatemala (Territorial Differendum Proposals from the OAS Facilitators)*, B-paragraph 9(c), www.belize-guatemala.gov.bz/

110 2002 *Cameroon* v. *Nigeria; Equatorial Guinea Intervening (Merits)* judgment, paragraphs 305–7.

111 2002 *Cameroon* v. *Nigeria; Equatorial Guinea Intervening (Merits)* judgment, paragraph 307 and operative paragraph 325.IV.(C)–(D), adopted unanimously by sixteen members, *supra* n. 26; Declaration of Judge Oda, paragraphs 22–3 and Dissenting Opinion of Judge ad hoc Ajibola, paragraph 172. The ICJ changed (by comparison to Cameroon's suggestion) the longitude of Point X by 4' (about 120m). For operative

As Sketch-Map No. 12 illustrated, the ICJ confined itself, in accordance with the intentions of both parties, to indicating the boundary's direction without fixing the Cameroon–Nigeria–Equatorial Guinea tripoint.[112]

It is to be hoped that, notwithstanding apparent drawbacks in development funding, the conduct of Nigeria and Ethiopia, which both likely intended to accelerate such funding, would be avoided in future to the advantage of the fulfilment by developing states of their Millennium commitment to resolving their disputes by 'peaceful means and in conformity with the principles of justice and international law', including bona fide respect for the final and binding decisions of the ICJ and other third party fora within the framework of the United Nations Charter.[113]

paragraph 325.IV.(A), see *supra* n. 72; and for operative paragraph 325.IV.(B), see *supra* n. 84. On the lack of geodetic datum, see *supra* n. 85.

[112] Sketch-Map No. 12 and *Cameroon* v. *Nigeria* Relevant Lines, *supra* n. 85.

[113] See views of ICJ Presidents Schwebel, Guillaume, and Shi, quoted *supra* nn. 10, 30 and UNGA Resolution 55/2 on United Nations Millennium Declaration of 8 September 2000, paragraph 4. See also UNGA Resolution 57/26 on Prevention and Peaceful Settlement of Disputes of 19 November 2002 and UN SC Presidential Statement on The Role of the Security Council in the Pacific Settlement of Disputes, UN Doc. S/PRST/2003/5, 13 May 2003, www.un.org/Docs/sc/

BIBLIOGRAPHY OF WORKS BY FLORENTINO FELICIANO

'Effects of Joint Wills' (1950) 25 *Philippine Law Journal* 629

'Pledges and Mortgages of Shares of Stock' (1950) 25 *Philippine Law Journal* 660

'The Anglo-Iranian Oil Dispute' (1951) 26 *Philippine Law Journal* 55

'Classification and Preference of Credits in Insolvency' (1951) 26 *Philippine Law Journal* 98

'On Vicarious Liability of the Employer' (1951) 26 *Philippine Law Journal* 413

'1951 Annual Survey of Philippine Law: Criminal Law: Criminal Liability and Specific Crimes' (1952) 27 *Philippine Law Journal* 283 (with A. M. Ceniza)

'On the Shareholders' Right of Preemption: Law and Practice' (1953) 28 *Philippine Law Journal* 443

'The Belligerent Occupant and the Returning Sovereign: Aspects of the Philippine Law of Belligerent Occupation' (1953) 28 *Philippine Law Journal* 645

Conflicting Orders and Appraisal of Resort to Coercion (Proceedings, American Society of International Law, 1959)

Studies in World Public Order (Yale University Press, 1961) (with Myres S. McDougal & Associates)

Law and Minimum World Public Order: The Legal Regulation of International Coercion (Yale University Press, 1961) (with Myres S. McDougal)

'On Territorial Waters of Archipelagoes' (1962) 1 *Philippine International Law Journal* 157

'The Functions of Judicial Review and the Doctrine of Political Questions' (1964) 39 *Philippine Law Journal* 444

'The Asian Development Bank' (1965) 4 *Philippine International Law Journal*

Comments on the Relevance of International Law to the Development Process (Proceedings, American Society of International Law 15, 1966)

'Legal Problems of Private International Business Enterprises: An Introduction to the International Law of Private Business Associations and Economic Development' (1966) 113 *Hague Recueil* 213

'Section 13(5) Problems: The Consequences of Obsolescence' in 165 *Aspects of Philippine Corporate Practice* (U.P. Law Centre, 1967)

'Some International Law Aspects of Economic Development' (1975) IV *Philippine Yearbook of International Law* 49

'The Principle of Non-Refoulement: A Note on International Legal Protection of Refugees and Displaced Persons' (1982) 57 *Philippine Law Journal* 598

'Coerced Movements of People Across State Boundaries: Some Problems of International Humanitarian Law' (1983) 58 *Philippine Law Journal* 256; also published in (1983): *Australian Yearbook of International Law* 113

'Regional Conceptions of Public Order: Some Reflections on the Development of an International Law for a New World Order' in *The Spirit of Uppsala*, Grahl-Madsen and Toman (eds.), (1984) (with E. D. Solidum)

'Role of Investment Agencies in Developing Countries in the Management and Negotiation of Contracts' in Horn (ed.), *Adaptation and Renegotiation of Contracts in International Trade and Finance* (Studies in Transnational Economic Law, Vol. 3, 1985)

'The Problem of Delay in the Philippine Court System' (1987) 62 *Philippine Law Journal* 201 (with E. L. Caparas)

'Reflections on the Voluntary Rescheduling Approach to the International Debt Problems: Framework and General Principles' (1987) II *Foreign Relations Journal* (October, no. 3)

'Process and Culture in Development Negotiations: The Management of Consent' 1990 V *Foreign Relations Journal* (October, no. 3)

Refugees in Southeast Asia: A Note on Philippine Practice and Recent Developments (with M. P. dela Cerna) (Proceedings of the 1990 Pacific Region and International Law (PRIL) Conference at the University of Melbourne); also published in (1990) VI *World Bulletin: Bulletin of the Institute of International Legal Studies* (November–December, no. 6)

Some Aspects of the Dispute Settlement Provisions of the 1982 United Nations Convention on the Law of the Sea (Selected Papers published by the Southeast Asian Programme in Ocean Law, Policy and Management (SEAPOL), delivered at SEAPOL Workshops in Phuket and Chiangmai, Thailand, 1989 and 1991), p. 41

'Marine Pollution and Spoliation of Natural Resources as War Measures: A Note on Some International Law Problems in the Gulf War' (1992) 14 *Houston Journal of International Law* 483

'The Application of Law: Some Recurring Aspects of the Process of Judicial Review and Decision Making' (1992) 37 *American Journal of Jurisprudence* (December)

Sovereign External Debt: A Note on Contemporary Legal Aspects (published under the title '1992 – La Dette Exterieure/The Present State of Research Carried Out by the English-speaking Section of the Centre for Studies and Research') (Hague Academy of International Law, April 1993)

'Qualities of a Good Judge' (1994) III (2) *Lawyers Review* (28 February 1994) 68

'The Doctrine of Sovereign Immunity from Suit in a Globalizing and Developing Economy: Philippine Experience and Caselaw' in N. Ando (ed.), *Japan and*

International Law: Past, Present and Future (International Symposium to mark the Centennial of the Japanese Association of International Law, 1999); also published in (1998) 3 *Austrian Review of International and European Law*

'Dispute Settlement under the Aegis of the World Trade Organization (WTO)' in *Odyssey and Legacy: The Chief Justice Andres R. Narvasa – Centennial Lecture Series* (Supreme Court of the Philippines and the College of Law, University of the Philippines, 1998), p. 179

'Dispute Settlement in the World Trade Organization: Institutions, Process and Practice' (with Peter Van den Bossche), in H. Schermers and N. Blokker (eds.), *Proliferation of International Organizations: Legal Aspects* (Kluwer, 2000); also published in (2000) 73 *Philippine Law Journal*

'Reflections on Good Governance, Development and Judicial Reform: Some Perspectives on the Problem of Judicial Corruption' in S. Schlemmer-Schulte and K. Y. Tung (eds.), *International Financial and Development Law, Liber Amicorum Ibraham F. I. Shihata* (Kluwer, 2001)

'Some Perspectives on the Problem of Corruption: The Nexus Between Reform and Control of Corruption and National Development Processes': Address delivered before the University of the Philippines Chapter, Phi Kappa Phi International Honor Society, 18 April 2001; published in Phi Kappa Phi UP Newsletter, January–March 2002

'Some Structural Features of the Dispute Settlement System of the World Trade Organization': Address delivered at the Conference of the WTO Research Institute of Shanghai, Peoples Republic of China, 18 May 2001; text in *The WTO and China: The Road to Free Trade*, published by the Hong Kong WTO Research Institute, p. 21 (2003)

INDEX